West Africa during the Atlantic Slave Trade

New Approaches to Anthropological Archaeology

Series editors

Thomas E. Levy, University of California, San Diego, Augustin F. C. Holl, University of Michigan, and Guillermo Algaze, University of California, San Diego

Anthropological Archaeology offers a methodologically refreshing approach to the study of cultural evolution. It recognizes the fundamental role that anthropology now plays in archaeology and also integrates the strengths of various research paradigms which characterize archaeology on the world scene today, including new or processual, post-processual, evolutionist, cognitive, symbolic, marxist and historical archaeologies. It does so by taking into account the cultural and, when possible, historical context of the material remains being studied. This involves the development of models concerning the formative role of cognition, symbolism and ideology in human societies to explain the more material and economic dimensions of human culture that are the natural purview of archaeological data. It also involves an understanding of the cultural ecology of the societies being studied, and of the limitations and opportunities that the environment imposes on the evolution or devolution of human societies. Based on the assumption that cultures never develop in isolation, Anthropological Archaeology takes a regional approach to tackling fundamental issues concerning past cultural evolution anywhere in the world.

This new series welcomes proposals from 'intellectual foragers' whose interests combine field research with theoretical studies of issues of cultural evolution in the past and in the ethno-archaeological present. The series differs from much theoretical discourse in archaeology today in that it is dedicated to publishing work firmly grounded in archaeological fact, while also venturing to explore more speculative ideas about how cultures evolve and change.

Forthcoming titles in the series:

Archaeology, Anthropology and Cult: The Sanctuary at Vilat, Israel, edited by David Alon and Thomas E. Levy

Early Urbanizations in the Levant: A Regional Perspective, Raphael Greenberg

Landscapes, Rock-Art and the Dreaming: An Archaeology of Preunderstanding, Bruno David

West Africa during the Atlantic Slave Trade

ARCHAEOLOGICAL PERSPECTIVES

Edited by

Christopher R. DeCorse

Leicester University Press
London and New York

Leicester University Press
A Continuum imprint
The Tower Building, 11 York Road, London SE1 7NX
370 Lexington Avenue, New York, NY 10017-6503

First published 2001

British Library Cataloguing-in-Publication Data
A catalogue record for this book is available from the British Library.

ISBN 0-7185-0247-7 (hardback)

Library of Congress Cataloging-in-Publication Data
West Africa during the Atlantic slave trade: archaeological perspectives / edited
by Christopher R. DeCorse.
        p. cm. — (New approaches to anthropological archaeology)
    Includes bibliographical references and index.
    ISBN 0-7185-0247-7
    1. Excavations (Archaeology)—Africa, West. 2. Africa, West—Antiquities. 3. Slave
  trade—Africa, West. I. DeCorse, Christopher R.   II. Series.

DT473. W47 2001
966'.01—dc21   00-056345

Typeset by CentraServe Ltd, Saffron Waldon, Essex
Printed and bound in Great Britain by The Cromwell Press.

Contents

List of Figures   vii

List of Tables   ix

List of Contributors   x

Foreword by Merrick Posnansky   xi

1 Introduction   1
   Christopher R. DeCorse

2 Tools for Understanding Transformation and Continuity in
   Senegambian Society: 1500–1900   14
   Susan Keech McIntosh, with a contribution by I. Thiaw

3 Historical Process and the Impact of the Atlantic Trade on Banda,
   Ghana, c. 1800–1920   38
   Ann Brower Stahl

4 The Effect of the Slave Trade on the Bassar Ironworking Society,
   Togo   59
   Philip Lynton de Barros

5 Change and Continuity in Coastal Bénin   81
   Kenneth G. Kelly

6 Kanem-Borno: A Brief Summary of the History and Archaeology
of an Empire of the Central *bilad al-sudan*   101

Detlef Gronenborn

7 State Formation and Enslavement in the Southern Lake Chad
Basin   131

Scott MacEachern

8 500 Years in the Cameroons: Making Sense of the
Archaeological Record   152

Augustin F. C. Holl

9 An Americanist Perspective on African Archaeology: Toward an
Archaeology of the Black Atlantic   179

Theresa A. Singleton

Index   185

List of Figures

1.1 West Africa: vegetation belts
1.2 West Africa: major ethnic groups
2.1 Features, regions, kingdoms, and archaeological sites mentioned in the text
2.2 Pottery from the Sine Ngayene area dated to the early second millennium and late second millennium pottery from the same area
2.3 Pottery from the Middle Senegal Valley dating to the recent period (AD 1600–1900)
3.1 Place names mentioned in text
3.2 Villages and sites in the Banda area
3.3 Plan map of Makala Kataa. Excavated areas shown in black
3.4 Iron Age 1 pottery from Makala Kataa
3.5 Iron Age 2 pottery from the 1982 Banda Survey
3.6 Woman headloading pottery, Banda-Ahenkro market, 1982
3.7 Locally made pipes from Early Makala
4.1 Bassar in West Africa. Relationship to states of the Middle Volta Basin and Hausa kola routes c. AD 1800
4.2 Bassar region showing iron ores, chiefdoms centered on Bassar and Kabu, and specialist villages at contact (1890s)
4.3 Smelting furnace nearly four meters tall at Nangbani
4.4 Bassar smithing equipment
4.5 Bassar region c. AD 1600–1750
4.6 Bassar region c. AD 1825/1850
4.7 Bassar ceramics

5.1 Map of the Bight of Bénin indicating the sites and towns discussed in text, historic states mentioned in text, and the location of modern nations
5.2 Complete locally manufactured cooking pots, bowl rims, and a complete bowl excavated at Savi
5.3 Decorated locally produced earthenware rims excavated at Savi
5.4 Complete urn-shaped vessel, an elaborate earthenware pedestal, and an earthenware foot, all excavated at Savi
5.5 Terracotta or clay figurines excavated at Savi
5.6 Stone and clay beads from Savi
5.7 Copper bell and copper ring excavated at Savi
5.8 Sample of the variety of sizes and decorations present among locally manufactured tobacco pipes recovered at Savi
6.1 The Central *bilad al-sudan* with sites mentioned in the text
6.2 Map of the Chad Basin reconstructed after Ibn Said from the thirteenth century AD
6.3 Plans of the capitals and palaces of the fourteenth to eighteenth centuries
6.4 Ngala. Plan of the palace (inset) and stratigraphy
6.5 The ruins of Birni Gazargamo in 1854
6.6 Pottery from site of Gambaru, Kukawa, and Dikwa

5.7 View of the wall of Kukawa in 1892

5.8 Plans of the capitals of the nineteenth and twentieth centuries

5.9 View of *dendal* in the western town of Kukawa around 1853

7.1 Traditional states of the Lake Chad Basin

7.2 Major ethnic groups in and around the Mandara Mountains

7.3 Defensive wall at the Iron Age site of Manaouatchi-Gréa, northern Cameroon

7.4 Landscape of defense and domestication in the Mandara Mountains of northern Cameroon

8.1 Location map of the selected regional cases studied: 1) The Lékié-Yaoundé region in the southern forested zone; 2) The Western Grassfields; 3) The Western Adamaoua; 4) The Upper Benue Basin and the Fali region; 5) The Chadian plain

8.2 The southern forested zone: 1) The Lékié settlement cluster; 2) Location of the Matomb settlement cluster; 3) Location of the Babimbi settlement cluster

8.3 Distribution of settlements in the Western Grassfields: 1) Glazed Sherd Industry (GSI) settlement cluster; 2) Ndop Plateau Industry (NPI) settlement cluster

8.4 Furnace types recorded in the Western Grassfields

8.5 Settlement patterns at the climax of the Ndop Plateau Industry and settlement pattern in the Glazed Sherd Industry cluster

8.6 The Mayo Wodeo and Mayo Oumiare catchment basins, in the Western Adamaoua: distribution of settlements and land-use patterns

8.7 The Mayo Darlé catchment basin in the Western Adamaoua: distribution of settlements and land-use patterns

8.8 The Upper Benue Basin and the Fali region: general distribution of recorded archaeological sites

8.9 Spatial organization of the cemetery of Barki-Ngoutchoumi in the Fali region

8.10 Walled cities of the Chadian plain and inferred territorial organization

List of Tables

2.1 Some important events of the second millennium in the Senegambia

8.1 Major smelting sites from the southern forested regions

8.2 Iron production sites in the Ndop Plateau Industry (NPI)

8.3 Iron production sites of the Glazed Sherd Industry (GSI)

8.4 Distribution of archaeological features in the Western Adamaoua

8.5 Some Chadian plain sites: walled cities with studied cemeteries

8.6 General aspects of the distribution of grave goods in tested mound sites

8.7 Slave trade on the Cameroonian coast as known from British Parliamentary Papers

List of Contributors

Philip Lynton de Barros is Associate Professor of Anthropology, Behavioral Sciences Department, Palomar College, San Marcos, California.

Christopher R. DeCorse is Associate Professor, Department of Anthropology, Syracuse University, New York.

Detlef Gronenborn is Adjunct Professor, Seminar für Vor- und Frühgeschichte, Johann Wolfgang Goethe-Universität, Germany.

Augustin F. C. Holl is Professor and Curator, Department of Anthropology, Center for Afroamerican and African Studies, Museum of Anthropology, University of Michigan, Ann Arbor.

Kenneth G. Kelly is Assistant Professor, Department of Anthropology, University of South Carolina, Columbia.

Scott MacEachern is Assistant Professor, Department of Sociology and Anthropology, Bowdoin College, Maine.

Susan Keech McIntosh is Professor, Department of Anthropology, Rice University, Texas.

Merrick Posnansky is Professor Emeritus, Department of History and Anthropology , University of California, Los Angeles.

Theresa A. Singleton is Associate Professor, Department of Anthropology, Syracuse University, New York.

Ann Brower Stahl is Professor, Department of Anthropology, State University of New York at Binghampton, New York.

Ibrahima Thidw is a Research Associate, Department of Anthropology, Rice University, Texas, and is currently excavating on Gorée Island.

Foreword

MERRICK POSNANSKY

Professor Emeritus, Department of History and Anthropology,
University of California, Los Angeles

In June 1995, in Harare, the capital of Zimbabwe, Historical Archaeology in Africa came of age. Its recognition came in the form of two sessions at the Tenth Pan African Prehistory Congress, when an historical archaeologist, Theresa Singleton, a specialist in African-American archaeology, was elected to the Council. This volume is further evidence of a maturing discipline, a synthesis of the achievements of archaeologists either working in the field, or speculating about the historical era in West Africa, using insights developed from archaeological research. Historical Archaeology in West Africa essentially has an Atlantic dimension. A dimension thrust upon it by the centrality of both the destructive and reconstructive nature of the Atlantic Slave Trade. A trade that displaced millions of Africans and transplanted them into a new world where they created vibrant cultures. With successful coping mechanisms, these New World communities kept alive the cultural traditions of their homelands in the face of a brutally imposed way of life, economic system, language, and technology. This volume provides the first fruits of the efforts of a dedicated generation of historical archaeologists to appreciate the broader dimensions of their work and materially add to our knowledge of one of the most significant eras in African history.

Their contributions convincingly demonstrate that there is a need for Historical Archaeology, and have provided much of the critical theory that was so obviously lacking in the early work that Chris DeCorse and I reviewed in 1986.[1]

As we rejoice in this volume in a new era of Historical Archaeology it is perhaps pertinent to glance at the history of our discipline. Before 1960 there were few archaeologists in Africa, in fact less than ten over the whole of tropical Africa. Most looked after museums that served whole countries, such as Desmond Clark at the Livingstone Museum in Northern Rhodesia (now Zambia), or myself at the Uganda Museum, and Bernard Fagg in Nigeria. We all had huge bailiwicks and extremely limited budgets for research. We covered countries bigger than most American states and we tried to do justice to all periods of time—from human origins to the colonial period—as well as collecting ethnographic items. As a consequence, a priority for research was placed on the need to discover more about the period which was completely unknown: the prehistoric period, which extended right into the middle of the second millennium AD and in some areas even into the nineteenth century. By the 1950s, however, in later archaeology there were three areas where the primary intention was to marry historical research with archaeological investigation. The objective was clearly changing from the incidental to the intentional. The first area was the East African seaboard, where James Kirkman had begun to explore stone ruins that were locally described as lost Arab towns. He documented coastal sites from Somalia to Mozambique[2] where ruined mosques and stone graves indicated past towns, and began a long-term investigation of the town of Gedi near Malindi on the Kenya coast. In a paper in the *Antiquaries Journal* for 1957 he called his work Historical Archaeology. His pioneer work was supplemented by that of Neville Chittick. At the same time, on the then Gold Coast, Professor A. W. Lawrence, of the University College of the Gold Coast (the very first Professor of Archaeology in tropical Africa), was recording the post-1482 European fortified trading posts.[3] He also perceived of his work as Historical Archaeology but his prime objective was the conservation and restoration of the monuments after clearance had taken place. In Uganda I was also calling my own studies of the principal sites of the Interlacustrine Kingdoms, where I was using oral history to locate and date sites, Historical Archaeology, after rejecting both 'protohistory' and 'ethnohistory' as defining terms.[4] I justified my use, and incidentally inculcated the same in my students, on the basis of the validity of the oral traditions of the Interlacustrine states. These traditions guided us to sites, provided topographical details, gave us genealogies, filled us in on interstate conflict, struggles for succession, aspects of the economy, and even supernatural events. All were remembered, and thus recorded, using elaborate (rather than haphazard) systems of passing information down through the generations. It was the memorable unnatural events, like eclipses, which enabled us to tie our oral chronologies to a universal time-scale. Imports from the coast, such as beads and cloth, and the diffusion of new foods and pastimes such as tobacco smoking, provided links with more accessible events of coastal history. Though these were intentional historical archaeological activities they did not involve the creation of a new body of critical theory. However, in the work of Peter Schmidt who followed some of my initiatives, this was clearly the intention nearly two decades later when he wrote his book on his Tanzania research, which he entitled *Historical Archaeology : A Structural Approach in an African Culture*.[5] Though the late 1960s witnessed an expanded use of oral traditions there was, in the early heady days of the newly independent states, an unwillingness to look at anything that smacked of colonial archaeology. The demand was for using archaeology to discover African roots, to discover the glorious days which preceded the arrival of the Europeans, to create an African history based on discoveries about previously neglected African polities. In many ways Historical Archaeology in Africa had to await the arrival of new scholarship, particularly from the USA, where Historical Archaeology had such a charged development in the 1970s. It was to this generation that Christopher DeCorse belonged, who in the mid-1980s resumed initiatives on the Ghana coast that had stalled in the late 1960s.

In 1984[6] I defined Historical Archaeology as 'archaeology undertaken in periods or for areas in which the principal source for contextual information is provided by documentary evidence.' This was a definition without chronological or geographical parameters. It could embrace an African as well as an American or Asian situation. It was obvious that as literacy patterns spread so Historical Archaeology would become more pervasive, but in my own interpretation of this definition the community being examined need not be literate to be considered historical though their chronological context required documentary underpinning. Historical archaeologists in Africa have convincingly shown the value of the oral tradition throughout Africa. Though many of its records may not be as concise chronologically as the writen documents, they nevertheless provide a chronological order that can both stand on its own and be complemented by actual written documents. I realize that there may have been a gross inconsistency in my earlier writings in that as an historian I have always argued for a continuum in African history and taught my introductory classes with the subject matter being the story of humans in Africa, yet for archaeology I am arguing for a stricter division between prehistoric and historic societies. I am thus ascribing a greater importance to the global nature of much of what has been considered as Historical Archaeology in Africa. There is also the qualitative factor that the material culture in Historical Archaeology is much more varied and representative of a wider number of locales than is the subject matter of the prehistorians. Using documentary sources we can date our material with ease by knowing the date or relatively short period of manufacture at the workshop. Being workshop-made, much of the material culture has less of the 'personality' or the fingerprints of their makers that we often ascribe to the products of prehistoric communities.

In recent years there has been a stress on the global dimension of Historical Archaeology, which owes a great deal to influential teachers such as Jim Deetz, Kathleen Deagan, Peter Schmidt, and myself, who have all transcended the constrictions of American Historical Archaeology. The number of graduate students wanting to work on topics away from the USA has continued to grow. Vestiges still remain, however, of an Eurocentric approach with too much research emphasizing the archaeology of European expansion at the expense of other themes. This is inevitable, as we work from the known to the unknown. There is just as much justification for considering both Islamic archaeology or the Chinese expansion in Asia as Historical Archaeology. One uses the same kind of source data as one might use in seventeenth-century North American situations: ceramics made in specialized workshops, coins, metal goods, beads, and religious items such as pilgrim bottles, all of which display a remarkable uniformity over thousands of miles. We may not be able to read the texts in Arabic or Chinese but it is still text-aided archaeology. There is often a population and cultural continuity from past to present just as in North American sites. African Historical Archaeology now has a distinctiveness and integrity separate from Historical Archaeology in North America that allows us to compare it directly with other non-Western historical archaeologies.

What is refreshing in the papers in this volume is the attempt to move on from the Eurocentric and structuralist approaches to a more convincing attempt to look outward from Africa with the Europeans as only one intrusive and disruptive element. In all these cases we are returning to the African oral sources as primary, with the written sources as largely secondary. We are empowering our interpretations by using ethno-archaeology to take us back into time, comparing what we find in the ground with comparisons from other societies obtained by asking much more of what had previously been thought of as a static material culture. It is this questioning of the nature of evidence, whether produced by archaeologists or from the work of scholars in other disciplines, which is the hallmark of the new African Historical Archaeology. We are moving from the simple descriptive questions of only a generation ago. These consisted of: What happened in the past? When did they occur? How did people live? What were the nature of their economic, social, and religious systems and lifestyles? The more interesting questions of power relationships, gender relationships, and symbolic significance are now helping to generate our research priorities, as they should as we move beyond the pioneering days of a little more than a generation ago. I suppose we have all been suffused in our scholarship by questions that derive from the softer of the social sciences and the advances in the behavioral sciences. We are interested in the value of imported materials not so much in purely functional terms but also in the ways they may have enhanced the status of their users. We are using documentary sources more effectively not just to amplify the archaeological record but to lead us to interpretations of motive and meaning and to address questions that recently were thought inaccessible. A further change from attempts at synthesis of only fifteen years ago has been the broadening of our geographical vision. At that time we looked at the era of the slave trade and Historical Archaeology from the perspective of the European coastal establishments. It was an Atlantic world that was in the vanguard of our perspectives. Our colleagues in the Americas have forced us to ask questions about what mental blueprints accompanied the slaves from Africa, how representative were the transplanted Africans of the societies they left behind. Our emphasis is firmly on the nature of the African societies that participated in the slave trade rather than on the mechanics of the trade. Superior prospection and dating techniques, multidisciplinary approaches, and a relentless search for comparative material to date previously undateable inland assemblages, have all facilitated access to and validation of Historical Archaeology in areas of the savanna and Sahel that we had relegated to the documentary historians. The editor, Christopher DeCorse, is to be complimented on bringing together a team of scholars who cover the whole of West Africa, from Senegal to Cameroon, and whose work represents the different faces of Historical Archaeology at the beginning of a new millennium. At a time when regional syntheses of African archaeology are all too rare, even for the longer-studied prehistoric period, it is exciting to welcome a volume devoted to the archaeology for the historical period of West Africa that will certainly stimulate a new generation of scholars.

Notes

1 Merrick Posnansky and Christopher DeCorse (1986) Historical Archaeology in Sub-Saharan Africa—a Review. *Historical Archaeology*, 20: 1–14.

2 James S. Kirkman (1964) *Men and Monuments on the East African Coast*, London: Lutterworth.

3 A. W. Lawrence (1963) *Trade Castles and Forts of West Africa*, London: Jonathan Cape.

4 Merrick Posnansky (1959) Progress and Prospects in Historical Archaeology in Uganda. In *Discovering Africa's Past*, edited by Merrick Posnansky, Uganda Museum, Occ. Paper no. 4, 31–41.

5 Peter R. Schmidt (1978) *Historical Archaeology: A Structural Approach in an African Culture*. Westport: Greenwood.

6 In a paper given at the Society for Historical Archaeology at Colonial Williamsburg and later published in Posnansky and DeCorse 1986.

1 Introduction

CHRISTOPHER R. DECORSE

The peoples of West Africa were an integral part of the dramatic transformations that shaped the world during the past five centuries. Yet the culture history of the region during this tumultuous period remains poorly investigated. In the wake of extensive research on the archaeological record of Colombian consequences in the Americas, the material record of many portions of West Africa is unstudied and even basic regional chronological syntheses are often lacking. This paucity of information is all the more striking in light of the fact that in some instances written and oral historical sources provide a poor chronicle of much of the area. Archaeology thus affords critical insight, as it offers both information and time-depth not accessible any other way.

This volume surveys West African culture history of the past five centuries from an archaeological perspective. The intended concentration is on the economic, social, and cultural transformations that unfolded during the period of the Atlantic slave trade. The objective is to assess the culture histories and the archaeological records of some of the areas from which enslaved Africans were taken, thus offering insight into the developments that occurred during this period and the possible impacts of the trade on West African societies, as well as providing a context for studies of the African Diaspora (see the concluding chapter by Singleton). Discussions, however, often extend well beyond the boundaries of direct African-European interactions and the period of the Atlantic trade. The past 500 years witnessed dramatic changes in West African societies, including the rise and decline of African states, the continued spread of Islam, changing environmental conditions, and a host of indigenously mitigated developments, as well as the advent of the Europeans, the growth and decline of the Atlantic slave trade, and the onset of colonial rule. Within this context of economic and sociopolitical transformation, it is notable the degree to which indigenous beliefs structured the form and direction of developments (DeCorse 2001; Thornton 1995). This is not to suggest that African societies were static or remained unaffected by the global transformations of which they were part. Indeed, the following chapters indicate that there were dramatic changes in economic relations, social organization, and cultural practices. Nevertheless, in many instances the unfolding of these events was interpreted and redefined by African cultural traditions. Hence, when considering sociopolitical transformations or the development of state society, it is reasonable to consider their African cultural underpinnings as well as the tapestry of broader economic and historical transformations of which they were part.

What is apparent from the discussions in the following chapters is that cultural interactions, the impetus for change, and the nature of West African transformations during the past 500 years were very complex indeed. Diversity in the nature and expression of culture contact and change are recurring concerns in the studies presented. The expanding Euro-centric economic system, of which the Atlantic trade was part, was only one aspect of an intricately textured mosaic of interactions extending much further back in time and involving a myriad of variables, many of them independent of Europe. While tantalizing clues are emerging, current archaeological, histori-cal, and ethnographic work in West Africa often allows for only partial, restricted views of how these unfolded.

The coverage of this volume has been made as holistic as possible. It is intended as a resource for West Africanists, as well as all researchers interested in indigenous responses in the age of European expansion and the African diaspora. The studies presented synthe-size archaeological research, including previous work and new material. All of the contributors were asked to concentrate on the culture his-tory of the regions they surveyed, and on the insights afforded by archaeological data. The book progresses from west to east and, within sub-regions, from the coast to the hinterland.

As in all edited volumes, the contributions are varied in terms of the material surveyed, the theoretical perspectives presented, and the conclusions drawn. This diversity is, however, only in part the result of the differing perspec-tives of the authors. In addition to variation arising from climatic, geographic, cultural, and historical diversity (which is briefly examined below), a substantial amount of variation results from the uneven nature of the archae-ological work that has been undertaken. Archaeological assessments of the economic, political, and cultural changes internal to Afri-can societies over the past 500 years are frus-tratingly incomplete. There is a paucity of work in many areas on the relevant time period. This problem pervades all of the following dis-cussions, some more than others. Senegal, Ghana, and Nigeria have comparatively well-developed research and educational infrastruc-tures, and this is reflected in a more regular tempo of research, though not all portions of these countries have received equal attention. In contrast, discussion of the cultural history of some regions can be no more than preliminary reviews of limited literature. The studies selected for this volume represent some of the more substantive research projects that have been undertaken.

The research surveyed is also indicative of the methodological and theoretical concerns that have been brought to the study of the West African past. Some of this variation is the result of the background and training of the archaeologists working in the region, who include Africans, Europeans, and Americans trained at a variety of institutions (Ellison *et al.* 1996; Musonda 1990; Posnansky 1982; Rob-ertshaw 1990; Shaw 1989). It is also reason-able to note distinctive trends within the former French and English colonies (de Barros 1990; Kense 1990). These distinctive traditions have shaped the topical and temporal foci of research, as well as the theoretical paradigms in which archaeologists have operated.

The volume's temporal focus on the past 500 years roughly marks the arrival of the Europeans on the coast. This period, how-ever, also coincides with important develop-ments in the interior—the implications of which are most clearly articulated in the con-tributions by McIntosh and Holl (Chapters 2 and 8). The contributions are all *historical* in that, to a varying extent, they all draw on oral histories and the documentary past to contextualize, evaluate, and interpret the archaeological record, though the specifics provided by these sources are highly variable in terms of the time-depth, content, and 'coign of vantage' represented. Although examples of indigenous writing systems can be noted, accounts by Arab and European visitors to the region provide the vast majority of the written accounts. Arabic sources for the Sahel extend back to the late first millennium AD, while the first European accounts for the coastal regions begin in the fifteenth century. These sources, while important, are incomplete and afford very limited insight into developments in many regions until the nineteenth or even twentieth century. In light of these lacunae it is not surprising that historians and archae-ologists alike have frequently turned to oral histories and traditions, linguistics, and ethno-graphic analogy to strengthen their interpreta-tions of the past (Ehret and Posnansky 1982; Henige 1982; Miller 1980; Vansina 1985). In fact, many researchers who have examined the West African archaeological record of the past 500 years have dealt with questions tradition-ally subsumed under the headings of ethno-history, ethno-archaeology, and historical anthropology (e.g. Agorsah 1990; Atherton

1983; DeCorse 1996; MacEachern 1996). With these observations in mind, the temporal boundary has been left flexible out of necessity. Indeed, recognition and discussion of what went before—of the population movements, events, and transformations that laid the foundation for future developments—is desirable and the majority of contributions delve into the context provided by earlier events.

In this context, it is striking to note the limited degree to which information from Arabic and European sources has been drawn on. Similarly, in many areas the roles of Arabic trade and European expansion have often not been emphasized or envisaged as the primary explanatory framework in archaeological studies. Examinations of African ethnic and cultural groups, indigenous development, and technological innovations have emerged as far more important considerations. There are good reasons for this. Developments ranging from brass casting technology to the rise of state-level societies and indigenous cosmology have at times been ascribed to external agency, despite evidence to the contrary. Interdisciplinary archaeological and ethnographic studies have afforded important methodological insights into archaeological interpretation, as well as the presentation of pasts more directly relevant to the component populations of African nations. Studies have traced the origins of ethnographically known polities; sought insight into the archaeological perception of culture, ethnicity, and social boundaries; and examined the development of indigenous technology and artistic traditions.

Given the diversity of peoples, culture histories, and archaeological research represented it is difficult—perhaps impossible—to neatly synthesize West African culture history of the past 500 years. Admirable surveys have been presented (e.g. Brooks 1993; Jones 1983; Law 1991; McCaskie 1995; Reyna 1990; Rodney 1970; Terray 1995; Wilks 1993). Yet even these syntheses, out of necessity, have concentrated on certain sub-regions, cultural groups, or polities. Local developments were highly variable, despite the ways in which they may have been shaped by broader historical, economic, and political processes. Hence, the studies presented here cannot be taken as general models, but considered in light of the diverse patterns of which they were part.

West Africa before the Europeans

West Africa is here considered to extend from the Senegambia in the west to Cameroon in the east, bordered by the Sahara desert in the north and the Atlantic Ocean in the south. Few non-specialists realize the region's vast size, an area that would incorporate most of the continental United States. The region subsumes tremendous climatic, geographical, and cultural diversity (Figs 1.1 and 1.2). Climatic regions extend in roughly parallel, east–west bands. The desert region in the north includes some of the driest places on Earth, while the annual rainfall in the tropical forests of the coast exceeds 250 inches of rain per year. Between eastern Ghana and Benin, open savanna vegetation extends all the way to the coast, dividing the tropical forest into western and eastern portions. The varying availability of natural resources in these different areas provided stimulus to trade and exchange, as well as conflict. Fluctuations in climatic conditions and the availability of water resources were critical variables to the societies of the Sahel and savanna, and they played pivotal roles in the movement of some populations.

Languages of the Niger Congo family predominate throughout the region, and various commonalities in cultural practices have been noted within various sub-families and ethno-linguistic groups (Greenberg 1966; Murdock 1959). However, this shared linguistic classification belies a great deal of variation in subsistence strategies, social organization, and cultural history. Plantations of cash crops have become increasingly common in many areas during the present century. In the past, however, subsistence farming based on swidden agriculture predominated. Rice is the staple of preference among the Mande and West Atlantic peoples in the west, while yam cultivation has been more typical further east. West Africa was an independent center of domestication, and a diversity of species is represented, including sorghum, African rice, millets, oil palm, and some sixty varieties of yams (see reviews and bibliographies in Shaw *et al.* 1993). Throughout the region, however, many American and Asian crops have been introduced since the fifteenth century. A variety of domesticated animals, including cattle, chickens, goats, sheep, ducks, and Guinea fowls are

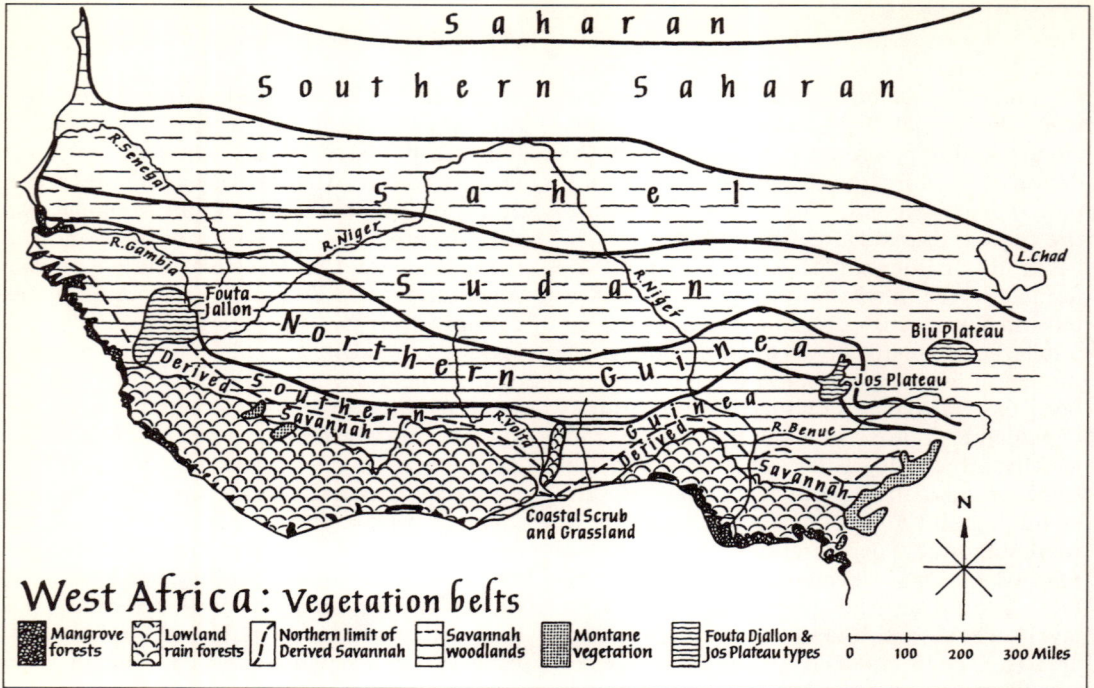

Figure 1.1 West Africa: vegetation belts. West Africa subsumes tremendous variation in climate and vegetation, ranging from tropical rain forest to some of the driest places on Earth (from *History of West Africa*, vol. 1, 2nd edition, edited by J. F. A. Ajayi and Michael Crowder, Columbia University Press, 1976).

commonly kept, and were exploited in the past. Although new varieties have been introduced, most of these animals were known well before the fifteenth century. Pastoralism is historically of particular importance to some groups, as for example the Fulani, who range widely over the savanna and Sahel. On the other hand, exploitation of shellfish and marine fishing were traditionally significant in the coastal regions. Various patterns of descent, marriage customs, age-grades, puberty rites, and cultural practices further distinguish individual ethnolinguistic groups.

Technological developments in West Africa were equally varied in their specifics and distribution. For the most part, with a few notable exceptions, the Late Stone Age was superseded by iron technology without any intervening Bronze or Copper Age (e.g. Kense and Okoro 1993). The earliest conclusive evidence of iron production comes from first millennium AD sites in Niger and Jos Plateau in Nigeria. Spectacular finds of copper alloy objects, produced using *cire perdue* (lost wax) casting, are known

from some sites dating to the ninth or tenth centuries AD. On the other hand, in some areas such as the Sierra Leone and Liberian hinterland, São Tomé, and the *firki* plains of northeast Nigeria evidence for iron smelting appears relatively late (approximately AD 700), and continues in association with Stone Age technology for several centuries.

West Africa did not exist in isolation during the millennia preceding the advent of the Atlantic trade. By the fifteenth century, when the first European arrived on the coast, West Africa was already linked by trade networks that extended throughout the coast and hinterland. There has been a tendency to conceptualize this trade as having been north to south in orientation: movement between the forest, savanna and Sahel and, later, between the European outposts on the coast and the interior hinterland. Clearly this was an important aspect of long-distance exchange. East–west trade patterns were, however, also important. By the first millennium AD inter- and intra-regional trade in resources such as

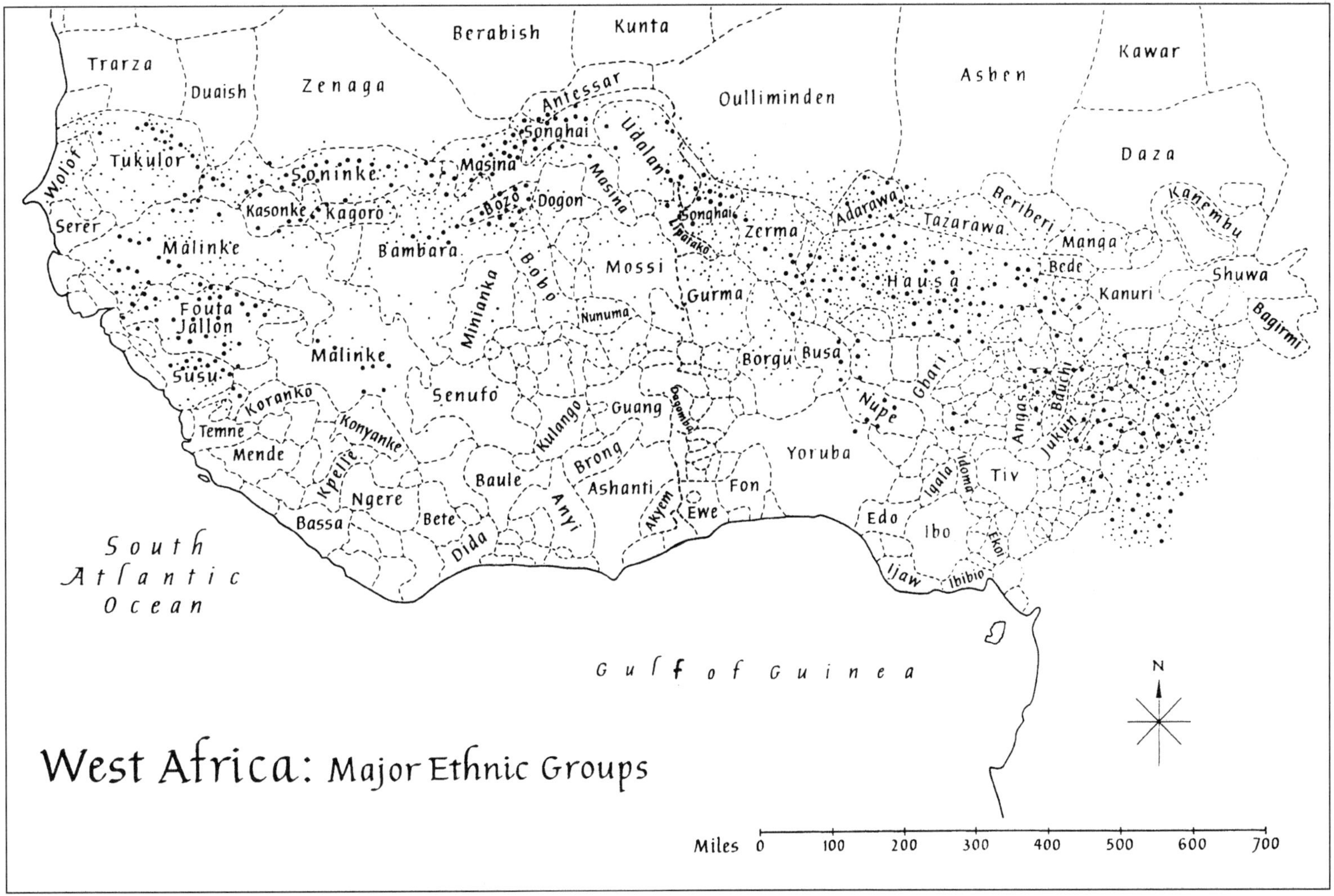

Figure 1.2 West Africa: major ethnic groups. This map only hints at the variation in cultural practices, subsistence strategies, social organization, and histories represented (from *History of West Africa*, edited by J. F. A. Ajayi and Michael Crowder, vol. 1, 2nd edition, Columbia University Press, 1976).

iron and gold moved through portions of the forest, savanna and Sahel (e.g. de Barros 1988; Sutton 1991). Along the coast, the lagoons between the Volta and the Niger facilitated local exchange that would complement, rather than compete with, the European marine trade (Law 1983).

The Arab trade with northern Africa was established by the end of the first millennium. Indeed, it is Islamic Arab travelers that provide the first documentary accounts of West Africa. Our perceptions of the nature of the trans-Saharan trade and the cultural interactions it engendered are primarily derived from these sources, limited as they are (Levtzion and Hopkins 1981). Arabic writings make reference to materials such as brass, beads, and natural resources, as well as slaves. Archaeological evidence for this trade is limited. Monad's study of a caravan site, dating to the early second millennium AD, is as unique as it is tantalizing (Monod 1964). For the most part, archaeological data are limited to isolated finds of Chinese porcelain, beads, glass, and brassware from northern Africa (e.g. DeCorse 1989b; Garrard 1980; Silverman 1980). Materials such as kola, fish, gold, salt, and slaves, often presumed to have been of critical importance, are difficult to assess from an archaeological standpoint.

Prior to the fifteenth century the nexus of sociopolitical developments appears to have been in the Sahel and savanna. This may, in part, result from lacunae in our knowledge of the archaeological record of the forest regions. Currently available information, however, suggests urbanism and sociopolitical complexity occurred earlier in the regions to the north. In the fifteenth century, areas such as the coast and coastal hinterlands of Sierra Leone, Liberia, Côte d'Ivoire, and Ghana probably had relatively low population densities compared to portions of the interior. Some models have viewed the trans-Saharan Arab trade as the stimulus for these developments. Yet the origins of many of the settlements and polities referred to in later Arabic and European accounts—including ancient Ghana and Mali, Asanti, and Benin—can be traced back to the first or early second millennium AD (see the chapters by McIntosh, Gronenborn, and MacEachern). Some polities extended over large regions. For example, the Kingdom of Benin was ruled by the Oba who controlled a powerful army and a network of adminis-

trators, through which his influence reached throughout much of south central Nigeria (Connah 1975). In contrast, evidence for urbanization and political stratification is limited in some regions and acephalous societies appear to have predominated both before and after the period of the Atlantic trade. Such appears to have been the case in the forests of Guinea, Sierra Leone, and Liberia, where evidence for centralized, state-level societies is limited (DeCorse 1989a). Oral histories and documentary records suggest that settlements remained autonomous, or loosely united under a charismatic leader or prominent war chief.

A critical aspect of north–south interactions was Islam, which was introduced into West Africa late in the first millennium AD. The nature of this introduction was highly variable, involving a variety of dynasties, schools of Islam, and ethnolinguistic groups (Hiskett 1984; Insoll 1996; McCall and Bennett 1971; Trimingham 1978). Islamic beliefs were adapted and modified, producing religious practices that were syncretic combinations of Islamic and indigenous African belief systems. In addition to religion, the Arab trade brought common language, writing, and legal systems. In some cases, particularly during the initial centuries, Islam was spread through merchants and the ruling class. However, in many instances, ranging from the Futa Jallon in the west to the Mandara Highlands in the east, Islamic states waged *jihads* or holy wars on neighboring non-Islamic populations and occupied their lands (see chapters by McIntosh, Holl, Gronenborn, and MacEachern). The reasons—and the outcomes—of these conflicts were not entirely religious. They were frequently driven by economic, political, and cultural motives.

Archaeological work on sites known from Arabic sources has often concentrated on narrowly focused historical questions, such as the identification and description of the Arab and African settlements mentioned in the documents (see chapter by Gronenborn; de Barros 1990). These studies serve to underscore the incomplete nature of the documents, which often provide such limited information that even the identification of the location and the organization of the settlements mentioned remain tenuous. Given these limitations, archaeological research can be important in refining our understanding of the events described in written and oral sources. Work on other sites has often dealt with questions of much broader interest, in terms of both theoretical implications and spatial focus.

The Atlantic trade

Europeans arrived on the West African coast in the fifteenth century. The Cape Verde Islands were settled during the middle of the fifteenth century, and São Tomé in the Bight of Benin was reached by the end of the century. Models of African–European interactions afford dramatic contrasts, both within West Africa and with other world areas. It was trade that brought the Europeans and it was within this arena that their activities took place (DeCorse 1998, 2001). Gold was the primary objective during the fifteenth and sixteenth centuries but other commodities, including ivory, pepper, redwood, and hides, became increasingly important. The slave trade, shifting in focus and volume through time, had major consequences in many regions. Some 12 to 15 million individuals were removed from Africa (e.g. Debien 1974; Geegus 1989; Gemery and Hogendorn 1979; Higman 1984; Inikori 1976, 1982; Manning 1997; Richardson 1980). The horror of the Middle Passage and the conditions enslaved Africans faced in the Americas have been treated in contemporary accounts and in more recent scholarship. However, many of the historical studies that have been undertaken have focused on the numbers of slaves or where the slaves were purchased, not their actual cultural or ethnic affiliations. As Lovejoy (1989:378) has noted: '. . . ethnicity under slavery tended to be identified with the commercial system through which the slaves passed in Africa; that is the region and/or port of export.' Names such as Congo, Gbe (Ewe-Fon), Yoruba, Igbo, Bambara, Akan, Mina, Angola, and Mozambique became glosses for broadly inclusive groups representing numerous, ethnically heterogeneous populations.

The ways in which captive Africans reached the trading enclaves on the coast varied a great deal. Although the European arrived on the coast in the fifteenth century, direct interaction with Europeans for the majority of West African societies was non-existent until the late nineteenth or twentieth centuries. On the Gold Coast more than 60 European trade posts, forts, and plantations had been established by 1800, but these were confined to the coastal margin and the total European presence never exceeded more than a few hundred (DeCorse 1992, 1993, 2001; Lawrence 1963; Posnansky and DeCorse 1986; Van Dantzig 1980). In the Senegal and Gambia river valleys, European traders reached farther inland, but their numbers remained small (Wood 1967). Many of the consequences of European expansion in both economic and cultural terms was played out far from the coast, with little direct European involvement, and within African sociocultural contexts. Even in the coastal enclaves the perceptions, goals, and motivations of the African populations frequently circumscribed the actions of the Europeans (Kelly 1997 and this volume). Until the late nineteenth century and the partition of Africa, Europeans frequently exercised limited control over the immediate hinterland and there was never a substantial settler population. These scenarios are very different from those encountered in South Africa and portions of the East African coast, where substantial European settlement and conscription of the indigenous population into the labor force was an integral part of the contact setting.

Given the nature of the contact setting, it is not surprising that many studies of European–West African relations of the pre-colonial period have focused on trade and economic relations (DeCorse 1998; cf. Curtin 1975; Daaku 1970; Dike 1966; Hopkins 1973; Jones 1983; Kea 1982; Polanyi 1966; Reynolds 1974; Rodney 1970; Wallerstein 1986). Although specific models of the economic transformations within West African societies vary, the region became increasingly enmeshed in an economic system that was ever-widening in scope and increasingly Eurocentric in orientation. The societies most immediately affected by the European trade were the coastal and riverine towns that were the sites of early Portuguese, French, Dutch, English, Swedish, Danish, and Brandenberger entrepots. Within the hinterland, trade in commodities and enslaved Africans gradually transformed the sociopolitical structure of societies involved. The economic focus shifted from the forest–savanna ecotone to the coast. Some of the polities of the Sahel declined, while other regions and the coastal states thrived along the new frontier of opportunity provided by the European trade.

While an holistic perspective of regional, inter-regional, and global developments is desirable, there is an equal need to recognize the varied consequences of local economic, political, and cultural variation, and the disparate contact settings represented. Although the panorama of an expanding Eurocentric economy provides a backdrop—a context—for the structure of African–European relations, the timing and nature of individual contacts varied, as did the specific European policies initiated, the materials exchanged, and the volume of trade. Local responses were diverse—some African polities enjoyed relatively harmonious relations with the Europeans, while others vigorously opposed or regulated European activities. Given the small number of Europeans on the coast, interactions were frequently dictated more by historical incident, distinctive local conditions, and personal relations than by any unified policy on the part of the European nations involved.

Africa is replete with illustrations of the varied nature of African–European interaction. The Portuguese settlements in North Africa, such as Qsar-es-Seghir, can be viewed as ill-fated colonial experiments: economic failures that remained isolated from the hinterland and the interior trade (Redman 1986). In contrast, the lucrative traffic along the West African coast was at first conducted from ships without any established bases. This remained the predominant pattern in areas such as Liberia and Ivory Coast throughout the pre-colonial period. On the other hand, gold was found relatively close to the coast of modern-day Ghana, and the Europeans established fortified outposts to secure trade and allow for the accumulation and storage of goods. Although the specific function of these outposts varied, they were primarily small military garrisons staffed by men. Often the garrison personnel were ethnically heterogeneous, consisting of individuals of various European nationalities, as well as Africans. For example in 1679, the complement of the Danish Fort Christiansborg consisted of the Danish commander, a Greek assistant, and 40 slaves. What sense of Danish cultural identity may have evolved in this setting is open to question. Despite their size, these communities were nevertheless crucial in drawing the coast and hinterland into the broadening Eurocentric economic system.

The most enduring monuments to European expansion are the forts and trade posts that dot the coast. Research undertaken at these sites has primarily focused on the identification of specific outposts, the histories of extant European buildings, and on preservation and restoration concerns (Bech and Hyland 1978; Bessac 1952; Bessac and Dfkeyser 1951; Courrèges 1987; Dahmen and van Elteran 1992; Diop 1993; Ephson 1970; Fage 1959; Flight 1968; Groll 1968; Hyland 1970, 1971; Jeppeson 1966; Joustra and Six 1988; Matson 1953; Mauny 1949, 1950, 1954; O'Neal 1951; Priddy 1977; Priestley 1956; Van Dantzig 1972, 1980; Van Dantzig and Priddy 1971; van den Nieuwenhof 1991; Varley 1952; Wood 1967). This work has generally not involved excavation, and archaeological data have been seen as incidental to historical and restoration interests. By far the most comprehensive work on European outposts in West Africa was undertaken by the late A. W. Lawrence between 1951 and 1957. Although Lawrence (1963, 1969) surveyed much of the West African coast, his work concentrated on the European forts and castles of Ghana. This area, encompassing the region historically known as the Gold Coast, was the site of more European trade posts than any other part of Africa. Lawrence's publications synthesize European archival material and field data to provide the seminal work on many structures and a limited amount of information on life in the forts. Lawrence provides virtually no discussion of the artifacts discovered in clearing the structures. His emphasis on building history is comparable to early work on European sites in other parts of Africa and, indeed, other world areas as well.

Work on other European sites in West Africa has similarly been motivated by restoration and preservation concerns. In Ghana, the Central Region Development Commission is currently directing work on some of the major European structures, including Cape Coast and Elmina Castles, and Fort St. Jago, where a limited amount of excavation has been undertaken to complement restoration work (Hyland 1995). Similarly, research in Sierra Leone has focused on Bunce Island, a small British trade post in the Sierra Leone estuary that was surveyed in 1993. In Benin, the Portuguese factory at Ouidah has been restored (Sinou 1992). Another case in point is Fort d'Estrees, on Goree Island off the Senegalese coast. With the help of international funding, the Senegalese government has been able to preserve much of the old townscape and renovated the Fort as the Historical Museum of Senegal. In Côte d'Ivoire no large European outposts were established prior to the nineteenth century. Scant archaeological work has been undertaken, but extensive restoration work has been done on French colonial buildings (e.g. Côte d'Ivoire 1985; Courrèges 1987).

A few European outposts have been the targets of systematic archaeological work. Funded through academic institutions, these projects were not driven by preservation concerns. Examples include Posnansky's 1976 excavations at Fort Ruychaver, a small seventeenth-century Dutch outpost on the Ankobra River, Ghana, and Calvocoressi's work at the supposed early Norman trading site at Bantoma near Elmina (Calvocoressi 1977; Posnansky and Van Dantzig 1976). More recently, a systematic survey of Danish forts and plantations in Ghana and excavations at Daccubie and Bibease were undertaken as part of a long-term study to examine culture change in coastal Ghana (DeCorse 1993), and to evaluate the nature of enslavement in a West African context (Bredwa-Mensah 1996; Bredwa-Mensah and Crossland 1997). The Danish plantations are interesting as they were, in part, established as an outgrowth of the abolitionist movement. They were, however, short lived and largely unsuccessful.

The continuing emphasis (as measured by funding) on the restoration and preservation of European structures is notable, as similar efforts have generally not been directed to African settlements. Most West African countries have only limited legislation protecting archaeological resources, and international funding to preserve or salvage sites has not been forthcoming. Multinational corporations have occasionally funded archaeological work on sites affected by development and mining activities, but these cases are the exception rather than the rule. The concentration on European structures is, in part, predicated by the need to strike a balance between preservation concerns and modern usage. Many European monuments served, and continue to serve, as government offices, prisons, and museums. More recently, European structures have been increasingly viewed as potential tourist attractions. The contrasting agendas represented makes interpretation and management of these structures difficult (Bruner 1996).

The preceding discussion illustrates the specialized nature of the European presence in West Africa and the dominance of historical and restoration concerns in research on European sites. Much more archaeological data could be usefully incorporated into restoration studies and interpretive displays. Further work on European sites also promises to provide important insights into European responses to varying contact settings and the nature of the European commodities' trade. Yet, while future research may provide valuable information, European sites can only offer insight into one side of the contact. In order to obtain a more holistic interpretation of West African culture dynamics, the associated African settlements and the vast hinterlands from which captive Africans were drawn need to be examined. This has been the focus of studies presented here.

Continuities and transformations

Relatively few studies have specifically concentrated on African settlements associated with European trade posts. Among the larger projects are the excavations undertaken at the early European trading sites of Elmina, Ghana (DeCorse 1992, 2001), and Savi in coastal Benin (Kelly this volume); in both instances the emphasis was placed on the interpretation of the associated African communities. These projects illustrate the limited amount of information afforded by European documentary accounts even in areas with long histories of African–European interaction. In terms of European source material, Elmina is one of the best described and illustrated sites in sub-Saharan Africa. It was the location of the first European trade post in the region, and the headquarters of both the Portuguese and Dutch in West Africa. The documentary evidence relating to the site is extensive. Nevertheless, specific information on life within the African settlement and African customs is far from complete. Like European illustrations of the settlement, the overwhelming emphasis is or the European presence and European concerns. Archaeological data have been used to illustrate cultural continuities in the midst of a great deal of technological and social change.

Sites such as Elmina and Savi have produced comparatively large amounts of trade items. However, more important than the number of trade items recovered is the inferences drawn from the appearance of European trade goods in the archaeological record. The presence or absence of certain categories of material goods does not automatically imply a particular stage of economic relations, certain sociocultural changes, or the assimilation of a certain suite of European cultural traits. European trade items were utilized in disparate ways. Archaeological data, nevertheless, afford an important means of assessing change in African societies. More important than the presence or absence of trade items, it is the changes in settlement patterns, defensive features, and settlement organization that testify most eloquently to the transformations that occurred in African societies. Given the general knowledge about the timing and foci of the Atlantic trade, and the relative numbers of captive Africans obtained in different areas that can be gleaned from the documentary record, we can turn to the archaeological record for evidence of the trade and its consequences. Direct evidence for slavery is exceedingly limited (DeCorse 1991). Assessment of this issue is dependent on a far better understanding of the archaeological record than is currently at hand, but the information does point to substantial change in many African societies between the fifteenth and the nineteenth centuries.

Examining West African archaeological sites, several researchers have noted radical changes in the material record of the post-European contact period. In coastal Ghana, for example, there are significant differences in form, decorative inventory, and manufacturing techniques between the pottery of the Late Iron Age/Early Historic Period and later assemblages. Data also indicate change in subsistence, as well as increasing urbanization and craft specialization (DeCorse 2001). Additional indications of change during the post-European contact period have been noted in the Birim Valley, 50 miles (80 km) west of Accra and Shai. On the basis of his excavations, Kiyaga-Mulindwa (1982) concluded that the earthworks found in this area 'may be regarded as a deterrent to small-scale attacks, petty slave-hunting forays, and kidnappings.' He further argues that increasing slave trading during the eighteenth century eventually led to the disappearance or displacement of the builders of the Birim earthworks.

Changes such as these have been widely reported in other parts of West Africa (DeCorse 1991). Archaeological data from northeastern Sierra Leone provide evidence of significant change during the eighteenth and nineteenth centuries. Settlements of the Limba, Yalunka, and Kuranko dating to this period were commonly surrounded by a variety of fortifications, including earthen walls, entrenchments, hedges of thorn bushes, and stockades of living trees (DeCorse 1989a). Oral traditions and limited documentary accounts indicate these measures were necessary protection from slave raids. Similar defensive sites dating to the last 400 years are common throughout the hinterland of the Guinea coast, and similar pressures may have precipitated the foundation of many of them.

Reasons for change in African societies during the past 500 years are clearly complex, as are archaeological perceptions of these changes. Although overarching analytical frameworks may suggest certain commonalities in response to inter-regional trends, there were variations in individual contact settings due to cultural, demographic, economic, environmental, and historical factors. While the European presence can be seen as a critical mechanism for sociocultural change in an entrepot like Elmina, other economic, social, and cultural interactions need to be considered in evaluating developments in the hinterland. Understanding the latter developments is dependent on the elucidation of indigenous relations, some of which were well underway long before the arrival of Europeans. It is the particularities of these transformations that this volume best illustrates.

References

Agorsah, E. K. (1990) Ethnoarchaeology: the search for a self-corrective approach to the study of past human behavior. *African Archaeological Review*, 8:189–208.

Atherton, J. (1983) Ethnoarchaeology in Africa. *African Archaeological Review*, 1:75–104.

Bech, N. and Hyland, A. D. C. (1978) *Elmina: A Conservation Study.* Faculty of Architecture, University of Science and Technology, Kumasi, Occasional Report, Number 17.

Bessac, H. (1952) L'emplacement des Forts de Portendick. *Notes Africaines,* 54:50–2.

Bessac, H. and Dfkeyser, P. L. (1951) Les ruines du Fort Merinaghen en marge de la mise en valeur du Senegal de 1817 a 1854. *Notes Africaines,* 49:18–21.

Bredwa-Mensah, Y. (1996) Slavery and plantation life at the Danish plantation site of Bibease. *EAZ Ethnography—Archaol,* 38:445–58.

Bredwa-Mensah, Yaw, and Crossland, Leonard B. (1997) A preliminary report on archaeological investigations at the Danish plantation settlements along the south Akuapem ridge, Ghana. *Papers of the Institute of Archaeology,* 8:59–71.

Brooks, George E. (1993) *Landlords and Strangers: Ecology, Society, and Trade in Western Africa, 1000–1630.* San Francisco: Westview Press.

Bruner, E. M. (1996) Tourism in Ghana: the representation of slavery and the return of the black Diaspora. *American Anthropologist,* 98 (2):290–304.

Calvocoressi, D. (1977) Excavations at Bantama, near Elmina, Ghana. *West African Journal of Archaeology,* 7:117–41.

Connah, Graham (1975) *The Archaeology of Benin.* Oxford: Clarendon Press.

Côte d'Ivoire, Ministère des Affairs Culturelles (1985) *Architecture Coloniale en Côte d'Ivoire. Inventaire des Sites et Monuments de Côte d'Ivoire,* Volume 1.

Courrèges, G. (1987) *Grand Bassam et les comptoirs de la côte.* Clermont-Ferrand: L'Instant Durable.

Curtin, Philip D. (1975) *Economic Change in Precolonial Africa: Senegambia in the Era of the Slave Trade.* Madison: University of Wisconsin Press.

Daaku, Kwame Yeboa (1970) *Trade and Politics on the Gold Coast 1600–1720.* London: Oxford University Press.

Dahmen, R. and van Elteran, S. (1992) *Forts and Castles of Ghana: The Future of Fort Batenstein.* Delft: Delft University of Technology.

de Barros, Philip (1988) Societal repercussions of the rise of large-scale traditional iron production: a West African example. *African Archaeological Review,* 6:91–113.

de Barros, Philip (1990) Changing paradigms, goals, and methods in the archaeology of francophone West Africa. In *A History of African Archaeology,* edited by Peter Robertshaw. London: James Currey, pp. 155–72.

Debien, Gabriel (1974) *Les Esclaves aux Antilles françaises (XVIIe–XVIIIe siècles).* Basse Terre: Société d'histoire de la Guadeloupe.

Dike, K. Onwuka (1966) *Trade and Politics in the Niger Delta 1830–1885.* Oxford: Clarendon Press.

DeCorse, C. R. (1989a) Material aspects of Limba, Yalunka and Kuranko ethnicity: archaeological research in northeastern Sierra Leone. In *Archaeological Approaches to Cultural Identity,* edited by S. J. Shennan. London: Unwin Hyman, pp. 125–40.

DeCorse, C. R. (1989b) Beads as chronological indicators in West African archaeology: a reexamination. *Beads: The Journal of the Society of Bead Researchers,* 1:41–53.

DeCorse, C. R. (1991) West African archaeology and the Atlantic slave trade. *Slavery and Abolition,* 12(2):92–6.

DeCorse, C. R. (1992) Culture contact, continuity, and change on the Gold Coast, AD 1400–1900. *African Archaeological Review,* 10:159–92.

DeCorse, C. R. (1993) The Danes on the Gold Coast: culture change and the European presence. *African Archaeological Review,* 11:149–73.

DeCorse, C. R. (1996) Documents, oral histories, and the material record: historical archaeology in West Africa. *World Archaeological Bulletin,* 7:40–50.

DeCorse, C. R. (1998) Culture contact and change in West Africa. In *Studies in Culture Contact,* edited by James Cusick. Carbondale: Southern Illinois University Press, pp. 358–77.

DeCorse, C. R. (2001) *An Archaeology of Elmina: Africans and Europeans on the Gold Coast, 1400–1900.* Washington, D.C.: Smithsonian Institution Press.

Diop, C. A. (1993) *Goree: The Island and the Historical Museum.* Dakar: I.F.A.N.

Ehret, Christopher and Posnansky, Merrick (1982) *The Archaeological and Linguistic Reconstruction of African History.* Berkeley: University of California Press.

Ellison, James, Robertshaw, Peter, Gifford-Gonzalez, Diane, McIntosh, Roderick J., Stahl, Ann B., DeCorse, Christopher R., Robbins, Larry H., Kent, Susan, Ngaba-Waye, Adoum, Sahnouni, Mohamed, and Segobye, A. K. (1996) The future of African archaeology. *African Archaeological Review,* 13(1):5–34.

Ephson, I. S. (1970) *Ancient Forts and Castles of the Gold Coast (Ghana).* Accra: Ilen Publications.

Fage, J. D. (ed.) (1959) A new check list of the forts and castles of Ghana. *Transactions of the Historical Society of Ghana,* 4(1):57–67.

Flight, C. (1968) The 'French Battery' at Elmina. *West African Archaeological Newsletter*, 10:20–3.

Garrard, Timothy F. (1980) *Akan Weights and the Gold Trade*. New York: Longman.

Geggus, D. (1989) Sex ratio, age and ethnicity in the Atlantic slave trade: data from French shipping and plantation records. *Journal of African History*, 30(1):23–44.

Gemery, H. A. and Hogendorn, J. S. (1979) *The Uncommon Market: Essays in the Economic History of the Slave Trade*. New York: Academic Press.

Greenberg, Joseph H. (1966) *The Languages of Africa*. Bloomington: Indiana University.

Groll, C. L. T. (1968) De monumenten van Europese oorsprong in Ghana. *Koninklijke Nederlandse Oudheidkundige Bond Bulletin*, 67(5):103–21.

Henige, David P. (1982) *Oral Historiography*. London: Longman.

Higman, Barry W. (1984) *Slave Populations of the British Caribbean, 1807–1834*. Baltimore: Johns Hopkins University Press.

Hiskett, Mervyn (1984) *The Development of Islam in West Africa*. New York: Longman.

Hopkins, A. G. (1973) *An Economic History of West Africa*. New York: Columbia University Press.

Hyland, A. D. C. (1970) *Documentation and Conservation*. Faculty of Architecture, University of Science and Technology, Kumasi, Occasional Report, Number 13.

Hyland, A. D. C. (1971) *The Castles of Elmina: A Brief History and Guide*. Ghana Museums and Monuments Board Series, Number 3.

Hyland, A. (1995) Monuments conservation practice in Ghana: issues of policy and management. *Journal of Architectural Conservation*, 2:45–62.

Inikori, J. E. (ed.) (1982) *Forced Migration: The Impact of the Export Slave Trade on African Societies*. New York: Africana Publishing Company.

Insoll, T. (1996) The archaeology of Islam in sub-Saharan Africa: a review. *Journal of World Prehistory*, 10(4):439–504.

Jeppesen, A. H. (1966) Danske plantageanlage pa Guldkysten 1788–1850. *Kobenhavns Universitets Geografiske Institute*, Publikation nr. 91.

Jones, Adam (1983) From Slaves to Palm Kernels: A History of the Galinhas Country (West Africa), 1730–1890. Wiesbaden: Franz Steiner.

Joustra, A. K. and Six, D. L. (1988) De oud-Europese forten aan de westkust van Afrika. *Koninklijke Nederlandse Oudheidkundige Bond Bulletin*, 87(6):256–60.

Kea, Ray (1982) *Settlements, Trade and Politics in the Seventeenth-Century Gold Coast*. Baltimore: Johns Hopkins University Press.

Kelly, Kenneth G. (1997) The archaeology of African-European interaction: investigating the social roles of trade, traders, and the use of space in the seventeenth- and eighteenth-century Hueda kingdom, Republic of Bénin. *World Archaeology*, 28(3):351–69.

Kense, François J. (1990) Archaeology in anglophone West Africa. In *A History of African Archaeology*, edited by Peter Robertshaw. London: James Currey, pp. 135–54.

Kense, F. J. and Okoro, J. Ako (1993) Changing perspectives on traditional iron production in West Africa. In *The Archaeology of Africa: Food, Metals and Towns*, edited by P. S. Thurstan Shaw, Bassey Andah and Alex Okpoko. London: Routledge, pp. 449–58.

Kiyaga Mulindwa, D. (1982) Social and demographic changes in the Birim Valley, southern Ghana. *Journal of African History*, 23:63–82.

Law, Robin (1983) Trade and politics behind the slave coast: the lagoon traffic and the rise of Lagos, 1500–1800. *Journal of African History*, 24:321–48.

Lawrence, A. W. (1963) *Trade Castles and Forts of West Africa*. London: Jonathan Cape.

Lawrence, A. W. (1969) *Fortified Trade-posts: The English in West Africa 1645–1822*. London: Jonathan Cape.

Levtzion, Nehemia and Hopkins, J. F. P. (eds), (1981) *Corpus of Early Arabic Sources for West African History*. Cambridge: Cambridge University Press.

Lovejoy, Paul E. (1989) The impact of the Atlantic slave trade on Africa: a review of the literature. *Journal of African History*, 30(3):365–94.

McCall, Daniel F. and Bennett, Norman R. (1971) *Aspects of African Islam*. Boston University Papers on Africa, Volume 5. Boston: African Studies Center, Boston University.

McCaskie, T. C. (1995) *State and Society in Pre-Colonial Asante*. Cambridge: Cambridge University Press.

MacEachern, Scott (1996) Foreign countries: the development of ethnoarchaeology in sub-Saharan Africa. *Journal of World Prehistory*, 10(3):243–304.

Manning, Patrick (1997) *Slavery and African Life: Occidental, Oriental, and African Slave Trades*. Cambridge: Cambridge University Press.

Matson, J. N. (1953) The French at Amoku. *Transactions of the Gold Coast and Togoland Historical Society*, 1(2):47–60.

Mauny, R. (1949) Une fortresse Portugaise du XVe siècle a l'embouchure du Senegal. *Notes Africaines*, 49:98–9.

Mauny, R. (1950) Un fort Hollandais du XVIIe siècle au Cap-Vert. *Notes Africaines*, 46:47.

Mauny, R. (1954) *Guide de Gorée*, 2nd edn. *I.F.A.N. Initiations Africaines*, VII: Dakar.

Miller, Joseph C. (ed.) (1980) *The African Past Speaks: Essays on Oral Tradition and History*. Hamden, Conn.: Archon.

Monod, T. (1964) Majabat al-Koubra. *Bull. I.F.A.N.*, 26(4):1,392–403.

Murdock, George Peter (1959) *Africa, Its Peoples and Their Culture History*. New York: McGraw-Hill.

Musonda, Francis (1990) African archaeology: looking forward. *African Archaeological Review*, 8:3–22.

O'Neal, B. H. St. J. (1951) 'Report on the Forts and Castles of Ghana'. Accra: Ghana Museum and Monuments Board (manuscript).

Polanyi, Karl (1966) *Dahomey and the Slave Trade: An Analysis of an Archaic Economy*. Seattle: University of Washington Press.

Posnansky, M. (1982) African archaeology comes of age. *World Archaeology*, 13:345–58.

Posnansky, M. and DeCorse, C. R. (1986) Historical archaeology in sub-Saharan Africa: a review. *Historical Archaeology*, 20(1):1–14.

Posnansky, M. and Van Dantzig, A. (1976) Fort Ruychaver rediscovered. *Sankofa*, 2:7–18.

Priddy, B. (1970) *Christiansborg Castle—Osu*. Accra: Ghana Museums and Monuments Board.

Priestley, M. A. (1956) A note on Fort William, Anomabu. *Transactions of the Gold Coast and Togoland Historical Society*, 2(1):46–9.

Redman, C. L. (1986) *Qsar es-Seghir: An Archaeological View of Medieval Life*. New York: Academic Press.

Reyna, S. P. (1990) *Wars Without End*. Hanover and London: University Press of New England.

Reynolds, Edward (1974) *Trade and Economic Change on the Gold Coast, 1804–1874*. London: Longman.

Richardson, David (1989) Slave exports from West and Central Africa, 1700–1810. *Journal of African History*, 30(1):1–22.

Robertshaw, Peter (ed.) (1990) *A History of African Archaeology*. London: James Currey.

Rodney, Walter (1970) *A History of the Upper Guinea Coast*. New York: Monthly Review Press.

Shaw, Thurstan (1989) African archaeology: looking back and looking forward. *African Archaeological Review*, 7:3–32.

Shaw, Thurstan, Sinclair, Paul, Andah, Bassey and Okpoko, Alex (eds) (1993) *The Archaeology of Africa: Food, Metals, and Towns*. New York: Routledge.

Silverman, Raymond A. (1983) 'History, Art and Assimilation: The Impact of Islam on Akan Material Culture (Ghana)'. Ph.D. dissertation, Fine Arts, University of Washington, Seattle.

Sinou, A. (1992) 'Architectural and Urban Heritage: The Example of the City of Ouidah, Benin'. Paper presented at the International Conference on Culture and Development held at the World Bank, Washington, D.C.

Sutton, I. B. (1981) The Volta River salt trade: the survival of an indigenous industry. *Journal of African History*, 22:43–61.

Terray, Emmanuel (1995) *Une histoire du royaume abron du Gyaman: des origines à la conquête coloniale*. Paris: KARTHALA.

Thornton, J. (1995) *Africa and Africans in the Making of the Atlantic World, 1400–1680*. New York: Cambridge University Press.

Trimingham, J. Spencer (1978) *Islam in West Africa*. Oxford: Clarendon Press.

Van Dantzig, A. (1972) A note on Fort 'Batenstein' and Butre. *Ghana Notes and Queries*, 12:16–19.

Van Dantzig, A. (1980) *Forts and Castles of Ghana*. Accra: Sedco Publishing.

Van Dantzig, A. and Priddy, B. (1971) *A Short History of the Forts and Castles of Ghana*. Accra: Liberty Press Limited.

van den Nieuwenhof, M. H. L. (1991) 'Vier Nederlandse Koopmanswoningen in Elmina, Ghana'. Unpublished Masters thesis, Eindhoven University of Technology, The Netherlands.

Vansina, Jan (1985) *Oral Tradition as History*. Madison: University of Wisconsin Press.

Varley, W. J. (1952) The castles and forts of the Gold Coast. *Transactions of the Gold Coast and Togoland Historical Society*, 1:1–15.

Wallerstein, I. (1986) *Africa and the Modern World*. Trenton, N. J.: Africa World Press.

Wilks, Ivor (1993) *Forests of Gold: Essays on the Akan and the Kingdom of Asante*. Athens: Ohio University Press.

Wood, W. R. (1967) An archaeological appraisal of early European settlement in the Senegambia. *Journal of African History*, 8:39–64.

2 Tools for Understanding Transformation and Continuity in Senegambian Society: 1500–1900

SUSAN KEECH MCINTOSH
with a contribution by I. Thiaw

This chapter describes what is currently known about the archaeological record of the Senegambia in the period between AD 1500 and 1900. During the seventeenth and the eighteenth centuries European writers reported on sociopolitical upheavals taking place in the interior, but in general they focused almost exclusively on the coastal areas and commercial enclaves where they resided. Archaeology offers an invaluable complementary perspective, providing abundant evidence on the ordinary aspects of everyday life left unrecorded by early observers. Recent research also offers useful insights into the social, economic, and political changes during the past 500 years.

The Senegambia (Figure 2.1) during the era of the Atlantic trade is highly contested terrain. An archaeologist sets foot upon it advisedly. Up to now, that terrain, with all its ideological minefields, has been the almost exclusive purview of historians, who have invested it with special attention, partly because the European historical sources for the Senegambia are comparatively rich, but also because no other area of Africa was exposed to the trade over a longer period of time. From the later fifteenth century until the early nineteenth century, James Island, Gorée, and St. Louis funneled human cargoes to European traders. The debates that animate and inform historical studies of the Senegambia during this period have a long history that can be traced back through two centuries of writing on the slave trade (Manning 1990:14). Curtin (1975) introduced a new rigor into the debates with his pathbreaking work, *Economic Change in Precolonial Africa: The Senegambia in the Era of the Slave Trade*, in which he attempted to evaluate the role of slaving in Senegambian society through

time by looking at changing prices and export volumes of the human commodity involved. Curtin's (1969, 1975) figures on numbers of slaves exported continue to be re-evaluated, disputed, and revised (for example Becker's revision upwards by over 50 percent for the French trade from the Senegambia—Becker 1986b: 668). But the broad interpretive polarities of recent historical debates over the magnitude of the European slave trade and its effects on West African society were set out by Rodney (1972) and Fage (1969). Rodney argued that the European slave trade entailed massive losses to Africa's labor force, producing population stagnation that in turn affected economic and technological development. Fage, on the other hand, argued that while the export of slaves may have slowed or even halted population growth, it did not produce significant social change. For certain regions, he suggested, it 'may have been more profitable to have exported the equivalent of its natural growth of population rather than to have kept it at home' (Fage 1969: 89). As

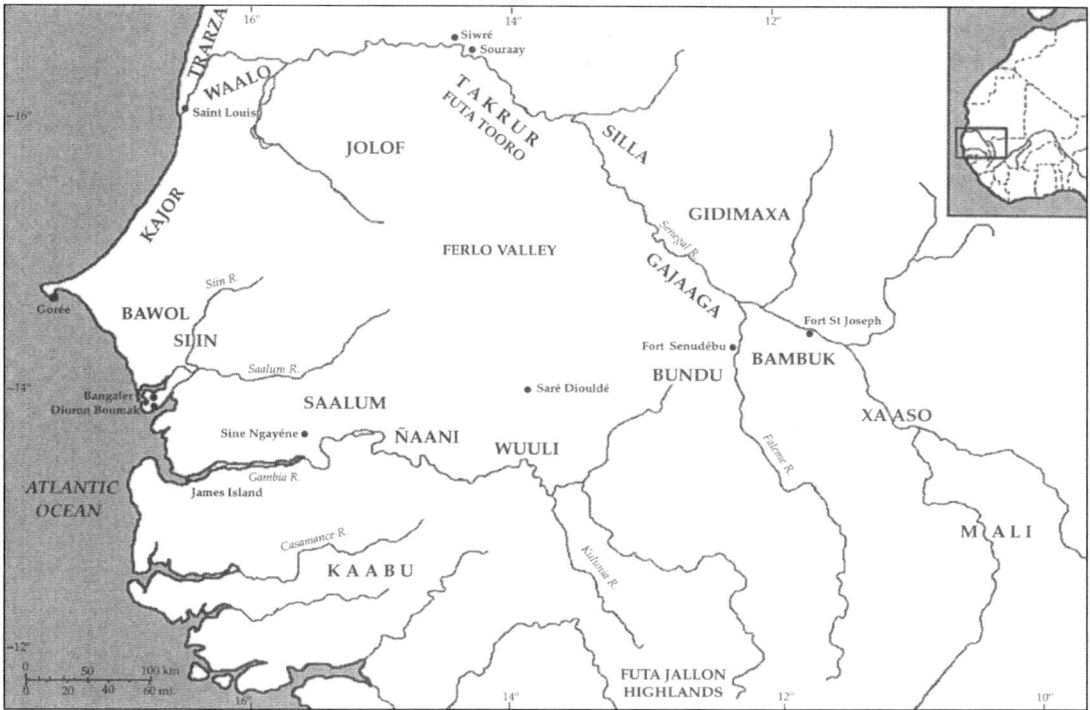

Figure 2.1 Features, regions, kingdoms, and archaeological sites mentioned in the text.

Manning (1990:14) pointed out, most of the recent studies of the social and demographic impact of slavery in Africa in general, and the Senegambia in particular, can be linked to support of one or the other of these theses (e.g. the recent re-enactment of the Fage–Rodney controversy involving Eltis (1987) and Lovejoy (1989)).

With regards to the Senegambia, it is not my intention to weigh in on one side or the other of this debate. I do want to propose, however, that an archaeological perspective which involves cross-cultural comparison and a deep-time framework that transcends the confines of the 'era of the Atlantic Trade' can offer some useful insights and, perhaps, ultimately help shape a less polarized field of historical interpretation. A social science view offers a counterpoint to potential particularist tendencies in detailed historical studies of single areas. Joined to the long-term diachronic perspective of archaeology, a comparative, systemic approach, concerned with identifying regularities in the operation of social systems involved in slave raiding and slave ownership, allows us to break down the polarities of the

Fage–Rodney theses and reframe the inquiry to ask: is significant social and political change a recurrent feature of societies involved in slave raiding and slave holding? If so, can the general principles of the dynamic driving these changes be identified? How did these play out within different historical, ecological, and cultural contexts within the Senegambia? And finally, to what extent does the social and political dynamic produced by the Atlantic trade appear to differ from that of earlier slave trading in Africa? This last question is particularly relevant to the 'underdevelopment hypothesis' of Rodney (1972) and others (e.g. Inikori and Engerman 1992), which postulates that the European slave trade changed the whole direction of development in the African societies affected by it, resulting in a deviation or slowing down when viewed against earlier trajectories of development and change. The thesis that the scale of the Atlantic trade and the new technologies of coercion that it introduced (i.e. firearms) had consequences so singular and novel as to constitute a dramatic rupture in the history and development of West Africa is accessible to empirical evaluation but only within a time-frame extending through the second millennium. This comparative and deep-time perspective liberates us from the tyranny of the European sources and their limited coastal perspective. The long-term perspective, while particularly suited to archaeology, is not unique to it. Among historians, A. Bathily (1989) and M. Klein (1977, 1998), for the Senegambia in particular, have cast their nets back to the early second millennium in an attempt to put the changes taking place after 1500 in some kind of historical perspective.

The Senegambia is particularly well suited to discussion of these issues. Of all the areas of the West African littoral, to which discussions of the Atlantic trade normally confine themselves, the Senegambia alone includes a significant area directly involved in the Saharan slave trade. Thus the Senegambia becomes, as Rodney (1966:442) recognized, an important test case for assessing the extent to which social transformations (such as domestic slavery on the West African littoral) can be attributed uniquely to the Atlantic trade, or whether they also occurred earlier in regions servicing the Saharan slave trade.

I begin then, with a long-term overview of slave trading in the Western Sudan. One detects in the literature a persistent tendency to downplay the significance of the Saharan slave trade in the history of the Western Sudan. To a certain extent, this is due to the near absence of data that would make estimates of the early desert trade possible (Austen 1992:214), but there is also an ideological element encouraging the assignment of a relatively minor status to it compared with the Atlantic trade. Rodney is instructive in this regard. Despite his acknowledgement (noted above) that the history of the slave trade in the Western Sudan prior to the beginning of the Atlantic trade was relevant to the evaluation of his thesis, his subsequent and far more strident work, *How Europe Underdeveloped Africa* (1972), virtually ignored slave trading as a factor in the emergence of Ghana, Mali, and Songhay between the eighth and sixteenth centuries. He contrasts the 'trickle of slaves from a few parts of West Africa across the Sahara' with the 'massive flow of the continent's peoples towards destinations named by Europeans' (Rodney 1972:59). More recent work has indicated that the true dimensions of

the desert slave trade were actually quite large, 'probably accounting for the uprooting of as many black Africans from their societies as did the trans-Atlantic trade' (Hunwick 1992:5).

Meillassoux (1991), in discussing the anthropology of slavery, suggests a decidedly central role for the slave trade in the development of the Sudanic states. It is worth quoting *in extenso* as a counterpoint to the dominant reconstruction of a political economy in the Sudanic kingdoms based primarily on taxes from the gold trade:

The Sahelo-Sudanese region, containing the great States which supplied slaves to the Mediterranean and the Sahara, with its long history of war, conquest and trade, was also the center of the development of an African slavery. el-Bekri refers briefly to its existence in the eleventh century. In the fourteenth century, Ibn Battuta remarks on it in the Sudanese States, and particularly in Mali. He notes slaves of both sexes, children and adults; especially palace servants, royal soldiers, and concubines. Some were employed as porters, others in the copper mines. They were subjected to corporal punishments and could be given as presents . . .

The Tarikhs el-Fettach and es-Sudan gave clearer information about the dominant forms of slavery in the kingdom of Gao in the sixteenth century. The documents refer to slaves on the land organized in plantations for the production of the material needs of the king, his followers and his army, and of 'the poor'. Slaves at court seem to have been extremely numerous . . .

. . . The period of domination by the medieval Sahelian States corresponded to the constitution and domination of an aristocratic class founded on wars of abduction. The evidence describes a slavery linked to these aristocratic forms of society: slavery at court, military slavery, slaves on the land: all intended for maintenance of the dominant class and the reproduction of its means of domination: war and the administration of war.

Although the captives' product was intended to be sold, it would be wrong to consider that the structures and destiny of this military class were based on trade. Its main activity was war; war shaped its social organization and the modes of domination of the aristocracy, as it shaped the nature of the slavery which grew up around the aristocracy. In fact the pillaging aristocrats, unlike the merchants, did not sell in order to buy other goods intended for sale. Their involvement in trade was usually limited to the purchase of use-goods. They were not in any sense intermediaries in the circuit of commodities. The African aristocracy, like most others, considered it beneath them to take part in venal activities. They merely transformed free individuals into commodities, through capture. It was the merchants who took over the products, lived by and profited from the trade and were organized socially in terms of this activity. (Meillassoux 1991:53)

As archaeological work by myself and Rod McIntosh has shown, the rapid establishment in the ninth and tenth centuries by Arabs and Berbers of well-integrated trans-Saharan and regional sub-Saharan transport networks for slaves and other commodities was made possible by the prior development of long-distance trade and specialized economies in parts of the Western Sudan (McIntosh 1995; McIntosh and McIntosh 1980, 1981). While there can be little doubt now that the emergence of complex exchange networks and large-scale communities substantially pre-dates the establishment of the trans-Saharan trade in some areas of sub-Saharan West Africa, it is also clear that the introduction of new systems of value and market demand, and new formal institutions of taxation and control, dramatically affected the nature of political organization in the Western Sudan. The improved efficiency of cavalry raiding and warfare—made possible by the introduction of innovations from the Arab world, such as the stirrup—made horses increasingly central to the political economy of the northern savanna. From Ghana in the eleventh century, to Mali (thirteenth and fourteenth centuries), and to Songhay (sixteenth century), there is a steady progression in the sophistication of statecraft, warcraft, and the imperial apparatus, and slave raiding, slave trading and the development of slave holding systems are important factors.

In considering the history of the slave trade in the Senegambia, it is necessary to recognize the extent to which Mandé concepts of governance, social organization, and power spread into the Senegambia through the agencies of migrant Soninké clans (documented in the Bawol, Kajor, the Futa Tooro, and Gajaaga) or the domination of Mali, which controlled much of the Senegambia in the fourteenth century (documented in Boulègue 1987). It was likely at this time that the Malinké title *Farba* (big chief) was borrowed by the Wolof (*buurba*), as was patrilineal succession, in contrast to all other Senegambian societies at the time (Boulègue 1987:45). Soninké and Malinké elements were ultimately Wolofized or Sereerized, such that concepts of caste, for example, which originated in the Mandé world (and which included the designation 'slave'), were incorporated into Wolof and Sereer language (Tamari 1991). Although Tamari puts a date as late as the thirteenth century on the development and spread of the caste system, I have suggested, based on archaeological evidence, that the caste system may have developed among the Soninké and spread up to three centuries earlier via an early phase of the Soninké trade diaspora (McIntosh 1981, 1995). Whatever the true date of their origins, it is clear that populations structured by principles of occupational caste and slave *vs.* freeborn status were organized into centralized polities in northern and western parts of the Senegambia centuries before the arrival of the Europeans on the West African coast.

Martin Klein (1977), in an analysis of servitude among the Wolof and Sereer that is very much informed by the long-term, comparative perspective advocated here, has provided a useful summary of how the emergence of a statutory servile group provides a new dynamic for social and political change:

> Servile relationships were a way for elites to assure themselves of goods and services in a society with scarce resources. Once the institution of the *jaam* (slave) came into being, *jaam* were increasingly called upon to meet varying personnel needs of the society. Economic and political functions were intimately related. Power gave wealth and wealth gave power. The *jaam* in any form were a kind of capital investment. They were also the most efficient way of increasing the scale of various lineages and polities. The individual enslaved could be an extra hand in the fields, an extra warrior in battle, and, if successful, even a chief who would be loyal because he was kinless. From an early date the individual enslaved could also be sold. Trade was a valuable source of both prestige goods and military equipment. Thus it was also a major source of social differentiation. The war

goods—horses, swords, and from the late 17th century on, guns—gave the elites greater control over their own societies. Prestige goods gave them a life-style distinct from that of the majority. (Klein 1977:358)

From this analysis, it is apparent how slave holding, once it emerged in a society, was likely to expand as a direct function of the desire of élites to expand their influence and power. In view of the widespread ethnographic distribution of slavery across all types of food-producing economies, Goody (1980) is confident that slavery in Africa is 'undoubtedly ancient and not a product of the European trade.' For areas that are land-rich but labor-poor, and characterized by low levels of agricultural intensification and productivity (as much of Africa is), slavery is one way that emerging élites can expand their resource base. Another is by expanding their lineage, through marriage and a whole range of other strategies for absorbing outsiders. Kopytoff and Meiers (1977:61, 64) have argued that the pervasive need of African households, kin groups, and whole societies for more people has created 'a particular kind of consumer society—one in which social groups have a driving urge to take in new persons.' African concepts of wealth and property thus tend to focus on people, in contrast to social systems such as those of feudal Europe and Asia, where land was the primary source of wealth (Goody 1971; Watson 1980). Where the struggle for control of land is paramount, kin systems tend to be exclusionary, so as to limit access rights to land. African systems, by contrast, are in general open, eventually absorbing slaves within kin groups (e.g. recognizing the offspring of a free man and a slave woman as a free member of the father's lineage—Kopytoff and Meiers 1977 provide numerous examples, but exceptions do exist). Where this kind of mobility out of the slave class exists, continuing violence and raiding are required to replenish the 'ever-emptying pool of forced labor' (Goody 1980:41).

Increased slave holding correlated with increases in polity size, in political violence related to raiding for captives, and in growth of the mechanisms of power. This is the historical pattern we see in the Western Sudan in the first half of the second millennium, and it is also the pattern we see in the Senegambia

during the era of the Atlantic trade. Becker (1985a, 1986a, 1988) has summarized the effects of the Atlantic trade on the Senegambia that can be documented historically: increased political violence and the rise of warrior states, leading to increased migration and depopulation of various regions, in response to violence and subsistence crises engendered by political instability; changes in social organization, for example, the multiplication of statutory groups; the growth of the mechanism of power; the growth of a captive class (see also Barry 1988, Bathily 1986, 1989 among many others). Some see this restructuring of Senegambian society as occurring *c*. 1700, during or just after the time when the development of sugar plantations in the West Indies caused a surge in the demand for slaves. Others (such as Barry 1985, 1988 and Boulègue 1987) believe the change began in the sixteenth century with the breakup of the Jolof empire and the emergence of smaller but more highly centralized states (Klein 1992:28). To orient readers, a table (Table 2.1) summarizing some of the important events of the second millennium in the Senegambia is included here.

The broad outlines of a process by which formerly acephalous, non-casted peoples became drawn into more hierarchically organized systems that sold and/or used slaves are suggested by Martin Klein's (1977) analysis of the Sereer of Siin and Saalum, who appear to have been influenced by their participation in the Wolof political system. It will be recalled that the Portuguese found slavery and the slave trade well developed among the Wolof when they first encountered them. Cadamosto (1937:30) wrote that the Wolof king 'supports himself by raids which result in many slaves from his own as well as neighboring countries. He employs these slaves in cultivating the land allotted to him, but he also sells many to the Azanaghi merchants in return for horses and other goods.'

We may reasonably ask whether the societies of the Middle Senegal Valley, which in the first millennium AD displayed no overt archaeological manifestations of centralized political organization or social stratification (McIntosh *et al*. 1992), were transformed in a similar fashion through contact with Mandé and Arab-Berber political systems in the period from the tenth to fourteenth centuries. The existence of slave-raiding societies in the Middle Senegal is attested by al-Idrisi in the twelfth century, who reports that the people of Silla (two days' travel from Takrur) raid the land of the Lamlam for captives, which they sell to visiting merchants. Idrisi indicates that gold and slaves were exported from Takrur (Levtzion and Hopkins 1981:107–8).

Although we typically imagine that the human cargoes in the desert trade were destined primarily for the Maghrib, a number of recent studies have documented the large numbers that were transported into servitude in the Sahel and Sahara in the eighteenth and nineteenth centuries (Klein 1992; McDougall 1992; Webb 1995). A long antiquity for this practice is suggested by al-Bakri's report that, prior to its sacking by the Almoravids in 1054, the north Sahelian town of Awdaghust was inhabited by Zanata Berbers, who owned slaves 'so numerous that one person from among them might possess a thousand' (Levtzion and Hopkins 1981:74). Slave populations could plausibly have been used in the varied productive sectors (metal working, glass making, ceramic production, textiles) attested by archaeological investigation at Tegdaoust, presumed site of Awdaghust (see especially Vanacker 1979). Although the identification of a servile population was not part of the archaeological investigations undertaken at Tegdaoust, it is worth emphasizing that archaeological techniques are well suited to this kind of inquiry, and can be usefully incorporated into research designs where skeletal remains may be anticipated. Through studies of burial customs, differential health and/or nutritional status revealed by osteological analysis and racial characteristics of the skull, it is potentially possible to identify the existence of a servile black population living among a population of Mediterranean (Berber or Arab) type.

Valuable insights arising from James Webb's (1995) remarkable study of the desert-sector trade of the western Sahel in the period 1600–1850 include the resistance of the desert-side horse-for-slave trade, which predated the Atlantic slave trade and persisted beyond it, the decline or reorientation during the period of the Atlantic trade, as well as the differential impact that the northward transfer of slaves had in different parts of the western Sahel. But most valuable of all is his demonstration of the extent to which changes in the rate and organization of the slaving enterprise were related to increasing aridity after 1600. This linkage of ecological crisis, political violence, and enslavement, as the resources of the interlocking subsistence systems of desert trader, pastoralist, and agriculturalist came under increasing pressure, offers important insights for understanding transformations of Sahelian societies during earlier climate downturns—such as that associated with the decline of Ghana in the late eleventh and twelfth centuries AD. Webb's compelling analysis also makes us far more aware that not all population displacement, political violence, and social reorganization subsequent to 1600 in the Senegambia can be attributed *a priori* to the effects of the Atlantic trade. Southward migrations from the Futa Tooro, the operation of Moroccan and Moorish armies in Bundu, as well as the Tubenan revolution, for example, may have closer linkages to the dynamic of the desert frontier. However, it is true that the two systems overlapped significantly, particularly on the Middle and Upper Senegal, making it difficult to tease apart their different effects.

While this discussion has emphasized, as is usual, changes associated with participation in the slave trade, there is another, equally interesting side to the story, which is less commonly discussed. That is the resistance of various non-hierarchically organized African groups to political centralization and participation in the slave trade. The dialectic between these societies (which include the Dogon on the middle Niger and (to different extents) the Sereer and Jola in the Senegambia) and the more centralized groups that raided them provided its own important dynamic in the history of the Western Sudan. Rodney's 1966 analysis focused on the Upper Guinea coast where a number of these societies, many of which are closely related linguistically, are concentrated. But it is Linares de Sapir's fine-grained analysis that shows us the extent of the resistance shown by the Jola to participation in the export slave trade, or in the domestic use of slave labor until very late in their history (and then only by some groups). She concludes that the source of this resistance was deeply rooted in their social institutions, since they lacked commercial institutions and marked social classes (Linares de Sapir 1987:129). This reasoning makes us all the more aware that we do not understand very well why some previously

Table 2.1 Some important events of the second millennium in the Senegambia

Time	Geographical Area		
	Senegal River Valley	Central Western	Senegal Oriental
10th century	Takrur polity established in the middle valley. Trans-Saharan trade develops exchanging gold and slaves for horses and luxuries.		Namandiru polity on Upper Senegal and Faleme, tributary to Ghana.
11th century	Takrur and Silla polities in middle valley. Takrur chief converts to Islam. Almoravid movement.		
12th to 14th centuries	Takrur absorbed by Jolof.	Jolof Empire founded by Njajan Njay. Waalo and Bawol polities established, tributary to Jolof.	Conquest by Mali of large area, consolidated as Kaabu Empire. Successive waves of Malinke settlement.
		Malian invasion defeats Jolof. Trade between Mali and Jolof grows.	
1444	Portuguese period begins. Diaz first sights Senegal River, learns of Jolof Empire. Slave trade develops: horses, brass, iron imported.		
c.1490	Koli Tengela Ba founds Kingdom of Futa Tooro.	Saalum kingdom established.	Ñaani and Wuuli kingdoms pay tribute to Kaabu.
c.1550		Jolof Empire collapses.	
early 1600s	French factories established on islands of Bocos and St Louis at mouth of Senegal; British develop Gambia trade.	Dutch factory and fort built on Gorée Island. Coastal kingdoms trade with Dutch, French, and British.	
1673–77	Tubenan religious revolution overthrows traditional rulers of Futa Tooro, Jolof, Kajor, and Waalo. Traditional dynasties, with French traders' help, defeat clerics. Jolof ruler remains loyal to Tubenan.		
1677–79		French drive out Dutch and establish coastal trade monopoly. British trade in Gambia.	
1690s			Migrations from Futa Tooro; Sy clerical dynasty established in Bundu. French forts built in Gajaaga, Bambuk, Bundu.
1700–1740s			Hostilities in Gajaaga involving French, Moroccan and Futanke forces.

Table 2.1 (*continued*)

Time	Geographical Area		
	Senegal River Valley	Central Western	Senegal Oriental
1750s–1760s			Chronic war between Gajaaga, Bundu, Bambuk, Xaaso. Control of Fort St Joseph passes into local hands.
1758–63	Seven Years' War; British eliminate French from Senegambia briefly.	Gorée returned to the French.	
1770s	Clerical revolution in Futa Tooro; Almamate established.	Rulers of Kajor, Bawol, Waalo and Jolof endorse Islamic reform movement and its new leaders.	
1778	St. Louis returned to French.		
*c.*1790	Futa Toro defeats Waalo and Trarza.	Kajor civil war; clerics lose.	Bundu civil war between cleric and secular factions; clerics lose.
1789–1815	French Revolution and ensuing wars disrupt Atlantic trade. France loses St. Louis and Gorée to British.		Bundu annexes part of lower Gajaaga, invades Futa Tooro, attacks Wuuli.
1814–15	Treaties of Paris and Vienna return Gorée and St. Louis to French; prohibit slave trade.		
1820s	French develop gum arabic trade as alternative to slave trade.		French presence re-established in Upper Senegal. Bambara raids depopulate Bambuk, affect Bundu.
1830s			Gajaaga split by warring factions. War between Gajaaga/Gidimaxa/Bundu. Civil war in Xaaso.
1840s	Slavery abolished on St. Louis and Gorée.	Groundnuts prove valuable export; revolutionize colonial commerce and indigenous economy.	
1845–64	Al-Hajj Umar Tal's militant Islamic reform movement dominates mainland politics.	Maba leads Islamic revolution and *jihad*.	Umarian conquests in Bundu, Gajaaga, Bambuk.
	Faidherbe, Governor of Senegal, launches first campaigns for colonial domination with support of French merchants.		
1870s–1890s	French colonial conquest wars and Senegalese civil wars.		

Sources: Colvin 1981; Curtin 1975, Volume 2.

non-hierarchical societies (for example, the Wolof, who are closely related linguistically to the Sereer) overcame this resistance fairly early and developed specialized economies and stratification, while other, neighboring groups did not, sometimes at the cost of decimation, assimilation, or migration. Linares de Sapir suggests that a refocus of analysis on the wide variety of slaving practices that did (and did not) develop among Upper Guinea groups would permit us to address 'the important question of what structural features and minimal conditions must have been present for different forms of slavery to have developed' (Linares de Sapir 1987:132).

Thus far, I have tried to show that when viewed within a long-term, comparative perspective, slaving systems in West Africa can be seen to be characterized by recurrent patterns of social and political change and transformation, which emerge from the political opportunities offered by slave raiding, slave holding and slave trading themselves. It also appears certain that the Mandé societies that were involved earliest and most directly in the Saharan trade developed political systems, social structures, and concepts of servitude, power, and leadership (some of which pre-date the Saharan trade) that spread through migration or conquest to the West Atlantic societies (Peul, Wolof) of the Senegambia. It is no coincidence that the first Senegambian groups to participate in the Atlantic trade—the coastal Wolof and Mandé groups (e.g. Mandingo) who had migrated along the Gambia River—shared this common heritage. Further south in the Casamance, groups such as the Jola encountered slaving for the first time in the context of the Atlantic trade.

This kind of analysis finds points of agreement and disagreement with both the Fage and Rodney camps, and consequently risks offending both to some degree. I will stick my neck out even further and suggest that sufficient comparative data are not currently available to permit evaluation of claims that the changes and transformations produced during the Atlantic slave trade were of a different magnitude or kind from those produced by the Saharan trade. Evaluating the nature and magnitude of changes during the past 500 years within the Senegambia requires detailed local and regional studies, aimed at reconstructing long-term histories extending back

beyond the debut of the Atlantic trade. Few such studies exist covering relevant topics such as changing patterns of settlement and migration, political organization and political economy, subsistence technology and economy, mode of production, nutritional status, material culture, and warfare. I have also suggested that the resistance of certain societies to centralization and slaving is a vital element for understanding the history of slavery in Senegambia. This too is an area where most of the work remains to be done.

The historical evidence available for these tasks is uneven. Internal (non-European) historical resources, including village and family traditions (describing migrations, settlement foundation, genealogies, etc.) and dynastic traditions focused on the leading families of former polities, provide a valuable counterbalance to European accounts for the period of the Atlantic trade. Regrettably, these have been generally underutilized and undercollected up to the present. This statement is not meant to diminish the significance of important collections and transcriptions of dynastic and village traditions that do exist for the Senegambia (e.g. Becker and Martin 1981a, 1981b, 1981c, 1984; Ba 1976; Bathily 1989; Boilat 1853; Brigaud 1962; Cissoko 1979; Curtin 1975; Diouf 1972; Dyâo 1864; Fall 1974; Gaden 1912; Golberry 1802; Gravrand 1983; Johnson and Robinson 1969; Kamara (forthcoming); Martin and Becker 1979; Robinson 1970, 1988; Rousseau 1933, 1941; Samb 1964; Sarr 1983; Soh 1913; Wade 1964; Wright 1977, 1979), but rather to emphasize the enormous lacunae that remain in the coverage of entire regions.

External sources, almost exclusively European, were long considered the true and unique basis of history, and consequently were privileged in historical research. The qualitative and quantitative importance of these texts varies greatly depending on time and place. In general, both the sources and the detail available on period maps demonstrate that European knowledge was limited to the coast and the valleys of the Senegal and the Gambia rivers. The earliest sources—fifteenth- and sixteenth-century Portuguese accounts—with their potential insights into Senegambian societies prior to the full development of the slave trade, are of particular interest (Alvares d'Almada 1733; Cadamosto 1937; Donelha 1977; Fernandes 1938, 1951; Gomes 1959;

Pacheco Pereira 1937; Texeira da Mota 1969; Zurara 1898–9). Yet their limited focus on the coast and on centralized societies with which they hoped to develop commercial relations, as well as the numerous interpretive problems these documents present, result in a very fuzzy and incomplete picture (Becker 1987b:157; Boulègue 1968:177).

In the seventeenth and eighteenth centuries, diverse archival documents become increasingly numerous, originating from the different European nations engaging in the Senegambian slave and gum arabic trades. Becker (1985a, 1987b) gives an excellent overview of these sources. While particularly well suited for a history of European establishment in Senegambia, Curtin (1975) and Moraes (1976) have shown that these sources provide interesting elements for a history of the Senegambia itself. The most numerous class of documents originates from European commercial enterprises and provides details on changing economic and political conditions locally. There are also reports by missionaries and scientists (e.g. the naturalist Adanson, see Becker 1981), many of which remain unpublished and little known. However, all European documents provide an outsider's view of Senegambian society, as Curtin (1975:xxiii) reminds us:

> They were mainly temporary residents of the trade enclaves Europeans maintained along the coast and rivers. Everything they wrote has kept the biases of their time, place and social status in Western society. Few indeed even tried to understand the African societies around them. For any historian, even present-day Senegalese or Gambian historians, these sources pose a constant threat of 'brainwashing' or unconsciously imposing their point of view.

While these sources do provide brief, selective, and often imprecise descriptions of local agricultural activities, customs, religions, and political leaders, they offer few details of territorial and political organization, settlement distribution, population size, and family or social structure. Thus, they provide little with which to evaluate the impact of the explosively expanding slave trade.

An enormous amount of primary data collection and analysis remains to be undertaken in the Senegambia before comparably detailed local and regional histories can be reconstructed for all parts of the region. Even when this is done, we can expect that gaps will remain and there will be a fall-off in detail the further back in time we go. Thus, for many of the topics of interest, archaeology provides us with the best possibility of developing comparable deep-time databases from different regions of the Senegambia. Regrettably, archaeology remains seriously undeveloped in the Senegambia, and the archaeology of the past 500 years is the period most poorly known. Work has focused on visually prominent remains, such as funerary mounds or megaliths and coastal shell middens, most of which appear to pre-date the era of the slave trade, although the chronology for these classes of sites rests on a very inadequate base of a few radiocarbon dates. Nevertheless, information from surveys and excavations in various regions provides preliminary insights into political organization, subsistence, material culture, and settlement patterns at various moments in time over the past two millennia. In the final section of this chapter, I summarize what we currently can say on these subjects and suggest various questions that merit archaeological investigation in the future.

Archaeology

Archaeology in the Senegambia is still poorly developed, with basic chronologies and culture history sequences lacking for most regions. The archaeology of the historic period is among the most neglected time periods, with virtually no published reports on excavations of any European site or of any regional capitals or seats of power. In 1967, Raymond Wood summarized his article 'An archaeological appraisal of early European settlement in the Senegambia' in these words:

> The excavation of [the] . . . early settlements discussed should provide trade goods which will be useful in identifying and dating native villages which were contemporaneous with them, thus establishing firm chronological horizons and the identification of native cultural units. It should also provide the basis for permitting more accurate estimates of the rate and nature of cultural change in the historic tribal groups.

Wood was, of course, quite correct in his appraisal of the kind of research programme required and its potential payoff, but the type of work he recommended is only beginning to be undertaken. The institutional structure of academic archaeology in Senegal, where it is housed within the Department of History at the University of Dakar-Ch. A. Diop, is implicated in this lack of interest in archaeology, as opposed to the texts and oral traditions, as a source of information about the period of the Atlantic slave trade. Excavations conducted by Guy Thilmans on Gorée Island a number of years ago may, ultimately, produce the kind of results Wood outlines, but thus far no report on the results or the progress of the analysis has appeared. A pioneering project of excavation and survey, aimed at recovering information on long-term change during the second millennium near the gold-producing region of the Faleme River Valley, has recently been completed (Thiaw 1999), and will be discussed later in this chapter. This project included excavation at Fort Senudébu, a trading post established by the French in the nineteenth century, and is very much informed by the agenda outlined by Wood.

Beyond historical sites with European presence, there are very few areas of the Senegambia where sites dating to the last 500 years have been identified and investigated, providing some preliminary information on material culture and some aspects of society. In the lower Casamance, Olga Linares de Sapir's (1971) work on the shell middens utilized an ecological perspective to shed light on changing settlement patterns and subsistence economies in the delta region. She succeeded in establishing a detailed, four-phase ceramic chronology, extending from 200 BC to the historic period. Interestingly, she presents us with a picture of considerable continuity through long periods of time, with pottery belonging to the same tradition as the modern Jola present from AD 200–300. Red-slipped, shell-tempered ware became increasingly common during the second millennium in the Casamance. Fernandes encountered it there in the early sixteenth century (cited in Linares de Sapir 1971:47). Pottery of a related, but more refined and highly decorated tradition comes from the shell middens of the Siin Saalum region, with a cluster of dates *c*. AD 900–1100 from the large midden of Dioron Boumak, and dates into the historic period from Bangaler (Descamps *et al.* 1974). The Siin Saalum middens differ from the Casamance middens both in size (those in Siin Saalum are vast, while the Casamance middens rarely exceed 40 meters in diameter), and in the presence of burial tumuli built of shell in the Siin Saalum. Nineteenth-century sources describe Sereer burials in the shell middens of the Joal-Fadiouth region (cited in Becker and Martin 1982:266–7):

'When a person dies, his body is carried to a cemetery and placed on a bed of shells under a straw hut, which is then covered with shells: these are tumuli of the shells of Oysters or Arca . . . When a relative dies, the tumulus is opened in order to place the body alongside those who preceded the deceased in death, then the opening is resealed. Offerings of millet and milk are made to the dead.'

This description fits well with the archaeological evidence for multiple sequential burials (up to 68 at Dioron Boumak) in each tumulus. However, study of the historical and ethnographic literature for information on pre-Islamic burial customs in Senegal shows clearly that, in addition to the Sereer, the Wolof and the Mandinka practiced tumulus burial during the sixteenth and seventeenth centuries (Becker and Martin 1982). Tumulus burial still exists among the Sereer, but the Wolof and Mandinka now follow Islamic practice. It is, therefore, unclear whether the shell tumuli of the Siin Saalum were all erected by Sereer, or whether some may have been created by the Mandinka who, Fernandes indicated, were engaged in the large-scale export of dried shellfish meat in the early sixteenth century. Alvarez d'Almada reported the presence of Sereer, whose oral traditions recall migration from the north, in the area at the end of the sixteenth century (cited in Descamps *et al.* 1974). Whether the two groups co-existed on the Petite Côte for some period of time is unknown. The ceramics from the Siin Saalum middens have not been studied in sufficient detail, nor have enough middens been excavated to permit reliable reconstruction of change through time or space in the ceramic assemblages. The excavator of Faboura shell midden, located 40 km from Dioron Boumak and nearly contemporaneous with it, describes a ceramic assemblage that differs significantly from previously described Siin Saalum coastal assemblages (Becker and Martin 1973). How best to interpret this is a question that will require expanded investigation of many more midden sites.

Burial in a variety of earthen or stone tumuli numbering in the thousands was also widespread in inland regions in the north and central parts of the Senegambia. Of the handful of excavated sites, one—Saré Diouldé—has produced a radiocarbon date with a range extending into the historic period (430 ± 130 BP, or cal. AD 1410–1650—Thilmans *et al.* 1980). The nature of the inhumations recorded from the tumulus is interesting for the insights they offer on social and political organization. In all, 56 skeletons were recovered from a single tumulus at Saré Diouldé (over 50 other tumuli exist at the site, but have not been excavated). The fact that the skeletons were still articulated and that numerous different skeletons were touching one another, rather than being separated by a layer of earth, indicates that some, if not all, of the bodies were simultaneously interred at or shortly after the time of death. The demographic composition of the buried group includes a very small percentage of children, which is the opposite of what is expected in mass deaths caused by epidemics. The excavators conclude that the dead at Saré Diouldé were most likely sacrificial victims (Thilmans *et al.* 1980). Fernandes, in the early sixteenth century, describes the burial of a coastal Manding chief, accompanied by his first wife and his servants, all of whom were entombed alive in an earthen tumulus (cited in Becker and Martin 1982:263). There are also several passages in sixteenth- and seventeenth-century texts describing the sacrifices of slaves at the burial of chiefs (but not in tumuli) in the coastal societies of present-day Guinea-Bissau (Becker and Martin 1982: 263–5). The available historical reports confirm basic archaeological postulates about the correlation of status with energy and resource investment in burial ritual. Chiefs and kings were buried in very large mounds, representing considerable labor investment, and human sacrifice is mentioned only in connection with chiefly burial. In Africa, where control of labor, rather than land, was a primary route to wealth and power, human sacrifice represented the ritual destruction of the ultimate productive resource. Its effectiveness in communicating the status of the chief so honored

was therefore considerable. Although historical sources are unlikely ever to mention the far-inland society which erected the Saré Diouldé tumuli, we are able to infer from the burials excavated there that it was hierarchically organized to the extent that labor controlled by its leaders was subject to ritual sacrifice. This kind of control suggests the existence of a captive or largely powerless sector within society, such as war captives, servants, or slaves. The fact that the teeth of the Saré Diouldé skeletons were found to have a high incidence of caries and enamel hypoplasias (Thilmans *et al.* 1980:128–31), indicative of compromised nutritional and/or health status, further supports the conclusion that these people had suffered hardship, due either to poor living conditions as captives or recurring crises (political instability, famine) that culminated in capture shortly before their deaths.

If we wished to inquire whether this situation represented a new condition that could be linked to the slave trade, we would have to look at other funerary monuments from earlier periods. Although the excavated sample is small, we find several instances of earlier monuments where multiple simultaneous burials, similar to those at Saré Diouldé, have been uncovered. Two of the megalithic circles at Sine Ngayéne, for example, produced 24 and 59 simultaneous inhumations. These skeletons also had an elevated frequency of dental pathology, although not so high or severe as at Saré Diouldé (Thilmans *et al.* 1980:128–31). The relevant radiocarbon date is 867 ± 117 BP (cal. AD 1020–1270). We can thus conclude that the conditions of hierarchical society and human sacrifice substantially pre-date the Atlantic trade. Information from Labat concerning the region around Bissao indicates that the earlier custom of strangling or interring alive a number of people with chiefs was nearly abolished by the early eighteenth century (Becker and Martin 1982:266), most likely owing to the influence of Islam (M. Klein, pers. comm.).

Sometime subsequent to the introduction of tobacco pipes into the Senegambia at the turn of the seventeenth century, pottery assemblages underwent fairly dramatic change over much of the northern and western tumulus and megalith zone, as well as in the Middle Senegal Valley. This fact, plus the fact that the changes involved broad similarities over this large area, were brought to light during two recent projects: the Middle Senegal Valley Project, involving excavation and survey at numerous sites in the central region of the valley between 1990 and 1992, and the Senegal Tumulus Survey Project, involving surface survey in different areas of the vast tumulus zone of the Senegambia.

Although the tumulus survey involved no excavation, only surface survey, it was possible to identify several distinctive ceramic assemblages that appear to be associated with different types of sites and different time periods. In the case of both the northern tumulus group and the southern tumulus/megalith group, pottery form, surface finish, decoration, and firing methods all change sometime after 1600. The pottery that we recovered from habitation sites with tobacco pipes was totally different from that associated with the earlier burial monuments (see McIntosh and McIntosh 1993 for a full discussion). The major unifying characteristic in both areas was a dramatic decline in the amount of labor or care invested in producing pottery. Pottery was crudely finished, with time no longer expended on smoothing the exterior surface, which remained ragged and uneven. Decoration largely disappeared (Figure 2.2). Slip, if applied, was slapped on haphazardly and allowed to dribble across the surface. Firing time was so brief that only a thin surface layer of clay was oxidized. The rest remained dark gray or black, due to the consumption of the available oxygen during firing by the large quantities of organic temper that also characterize this period. In both areas a similar, but not identical, range of pottery forms appears, dominated by simple, closed vessels with a high proportion of bevelled rims.

A detailed study of contact-period pottery was conducted as part of the Middle Senegal Valley Project (Gueye 1991). In the Middle Senegal Valley, the time horizon for tobacco pipes extends from their introduction c. 1600 to approximately 1850. Although in some areas pipes may have been used prior to the sixteenth century for smoking indigenous plants, such as Datura, extensive excavations in the Inland Niger Delta and the Middle Senegal Valley indicate that pipes were not present in the first or early second millennium AD. We thus consider Mauny's (1961) idea that smoking pipes were introduced to the Western

Sudan at the time of the Moroccan invasion of 1591 to be essentially correct for these two areas. Pipe smoking declined when the *jihad* movement of El Hadj Omar, which forbade tobacco to members of this Tidjani sect, became widespread in Senegal (Gueye 1991). On the basis of association with tobacco pipes on the surface of sites within the Middle Senegal Valley, Thilmans and Ravisé (1980) had identified a ceramic group they called 'Toucouleur subactuel'. Subsequent excavation by Gueye (1991) at two Middle Senegal Valley sites, Souraay and Siwré, produced archaeological deposits with pipes and characteristic pottery of this group, which permitted an expanded understanding of the nature of these recent assemblages. While we still have much to learn about how these contact-period assemblages evolved through time, this work provides a preliminary framework to guide future research.

Contact-period pottery in the Middle Senegal Valley is highly characteristic in possessing the following group of traits: it is frequently thin-walled (average 5–7 mm) and made of a fine but extremely porous paste, from the abundant use of organic (chaff and straw) temper. Firing conditions caused much of the temper to burn off, leaving masses of voids. The open-air firing of the pottery was apparently brief enough that most of the available oxygen was consumed by the burnoff of the vegetable temper. Consequently the paste is an unoxidized dark gray color throughout, or oxidized to a reddish-orange only on the surface, with a black unoxidized core. The pottery represents a very limited range of simple globular forms, with lips that are either simple and uninflected, sometimes with a bevelled edge, or everted, or straight and narrow, like a short tube perched atop a sphere (Figure 2.3). Over half of all rim and body sherds are either plain or slipped, with no other decoration. The commonest decorative motif, after slip, is twisted and rolled twine roulette, followed by linear incision with something the size of a straight pin ('pin incision'), and raised cordons marked by fingernail impressions.

Compared to both earlier assemblages in the Middle Senegal Valley and the pottery produced today by Tukolor potters in the region, one can see in this assemblage a reduction of labor investment in potting (Gueye 1991:152). Time-consuming elements, such as

Figure 2.2 Pottery from the Sine Ngayene area dated to the early second millennium (top) shows careful preparation and decoration. Late second millennium pottery (bottom) from the same area shows how poorly prepared and finished these vessels were.

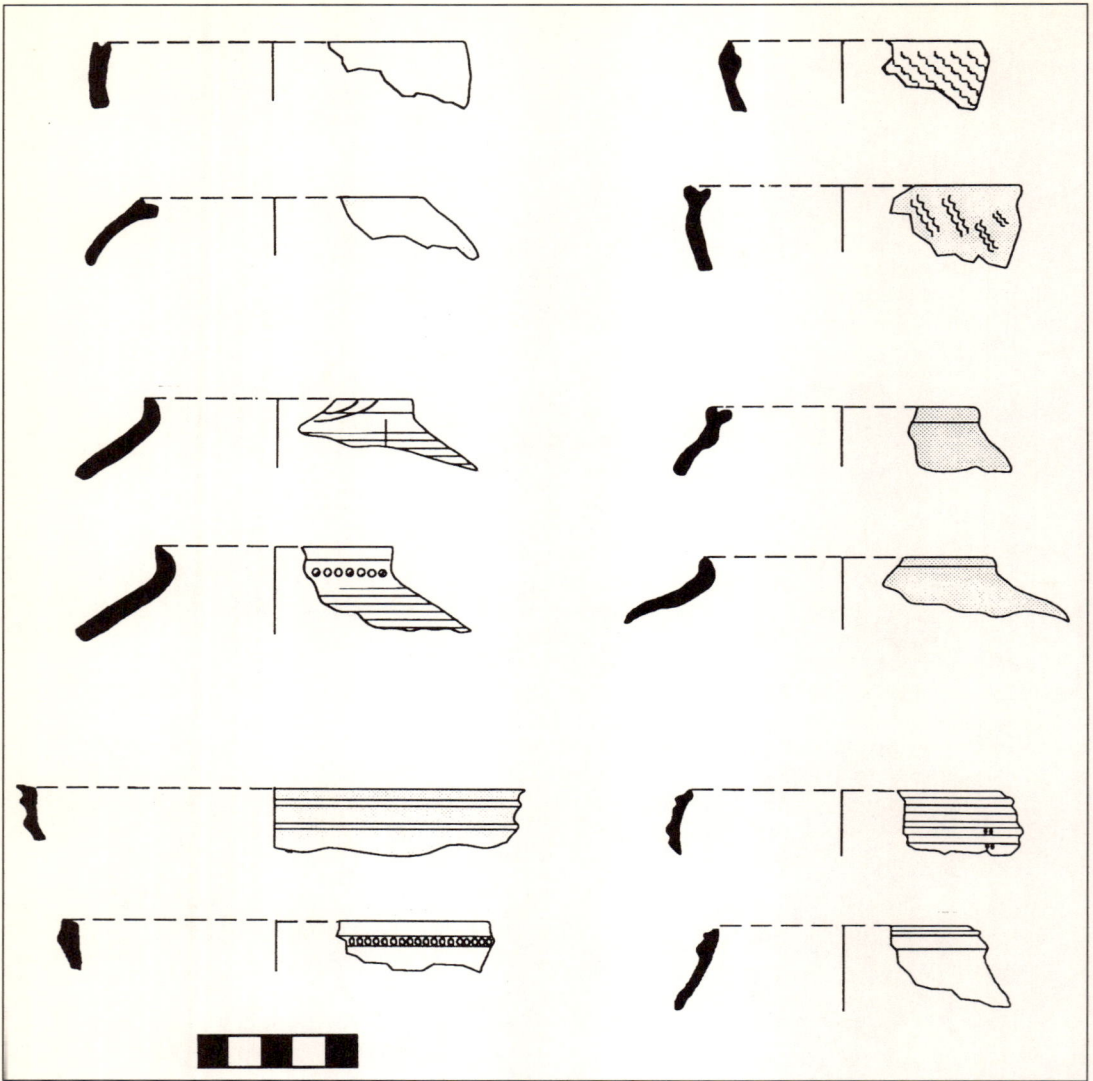

Figure 2.3 Pottery from the Middle Senegal Valley dating to the recent period (AD 1600–1900). Vessels with a bevelled lip are highly diagnostic (top four). Commonly, these are undecorated or covered with red slip (stippled), but may have rolled twine decoration. Globular vessels with a short, vertical lip are also diagnostic (middle four). These may be decorated with pin incision, slip, and/or a zone of twine roulette. Simple open or closed vessels with one or more raised cordons are another distinctive class of subactuel pottery (bottom four). These are often slipped and sometimes decorated with fingernail impressions on the cordon. (Redrawn from Gueye, 1991).

crushing and sieving of pottery temper and kneading the clay, have been eliminated, resulting in a porous, friable, and weak paste. Both form and decor are limited in variety. Among the possible factors accounting for this precipitous decline in the quality of pottery production are slave raiding (which was a major activity along the Senegal River in the period under discussion (1600–1850)), political unrest, civil wars, and population movements related to Islamic militancy, beginning with the war of the marabouts in 1673–77, the tooroodo revolution of 1776, and leading up to the eve of the Tukolor *jihad* movement of El Hadj Omar in 1850 (Gueye 1991). While it is tempting to attribute the extreme and repeated disruption of Middle Senegal Valley society during the seventeenth and eighteenth centuries to the presence of slave traders on the Senegal River, it is important to recall that recurrent severe droughts characterized this period, which brought desert nomads and pastoralists into increased conflict over the water sources and pasture in the Middle Senegal Valley in a scenario that has been played out many times over the past two thousand years. There is also the consideration that slave raiding has been present in the Middle Senegal Valley since at least the twelfth century, when it is mentioned by al-Idrisi.

What appears to have been unique about this time period is the spread, for the first time, of similar, related ceramic assemblages throughout western and northern Senegal. From the Middle Senegal Valley south to the Saluum area we find, on sites occupied between AD 1600 and 1850, poorly made organic tempered pottery that shows the same range of simple forms and careless decoration as the Middle Senegal Valley sites. This represents a definite change, as far as we understand it, from an earlier situation characterized by numerous distinct regional ceramic traditions within this same area. Oddly, it was during an earlier period (thirteenth–fifteenth century) that a single identifiable political entity—the Jolof confederation—existed between the lower Senegal and Gambia rivers. The Jolof hegemony came apart at the end of the fifteenth century, largely owing to large-scale movements of Peul from the east, led by Koli Tengella. Tengella established the Denyanké dynasty in the Middle Senegal in the fifteenth century, and moved south on a path of conquest that extended south of the Gambia into the Fuuta Jallon, and back north to the Upper Senegal. The disruption that followed this invasion is described in oral tradition recounted by Yoro Dyao (cited in Boulègue 1987:161):

'having become . . . the uncontested master of the Futa [Middle Senegal Valley], Koli attacked the Namandiru [in the Ferlo Valley]. The inhabitants of Namandiru fled to the Jolof, the Siin and the Saalum, and their homeland became the desert which today separates the Futa from the Jolof.'

While it is tempting to speculate that the widespread distribution of this type of pottery reflects Peul movements and shifting centers of dominance, we really have too little data at present to evaluate such hypotheses. We are missing crucial information, for example, on the contact-period sequences on the coast, where Peul were not dominant, and in the Futa Jallon, where they established an important regional hegemony. In a recent thesis, Gueye (1998) attributes the spread of this subactuelle assemblage throughout the Middle Senegal Valley to circulation of pottery via various forms of exchange among Peul/Tukolor networks, as well as via Peul seasonal transhumance.

As mentioned earlier, only one region in Senegal has been the focus of systematic archaeological investigation of sites dating to the last 500 years—the Falemme region of the Upper Senegal drainage system. In the final part of this section devoted to archaeology as a source of information on this period, Ibrahima Thiaw summarizes the results of his pioneering research.

Processes of change in the Falemme: AD 500–1900, by Ibrahima Thiaw

In 1996/7, the Falemme Archaeological Research Project conducted survey and excavation along a previously unexplored 50 km segment of the Falemme River. Although economically marginal today, the area was historically linked to both the trans-Saharan and the Atlantic trade, and thus had great potential to illuminate processes of change in an area remote from the shores of both the Atlantic and the Sahara. The research included extensive surface survey (resulting in the mapping of 154 previously unknown sites), plus excavation at three sites: Arondo, a late first and early second millennium site at the Senegal/Falemme confluence; the French trading post of Fort Senudébu; and Tata Almamy—two nineteenth-century sites located about 45 km up-river from the confluence. Tata Almamy was a palace for the local leader, or *Almamy*, of Bundu and was established atop an escarpment immediately adjacent to Fort Senudébu (Flize 1857). The objectives of the research were to recover information on change in subsistence, site density, craft production, land use, trade, and material culture to provide direct evidence relevant to an understanding of change in the region during the second millennium AD.

From this work, it emerges that from 500 to 1500, the lower Falemme was sparsely occupied (only 18 sites in the survey region date to this period) and involved in limited long distance trade. Copper and beads were being imported as prestige items from across the Sahara, and were exchanged against gold from the nearby goldfields of Bambuhu and Buure, as well as slaves and grains that fed the southern Sahara trade entrepôts (Bathily 1989; Thiaw 1999). Many of the sites dating to this period yielded spindle-whorls, indicating the presence of a weaving industry. Production of marketable surpluses in grains and cloth eventually led to an increased reliance on slave labor, perhaps by the first half of the second millennium AD. But at Arondo from AD 500 to 1000, subsistence remains indicate a reliance on both domesticated and wild plant and animal resources. Settlement during this period was organized on levees along the river, with little evidence of hierarchy or urban development. The largest site is only eight hectares, and over 75 percent of the sites measure less than one hectare.

In the late fifteenth and early sixteenth centuries, the Portuguese were aware of the commercial potential of the Upper Senegal. They penetrated the region and erected an outpost at the Felu Falls, at the gate of the gold mines of Bambuhu (Boulègue 1987; Hair 1984). However, the success of local merchants (juula) as middlemen in the international commerce depended on their monopoly on inland trade networks. Portuguese settlement in the region was short lived as a result of the combined hostility of the juula traders, inclement climate, and disease.

Beginning in the eighteenth century, however, repeated expeditions by the French and British from their coastal bases increasingly opened the Upper Senegal to the Atlantic system, ultimately deflecting most of the traffic toward that region (Chambonneau 1898; Hodges 1924; Jobson 1968; Park 1960). At that time, the French chartered companies established a number of trading outposts along the Senegal and Falemme rivers but repeatedly failed to eradicate the trade that local merchants entertained with the British on the Gambia (David 1974; Delcourt 1952; Dodwell 1916; Gray 1966).

Settlement patterns, site structural/functional variability, and material culture traced to this period differ fundamentally from that of earlier periods. Contacts with the Sahara were maintained willingly or unwillingly, as Moroccan expeditionary forces and Mauritanian emirates of Brakna and Trarza permanently forayed for slaves, cattle, and grains in the entire region (Bathily 1989; Curtin 1975; Delcourt 1952). But the assemblages encountered show a dramatic increase in European imports and a decline in Saharan trade imports. European glass beads and metal imports were particularly popular. The growth in European iron bar imports is directly linked to the development of commercial agriculture. A large number of slaves were locally employed in producing marketable commodities that were sold to the Europeans (Manchuelle 1997). This activity was more profitable to the local élites and traders, who sold only their surplus in slaves to the Europeans.

Some trade items had a major impact on the lifestyle of the Africans. The presence of wine bottles in contexts associated with indigenous occupation, both at Fort Senudébu and Tata Almamy, is quite intriguing. We know from historical sources that Almamy Boubakar Saada settled at Fort Senudébu after the French evacuated in the 1860s (Gomez 1992).

One other critical aspect of the lower Falemme nineteenth-century assemblages is the dominance of British manufactured products, including musket balls, beads, ceramics, etc. This period of rapidly changing tastes influenced by European manufacture is also characterized by dramatic changes in local crafts and productive technologies. The pottery assemblages are dominated by the subactuelle pottery described in the preceding section (Chavane 1985; Gueye 1991, 1998; McIntosh and McIntosh 1993; Thilmans and Ravisé 1980). Subsistence economies, too, attest to changes. At Fort Senudébu and Tata Almamy, sheep/goat and cattle had largely displaced wild animal resources, although both wild and domesticated plant resources continued to be exploited. Interestingly, ovicaprine teeth show a high number of individuals culled at a young age. This pattern, combined with the predominance of cattle and sheep, can be linked either to livestock raiding conducted by the French colonists and Almamy Saada, or the arrival of specialized herding economies and increased trade in livestock (Watson 1999).

The nineteenth century is partially illuminated by historical sources, in which there are indications that commercial agriculture reached a tremendous peak of development during this period (Bathily 1986, 1989; Brooks 1975; Curtin 1975; David 1974; Delcourt 1952; Gomez 1992; Manchuelle 1989, 1997; Moitt 1989; Swindell 1980). Commercial agriculture relied heavily on domestic slavery and was cornered by the local élites and *juula* traders, who supplied grains, peanuts, indigo, tobacco, and cotton to the French colonists, their domestics, and slaves. After the imposition of the colonial government in the late nineteenth century the axis of economic activities was redeployed to the coastal Atlantic regions, affecting severely the economy and demography of the Upper Senegal valley.

Parallel with trade and exchange relations, major changes are noted in settlement pattern. Along with French European outposts, new local sites known as *tata*, which were fortified strongholds, were being built in the region. *Tata* were simple city walls or defensive sites built out of mud or stones. Both European outposts and *tata* were preferentially located on higher topographic elevations including levees and escarpments. The majority of sites dating to this period (30 out of 57 in total) were, however, established on the lowland within the floodplain and are known in the Middle Senegal valley as *plages* (Thilmans and Ravisé 1980). This pattern is interpreted in relation to the expansion of the Atlantic system and correlated with the development of slavery and increased political violence. The erection of *tata* reflects the success, wealth, and prestige of the local élites and traders who drew tremendous profits from the Atlantic trade, competing with the Europeans. Many historical sources linked these structures with increased social differentiation, political control, slave raiding, war and resistance (Faidherbe 1889; Leblanc 1822; Park 1960; Raffenel 1846). In contrast, the *plages* were relegated to the defenseless populace, including ordinary yeomen and slaves.

In the western Lower Falemme, the number of sites provisionally dated to the eighteenth and nineteenth centuries is double the number of sites dating to the period 500–1500. Even so, it is clear that a large number of peoples were displaced as a result of slavery, *jihad* wars and French colonial conquest (Bathily 1970, 1972; Clark 1994, 1996; Marty 1925; Nyambarza 1969; Robinson 1985, 1987). Regional out-migration was accelerated in the late nineteenth and early twentieth centuries as the French redeployed their commercial and economic activities toward the coastal regions, but also, in certain areas, as a result of the official abolition of slavery (Brooks 1975; Clark 1994; Manchuelle 1989; Moitt 1989; Roberts and Klein 1980; Swindell 1980).

The Lower Falemme evidence suggests that the Upper Senegal societies were profoundly affected by slavery. However, the long-term experience of the local population with interregional commerce permitted them to maximize their profits during the Atlantic era. Their capitalization on commercial agriculture and slave labor tremendously limited European slave imports against which they competed. Available archaeological evidence indicates that the expansion of the Atlantic system in the Upper Senegal had a major impact on the local economy and demography of the region.

Conclusions

At the beginning of this chapter, it was pointed out that some highly polarized debates exist regarding the impact and consequences of the Atlantic slave trade on Africa in general and the Senegambia in particular. I have argued that, without a deeper time perspective on the changes accompanying the earlier incorporation of the Sudanic zone into the Saharan slave trade, assessing claims that the Atlantic slave trade had unprecedented and unique consequences is impossible. This is not to deny the extremely strong case that has been made for the major impact of the Atlantic trade on Senegambian societies in the seventeenth and eighteenth centuries especially: Charles Becker has gathered the compelling evidence for the growth of warrior states, political instability, and famine that prompted increased population movements as people re-aligned themselves to participate in or to protect themselves from the trade in slaves. That other factors, such as climate change and shifting patterns of desert-side trade, may have contributed to these changes is not to deny the fundamental importance of the Atlantic trade to understanding them.

Lovejoy (1983, 1989) and Klein (1992) have argued that in the long history of slavery in West Africa, the Atlantic slave trade had a transforming effect because it succeeded in making slavery basic to the political economy, exemplified by dependence on a slave mode of production, which emerged for the first time in local economies by the nineteenth century. In the course of this transformation, it is argued, African use of slaves shifted from the agricultural sector to specialized production of trade commodities. There is evidence from Tegdaoust in the eleventh century for specialized production of trade commodities by massive slave populations, and from the Mali Empire in the fourteenth century for immense slave plantations. African slavery varied from place to place and from one time period to another in the scale of enslavement and the uses to which slaves were put. In the first half of the second millennium, slaves were used in raw material extraction (gold, copper, salt), warfare, agriculture, the household, and transport. The fact that African kin systems absorbed slaves, especially women who bore children to freemen, and the children of these unions, suggests that the violent cycle of continual raiding for new slaves has a long time-depth in West Africa. Is the pattern of loosely confederated polities such as Wolof fragmenting in the face of this violence, and being replaced by smaller, more centralized polities really new to the Atlantic trade? Or are we seeing a continuation of the alternating alliance-building/consolidation *vs.* fragmentation cycle that began with the Ghana kingdom and accelerated as new technologies for warfare became available?

Consideration of these issues leads us to conclude that the history of the slave trade writ large must be built up from numerous local and regional histories. Our brief review of the available historical sources concludes that external sources have too many gaps for this purpose and must be complemented by internal sources, such as provincial, dynastic, and village traditions. We have emphasized the tremendous amount of work that remains to be undertaken in collecting and analyzing this type of material. Archaeology likewise provides a powerful tool for collecting data for inter-regional comparisons through time on settlement patterns, subsistence economy, nutritional and health status of groups within societies, material culture, technology, craft production, and warfare. The funerary monuments (tumuli and megaliths) that attracted considerable research interest between the 1960s and the 1980s are excellent candidates for physical anthropological analyses of health, nutritional status, and incidence of trauma that would inform us on differentials in diet and violence through time. This kind of analysis has not yet been applied to the skeletons recovered from excavated monuments.

The archaeology of the past 500 years in the Senegambia is woefully underdeveloped at present. Surveys along the Middle Senegal Valley (Deme 1991; Gueye 1991; Martin and Becker 1974, 1977; Thilmans and Ravisé 1980) and in the northwest quadrant of the Senegambia (Diop 1985; McIntosh and McIntosh 1993) have demonstrated that site density is relatively low during this period, in comparison with the many sites that were occupied in the region during the first and early second millennia.

In the lower Falemme, by contrast, site density is remarkably low between AD 500 and 1500, with only 18 sites (most under one hectare in area) providing surface material dating to this period. The survey evidence does not support the claim (Bathily 1989) that the Upper Senegal was urban in character in the early second millennium. Material from the period 1500–1900 is present on 57 sites, some quite large (18–20 hectares). This suggests that very different long-term trajectories characterize the Middle and Upper Senegal regions. Given the more limited agricultural zone in the Upper Senegal drainage, population expansion may not have peaked until pastoral economies were implanted in the region by the Peul in the second half of the second millennium. The increase in settlement numbers may be attributed to increasing mobility in an atmosphere of political violence, in which new settlements are founded frequently, and occupied only briefly by refugee populations. Alternatively, population on the narrow river flood plain may have grown and land use intensified due to the development of slave-based agricultural production for export. Future archaeological research should permit assessment of these various possibilities. In any event, however, it is clear that the notion of a large-scale and urbanized landscape that was dramatically decimated during the era of the Atlantic trade cannot be sustained for the Upper Senegal/ Falemme confluence zone.

Once dated archaeological sequences of material culture can be established (as in the Middle Senegal Valley—McIntosh *et al.* 1992, and the lower Falemme—Thiaw 1999), it is possible to undertake systematic foot surveys in order to reconstruct shifting patterns of settlement through time. This can reveal episodes of abandonment throughout an entire area (as, for example, in the Mema region of Mali *c.* AD 1400—Togola 1996), for which multiple hypotheses, including slave raiding, must be considered. Through systematic survey and excavation, it is also possible to look at changing patterns of artisanal production and relative wealth within a region, by plotting numbers and distributions of the materials of production (spindle-whorls, loom weights, brass casting molds, etc.) and trade goods (beads, brass, gold) through time. An approach integrating these archaeological aspects with collection and analysis of local traditions offers our best hope of reconstructing shifts in the regional political economy through time. Needless to say, this will require tremendous effort, time, and resources, but a reliable and complete history of the Senegambia in the era of the Atlantic slave trade cannot be written any other way.

Acknowledgments

I am grateful to Charles Becker for his customary generosity in providing access to his published and unpublished papers and his bibliographic archives, all of which were fundamental to the writing of the original version of this chapter. I regret deeply that the historical sections to which he contributed so significantly had to be drastically abbreviated as a result of the switch in publishers from Smithsonian to Leicester. Charles Becker read and commented on a preliminary draft, and Martin Klein provided helpful comments on a later draft. I extend my thanks to them both. Any errors, inconsistencies, or plain wrongheadedness that might remain, despite their best efforts, are attributable to me alone.

References

Alvares d'Almada, A. (1733) *Relação e descripção de Guiné, na qual se trata das varias naçoens de negros.* Lisbon. (Reprinted in *Monumenta Missionaria Africana*, edited by Antonio Brasio, 2nd series, volume 3).

Austen, Ralph (1992) The Mediterranean Islamic slave trade out of Africa: a tentative census. In *The Human Commodity: Perspectives on the Trans-Saharan Trade*, edited by E. Savage. London: Frank Cass, pp. 214–48.

Ba, A. B. (976) Essai sur l'histoire du Saloum et du Rip. *Bulletin de l'Institut Fondamental d'Afrique Noire* (series B), 38(4):813–60.

Barry, Boubacar (1985) *Le Royaume du Waalo: le Sénégal avant la conquête.* Paris: Karthala.

Barry, Boubacar (1988) *La Sénégambie du XVe au XIXe siècles: traite négrière, Islam et conquête coloniale.* Paris: L'Harmattan.

Bathily, A. (1970) Mamadou Lamine et la résistance anti-impérialiste dans le Haut-Sénégal (1885–1887). *Notes Africaines*, 125:20–32.

Bathily, A. (1972) La conquête française du Haut-Fleuve (Sénégal) 1818–1887. *Bulletin de l'Institut Fondamental d'Afrique Noire* (series B), 34(1):67–112.

Bathily, A. (1986) La traite atlantique des esclaves et ses effets économiques et sociaux en Afrique: le cas de Galam, royaume de l'hinterland sénégambien au dixhuitième siècle. *Journal of African History*, 27:269–93.

Bathily, A. (1989) *Les Portes de L'Or: le royaume de Galam de l'ère musulmane au temps de négriers (VIIIe–XVIIIe siècles).* Paris: L'Harmattan.

Becker, Charles (1981) Cartes inédites d'Adanson sur le Sénégal. *Notes Africaines*, 172:93–100.

Becker, Charles (1985a) Histoire de la Sénégambie du XVe au XVIIIe siècles: un bilan. *Cahiers d'études Africaines*, 25(2):213–42.

Becker, Charles (1985b) Notes sur les conditions écologiques en Sénégambie aux 17e et 18e siècles. *African Economic History*, 14:167–216.

Becker, Charles (1986a) Conditions écologiques, crises de subsistance et histoire de la population à l'époque de la traite des esclaves en Sénégambie (17e–18e siècle). *Revue Canadienne des Études Africaines*, 20(3):357–76.

Becker, Charles (1986b) Note sur les chiffres de la traite atlantique française au dixhuitième siècle. *Cahiers d'Etudes Africaines*, 26:633–79.

Becker, Charles (1987a) 'La Place de la Sénégambie dans la traite atlantique française du 18e siècle'. Communication au 2e Congrès International de Démographie Historique de Paris.

Becker, Charles (1987b) Reflexions sur les sources de l'histoire de la Sénégambie. *Paideuma*, 33:147–230. Special issue on *European Sources for Sub-Saharan Africa Before 1900: Use and Abuse*, B. Heintze and A. Jones (eds).

Becker, Charles (1988) Les effets démographiques de la traite des esclaves en Sénégambie. Esquisse d'une histoire des peuplements du XVIIe à la fin du XIXe siècles. In *De la traite à l'esclavage du XVIIIe au XIXe siècle*, edited by S. Daget. Nantes-Paris: Société française d'Histoire d'Outre-Mer., pp. 70–110.

Becker, C. and Martin, V. (1973) *Historique des recherches sur la protohistoire sénégambienne*. Kaolack Senegal: multigr.

Becker, C. and Martin, V. (1981a) *Traditions villageoises du Saalum: Arrondissement de Ouadiour*. Kaolack, Ms. in possession of the author.

Becker, C. and Martin, J. (1981b) *Traditions villageoises du Saalum: Arrondissement de Kahone*. Kaolack, Ms. in possession of the author.

Becker, C. and Martin, V. (1981c) *Traditions villageoises du Saalum: Commune de Kaolack*. Kaolack, Ms. in possession of the author.

Becker, C. and Martin, V. (1982) Rites de sépulture préislamiques au Sénégal et vestiges protohistoriques. *Archives Suisses d'Anthropologie générale*, 46(2):261–93.

Becker, C. and Martin, V. (1984) *Traditions villageoises du Siin: Arrondissement de Niakhar*. Kaolack, Ms. in possession of the author.

Boilat, P. D. (1853) *Esquisses sénégalaises*. Paris: Bertrand.

Boulègue, J. (1968) *La Sénégambie du milieu du XVe siècle au début du XVIIe siècle*. Paris: Université de Paris I.

Boulègue, J. (1987) *Le Grand Jolof (XIIIe-XVIe siècle)*. Paris: Karthala.

Brigaud, F. (1962) *Histoire traditionnelle du Sénégal*. Saint-Louis: Centre de recherches et de documentation du Sénégal, Études Sénégalaises. Connaissance du Sénégal, IX.

Brooks, G. (1975) Peanuts and colonialism: consequences of the commercialization of peanuts in West Africa, 1830–70. *Journal of African History*, 16(1):29–54.

Cadamosto, A. da (1937) *The Voyages of Cadamosto*. (Trans. G.R. Crone) London.

Chambonneau (1898) Relation du Sr Chambonneau, commis de la compagnie de Sénégal, du voyage par luy fait en remontant le Niger (Juillet 1688). *Bulletin de Géographie historique et descriptive*, Number 2:308–21.

Chavane, B. A. (1985) *Villages de l'ancien Tekrour: recherches archéologiques dans la moyenne vallée du fleuve Sénégal*. Paris: Karthala.

Cissoko, S. M. (1979) 'Contribution à l'histoire politique des royaumes du Khasso dans le Haut Sénégal, des origins à la conquête française (XVIIe Siècle – 1890)'. Paris: Université de Paris I. Thèse de doctorat d'état.

Clark, A. F. (1994) Internal migrations and population movements in the Upper Senegal Valley (West Africa), 1890–1920. *Canadian Journal of African Studies*, 28(3):399–420.

Clark, A. F. (1996) The Fulbe of Bundu (Senegambia): from theocracy to secularization. *The International Journal of African Historical Studies*, 29(1):1–23.

Colvin, L. G. (1981) *Historical Dictionary of Senegal*. Metuchen, N. J.: Scarecrow Press.

Curtin, P. D. (1969) *The Atlantic Slave Trade*. Madison: University of Wisconsin Press.

Curtin, P. D. (1975) *Economic Change in Precolonial Africa. I. Senegambia in the Era of the Slave Trade. II. Supplementary Evidence*. Madison, University of Wisconsin Press, 2 vols.

David, P. (1974) *Journal d'un voiage fait en Bambouc en 1744*. Paris: Société française d'histoire d'Outre-Mer.

Delcourt, A. (1952) *La France et les establissements français au Sénégal entre 1713 et 1763*. Paris: Mémoire de l'Institut Fondamental d'Afrique Noire, 17.

Deme, A. (1991) 'Evolution climatique et processus de mise en place du peuplement dans l'Ile à Morphil'. Mémoire de Maîtrise, Université Ch. Anta Diop de Dakar.

Descamps, C., Thilmans, G. and Thommeret, Y. (1974) Données sur l'édification de l'amas coquillier de Dioron Boumak (Sénégal). *Bulletin de l'Association Sénégalaise pour l'Etude du Quaternaire Africane*. 41:67–83.

Diop, B. (1985) 'Les sites archéologiques du Bawol: approche ethnographique'. Mémoire de Maitrîse, Université de Dakar.

Diouf, N. (1972) Chronique du royaume du Sine. *Bulletin de l'Institut Fondamental d'Afrique Noire*, (series B), 34(4):702–32.

Dodwell, H. (1916) Le Sénégal sous la domination anglaise. *Revue d'Histoire des Colonies Françaises*, 4:267–300.

Donelha, A. (1977) *Descrição da Sierra Leoa e dos Rios de Guiné do Cabo Verde (1625)*. Edited by A. Texeira da Mota, English trans. P. E. H. Hair. Lisbon.

Dyâo, Y. (1864) Histoire des damels du Cayor. *Moniteur du Sénégal et Dépendances*, 448: 148–50; 449:153–4; 450:156–7; 451:151–62; 452:165–6; 453:169–70.

Eltis, David (1987) *Economic Growth and the Ending of the Transatlantic Slave Trade*. New York: Oxford University Press.

Fage, J. D. (1969) *A History of West Africa*. Cambridge: Cambridge University Press.

Faidherbe, L. L. C. (1889) *Le Sénégal. La France dans l'Afrique Occidentale*. Paris: Librairie Hachette et Cie.

Fall, T. L. (1974) Recueil sur la vie des Damel. *Bulletin de l'Institut Fondamental d'Afrique Noire* (series B), 36(1):98–140.

Fernandes, V. (1938) *Description de la côte d'Afrique de Ceuta au Sénégal*. Edited by P. de Cenival and T. Monod. Paris: Larose.

Fernandes, V. (1951) *Description de la côte occidentale d'Afrique (Sénégal au Cap de Monte, Archipels)*. Edited by T. Monod, A. Texeira da Mota and R. Mauny. Bissau: Memoirell, Centro de estudio da Guiné portuguesa.

Flize, L. (1857) Le Boundou (Sénégal). *Revue Coloniale*, 17:175–8.

Gaden, H. (1912) Légendes et coutumes sénégalaises, d'après Yoro Dyâo. *Revue d'Ethnographie et de Sociologie*, 3 (3–4) 119–37; (5–8) 191–201.

Golberry, S. M. X. (1802) *Travels in Africa during the Years 1785, 1786, 1787 . . .* Trans. F. Blagden (2 vols). London: B. McMillan.

Gomes, Diogo (1959) *De la première découverte de la Guinée*. Trans. and annotated by T. Monod, R. Mauny and G. Duval. Bissau: Centro de estudio de Guiné portuguesa.

Gomez, M. A. (1992) *Pragmatism in the Age of Jihad: The Precolonial State of Bundu*. Cambridge: Cambridge University Press.

Goody, J. (1971) *Technology, Tradition and the State in Africa*. London: Oxford University Press.

Goody, J. (1980) Slavery in time and space. In *Asian and African Systems of Slavery*, edited by J. L. Watson. Berkeley: University of California Press, pp. 16–42.

Gravrand, H. (1983) *La Civilisation sereer. Cosaan. Les origines*. Dakar-Abidjan: Nouvelles éditions Africaines.

Gray, J. M. (1966) *History of the Gambia*. London: Frank Cass & Co.

Gueye, Ndeye Sokhna (1991) 'Étude de la céramique subactuelle et de ses rapports avec la céramique de Cuballel'. Mémoire de Maîtrise, Université de Dakar.

Gueye, Ndeye Sokhna (1998) 'Poteries et peuplement de la moyenne vallée du Fleuve Sénégal du XVIe au XXe: approche ethnoarchéologique et ethnohistorique'. Thèse pour le Doctorat ès Lettres, Université de Paris X.

Hair, P. E. H. (1984) The Falls of Félou: a bibliographical exploration. *History in Africa*, 11:113–30.

Hodges, C. (1924) The journey of Cornelius Hodges in Senegambia, 1689–90. Published by G. Stone. *English Historical Review*, 39:89–95.

Hunwick, John (1992) Black slaves in the Mediterranean world: introduction to a neglected aspect of the African diaspora. In *The Human Commodity: Perspectives on the Trans-Saharan Trade*, edited by E. Savage. London: Frank Cass, pp. 214–48.

Inikori, J. E. and Engerman, S. L. (eds) (1992) *The Atlantic Slave Trade*. Durham, N.C.: Duke University Press.

Jobson, R. (1968) *The Golden Trade. London 1623. Or a Discovery of the River Gambia, and the Golden Trade of the Aethiopians*. Amsterdam: Da Capo Press.

Johnson, J. and Robinson, D. (1969) Deux fonds d'histoire orale sur le Fouta Toro. *Bulletin de l'Institut Fondamental d'Afrique Noire* (series B), 31:120–37.

Kamara, Shaikh Musa (forthcoming) *Zuhural Basatin*, Volume 1 (introduction by J. Schmitz).

Klein, Martin (1977) Servitude among the Wolof and Sereer of Senegambia. In *Slavery in Africa: Historical and Anthropological Perspectives*, edited by I. Kopytoff and S. Meiers. Madison: University of Wisconsin Press, pp. 335–66.

Klein, Martin (1992) The impact of the Atlantic slave trade on the societies of the western Sudan. In *The Atlantic Slave Trade*, edited by J. E. Inikori and S. L. Engerman. Durham N.C.: Duke University Press, pp. 25–47.

Klein, Martin (1998) *Slavery and Colonial Rule in French West Africa*. Cambridge: Cambridge University Press.

Kopytoff, I. and Meiers, S. (1977) African 'slavery' as an institution of marginality. In *Slavery in Africa: Historical and Anthropological Perspectives*, edited by I. Kopytoff and S. Meiers. Madison, University of Wisconsin Press, pp. 3–84.

Leblanc (1822) Voyage à Galam. *Annales Maritimes et Coloniales*, 1:133–59.

Levtzion, N. and Hopkins, J. (1981 *Corpus of Early Arabic Sources for West African History*. Cambridge: Cambridge University Press.

Linares de Sapir, Olga (1971) Shell middens of lower Casamance and problems of Diola protohistory. *West African Journal of Archaeology* 1:23–54.

Linares de Sapir, Olga (1987) Deferring to trade in slaves. *History in Africa*. 14:112–39.

Lovejoy, Paul (1983) *Transformations in Slavery: A History of Slavery in Africa*. Cambridge: Cambridge University Press.

Lovejoy, Paul (1989) The impact of the slave trade on Africa in the eighteenth and nineteenth centuries. *Journal of African History*, 30:365–94.

Ly, A. (1991) *L'Épopée de Samba Guéladiégui*. Dakar: IFAN/UNESCO: Editions Nouvelles du Sud.

McDougall, E. A. (1992) Salt, Saharans, and the trans-Saharan slave trade: nineteenth century developments. In *The Human Commodity: Perspectives on the Trans-Saharan Trade*, edited by E. Savage. London: Frank Cass, pp. 61–88.

McIntosh, S. K. (1981) A reconsideration of Wangera/Palolus, Island of Gold. *Journal of African History*, 22:145–58.

McIntosh, S. K. (1995) Conclusion: the sites in regional context. In *Excavations at Jenné-jeno, Hambarketolo and Kaniana: The 1981 Season*, edited by S. K. McIntosh. Berkeley: University of California Press, pp. 360–412.

McIntosh, S. K. and McIntosh, R. J. (1980) Prehistoric investigations in the region of Jenné, Mali. *Cambridge Monographs in African Archaeology*. Oxford: British Archaeology Reports, 2 vols.

McIntosh, S. K. and McIntosh, R. J. (1981) The inland Niger Delta before the Empire of Mali: evidence from Jenne-jeno. *Journal of African History*, 22:1–22.

McIntosh, S. K. and McIntosh, R. J. (1993) Field survey in the tumulus zone of Senegal. *African Archaeological Review*, 11:73–107.

McIntosh, S. K., McIntosh, R. J. and Bocoum, H. (1992) The middle Senegal Valley project: preliminary results from the 1990–91 field season. *Nyame Akuma*, 38:47–61.

Manchuelle, F. (1989) The 'patriarchal ideal' of Soninke labor migrants: from slave to employers of free labor. *Canadian Journal of African Studies*, 23(1):106–25.

Manchuelle, F. (1997) *Willing Migrants: Soninke Labor Diasporas, 1848–1960*. Athens: Ohio University Press.

Manning, Patrick (1990) *Slavery and African Life: Occidental, Oriental and African Slave Trades*. Cambridge: Cambridge University Press.

Martin, V. and Becker, C. (1974) Vestiges protohistoriques et occupation humaine au Sénégal. *Annales de Démographie Historique*: 403–29.

Martin, V. and Becker, C. (1977) Sites protohistoriques de la Sénégambie. In *Atlas National du Sénégal*, edited by R. Van Chi. Paris: IGN, pp. 48–51.

Martin, J. and Becker, C. (1979) Documents pour servir à l'histoire des îles du Saluum. *Bulletin de l'Institut Fondamental d'Afrique Noire*, (series B), 41(4):722–72.

Marty, P. (1925) L'establissement des français dans le Haut-Sénégal (1817–1822). *Revue d'Histoire des Colonies Françaises*, 13:51–118, 210–68.

Mauny, Raymond (1961) *Tableau géographique de l'ouest africain au Moyen-Age d'après les sources écrites, la tradition et l'archéologie*. Dakar: L'Institut Fondamental d'Afrique Noire.

Meillassoux, Claude (1991) *The Anthropology of Slavery*. Trans. A. Dasnois. Chicago: University of Chicago Press.

Moitt, B. (1989) Slavery and emancipation in the Senegal's peanut basin: the nineteenth and twentieth centuries. *International Journal of African Historical Studies*, 22(1):27–50.

Moraes, Nize I. de (1976) *Contribution à l'histoire de la Petite Côte (Sénégal) au XVIIe siècle*. Paris: Sorbonne, 6 vols.

Nyambarza, D. (1969) Le marabout El Hadj Mamadou Lamine d'après les archives françaises. *Cahiers d'Etudes Africaines*, 9: 124–45.

Pacheco Pereira, Duarte (1937) *Esmeraldo de situ orbis*. Trans. G. H. T. Kimble. London: Hakluyt Society.

Park, M. (1960) *Travels of Mungo Park*. Edited by R. Miller. London: J. M. Dent and Sons.

Pelissier, P. (1966) *Les Paysans du Sénégal: les civilisations agraires du Cayor à la Casamance*. Saint-Yrieix: Fabrègue.

Raffenel, A. (1846) Le Haut Sénégal et la Gambie en 1843 et 1844. *Revue Coloniale*, 8:309–40.

Roberts, R. and Klein, M. (1980) The Banamba slave exodus of 1905 and the decline of slavery in the Western Sudan. *Journal of African History*, 21:375–94.

Robinson, D. (1970) Supplément au Fonds Robinson d'histoire orale du Fouta Toro. *Bulletin de l'Institut Fondamental d'Afrique Noire* (Series B), 32(3):766–9.

Robinson, D. (1985) *The Holy War of Umar Tal: The Western Sudan in the Mid-Nineteenth Century*. Oxford: Clarendon Press.

Robinson, D. (1987) The Umarian emigration of the late nineteenth century. *International Journal of African Historical Studies*, 20(2): 245–70.

Robinson, D. (1988) Un historien et anthropoloque Sénégalais: Shaikh Musa Kamara. *Cahiers d'Etudes Africaines*, 28(1):89–116.

Robinson, D., Curtin, P. and Johnson, J. (1972) A tentative chronology of Futa Toro from the sixteenth through the nineteenth centuries. *Cahiers d'Etudes Africaines*, 12(4), 48:555–92.

Rodney, Walter (1966) African slavery and other forms of social oppression on the Upper Guinea Coast in the context of the Atlantic slave trade. *Journal of African History*, 7(3):431–43.

Rodney, Walter (1972) *How Europe Underdeveloped Africa*. New edn 1982. Washington, D.C.: Howard University Press.

Rousseau, R. (1933) Étude sur le Cayor. Cahiers de Yoro Dyâo. *Bulletin du Comité d'Etudes historiques et scientifiques de l'Afrique occidentale française*, 16(2):235–98.

Rousseau, R. (1941) Le Sénégal d'autrefois. Seconde étude sur le Cayor. *Bulletin de l'Institut Fondamental d'Afrique Noire*, 3(1–4): 79–144.

Samb, A. M. (1964) *Cadior Demb: Essai sur l'histoire du Cayor*. Dakar: Imp. A. Diop.

Sarr, A. (1983) Histoire du Sine-Saloum. Edited by C. Becker. *Bulletin de l'Institut Fondamental d'Afrique Noire* (series B), 45 (1).

Soh, S. A. (1913) *Chronique du Foûta sénégalais*. Edited by M. Delafosse and H. Gaden. Paris: Leroux.

Swindell, K. (1980) Serawoollies, Tillibunkas and strange farmers: the development of migrant groundnut farming along the Gambia River, 1848–95. *Journal of African History*, 21: 93–104.

Tamari, Tal (1991) The development of caste systems in West Africa. *Journal of African History*, 32:221–50.

Texeira da Mota, A. (1969) Un document nouveau pour l'histoire des Peuls au Sénégal pendant les XV et XVI siècles. *Bol. Cult. Guiné Portuguesa*, 24:781–860.

Thiaw, I. (1999) *An Archaeological Investigation of Long-term Culture Change in the Lower Falemme (Upper Senegal Region) AD 500–1900*. Ph.D thesis, Rice University.

Thilmans, G. and Ravisé, A. (1980) *Protohistoire du Sénégal. Recherches archéologiques. Vol. 2, Sincu Bara et les sites du fleuve*. Dakar: Papers of l'Institut Fondamental d'Afrique Noire, number 91.

Thilmans, G., Descamps, C. and Khayat, B. (1980) *Protohistoire du Sénégal. I. Les sites mégalithiques*. Dakar: L'Institut Fondamental d'Afrique Noire.

Togola, T. (1996) Iron Age occupation in the Méma region, Mali. *African Archaeological Review*, 13(2):91–110.

Vanacker, C. (1979) *Tegdaoust II: recherches sur Aoudaghost. Fouille d'un quartier artisanal*. Nouakchott: Institut Mauritanien de la Recherche Scientifique.

Wade, A. (1964) Chronique du Wâlo sénégalais (1855). Edited by V. Monteil. *Bulletin de l'Institut Fondamental d'Afrique Noire* (series B), 26(3–4):440–98.

Watson, D. (1999) The Faleme Valley faunal assemblages. Appendix E in I. Thiaw, *An Archaeological Investigation of Long-term Culture Change in the Lower Falemme (Upper Senegal Region) AD 500–1900*, pp. 371–83.

Watson, J. L. (1980) Slavery as an institution: open and closed systems. In *Asian and African Systems of Slavery*, edited by J. L. Watson. Berkeley: University of California Press, pp. 1–15.

Webb, J. A. (1995) *Desert Frontier: Ecological and Economic Change along the Western Sahel 1600–1850*. Madison: University of Wisconsin Press.

Wood, W. R. (1967) An archaeological appraisal of early European settlement in the Senegambia. *Journal of African History*, 8(1):39–64.

Wright, D. R. (1977) *The Early History of Niumi: Settlement and Foundation of a Mandinka State on the Gambia River*. Athens: Ohio University Press.

Wright, D. R. (1979) *Oral Traditions from the Gambia*. Athens: Ohio University Press.

Zurara, G. Eanes de (1898–99) *The Chronicle of the Discovery and Conquest of Guinea*. Edited by C. R. Beazley and E. Prestage, 2 vols. London: Hakluyt Society.

3 Historical Process and the Impact of the Atlantic Trade on Banda, Ghana, c. 1800–1920

ANN BROWER STAHL

This chapter explores two themes through a case study of the Banda area, west central Ghana: 1) the need to balance regional perspectives on the Atlantic trade with insights into its variable effects at the local level; and 2) the importance of considering temporal context and change through time in our efforts to shed light on the cultural heritage of Africans in the diaspora. Banda is an ethnically complex chieftaincy situated between large forest states to the south and savanna states to the north. The nineteenth century, the period of focus, witnessed a waxing and waning of external authority over Banda, first by Asante and later by the British. I explore the impact of these historical forces on nineteenth-century material culture and settlement structure, paying special attention to the role of Banda in the slave trade and to the impact of a market economy on local life.

This chapter examines the effects of the Atlantic trade on a small region of west central Ghana in the period from the eighteenth through the early twentieth centuries. I assume that readers of this volume are motivated by one of two broad interests: a general interest in how the Atlantic trade affected African societies; or an interest in how African societies can inform the lives of Africans in the diaspora. With that readership in mind, I develop two themes through a discussion of the Banda case study: the need to balance regional perspectives with insights into the variable effects of the Atlantic trade at the local level; and the need for temporally sensitive perspectives that balance an interest in cultural continuity with an awareness of change (cf. Holloway 1990). Africanist historians have devoted considerable attention to general features of the Atlantic trade, describing the roles of Europeans and Africans, documenting proc-

esses of enslavement, and debating the demographic effects of the slave trade (e.g. Curtin 1975; Fage 1982; Inikori 1982; Lovejoy 1983; Thornton 1992). These studies are typically based in documentary evidence, and adopt a regional perspective. They provide an important context within which to view the Atlantic trade and its effects, but regional analyses need to be balanced by local perspectives that examine the effects of the Atlantic trade at different points in time (e.g. Manning 1987). We know, for example, that the effects of the slave trade were uneven—some societies were the object of slave raids, others involved in the capture and sale of slaves, and others absorbed slaves internally (Van Dantzig 1982:188). A single society might be involved in multiple capacities at different points in time. The coastal bias of documentary sources has made it especially difficult to gain insight into the effects of the Atlantic trade on the interior societies whose

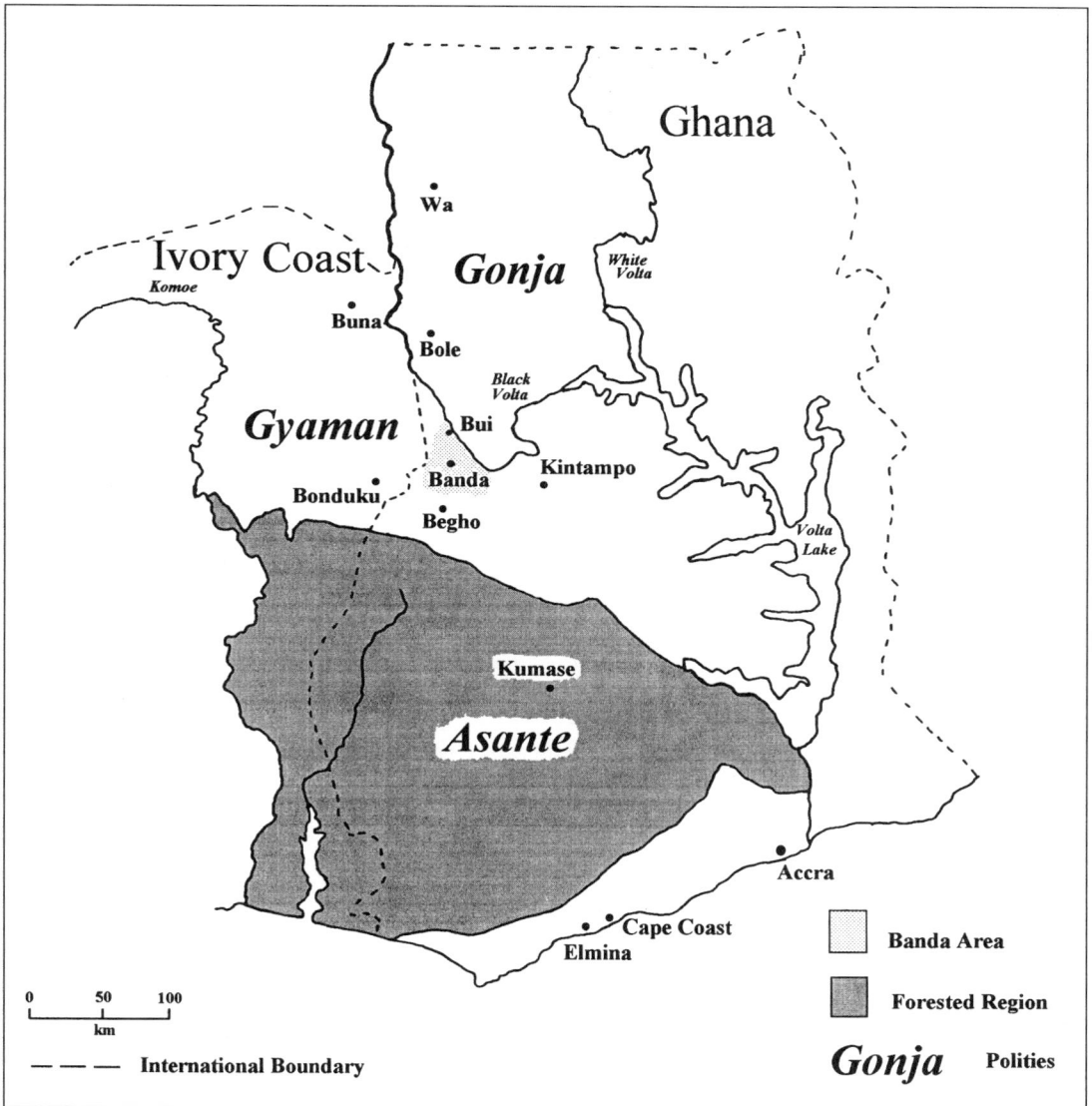

Figure 3.1 Place names mentioned in text.

personnel were consumed by the slave trade. Because documentary evidence focuses primarily on the external trade, less attention has been paid to the internal trade and its effects (*cf*. Miers and Roberts 1988). Oral historical sources have played an important role in exploring these issues in the interior (e.g. Haight 1981), but until recently, archaeology has played a relatively minor role in helping us to understand how the Atlantic trade affected daily life at the local level. Through a case

study of Banda over the past several centuries, I attempt to demonstrate the value of archaeological evidence in developing local perspectives on these issues.

Banda lay on the frontier between the Akan world of the forest and the Guang societies of the northern savanna (Figure 3.1), its fortunes affected by its more powerful neighbors to the north and south. This forest–savanna ecotone was home to a series of entrepôts from at least the thirteenth century.

These served as conduits for the northward flow of forest products at the height of the trans-Saharan trade, as well as staging points in the southward flow of savanna resources (including slaves) to Atlantic ports. The ethnic complexity of the area today attests a long period of external contacts and the forging of a distinctive society in the interstices of neighboring states, a process common to internal frontiers throughout Africa (Kopytoff 1987, 1999). Frontier societies like Banda have been relatively invisible in the anthropological literature. Anthropologists were drawn instead to societies that best fit the model of a homogeneous tribe. 'Instead of a primordial embryo—a kind of tribal homunculus—maturing through history while preserving its ethnic essence, what we have here is a magnet that grows by attracting to itself the ethnic and cultural detritus produced by the routine workings of other societies' (Kopytoff 1987:6–7). Thus contemporary cultural expressions cannot be assumed to reflect past variation adequately (David and Sterner 1999; Guyer and Belinga 1995; Wolf 1984). Culture, particularly in frontier contexts like Banda, must be viewed as active, fluid, subject to change, rather than as anachronistic reflection of ancestral practice. I hope to show that through judicious consideration of oral historical and archaeological evidence, we can gain fuller appreciation of the historical forces that conditioned rural African life, and to discern something of the fluidity of cultural practice in the period of the Atlantic trade.

Banda and its involvement in the Atlantic trade

The Banda Traditional Area today incorporates 25 villages under the auspices of the Banda Paramount Chieftaincy. Ghana has two parallel, but not equally powerful, systems of government: a centralized national government, which has ranged since independence from a parliamentary system to a military government; and 'traditional' governance by chiefs and councils of elders that varies in local form. Traditional councils are integrated at the regional and national levels by deliberative bodies that deal with chieftaincy disputes and other matters relating to 'traditional' rule. This dual system is a product of the colonial period

when British officials attempted to rule their West African colonies indirectly (Lugard 1965). Though indirect rule was a conservative strategy aimed at preserving African institutions, it had the effect of transforming the very institutions that the British hoped to preserve because it relied on traditional African leaders to implement British policy (Kuklick 1979:44; see also Adas 1995).

The villages of the Banda Paramount Chieftaincy comprise members of five ethnic-linguistic groups (Stahl 1991). The chieftaincy is dominated by the Nafana, who trace their origins to the Ivory Coast. The Nafana recount that they migrated to Banda because of a chieftaincy dispute in their homeland, probably sometime late in the seventeenth century. In Banda, they encountered an autochthonous people, the Kuulo (or Dumpo), who were incorporated into the newly founded Nafana (Banda) chieftaincy. Over time, the Banda chieftaincy incorporated other immigrants and refugees, some of whom retained distinctive identities (i.e. the Muslim Ligby and the Ewe), and others who adopted Nafana identity (see Stahl 1991, 2001 for details).

Banda has a long and varied history of external relations. From roughly the thirteenth century, entrepôts like Begho, located on Banda's southern margin, linked the forest with merchant centers along the Niger River (Posnansky 1973, 1987; Wilks 1982a). Begho was a thriving commercial settlement into the eighteenth century that was occupied by merchants and artisans of diverse ethnic origins. With the rise of the Atlantic trade, Begho's commercial importance diminished, and a series of military campaigns dispersed its population (Garrard 1980: 45–6; Posnansky 1987; Wilks 1982b; Wilks et al. 1986:15). This southward shift in the gravity of exchange coincided with a development of states throughout the forest regions of western Africa. In Ghana, the former Gold Coast, Asante dominated the forested regions from the early decades of the eighteenth century, and expanded its dominion over societies in the wooded savanna during the second half of that century (Wilks 1975:243–304). Asante levied annual tribute in slaves, gold, and other commodities; however, its ability to collect tribute varied, depending on conditions in Kumase, the Asante capital. Successions between Asante rulers were often disputed, and subject states took advantage of dissent in Kumase to rebel. Asante lost control of its northern provinces in the last decade of the nineteenth century, when British agents entered into treaty agreements with a number of northern states. Kumase itself succumbed to a British military force in 1896. This marked the beginning of a formal colonial era in Asante's northern hinterland. In the early decades of the twentieth century, British officials worked to forge infrastructural links (telegraph, roads) between the savanna and coast in order to encourage British investors to develop the resources of the Gold Coast hinterland (Boahen 1987:58; Constantine 1984:10–23). The increased exchange that followed in the wake of motor transport (Heap 1990) eroded some local industries, and ensured that rural inhabitants would become increasingly enmeshed in a cash economy.

The history of an autonomous Banda chieftaincy is difficult to reconstruct, for it was only when Banda became subject to Asante late in the eighteenth century (1773–74; Yarak 1979) that it began to figure in European documents and the oral traditions of its Akan neighbors (e.g. Wilks 1975:54, 72, 77). Nevertheless, limited evidence suggests that the Banda chieftaincy emerged in the vacuum created along the forest–savanna margin by the demise of Begho, Bono Manso, and other historically documented entrepôts. The *Kitāb Ghanjā*, or Gonja Chronicles, suggest that the Banda polity was in existence by *c.* 1751. These locally authored chronicles, written in Arabic, note the death of the Fula king ShYTAQ in July 1751. Fula is the Juula term for Banda, and scholars take this to be a reference to the Banda chief known as Sielɔngɔ in Banda traditions (Wilks *et al.* 1986: 98, 141). Sielɔngɔ is recognized as one of the first chiefs of Banda who, the Chronicles suggest, ruled for some 30 years. The implication is that the Banda polity existed in some form as early as 1720, consistent with the view that the Banda chieftaincy took root in the circumstances of uncertainty that prevailed after Begho's demise. From an historical vantage, then, Banda is a society that coalesced along a frontier during the period of the Atlantic trade (Stahl 2001). What was its role in that trade, and did Banda participate in the slave trade, either as a source or conduit for slaves?

In his authoritative study of nineteenth-century Asante, Wilks (1975:43–64) drew a distinction between inner and outer provinces of Asante. Inner provinces were distinguished by their subject, rather than tributary status. They were liable for taxes levied by Kumase (a head tax levied in gold dust late in the nineteenth century), but were not required to supply annual tribute (Wilks 1975:69–70). Most of the inner provinces were Akan societies, culturally and linguistically related to the Asante. Conversely, the more distant outer provinces were culturally and linguistically distinct from Asante, and were required to provide an annual tribute to Kumase. Asante levied tribute in slaves, livestock, and cloth against large outer provinces like Dagomba and Gonja. The size of their slave levy is unknown for the period of the Atlantic trade; however, during the nineteenth century each of these northern provinces supplied an estimated 1000 slaves annually to Kumase (Arhin 1974:100; Wilks 1975:67). Gonja and Dagomba acquired slaves by raiding small-scale, so-called acephalous societies that occupied the interstices between states (i.e. the Lobi, Grunsi, etc.). War captives taken during disputes with neighboring chieftaincies were another source of slaves. Whereas in theory raiding and military expeditions were confined to areas outside Greater Asante (Wilks 1975:70–1), in practice there was considerable strife between Asante's northern provinces during the nineteenth century. Asante's influence over its northern provinces waxed and waned, especially during periods of succession between heads of state, or Asantehenes. Confusion and strife in Kumase enabled both inner (i.e. Gyaman, Nkoranza) and outer (Gonja, Dagomba) provinces to pull away, and was often associated with rebellion and warfare among neighboring provinces.

Evidence adduced by Wilks (1975:54) suggests that Banda was an inner province of Asante, despite the fact that Banda peoples were ethnically and linguistically distinct from the Akan (Bravmann 1972; Stahl 1991). Banda was forcibly incorporated into Asante in the dry season of 1773–74, and it was in commenting on the large number of slaves generated by this campaign that a Dutch official at Elmina documented the existence of the Banda polity (Yarak 1979). Thus, some Banda kinsmen found themselves in coastal ports, awaiting the horrors of the middle passage, while others were probably consumed by the internal market for captives. After its defeat, Banda signaled homage to Asante, by sending seven sheep to Kumase during the annual Odwira or yam festival (Ameyaw 1965). There is no evidence that Asante levied an annual tribute in slaves against Banda, and, because it was incorporated into Asante only 25 years before the English moved to abolish the trans-Atlantic trade, it is unlikely that Banda was a major supplier of slaves to the Atlantic trade.

Although Banda's role in the Atlantic trade was probably limited, there is evidence that Banda, like many other West African societies, both consumed and supplied slaves destined for the internal trade during the nineteenth century. A pair of leg shackles, bonded together by a rigid iron bar, hang on an office wall at the Bui National Park, located adjacent to the Banda area. Found by a Game and Wildlife Officer in the bush near the abandoned village of Kasa on lands that formerly belonged to the Banda chieftaincy, the manacles represent the only material trace of a traffic in humans that influenced the social and economic landscape of Banda.

The internal slave trade in the nineteenth century

The enslavement of Africans continued after the British abolished the Atlantic trade in 1807 (Roberts and Miers 1988). An illicit trade in slaves continued to supply New World plantations into the first half of the nineteenth century (e.g. Gray 1958:649; Smith 1985:101–2). However, a bigger market for slaves existed within Africa itself. Most complex societies in West Africa practiced some form of domestic slavery through the nineteenth and into the early twentieth centuries. Ironically, the shift to 'legitimate' trade in agricultural commodities advocated by abolitionists probably contributed to the expansion of internal slavery, for slaves were used to produce and transport export crops such as oil-palm and cocoa (Lovejoy 1983: 136, 160).

Recent literature stresses the myriad forms of dependency that were glossed by nineteenth- and early twentieth-century references to domestic slavery (Kopytoff 1988; Roberts and Miers 1988). In Asante, for example, the English word 'slave' glossed at least five Akan terms for servitude that ranged from chattel

slavery to debt pawns (Dumett and Johnson 1988:75–7; Rattray 1929:33–55). Dumett and Johnson (1988:77) distinguished a variety of economic relations that corresponded to these Akan terms, some of which were distinguished by residence:

1) household slaves held by small-scale farmers;
2) plantation slaves who lived in hamlets;
3) slaves owned by merchants, some of whom served as porters in the caravan trade; and
4) court slaves who were either part of a chief's retinue or were engaged in production for the court.

Some forms of domestic slavery were distinguished from New World practices by the fact that slave status was not inherited—the children of slaves were free, and slave descendants were gradually assimilated into the larger society (Lovejoy 1983:109–34, 168–9; Morrison 1982:54–5; cf. McSheffrey 1983).

Slaving was thus a well-documented feature of the political economic landscape during the nineteenth century, and was linked to the shifting power relations among Volta basin polities. Northern provinces, including Gonja, Gyaman and Nkoranza, rebelled during periods of political chaos in Kumase, while Banda reportedly remained loyal to Asante. Banda's allegiance to Asante in the 1819 war against Gyaman was reported by Dupuis (1966:76–81), who visited Kumase in 1820 in an effort to establish trade relations between the British and Asante. Dupuis witnessed a public meeting, during which the Bandahene (Banda chief), whose entourage included slaves, came to claim his share of war spoils from the Gyaman campaign—which reportedly included 4700 captured men, women, and children (Dupuis 1966:81). Though the number may be exaggerated, Asante was experiencing a glut in the number of captives in the aftermath of Britain's abolition of the slave trade (McSheffrey 1983:366–7), which could account for the Asantehene's generosity.

During other wars among Asante's northern provinces, Banda found itself on the losing side, with its citizens enslaved after being captured. For example, after the British occupied Kumase in 1874 (Wilks 1975:287–301), Asante influence in the north diminished. At about this time a dispute broke out between

Banda and Gyaman, which caused Banda peoples to flee their territory and take refuge to the east (Arhin 1974:35). A later dispute (1893–94) pitted Banda against Nkoranza and its Mo allies. The heir to the Banda stool was killed, and a number of Banda citizens taken captive (Arhin 1974:39–41, 133–4; Hodgson 1894). At this time Banda was reportedly not engaged in slave raiding. In 1894, Ferguson noted that 'With the exception of Nkoranza and Banda, the more northern countries raid their weak neighbours for cattle and slaves' (Arhin 1974:100). However, in a later confrontation with neighboring Mo people, the Banda Nafana reportedly took a number of Mo captives and sold them as slaves (Ameyaw 1965:2; Ferguson 1896; see also Arhin 1974:116–34).

Later nineteenth-century slaving in the Volta basin is most closely associated with the Almami Samori Turé, who forged an empire that included areas extending from northern Sierra Leone to northern Ghana (Holden 1970; Muhammed 1977). Samori deployed his mounted *sofa* soldiers in wars of conquest throughout the savanna and savanna woodland from 1861–98. As he came under increasing pressure from French forces, he shifted his base of operations eastward, to the margins of the Volta basin, in the 1890s. He captured the trade centers of Buna and Bonduku (Figure 3.1), and, under the command of his son, Sarankye-More, dispatched forces eastward to Wa and Gonjaland. Although Banda was not occupied by Samori's troops, Samori reportedly warned Banda peoples to quit their settlements along the Black Volta River. Not all of the inhabitants heeded the warning, and those who remained in the riverside settlement of Bue (Bui) were taken captive by Samori and sold into slavery (Ameyaw 1965:12–13). An alternate version of the story suggests that the Nafana who were enslaved had been living in Gonjaland, and sought refuge in Banda as Samori pressed eastward. Samori threatened to attack Banda if these people were not returned. Fell (1913) was told that 120 people were handed over to Samori and never heard from again. By 1896, the British, concerned that an alliance between Samori and Kumase would strengthen Asante's resistance, dispatched forces to the north with the aim of stopping Samori's troops. British agents reported that Samori's troops had raided villages for food and slaves, and caused significant

dislocation in the Asante hinterland. Food was in short supply and there were numerous refugees (Hodgson 1897; Fell 1913). Using Bui in the Banda area as a base (Northcott 1897), the British pushed Samori's men west of the Black Volta River, but not without casualties—George Ferguson, the Fanti official who had pioneered British penetration of the Asante hinterland, was fatally wounded in a skirmish with Sarankye-More's troops near Wa (Henderson 1897).

Several lines of evidence document domestic use of captives in Banda. During 1986, James Anane and I collected oral histories from a number of Banda families, most of whom identified themselves as Nafana (Stahl and Anane 1989). One family related that their ancestors had purchased large numbers of slaves to rejuvenate their *katoo* ('house') after experiencing heavy war casualties (Stahl and Anane 1989:28). Many men had been lost during a war against the Fanti, and they had lost many women in other hostilities. A rich family member purchased slaves to rejuvenate the family; however, disaster ensued because one of the female slaves was a sorceress who planned to kill the few remaining family members. All but one of the remaining women succumbed to an epidemic instigated by the slave sorceress. This story suggests that, despite her slave origins, the accused woman was conceptualized as a family member, for sorcery is effective primarily against relatives.

Other Banda families are rumored to have slave origins. Many, but not all, Nafana trace their origins to the village of Kakala in the Ivory Coast, and most who do provided a long list of former male and female heads of family (i.e. eight to twelve) during our 1986 interviews. A second group of Nafana families say that their ancestors came from other ethnic groups—Gonja or Kulango—fleeing their homelands and seeking refuge in Banda owing to inheritance disputes, accusations of sorcery, etc. (See also Kopytoff 1987:18–22.) Elsewhere (Stahl 1991:264–7) I suggested that this influx of refugees probably occurred during the second half of the nineteenth century, and resulted from political instability in the Volta basin. A third group of Nafana families report that they derive from Kakala, the Nafana homeland, but these families provided significantly shorter genealogies (i.e. three or four former heads) than the families mentioned above. Village gossip identifies this third group as families with slave origins, and their short genealogies are consistent with the idea that they were more recently incorporated into Nafana society.

Another line of evidence that substantiates the domestic consumption of captives in Banda is the presence of a *Gyase* family in Banda. Rattray (1929:90–2) first described the *Gyasefo* among the Asante. *Gyase* is an Akan word meaning 'below the hearth,' and the *Gyasefo* among the Asante were the 'people around the hearth.' They included the retainers and servants of the Chief, whom Rattray (1929:57) characterized as 'slaves and pawns.' The *Gyasefo* were headed by the *Gyase Hene* whose 'stool,' or position, was inherited through the male line (Rattray 1929:90–1), an anomaly, for virtually all other positions were reckoned through the mother's line. New recruits came to the *Gyasefo* through enslavement, or by birth to a *Gyase* woman. Banda traditions relate that war captives were adopted into the *Gyase* family, which was directly under the Paramount Chief. Today, this is one of the largest families in Banda-Ahenkro, the seat of the Banda chieftaincy, and interviewees attributed this to the policy of adopting war captives (Stahl and Anane 1989:12). Several versions of Banda traditions collected during the twentieth century make at least passing reference to war captives (Ameyaw 1965; Fell 1913), and it is likely that they were assimilated into Nafana society by being adopted into the *Gyase* family. See Roberts and Miers 1988 for a general discussion of this.)

Oral historical sources thus suggest that Nafana society expanded by assimilating non-Nafana peoples, some of whom were captive in origin. This process of incorporating people of diverse origins is further overlaid by a veneer of 'Akanization,' as Banda peoples adopted elements of Akan political style, Akan day names, and so on (Stahl 1991:262–4). This process probably began when Banda was forcibly incorporated into Asante in the late eighteenth century, but it became more marked during the British colonial period as British officers attempted to make indirect rule easier by creating uniformity among Asante's former provinces (see Adas 1995 for a discussion of how this was linked with the idea of re-establishing eroded traditions). As a result, a number of positions or stools within Banda are of recent origin, and date to the period of British influence (Stahl 1991:263). Significantly, the *Gyase* stool is associated with a short genealogy (three former male heads; Stahl and Anane 1989:12), and may have been created in the period when domestic slavery ceased (early twentieth century; Miers and Roberts 1988).

In sum, while some Banda captives were funneled southward to the slave ports at the time of Banda's incorporation into Asante, the Banda chieftaincy was probably not a major player in the Atlantic slave trade. However, it was both a source and a consumer in the internal slave trade.

While historians debate the impact of the Atlantic slave trade on African societies—some argue that it had a dramatic demographic effect, especially on the so-called 'middle belt,' while others minimize its effects—there has been less discussion of the localized demographic implications of the internal trade (Manning 1987). An exception is Haight's (1981) study of the Bole Division of Gonja, which lies immediately north of the Banda area. Haight stressed the dramatic effects of *sofa* armies under Sarankye-More on the Bole district. British accounts from the 1880s and 1890s comment on the large number of ruined villages and devastated fields. The effects were particularly marked and long lasting in light of the poor soils in the area. Population levels in areas around Buna and Bonduku were also significantly affected by Samori's occupation. Conversely, oral historical and archival sources suggest that Banda, which occupies a geographically intermediate position between Bole, Bonduku and Buna (Figure 3.1), may have *gained* demographically by absorbing refugees from surrounding areas (Stahl 1991:264–7). Thus, we need to consider the effects of slaving on a regional basis, and recognize that those societies which captured and sold slaves during one period may have been the source of slaves during another (e.g. Gonja in the early nineteenth century, compared to late nineteenth century).

The colonial market economy

The British officers who spearheaded the British occupation of the Asante hinterland commented on the disruption created by Samori's *sofa* army. His forces pursued a scorched-earth policy, and large areas of western Gonja lay in ruins (Davidson-Houston 1896; Northcott 1898, 1899b:14–16, 27). The British claimed the Northern Territories in 1897, claiming land east of the Black Volta River from Kintampo north to the eleventh parallel (Figure 3.1; Northcott 1899b:7). British priorities in the period 1896–98 were to oust Samori's forces from those areas of the Volta basin that had been allotted to Britain at the Berlin Conference of 1884–85, and to re-establish trade disrupted by the unstable conditions of the 1880s and 1890s. By the end of 1898, Samori's empire had collapsed. The Almami was deported by the French to Gabon where he remained until his death in 1900 (Person 1970:107–11). With the threat of armed resistance in the Volta basin diminished, the British turned their attention to administering Asante. The Northern Territories remained under nominal British control, but it was not until the early decades of the twentieth century that the British established a significant administrative presence in the lands north of Asante.

British acquisition of Asante and its northern hinterland was a small component of a much larger colonial expansion, fueled by political economic circumstances in Europe generally, and Britain in particular. Contracting economies and labor unrest in the final decades of the nineteenth century spurred British officials to pursue protectionist economic policies. Politicians worked to convince British voters that investments in colonial expansion would be rewarded with guaranteed supplies of raw materials, captive markets for British goods, and job security at home (Constantine 1984:10–29). However, colonies were expected to be self-supporting. The Treasury scrutinized colonial investment (e.g. Gann and Duignan 1978:45–70; Colonial Office 1899; Treasury 1899), ensuring that individual colonies directed funds to infrastructural projects that would attract private investors to develop colonial resources (i.e. gold; see Kay 1972).

With the imposition of British control, Volta-basin trade resumed—and in fact expanded—because Asante restrictions on the movement of traders were no longer in force (Arhin 1976/77:456–57). The first priority of the colonial government was to create an infrastructure—establishing telegraphic communication, widening roads, and building bridges—that would make it possible for pri-

vate investors to develop the resources of the interior (Constantine 1984:10). Not only did the British hope to extract raw materials from the newly defined Northern Territories, but they also hoped to expand the market for British manufactured goods. Systematic expansion of trade required monetization and a uniform currency (Carland 1990; Guyer 1995), and British officials were anxious to substitute British coinage for the variety of local currencies circulating at the end of the nineteenth century (primarily cowrie shells and gold dust; Grier 1981). Colonel Northcott, the first administrator of the Northern Territories, reported that

> At first there was some difficulty in persuading the natives to accept the new medium as an equivalent for a specific number of cowries. They were disposed to regard the coins as curiosities, or to convert them into rings and other ornaments, but the necessity of paying taxes and fines in English coin and of employing it in the purchase of trade goods, soon familiarized them with its use. (Northcott 1899a)

Although the pace of mercantile expansion may have seemed slow to the British, an increasing range of manufactured products found their way into the Gold Coast hinterland, and goods that were considered prestigious during the nineteenth century became necessities in the twentieth (Arhin 1976/77:459–60).

While historians have acknowledged the growing importance of consumer goods in the twentieth-century Gold Coast economy (e.g. Arhin 1979; Steiner 1985), there is little evidence for how the growth of a market economy affected local industries, or for how colonial policies affected the contours of daily life (*cf.* McCarthy 1983). Some attention has focused on how indigenous iron production was affected by competition with imported metal (e.g. Goucher 1981; de Barros this volume). Although initial imports of British iron were considered inferior, local smelting decreased due to the combined effects of readily available, cheap imported metal, and a shortage of fuel because of deforestation; however, smithing increased as blacksmiths reworked scrap metal to local standards. The effects on cloth production were uneven, with indigenous production expanding in some

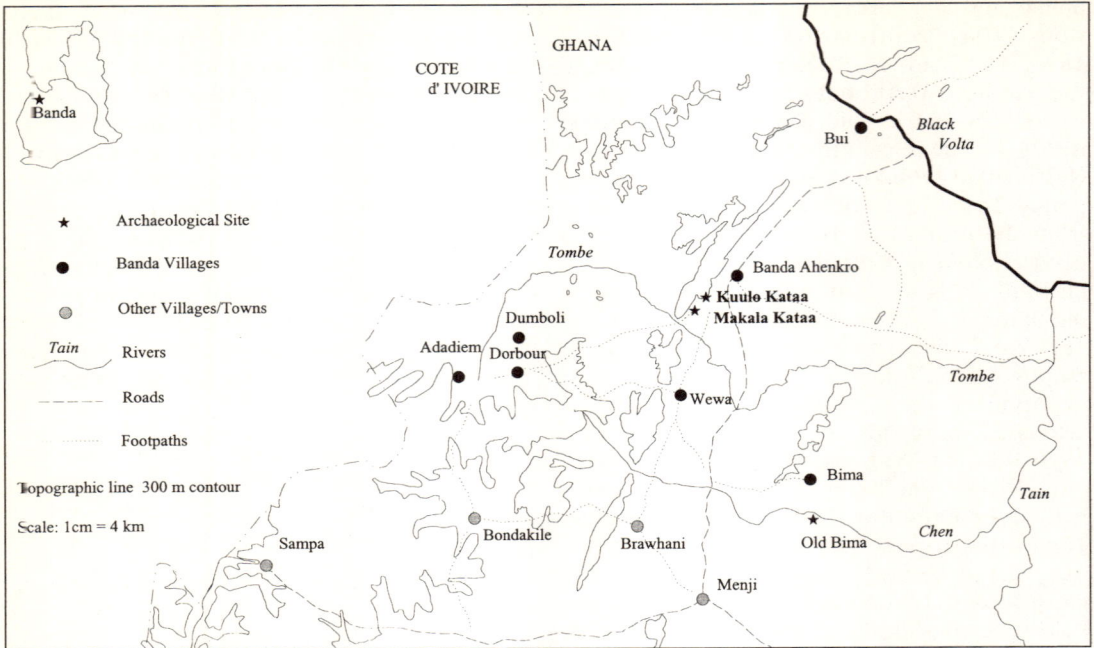

Figure 3.2 Villages and sites in the Banda area.

areas and contracting in others (Isaacman and Roberts 1995). Less attention has focused on the effects of a market economy on craft industries such as potting. Although traveling district commissioners mentioned crafts in passing, the written record is frustratingly limited. Similarly, we have a limited understanding of how British village planning policies affected individual towns. These issues can usefully be addressed through archaeological investigations, which help illuminate the local effects of the Atlantic trade and colonial policy.

The effects on local life: insights from Makala Kataa

By 1920 there was a growing British administrative presence in the Asante hinterland. District commissioners, the 'men on the scene,' were charged with a variety of tasks, including establishing a colonial presence and maintaining law and order; establishing boundaries; eliminating repugnant practices; collecting taxes and conducting censuses; and building roads, overseeing public works and sanitation (Kuklick 1979:108). The towns where district commissioners resided received greatest scru-

tiny; however, a good district commissioner was expected to spend much of his time touring his district. Thus, the district commissioner periodically visited outlying villages, inspecting roads, and reporting on the state of the countryside. Reports indicate that district commissioners were very concerned with the issue of village planning, and made an effort to convince villagers to abandon existing villages and establish new settlements consistent with British planning principles (e.g. Gold Coast Colony 1918:20; 1920:16; and see Boyle 1968:30, 50, 58 for examples of how one district commissioner encouraged rebuilding).

The archaeological site of Makala Kataa (8°8'15"N; 2°23'15"W; Figure 3.2) represents one such village in Banda, abandoned early in the twentieth century when a British official, locally known as the 'breaker of walls,' convinced Banda peoples to rebuild their villages (Stahl 1994, 1999a). The site is located adjacent to the contemporary village of Makala, and several elderly inhabitants of Makala recall living on the site as children. The site has two occupation foci (Figure 3.3): a terminal nineteenth- to early twentieth-century occupation on the southwest margin of the contemporary village (Late Makala); and a late

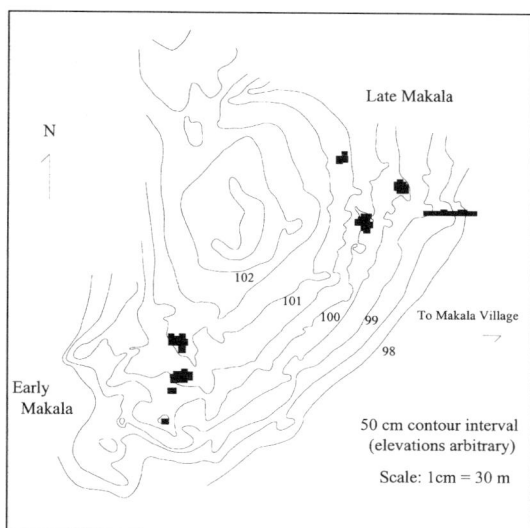

Figure 3.3 Plan map of Makala Kataa. Excavated areas shown in black.

eighteenth- to early nineteenth-century occupation to the southwest (Early Makala). The Banda Research Project has conducted three seasons of excavations that have sampled the early and late occupations in comparable proportions (see Stahl 1994, 1999a, 2001 for details). Results demonstrate contrasts in the ubiquity of trade goods; the character of the ceramic assemblage; and the nature of settlement between these two occupations. Here I focus on the character of the pottery and pipe assemblages, and what they tell us about the changing character of craft specialization in the Banda area; the nature of the exchange economy through time; and preliminary insights into differences in settlement morphology. For purposes of contrast, I also make reference to our most recent work at the earlier site of Kuulo Kataa (8°8′45″N; 2°22′30″W), located immediately north and east of Makala Kataa along the same ridge (Figure 3.2). This site was the focus of test excavations during the summer of 1995, and dates to the period *c.* AD 1300–1650 (Stahl 1999a). Kuulo Kataa is thus contemporary with Begho, and the site contrasts in many respects with Makala Kataa.

Chronology and classification

There are at least two distinct occupations represented by the archaeological deposits at Ma-

kala Kataa. The area immediately west of the contemporary village is characterized by a series of low circular mounds that resulted from the collapse of houses abandoned early in the twentieth century. We refer to this late nineteenth- to early twentieth-century occupation as Late Makala, or Makala Phase 1 (Figure 3.3). Associated ceramics differ from those found in the more substantial mounds that characterize the southwestern area of the site. This earlier occupation, referred to as Early Makala, or Makala Phase 2, dates to the end of the eighteenth, and early decades of the nineteenth century, an insight based on imported objects, oral sources, and thermo-luminescence dates (Stahl 1999a:12–16). Both occupation phases at Makala Kataa (Phase 1 and 2) fall within the bounds of a ceramic tradition that I have called Iron Age 1 (Stahl 1985:69–136; 1992:134–5; 1999a). Iron Age 1 ceramics are frequently surface treated with roulette-impression, either a cord-wrapped stick or a maize cob. Grooving and punctates (circular or triangular) are also common (Figure 3.4). Evidence from Makala Kataa suggests that the Iron Age 1 tradition can usefully be subdivided into two discrete temporal phases, represented at the discrete occupational loci. Ceramics associated with these loci are somewhat distinct. The primary distinction is that the earlier assemblage (Makala Phase 2) includes both cord and maize cob roulette-impressed ceramics, whereas the more recent assemblage (Makala Phase 1) is dominated by maize cob roulette-impressed pottery. Yet there is similarity in the grammar of design. Routlette-impression typically occurs on jars, and is commonly confined to the area below the shoulder/carination of the vessel, often offset by a shallow grooved (channeled) line (Stahl 1999a:47). Maize cob thus appears to have been substituted for cord roulette-impression during the course of the Makala Phase 2 occupation (Stahl 1994, 1999a; for a fuller analysis of the Makala ceramics see Cruz 2001).

Iron Age 2 pottery was recovered from a separate set of sites in the 1982 survey (Stahl 1985:120–7; 1992:135), a pattern confirmed by a more detailed survey in 1998 (Smith 1998). Iron Age 2 ceramics show affinities with Crossland's Begho ware (Crossland 1989:13–48), recovered from excavations at Begho, located just south of the Banda area

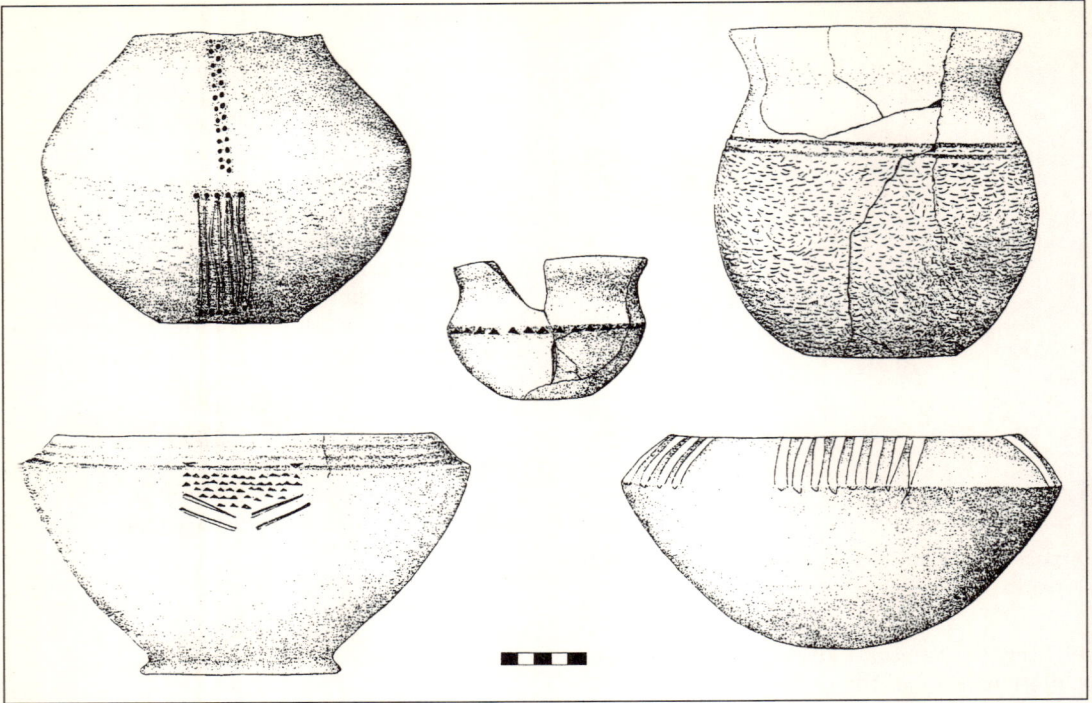

Figure 3.4 Iron Age 1 pottery from Makala Kataa. Scale in cm.

(Figure 3.1). Triangular punctates are rare and maize cob roulette virtually nonexistent. Cord roulette is commonly applied as a surface treatment; a variety of other surface treatments are less common, and may represent mat or roulette treatments. Comb/dentate roulette and wavy line roulette (stamped wavy line) decorations are distinctive to ceramics on this group of sites, as are rare carved roulette impressions (Figure 3.5; Stahl 1992:135), and mica-slipped or painted sherds. Several sites in the Banda area exhibit Iron Age 2 ceramics, including the site of Kuulo Kataa (referred to as Banda 7 in Stahl 1985:309), which was the focus of Banda Research Project investigations in 1995. We now refer to these ceramics and sites that have yielded them as the Kuulo phase (Stahl 1999a:23–7). Radiocarbon and thermoluminescence dates suggest that Kuulo Kataa was occupied sometime between c. AD 1300–1650 (Stahl 1999a), making it contemporary with the entrepôt of Begho. Kuulo Kataa is characterized by massive midden mounds that have yielded significantly higher densities of material than either occupation at Makala Kataa. While it is large by comparison to local

Iron Age 1 sites, it is considerably smaller than the Hani Begho sites investigated by Posnansky (1973, 1987).

The ceramic assemblage at Makala Kataa

Pottery is still made and used in the Banda area, although today it is produced by specialists who reside in several villages (Bondakile, Dorbour, and Adadiem) west of the Banda hills (Crossland 1989:51–82; Crossland and Posnansky 1978; Cruz 1996, 2001; Stahl and Cruz 1998). Ceramics are still headloaded from Dorbour to villages on the eastern margins of the Banda hills (Figure 3.6; Crossland and Posnansky 1978:87). Ceramics produced in these potting villages are relatively homogeneous in form and decorative treatment, despite the fact that women from two distinct ethnic-linguistic groups make the pottery. Several jar and bowl forms are sharply carinated at the shoulder, and decorative treatment consists predominantly of maize cob roulette, grooving, and occasional punctates (Crossland and Posnansky 1978:82–5; Cruz 2001). Archaeological ceramics from Late Makala (Makala Phase 1)

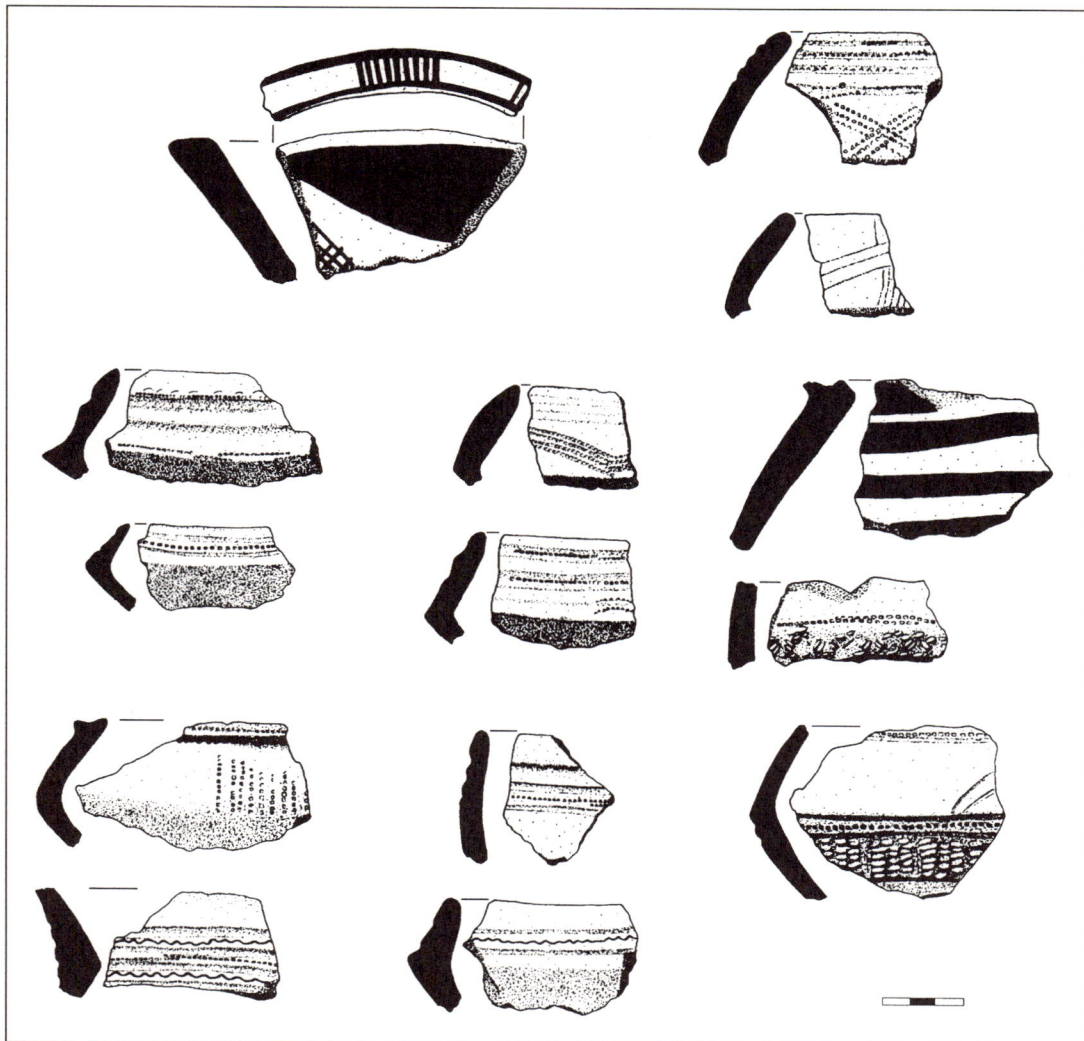

Figure 3.5 Iron Age 2 pottery from the 1982 Banda Survey (Stahl 1985). Scale in cm.

display clear affinities with contemporary ceramics, although subtle stylistic contrasts suggested changes in craft specialization (Stahl 1994) that have been confirmed through neutron activation analysis and oral historical sources (Cruz 1996, 2001; Stahl 1999a; Stahl and Cruz 1998).

The pottery assemblage from Makala Kataa provides insight into the character of nineteenth-century ceramic production. There is no evidence in the form of wasters that pottery was made at either the early or late occupations at Makala Kataa. Increased stylistic homogeneity suggests increased specialization

in ceramic production through time. The sample of ceramics from the early occupation (Makala Phase 2) showed greater diversity of decorative combinations (117 distinct combinations in all), compared to the later occupation (Makala Phase 1), which displayed far fewer (60 combinations; see Stahl 1994 for a discussion of sampling and its significance). But if ceramic production became an increasingly specialized activity, restricted to a smaller number of villages, this should be reflected in variables other than just decorative treatment.

Cruz's (1996, 2001) pioneering neutron activation study of Banda ceramics and clays

Figure 3.6 Woman headloading pottery, Banda-Ahenkro market, 1982.

demonstrated that clays east and west of the Banda hills have distinct chemical signatures. Moreover, clays used by Nafana potters in Dorbour and Adadiem could be distinguished from those used by Mo potters in Bondakile, both west of the Banda hills. Cruz's initial study included archaeological ceramics from Early and Late Makala (Cruz 1996), a sample that was expanded in a later study (Neff and Glascock 1997; Stahl 1999a:23–5, 47–9, 64). In brief, the neutron activation data document changes in the sites of production of pottery consumed by residents of Early and Late Makala. In the sample of analyzed sherds from Early Makala (n=55), jars and bowls displayed distinct chemical signatures. Jars were made from clays chemically similar to those of Dorbour and Adadiem (west of the Banda hills), while bowls were made from an unprovenanced clay source that Neff and Glascock (1997) place east of the Banda hills, based on its chemical similarity to an eastern source (Stahl 1999a:47–9). These data suggest

regional trade in finished pottery between villages east and west of the Banda hills. Other ceramic objects were produced from different clay sources than pottery. A small sample of spindle-whorls were made from an unprovenanced clay, again thought to be located east of the hills based on its chemical composition, while analyzed smoking pipes (n=7) were made from diverse clay sources, both east and west of the Banda hills (Stahl 1999a:50).

The neutron activation analysis of Late Makala ceramics produced a very different pattern. Half of the analyzed sherds (n=56), both bowls and jars, derived from provenanced clay sources east of the Banda hills. Pottery made from the Adadiem–Dorbour source west of the hills was far less common. Spindle-whorls (n=3) showed the same chemical composition as those at Early Makala. These data suggest changes in ceramic consumption: whereas Early Makala residents obtained jars from one source and bowls from another, Late Makala villagers obtained bowls and jars from the same locales and favored production sites east of the Banda hills.

Two factors may have contributed to changes in sources of pottery for Makala residents: the turmoil that characterized the central Volta basin during the nineteenth century; and the growing impact of a market economy that supplied alternatives to locally produced goods. Through time, potting has become increasingly localized, and is concentrated in the hands of a relatively small number of specialists. This relates in part to reduced demand brought about by the increased availability of alternative vessels (e.g. metal pots). There is little published information on the importation of metal vessels; however, advertisements in colonial handbooks illustrate vessels manufactured specifically for the colonial market (Gold Coast Colony 1928). Although there is no archaeological evidence for metal pots at either occupation of Makala Kataa (aside from a single enameled vessel recovered from Late Makala), the increased homogeneity of later ceramics (Makala Phase 1) coincides with a substantial increase in the number of other imported items that signals expanded petty trading late in the nineteenth century. While Early Makala yielded only a few imported beads and gun flints, European imports were ubiquitous at Late Makala, including beads, bottle glass, kaolin pipes, metal ornaments, and gun flints (Stahl 1999a:69–71). Based on our current understanding, it is significant that the effects of increased external exchange (presumably related to the British defeat of Asante) were felt before the British established a significant administrative presence in western Brong-Ahafo (Stahl 1994). Cruz has also conducted ethnographic work at contemporary potting villages that suggests that changes in marketing strategies were associated with some of these changes in production (Cruz 2001; Stahl and Cruz 1998). Increasingly, women from the potting villages have been forced into a pattern of itinerant trading, as demand for pots diminished and consumers stopped traveling to the potting villages to obtain ceramic wares.

Still, potting continues as a relatively vibrant, although undoubtedly altered craft despite competition with imports. Other crafts were not as resilient. Perhaps the most dramatic shift between Early and Late Makala is the replacement of locally produced ceramic pipes by European imports. The locally made pipes from Early Makala (n=175 fragments) were typical of nineteenth-century assemblages (Stahl 1994, 1999a:50). Most were single-angled forms (i.e. the base of the pipe stem was joined to the base of the bowl in a continuous surface), and some had lobed (quatrefoil) bases or stems (Figure 3.7). Yet the morphology and decorative treatment among the pipes varied considerably. Some pipe fragments were fashioned from fine-grained clays burnished to a high gloss and elaborately decorated, while others were roughly molded from coarsely tempered fabrics and showed little or no decorative treatment. Stylistic heterogeneity appears to have been valued. Drawing on the analogy of cloth—the quality and design of which convey prestige—it may be that the degree and quality of finishing on pipes was linked to practices of social distinction (Stahl 1999b).

The variety and abundance of locally produced clay pipes at Early Makala contrasts sharply with Late Makala. Here, only five local pipe fragments were recovered, compared with 130 fragments of imported ball clay pipes. This suggests a virtual replacement of a local product by an imported one, unlike pottery and cloth where locally produced forms persisted alongside imported alternatives (see Stahl and

Cruz 1998 on the intersection of gender and craft specialization).

In sum, a vibrant tradition of regional craft production was represented at the late eighteenth- to early nineteenth-century occupation at Early Makala. The relatively diverse pottery assemblage came from a variety of local sources, east and west of the Banda hills. An equally vibrant tradition of pipe manufacture is evidenced by the Early Makala pipe assemblage. Both crafts were affected by the growing availability of imported items in the late nineteenth and early twentieth centuries (Late Makala). Potting persisted, but appears to have become more localized. Pots originated disproportionately from sources closer to Makala Kataa, a factor that may reflect disruption of previous trade patterns by the political upheavals during the second half of the nineteenth century (Stahl 1999a, 2001). Decorative treatment on ceramics was more homogeneous. Conversely, pipe manufacture seems to have disappeared altogether under the pressure of competing imports. Two interesting questions that remain are: 1) whether there was a gendered division of labor in the production of pots and pipes, and hence differential impact on craft production by men compared with women; and 2) the role of prestige in determining which crafts were eliminated by competing imports (pipes), compared with the persistence of more mundane objects (pots) (Stahl 1999b).

The contrasting character of occupation mounds at Early and Late Makala lends insight into the changing character of village life during the nineteenth century. The mounds that resulted from the collapse of houses at Early Makala are relatively substantial, and often L-shaped. Excavation has revealed the presence of substantial gravel floors, episodes of rebuilding (witnessed by superpositioning of floors), and overburden consistent with the collapse of relatively substantial earthen walls (Stahl 1999a:41–6). The L-shape of some of the mounds and the relationship between kitchen deposits and associated floors presumed to be the remains of sleeping rooms suggest that structures were fairly substantial and included several residential units (i.e. joined together in compounds). These data suggest a relatively long-lived settlement in which buildings were augmented by the addition of rooms. This is consistent with the substantial midden mounds

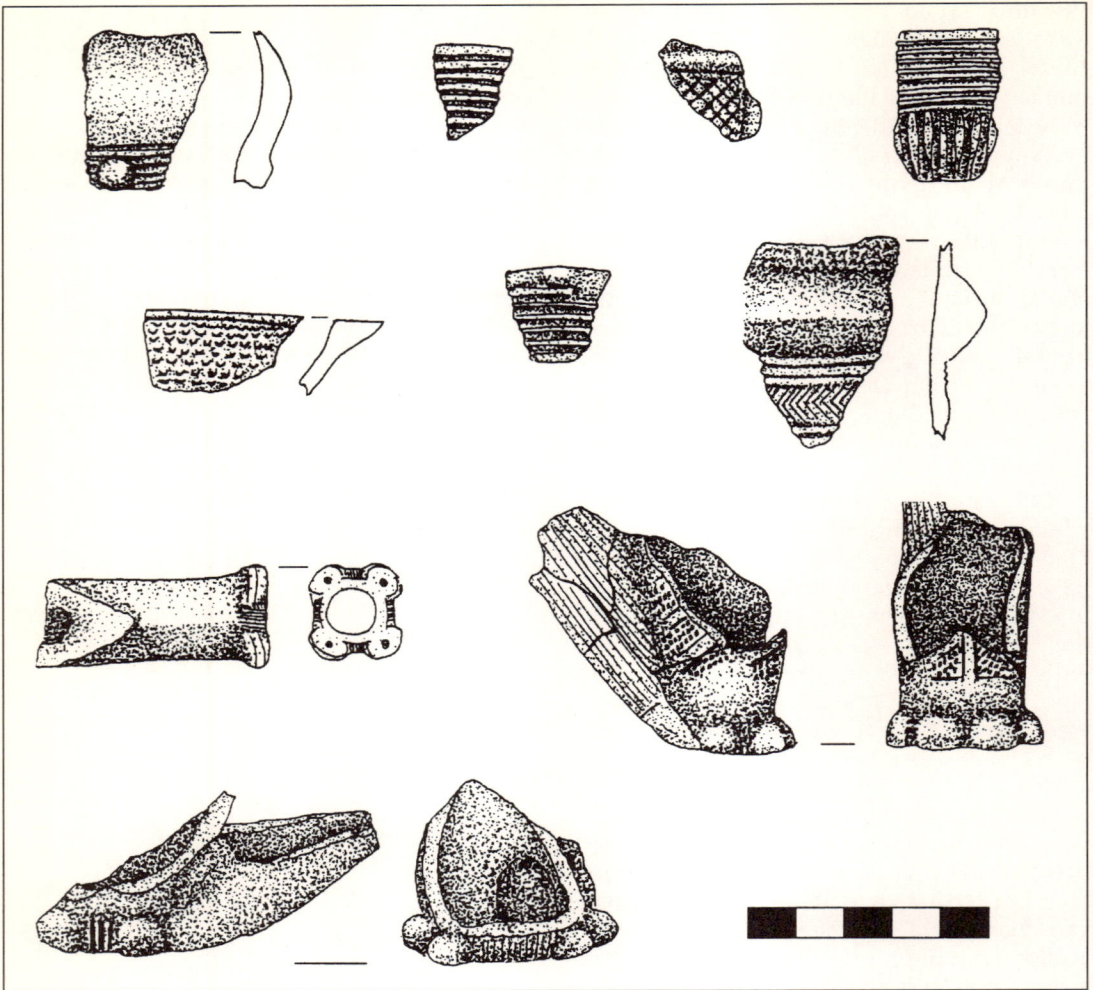

Figure 3.7 Locally made pipes from Early Makala. Scale in cm.

associated with Early Makala (Stahl 1994). Yet this area of the site appears to have been abandoned abruptly—kitchen deposits reveal useable pots and grindstones left in place, a pattern that suggests sudden abandonment (Stahl 1999a:44). Had the area been gradually abandoned with people relocating close by, we would expect such useable materials to be salvaged, as is the practice today (see also Cameron and Tomka 1993). Oral histories are replete with mention of warfare and political upheaval that caused Banda peoples to leave their homes, and the evidence for abrupt abandonment at Early Makala corroborates these scenarios.

Conversely, Late Makala represents a rela-

tively short-lived occupation. Here mounds are significantly smaller, and the limited evidence of structural features suggests a more ephemeral form of architecture. We encountered several packed gravel floors, but the amount of wall collapse appears to have been less substantial. That, combined with the evidence of post holes in the base of units, suggests a wattle-and-daub form of architecture rather than the more substantial coursed earth style construction that is only now being replaced by cement block constructions. This is consistent with the interpretation that Late Makala was established after the initial period of British occupation (at Bui in 1897) and the ousting of Samori's troops from neighboring areas, and was therefore occupied for only two decades when the British encouraged resettlement (Stahl 1994). Further, few useable items were left in place at Late Makala when it was abandoned in the 1920s, which is consistent with a more gradual, planned abandonment and relocation to the new village adjacent to the site (Cameron and Tomka 1993). The temporary character of Late Makala may explain the apparent lack of resistance of villagers to comply with British demands that they 'lay out' their towns (Stahl 1999a:62).

The effects of the Atlantic trade and implications for diaspora studies

The identity of the British officer (or officers) locally known as the 'breaker of walls' remains unknown. Whoever he was, he would have first visited the village represented by the Phase 1 deposits at Makala Kataa sometime late in the 1910s or early 1920s. Archaeological evidence suggests that the village that he saw and the daily lives of its inhabitants had felt the effects of the Atlantic trade and its reverberations. Some changes had occurred within the generation that separated occupation of Early and Late Makala. Other changes happened earlier, and differentiated the lives of the inhabitants of Kuulo Kataa from those of Makala Kataa. Yet even at Kuulo Kataa, villagers had begun to experiment with New World crops like maize (Stahl 1999a:35–7). While neutron activation suggests that potting was an important craft practiced at Kuulo Kataa, Early Makala villagers relied on potting villages to the west of the hills to obtain ceramics. There was a vibrant tradition of pipe manufacture. Pipes were well made and highly variable, suggesting that this type of material culture differentiated individuals. The village appears to have a long occupation, with people investing labor and resources in rebuilding and renewing their dwellings. But village life at Early Makala ended abruptly, probably a material expression of the upheavals that characterized the second half of the nineteenth century in the Volta basin (Stahl 2001). Traditions suggest that Banda people moved out of the area for a time (Ameyaw 1965), and toward the end of the century concentrated themselves along the Volta River (i.e. at Bui; Ameyaw 1965; York 1965).

Late Makala is probably the expression of a reoccupation of Banda territory that took place after the British and French ousted Samori's troops from the Volta basin. The lives of those who resettled—and they perhaps included some who had fled Early Makala as children, returning as adults to establish Late Makala–differed from those of their counterparts who lived 100 meters down the ridge earlier in the century. Local exchange networks were altered, possibly affected by the political economic turmoil that characterized the area in the later nineteenth century. Now most of the pottery was produced from sources close to home, east of the hills. Some local crafts withered in the face of competition from imports (i.e. local pipe production). Involvement in subcontinental exchange flourished, as evidenced by ubiquitous European imports. But those who resettled probably also included refugees from the north as well as captives who were subsequently incorporated into Nafana society, with implications for Nafana cultural practices and ethnic style (see Stahl 1991, 2001 for details). The architecture of this occupation suggests fairly ephemeral wattle-and-daub buildings, a construction technique used in the area today to construct kitchen or farm shelters, or by those unable to muster the resources to construct a more substantial coursed wall dwelling. If we take the structures represented at Kuulo Kataa and Early Makala as the standard, Late Makala dwellings appear anomalous, not reflective of village construction in peaceful periods. Yet the 'breaker of walls' would have perceived them as 'traditional' construction.

The 'breaker of walls' would also have confronted a society whose political forms and style had been influenced by Banda's incorporation into Asante, but whose details did not correspond to an Akan model as it does today. That isomorphism would come from later British efforts to reconstitute the Asante confederacy along traditional lines as they struggled to implement indirect rule during the 1930s (Stahl 1991; and see Adas 1995 for a general discussion).

What lessons can those interested in diaspora studies draw from a case study of a relatively remote rural area of west central Ghana? While we should expect the effects of the Atlantic trade to vary and be uneven (*cf.* DeCorse's 1992 insights into life at Elmina on the coast with Kense (1987) on Daboya in northern Ghana), the societies documented by missionaries or ethnographers early in the twentieth century had lived in sustained relationship with the Atlantic world for centuries. This relationship evoked changes in African societies (see for example Ekeh's (1990) provocative reflections on the relationship between lineage systems and the slave trade), and these changes must be taken into account in efforts to draw connections between the world occupied by those who endured the middle passage and that inhabited by African villagers in the twentieth century, no matter how 'traditional' those villages might appear. Efforts to discern continuities of practice between Africans in the diaspora and on the continent have often failed to take time and change into account (Thomas 1995:151–2). These problems commonly plague the use of ethnographic analogues in archaeological interpretation (Stahl 1993). We must critically evaluate the sources of our ethnographic models, and adopt a comparative approach to their application so that we do not naively project twentieth-century patterns into a more distant past (Stahl 1993; Wylie 1985). This requires attention both to continuities *and* to discontinuities that flowed from Africa's involvement in the Atlantic trade and the imposition of colonial rule (*cf.* Guyer and Belinga 1995).

I hope the case study also speaks to historians and anthropologists interested in the problem of the Atlantic trade, demonstrating the value of archaeological evidence in discerning how regional and extra-regional developments played out at the local level. By undertaking carefully controlled comparisons between sites in the same area occupied at different points in time, as well as between contemporary sites in different areas (i.e. the coast *vs.* the interior), archaeologists can make a substantial contribution to our understanding of the local effects of global connections, opening the way for archaeology to make a meaningful contribution to historical anthropological studies of how life in Africa has changed in the wake of the Atlantic trade, as well as into Africa's legacy in the diaspora (Stahl 2000).

Acknowledgments

The archaeological research was supported by the Wenner-Gren Foundation for Anthropological Research (G-5133; 1989), the National Geographic Society (Grant #4313–90; 1990), and the National Science Foundation (Grant SBR-9410726; 1994–96). Neutron activation analysis was supported by the National Science Foundation through the Archaeometry Laboratory at the University of Missouri Research Reactor and Sigma Xi funds awarded to Maria Cruz. Oral historical research was supported by the British Academy. All research was conducted under license by the Ghana Museums and Monuments Board.

I acknowledge the kind support of colleagues in Ghana, including Dr. I. Debrah, Acting Director, Ghana National Museum, and Professor J. Anquandah, Department of Archaeology, University of Ghana. Special thanks to (now former) Tolee Kofi Dwuru III, Bandahene, and his council of elders, who have graciously allowed me and my students to pursue research in the Banda area since 1982. Special thanks to James Anane, Sampson Attah, and their families, whose support and kindness have made my visits to Banda comfortable. Simon Opoku and Peter and Ama Shinnie have provided valuable logistical support and friendship. Ideas expressed in this chapter arise in part from discussion among those involved in the Banda Research Project, including Andrew Black, Alex Caton, Maria das Dores Cruz, and Leith Smith. Alex Caton illustrated the ceramics and pipes in Figures 3.4 and 3.7. I am grateful to Chris DeCorse for his insights on the imported artifacts from Makala Kataa. Thanks to Chris DeCorse, Ada Demlietner, Rob Mann, Laurie Miroff, Spyros Spryou, and Brian Thomas for valuable comments on drafts of this chapter, and Peter Stahl for invaluable input and support.

References

Adas, Michael (1995) The reconstruction of 'tradition' and the defense of the colonial order: British West Africa. In *Articulating Hidden Histories: Exploring the Influence of Eric R. Wolf*, edited by J. Schneider and R. Rapp. Berkeley: University of California Press, pp. 291–307.

Ameyaw, K. (1965) Tradition of Banda. In *Traditions from Brong-Ahafo*, nos 1–4. Institute of African Studies, University of Ghana, Legon.

Arhin, K. (ed.) (1974) *The Papers of George Ekem Ferguson: A Fanti Official of the Government of the Gold Coast, 1890–1897*. African Social Research Documents, Vol. 7. African Studies Centre, Cambridge University, Cambridge.

Arhin, K. (1976/77) The pressure of cash and its political consequences in Asante in the colonial period. *Journal of African Studies*, 3:453–68.

Arhin, K. (1979) *West African Traders in Ghana in the Nineteenth and Twentieth Centuries*. London: Longman.

Boahen, A. A. (1987) *African Perspectives on Colonialism*. Baltimore: Johns Hopkins University Press.

Boyle, L. (1968) *Diary of a Colonial Officer's Wife*. Oxford: Alden Press.

Bravmann, R. A. (1972) The diffusion of Ashanti political art. In *African Art and Leadership*, edited by D. Fraser and H. M. Cole. Madison: University of Wisconsin Press, pp. 153–71.

Cameron, C. M. and Tomka, S. A. (eds) (1993) *Abandonment of Settlements and Regions: Ethnoarchaeological and Archaeological Approaches*. Cambridge: Cambridge University Press.

Carland, J. M. (1990) The Colonial Office and the first West African note issue. *International Journal of African Historical Studies*, 23:495–502.

Colonial Office (1899) CO 879/58 No. 585, African (West) Gold Coast. No. 10, Colonial Office to the Treasury. Further Correspondence relating to the Northern Territories. Public Record Office, London.

Constantine, S. (1984) *The Making of British Colonial Development Policy 1914–1940*. London: Frank Cass.

Crossland, L. B. (1989) *Pottery from the Begho-B2 Site, Ghana*. African Occasional Papers No. 4. Calgary: University of Calgary Press.

Crossland, L. B. and Posnansky, M. (1978) Pottery, people and trade at Begho, Ghana. In *The Spatial Organisation of Culture*, edited by I. Hodder. Pittsburgh: University of Pittsburgh Press, pp. 77–89.

Cruz, M. das Dores (1996) Ceramic production in the Banda area (West-Central Ghana): an ethnoarchaeological approach. *Nyame Akuma*, 45:30–7.

Cruz, M. das Dores (2001) 'Shaping the quotidian: ceramic production and consumption in Banda, Ghana *c.* 1780–1994.' Unpublished doctoral dissertation, Department of Anthropology, State University of New York at Binghamton.

Curtin, P. (1975) *Economic Change in Precolonial Africa: Senegambia in the Era of the Slave Trade*, 2 vols. Madison: University of Wisconsin Press.

David, Nicholas and Sterner, Judy (1999) Wonderful society: the Burgess Shale creatures, Mandara polities and the nature of prehistory. In *Beyond Chiefdoms: Pathways to Complexity in Africa*, edited by Susan Keech McIntosh. Cambridge. Cambridge University Press, pp. 97–109.

Davidson-Houston (1896) CO 879/45 No. 506, African (West) Correspondence (1896) relative to boundary questions with France in the Bend of the Niger. Enclosure in no. 114, Acting Governor Hodgson to Mr. Chamberlain. Public Record Office, London.

DeCorse, C. (1992) Culture contact, continuity and change on the Gold Coast, AD 1400–1900. *African Archaeological Review*, 10:163–96.

Dumett, R. and Johnson, M. (1988) Britain and the suppression of slavery in the Gold Coast colony, Ashanti, and the Northern Territories. In *The End of Slavery in Africa*, edited by S. Miers and R. Roberts. Madison: University of Wisconsin Press, pp. 71–116.

Dupuis, J. (1966) *Journal of a Residence in Ashantee*. 2nd edition. London: Frank Cass. (First published 1824.)

Ekeh, Peter P. (1990) Social anthropology and two contrasting uses of tribalism in Africa. *Comparative Studies in Society and History*, 32:660–700.

Fage, J. D. (1982) Slavery and the slave trade in the context of West African History. In *Forced Migration: The Impact of the Export Slave Trade on African Societies*, edited by J. E. Inikori. London: Hutchinson University Library for Africa, pp. 154–66.

Fell, T. E. (1913) Notes on the History of Banda. Rattray Papers, MS101:7, paper 7. Royal Anthropological Society, London.

Ferguson, G. W. (1896) CO 879/45 No. 506, African (West) Correspondence (1896) relative to boundary questions with France in the Bend of the Niger. Enclosure in no. 130, Acting Governor Hodgson to Mr. Chamberlain. Public Record Office, London.

Gann, L. H. and Duignan, P. (1978) *The Rulers of British Africa 1870–1914*. London: Croom Helm.

Garrard, T. F. (1980) *Akan Weights and the Gold Trade*. London: Longman.

Gold Coast Colony (1918) Report on Ashanti,

1918. *Gold Coast Colony Departmental Reports for 1918*, CO 98/30. Public Record Office, London.

Gold Coast Colony (1920) Report on Ashanti for 1920. *Government of the Gold Coast Annual Report for 1920*. CO 98/34. Public Record Office, London.

Gold Coast Colony (1928) *The Gold Coast Handbook*. Government Printing Office, Accra.

Goucher, C. L. (1981) Iron is iron 'til it is rust: trade and ecology in the decline of West African iron-smelting. *Journal of African History*, 22:179–89.

Gray, L. C. (1958) *History of Agriculture in the Southern United States to 1860*, vol. 2. Glouster, MA: Peter Smith.

Grier, B. (1981) Underdevelopment, modes of production, and the state in colonial Ghana. *African Studies Review*, 24:21–47.

Guyer, Jane I. (ed.) (1995) *Money Matters: Instability, Values and Social Payments in the Modern History of West African Communities*. Portsmouth, NH: Heinemann.

Guyer, Jane I. and Belinga, Samuel M. Eno (1995) Wealth in people as wealth in knowledge: accumulation and composition in Equatorial Africa. *Journal of African History*, 36:91–120.

Haight, B. (1981) 'Bole and Gonja: contributions to the history of northern Ghana.' Unpublished Ph.D. dissertation, Department of History, Northwestern University, Evanston, IL.

Heap, S. (1990) The development of motor transport in the Gold Coast, 1900–39. *Journal of Transport History*, 11:19–37.

Henderson, F. B. (1897) CO 879/50 No. 538, African (West), Further Correspondence relative to boundary questions in the Bend of the Niger. No. 136. Public Record Office, London.

Hodgson, F. (1894) CO 879/39, No. 478, African (West), Further Correspondence relating to affairs in Ashanti. No. 57, Acting Governor Hodgson to Marquess of Ripon. Public Record Office, London.

Hodgson, F. (1897) CO 879/50, No. 538, African (West), Further Correspondence relative to boundary questions in the Bend of the Niger. No. 592, Acting Governor Hodgson to Mr. Chamberlain. Public Record Office, London.

Holden, J. (1970) The Samorian Impact on Buna: an essay in methodology. In *African Perspectives: Papers in the History, Politics and Economics of Africa Presented to Thomas Hodgkin*, edited by C. Allen and R. W. Johnson. Cambridge: Cambridge University Press, pp. 83–108.

Holloway, J. E. (ed.) (1990) *Africanisms in American Culture*. Bloomington: Indiana University Press.

Inikori, J. E. (1982) Introduction. In *Forced Migration: The Impact of the Export Slave Trade on African Societies*, edited by J. E. Inikori. London: Hutchinson University Library for Africa, pp. 13–60.

Isaacman, A. and Roberts, R. (eds) (1995) *Cotton, Colonialism, and Social History in Sub-Saharan Africa*. Heinemann: Portsmouth, NH.

Kay, G. B. (1972) Introduction. The political economy of colonialism in Ghana. In *The Political Economy of Colonialism in Ghana: A Collection of Documents and Statistics 1900–1960*, edited by G. B. Kay. Cambridge: Cambridge University Press, pp. 3–37.

Kense, F. J. (1987) The impact of Asante on the trade patterns of northern Ghana and Ivory Coast. In *The Golden Stool: Studies of the Asante Center and Periphery*, edited by E. Schildkrout. Anthropological Papers, Vol. 65, Part 1. New York: American Museum of Natural History, pp. 143–55.

Kopytoff, I. (1987) The internal African frontier: the making of African political culture. In *The African Frontier: The Reproduction of Traditional African Societies*, edited by I. Kopytoff. Bloomington: Indiana University Press, pp. 3–84.

Kopytoff, I. (1988) The cultural context of African abolition. In *The End of Slavery in Africa*, edited by S. Miers and R. Roberts. Madison: University of Wisconsin Press, pp. 485–503.

Kopytoff, I. (1999) Permutations in patrimonialism and populism: the Aghem chiefdoms of western Cameroon. In *Beyond Chiefdoms: Pathways to Complexity in Africa*, edited by Susan Keech McIntosh. Cambridge: Cambridge University Press, pp. 88–96.

Kuklick, H. (1979) *The Imperial Bureaucrat: The Colonial Administrative Service in the Gold Coast, 1920–1939*. Palo Alto, CA: Hoover Institution Press, Stanford University.

Lovejoy, P. E. (1983) *Transformations in Slavery: A History of Slavery in Africa*. Cambridge: Cambridge University Press.

Lugard, Lord (1965) *The Dual Mandate in British Tropical Africa*. Hamden, CT: Archon Press.

McCarthy, M. (1983) *Social Change and the Growth of British Power in the Gold Coast: The Fante States 1807–1874*. New York: University Press of America.

McSheffrey, G. M. (1983) Slavery, indentured servitude, legitimate trade and the impact of abolition in the Gold Coast, 1874–1901: a reappraisal. *Journal of African History*, 24:349–68.

Manning, P. (1987) Local versus regional impact of slave exports on Africa. In *African Population and Capitalism: Historical Perspectives*, edited by D. D. Cordell and J. W. Gregory. Boulder: Westview Press, pp. 35–49.

Miers, S. and Roberts, R. (eds) (1988) *The End of Slavery in Africa*. Madison: University of Wisconsin Press.

Morrison, M. K. C. (1982) *Ethnicity and Political Integration: The Case of Ashanti, Ghana*. Syracuse, NY: Maxwell School of Citizenship and Public Affairs, Syracuse University.

Muhammed, A. (1977) The Samorian occupation of Bondoukou: an indigenous view. *International Journal of African Historical Studies*, 10:242–58.

Neff, H. and Glascock, M. D. (1997) Compositional Analysis of Ceramics from the Banda Area, Ghana (update). Report on file with author.

Northcott, H. P. (1897) CO 879/52 No. 549. African (West) Gold Coast. Correspondence relating to the Northern Territories, January to June 1898. Enclosure in no. 102, Acting Governor Hodgson to Mr. Chamberlain. Public Record Office, London.

Northcott, H. P. (1898) CO 879/54 No. 564. African (West) Gold Coast. Further Correspondence relating to the Northern Territories, Enclosure 2 in no. 84, Governor Hodgson to Mr. Chamberlain. Public Record Office, London.

Northcott, H. P. (1899a) CO 879/58 No. 585, African (West) Gold Coast. Further Correspondence relating to the Northern Territories. Colonel Northcott to the Colonial Office, no. 96, Report on his tenure. Public Record Office, London.

Northcott, H. P. (1899b) Report on the Northern Territories of the Gold Coast. Intelligence Division, War Office. Her Majesty's Stationery Office, London.

Person, Y. (1970) Samori and resistance to the French. In *Protest and Power in Black Africa*, edited by R. I. Rotberg and A. A. Mazrui. New York: Oxford University Press, pp. 80–112.

Posnansky, M. (1973) Aspects of early West African trade. *World Archaeology*, 5:149–62.

Posnansky, M. (1987) Prelude to Akan civilization. In *The Golden Stool: Studies of the Asante Center and Periphery*, edited by E. Schildkrout. Anthropological Papers, Vol. 65, Part 1. New York: American Museum of Natural History, pp. 14–22.

Rattray, R. S. (1929) *Ashanti Law and Constitution*. London: Constable.

Roberts, R. and Miers, S. (1988) The end of slavery in Africa. In *The End of Slavery in Africa*, edited by S. Miers and R. Roberts. Madison: University of Wisconsin Press, pp. 3–68.

Smith, J. F. (1985) *Slavery and Rice Culture in Low Country Georgia 1750–1860*. Knoxville: University of Tennessee Press.

Smith, J. N. Leith (1998) 'Occupation of the hinterland: a preliminary assessment of settlement patterns in the Banda region of west central Ghana.' Paper delivered at the 14th Biennial Conference, Society of Africanist Archaeologists, May 1998, Syracuse, NY.

Stahl, A. B. (1985) 'The Kintampo culture: subsistence and settlement in Ghana during the mid-second millennium BC.' Unpublished Ph.D. dissertation, Department of Anthropology, University of California, Berkeley.

Stahl, A. B. (1991) Ethnic styles and ethnic boundaries: a diachronic case study from West Central Ghana. *Ethnohistory*, 38:250–75.

Stahl, A. B. (1992) The culture history of the central Volta Basin. In *An African Commitment: Papers in Honour of Peter Lewis Shinnie*, edited by J. Sterner and N. David. Calgary: University of Calgary Press, pp. 123–42.

Stahl, A. B. (1993) Concepts of time and approaches to analogical reasoning in historical perspective. *American Antiquity*, 58:235–60.

Stahl, A. B. (1994) Change and continuity in the Banda area, Ghana: the direct historical approach. *Journal of Field Archaeology*, 21:181–203.

Stahl, A. B. (1999a) The archaeology of global encounters viewed from Banda, Ghana. *African Archaeological Review*, 16(1):5–81.

Stahl, A. B. (1999b) 'Pipes, beads, bottles, and cloth: embodying colonial change in Banda, Ghana.' Paper delivered at the 64th Annual Meeting of the Society for American Archaeology, Chicago, April 1999. Under revision for publication.

Stahl, A. B. (2000) What is the use of archaeology in historical anthropology? In *The Entangled Past: Integrating History and Archaeology*. Proceedings of the 30th Chacmool Conference, edited by Matthew Boyd. Calgary: University of Calgary, pp. 4–11.

Stahl, A. B. (2001) *Making History in Banda: Anthropological Visions of Africa's Past*. Cambridge: Cambridge University Press.

Stahl, A. B. and Anane, A. (1989) 'Family histories from the Banda traditional area, Brong-Ahafo region, Ghana.' Ms. on file with the

Institute of African Studies, University of Ghana, the Ghana National Museum, and the Banda Traditional Council.

Stahl, A. B. and Cruz, M. das D. (1998) Men and women in a market economy: gender and production in West Central Ghana c. 1700–1995. In *Gender in African Prehistory*, edited by Susan Kent. Walnut Creek, CA: Altamira Press, pp. 205–26.

Steiner, C. B. (1985) Another image of Africa: toward an ethnohistory of European cloth marketed in West Africa 1873–1960. *Ethnohistory*, 32:91–110.

Thomas, B. W. (1995) Source criticism and the interpretation of African-American sites. *Southeastern Archaeology*, 14:149–57.

Thornton, J. (1992) *Africa and Africans in the Making of the Atlantic World, 1400–1680*. Cambridge: Cambridge University Press.

Treasury (1899) CO 879/58 No. 585, African (West) Gold Coast. Further Correspondence relating to the Northern Territories. No. 19, Correspondence from the Treasury to the Colonial Office. Public Record Office, London.

Van Dantzig, A. (1982) Effects of the Atlantic slave trade on some West African societies. In *Forced Migration: The Impact of the Export Slave Trade on African Societies*, edited by J. E. Ini-

kori. London: Hutchinson University Library for Africa, pp. 187–201.

Wilks, I. (1975) *Asante in the Nineteenth Century: The Structure and Evolution of a Political Order*. Cambridge: Cambridge University Press.

Wilks, I. (1982a) Wangara, Akan and Portuguese in the fifteenth and sixteenth centuries. I. The matter of Bitu. *Journal of African History*, 23:333–49.

Wilks, I. (1982b) Wangara, Akan and Portuguese in the fifteenth and sixteenth centuries. II. The struggle for trade. *Journal of African History*, 23:463–72.

Wilks, I., Levtzion, N. and Haight, B. M. (1986) *Chronicles from Gonja: A Tradition of West African Muslim Historiography*. Cambridge: Cambridge University Press.

Wolf, E. R. (1984) Culture. Panacea or problem? *American Antiquity*, 49:393–400.

Wylie, A. (1985) The reaction against analogy. In *Advances in Archaeological Method and Theory*, vol. 8, edited by M. B. Schiffer. New York: Academic Press, pp. 63–111.

Yarak, L. (1979) Dating Asantehene Osei Kwadwo's campaign against the Banna. *Asantesem*, 10:58.

York, R. N. (1965) Excavations at Bui: a preliminary report. *West African Archaeological Newsletter*, 3:18–21.

4 The Effect of the Slave Trade on the Bassar Ironworking Society, Togo

PHILIP LYNTON DE BARROS

The Bassar were one of the most important iron-producing peoples of West Africa. Using their rich hematite ores, they produced numerous items for regional trade as early as the thirteenth century, and by the early seventeenth century were producing iron tools and weapons for most of the populations of Togo, west central Benin, and eastern Ghana. The influence of the slave trade eventually penetrated northern Togo during the late eighteenth century, leading to the total depopulation of the Bassar peneplain and the creation of refugee populations near Mounts Djowul, Kabu, and Bassar; the dislocation and movement of iron production centers to new areas; and the interruption of iron production during the long siege of Bassar by the slave-raiding Dagomba in the 1870s. Other effects of slave raiding included the need to relocate and adjust to new clay sources for the production of Bassar pottery, the periodic interruption of regional and long-distance trade routes, and the probable development of a more formalized and centralized form of political organization, the Bassar chiefdom.

Introduction

This paper has two major goals: to present a culture history of the Bassar ironworking society, and to demonstrate the effects of the slave trade on this society, especially after *c.* AD 1750. These presentations are based on a combination of ethnographic, ethnohistorical, archival, and, especially, archaeological data.

Nearly all written sources on the Bassar region date from the 1890s onward, and consist primarily of German and French accounts by scientists, explorers, missionaries, and colonial administrators, including data from the German and French archives. A good deal of this material was examined, but additional work at the German archives in Lomé would prove useful for a greater understanding of the Bassar region between 1894 and 1914. Some information was also provided from English sources from Ghana. Additional data on contacts between the Bassar and neighboring peoples to the west may be available from David Tait's manuscripts on the Konkomba of Ghana (as noted in Wilks 1975:305), and from the drum chants and Muslim chronicles of the former Gonja and Dagomba states to the west (see Levtzion 1968; Tait 1961:9, 11; Tamakloe 1931:260). These sources were not directly consulted, in part because they do not focus on the Bassar; however, they may contain important information about the extent to which the Bassar were raided by the Dagomba and Gonja states during the sixteenth and seventeenth centuries.

Local oral traditions extend back to the

origins of the Bassar and Kabu chiefdoms in the late eighteenth and mid-nineteenth centuries, respectively, and these have been recorded by the French (Cornevin 1962a; Froelich and Alexandre 1960), Togolese (Gbikpi-Benissan 1976, 1978, 1979; Gnon 1967; Kuevi 1975), and myself (de Barros 1985:723–9). Elsewhere in the region, oral traditions consist primarily of brief migration stories, but little detail is available for more than three to four generations back (Cornevin 1962a; Martinelli 1982). A detailed, integrated history of clan and lineage migrations of the Bassar during the last two centuries has yet to be written, and would require a long-term genealogical study in the more than 20 villages and towns of the region.

Written and oral sources were useful primarily for studying developments after *c.* AD 1800–50. Ethnohistorical sources, used in combination with ethnographic data collected in the field, were particularly useful in reconstructing the regional and long-distance trade of Bassar iron and iron products. Archaeological data were indispensable for understanding the evolution of Bassar ironworking and its effects on demography and settlement patterns during most of the last two millennia. Nevertheless, the interpretation of the archaeological record of past ironworking technology, production, and exchange was greatly aided by ethnohistorical accounts of Bassar ironworking (Hupfeld 1899), and information from Bassar informants about smelting and smithing procedures, furnace types, slag types, sizes of typical iron blooms, tool types, and tool uselife.

The Bassar region

The Bassar region is located in north central Togo about 355 km (220 miles) from the coast (Figures 4.1 and 4.2). Situated on the western periphery of the Atakora Mountains (Togo Hills), just over 9° north of the equator, Bassar has a tropical climate dominated by alternating rainy (April–October) and dry (November–March) seasons. Annual rainfall is about 127–140 cm (50–55 inches), producing a savanna–woodland landscape. The physical landscape is characterized by the 24–29-km (15–18-mile)-wide Bassar peneplain incised by the Katcha River and bordered on the west and east by discontinuous, frequently iron-rich, chains of hills and mountains. Iron ores range from the nearly pure hematite at Bandjeli, which is relatively free from silica and phosphorus impurities, to lower-grade ores found in many of the small hills near Bitchabe, Kabu-Sara, Nababun, and Bassar, to lateritic sources, which were apparently little used (Kachinsky 1933; Koert 1906; Kouriatchy 1933; Lawson 1972; Simpara 1978). From a broad regional perspective, Bassar-region ores were more substantial and richer than most ore deposits found within a 150- to 300-km radius (de Barros 1985:129–33).

The Bassar, a name derived from a deity associated with Mount Bassar, which rises 460 m (1,500 feet) above the peneplain, call themselves the *Bi-tchambe*. Since the early to mid-nineteenth century, most Bassar have lived in the four population centers of Bassar (20,000 inhabitants), Kabu-Sara, Bandjeli, and Bitchabe (Sprigade 1908; Figures 4.1 and 4.2). The present-day Bassar are an amalgam of indigenous groups and substantial numbers of immigrants, attracted to the region by its iron-working industry and as a place of refuge from the slave-raiding Dagomba and Tyokossi. Most of the indigenous lineages near the town of Bassar claim to come from the Dikre sacred forest 5 km (3 miles) to the northwest (Figure 4.2).

Subsistence is based on shifting agriculture with yams (in richer soils), groundnuts, and sorghum rotated in two- to three-year cycles, followed by a fallow period of up to eight years. Other crops include millet, brown beans, cassava, okra, peppers, kapok, and shea butter nuts (*karite*). Bassar is a relatively rich agricultural region compared to its neighbors. Neighboring populations, such as the Tyokossi and Kabiye from the north and northeast, and the Kotokoli (Tem) from the east, have been importing sorghum and other foods in exchange for cloth, charcoal, slaves, and cattle for centuries (Cornevin 1962a:98–9; de Barros 1985:54, 62–4; Frobenius 1913:455).

Communities are made up either of a single localized exogamous kin group or clan or, more frequently, an amalgam of several residence groups or lineages (*ketemgban*) belonging to one or more clans. Many clans are split up among a number of different residence groups or villages, such as the Bissibe (primarily smelters) and the Koli (primarily smiths). Each extended family lives within its own house-

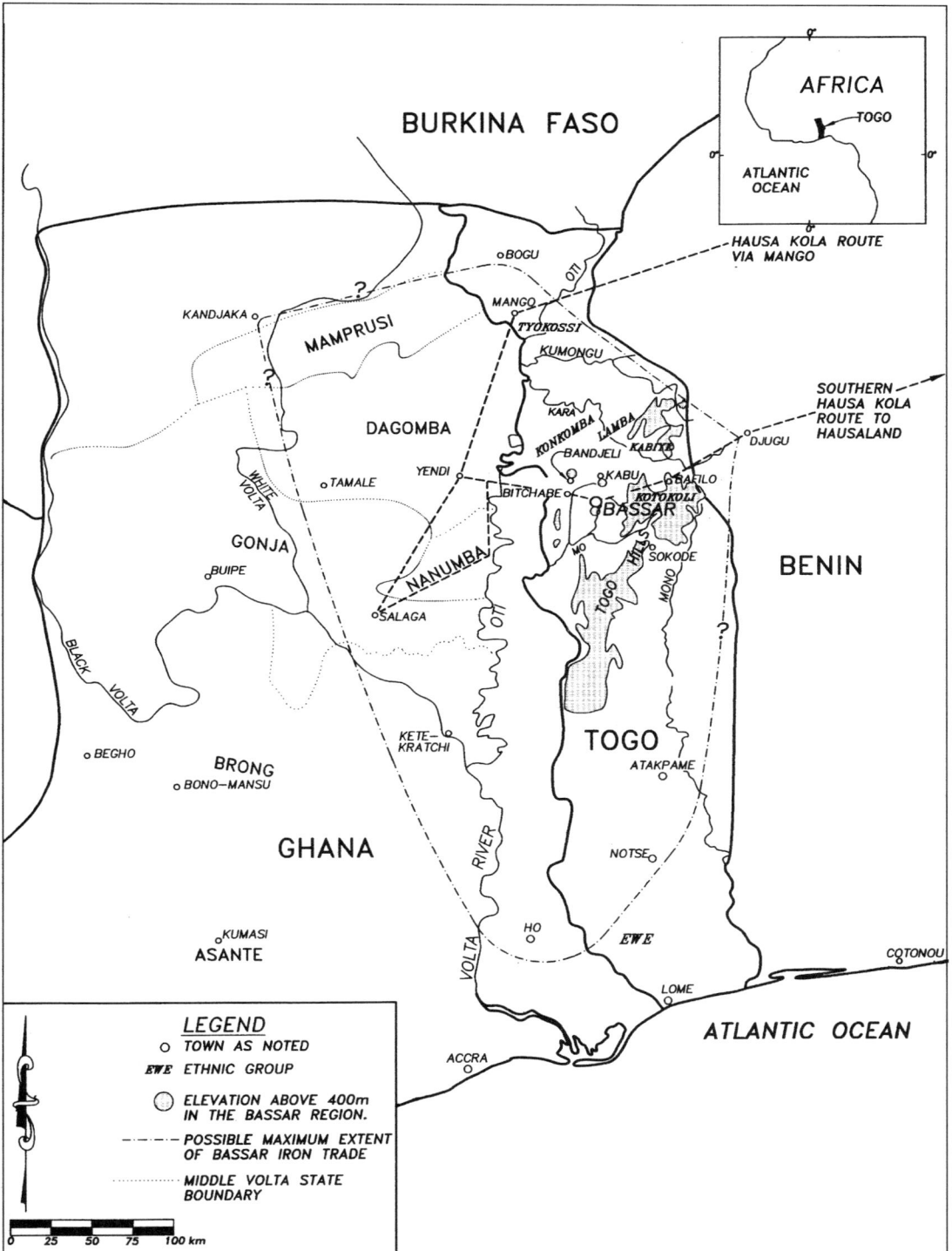

Figure 4.1 Bassar in West Africa. Relationship to states of the Middle Volta Basin and Hausa kola routes *c.* AD 1800.

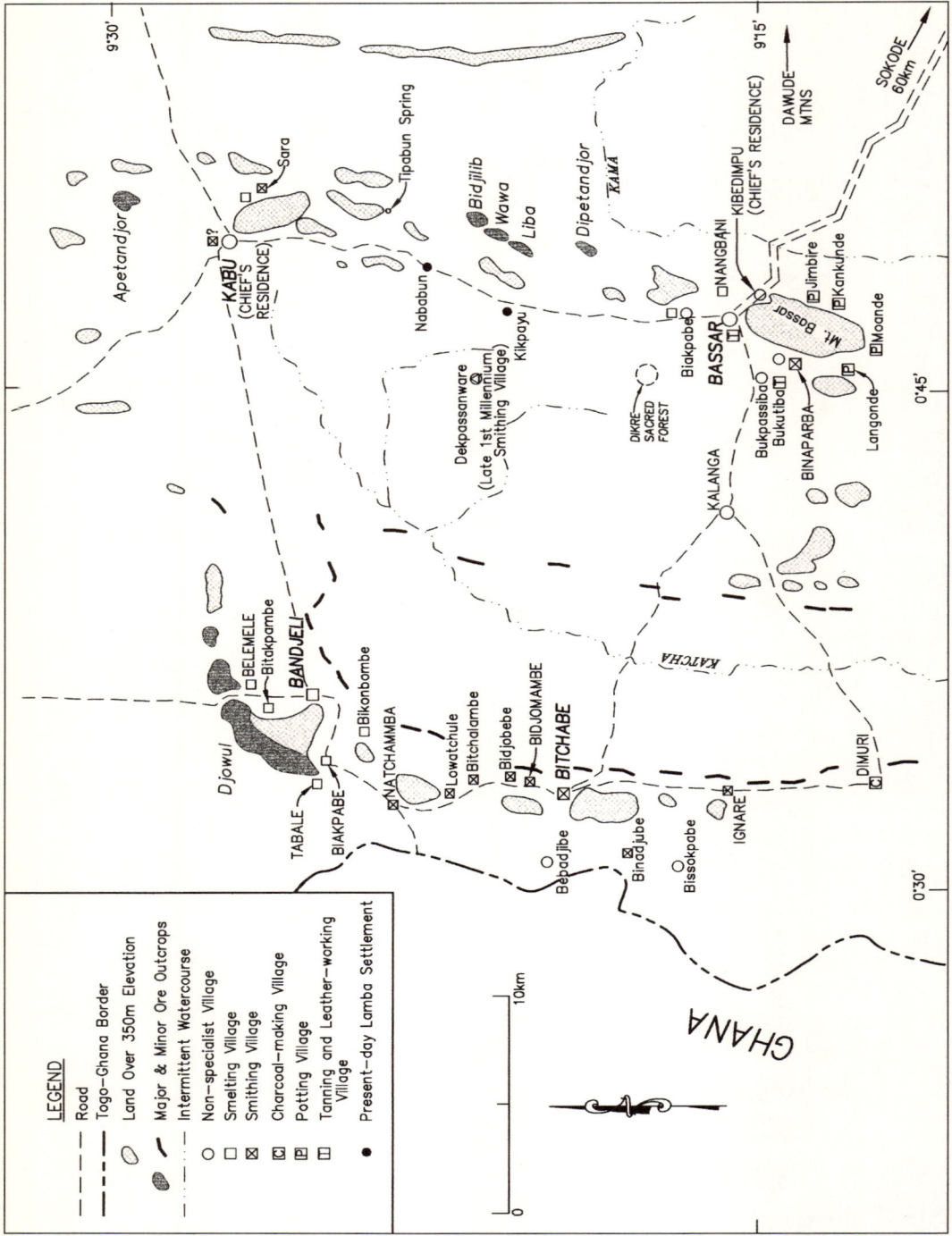

Figure 4.2 Bassar region showing iron ores, chiefdoms centered on Bassar and Kabu, and specialist villages at contact (1890s). The late first millennium smithing village of Dekpassanware is also shown.

hold (*soukala*). Aside from farming, most villages at the time of European (German) contact in the 1890s specialized in a particular activity such as smelting, smithing, charcoal production, potting, and the like (Figure 4.2).

At the time of contact with the Germans in the 1890s, Bassar political organization consisted of the Bassar and Kabu chiefdoms and the relatively autonomous western region running from Bandjeli to Bitchabe to Dimuri. Western-region villages were apparently presided over by a council of elders and a headman, generally the *chef de terre* (earth priest) from the founding lineage. It does not appear that a 'big man' system existed in western Bassar involving competition between village headmen for political power through the manipulation of production and/or exchange (see Fried 1967; Johnson and Earle 1987; Strathern 1969, 1971).

Culture history

Numerous Late Stone Age sites are known in Togo (Davies 1964; de Barros 1985, 2000a; Posnansky and de Barros 1980). About 6,500 years ago, pottery and ground (and polished) stone axes and hoe-like artifacts make their appearance in West Africa (Anquandah 1982:58–60; Phillipson 1993:144–6; Stahl 1994:71). The Agarade rockshelter in the Kotokoli region east of Bassar has produced a rich microlithic assemblage dated between 4,200 and 2,600 years ago, along with pottery and an edge-ground axe (de Barros 1992, 1999). Evidence for farming in West Africa dates only to the last 4,000 years, particularly as defined by the Kintampo culture in neighboring Ghana at about 1700 BC (Flight 1976; Phillipson 1993:147; Stahl 1985, 1994:72–9). The chronology of domestication in the Bassar region (and Togo generally) is unknown, but pottery and ground stone probably date back at least 3,500 years and possible contact with the Kintampo culture has been tentatively documented (de Barros 1983). The earliest Bassar habitation sites are small (<1,000 m², 1,200 square yards), suggesting extended family residences or seasonal camps (de Barros 1985:379, 399). These Late Stone Age inhabitants may have practiced a combination of hunting and gathering and rudimentary horticulture or vegeculture (de Barros 1988:97).

Later, there is a marked shift toward hamlet-sized settlements of just over a hectare in size. This may indicate a shift toward farming as the dominant mode of subsistence, resulting in a more sedentary lifestyle (de Barros 1988:97–8).

Two striking features of West African prehistory are the direct transition from the Stone Age to the Iron Age and the mosaic pattern of adoption of ironworking. Current data suggest ironworking appeared between 900 and 800 BC with the earliest evidence from southern Cameroon (Essomba 1992:219), Gabon (Clist 1989:71), and the Great Lakes region of East Africa (Schmidt and Childs 1985; Van Grunderbeek et al. 1982; Van Noten 1979). It was well established in West Africa by 500–400 BC in Niger and Nigeria (Calvocoressi and David 1979; Grébenart 1983). However, ironworking was not widely adopted in many parts of coastal (southern) West Africa until the middle centuries of the first millennium AD (Phillipson 1993:177). It was probably introduced into the Bassar region sometime after AD 500 (de Barros 1986:158). The regional ethnographic literature strongly suggests that traditional smelting and smithing were two separate technical operations carried out by distinct groups of specialists (Kense and Okoro 1993:458; Martinelli 1982:25–37). The archaeological data from Bassar tend to support this view (de Barros 1985:176–84). Ancestors of the neighboring Kabiye may have introduced smithing to eastern Bassar before the region became a major smelting center (de Barros 1985:157–58, 541–93; Delord 1961).

The development of a major smithing industry during the late first millennium AD had important effects on demography and settlement patterns in the eastern Bassar region (de Barros 1988): a general tendency toward higher population densities, larger habitation sites, and ultimately a settlement pattern composed of a large village (c. 15 hectares, 37 acres) at Dekpassanware (Figure 4.2) and satellite hamlets (not shown). Dekpassanware was probably a major market for iron products, but it is not known whether its leadership lay with the equivalent of a local big man or an hereditary chief (de Barros 1988:100).

Figure 4.3 Smelting furnace nearly four meters (13 feet) tall at Nangbani. This type of large furnace was developed in the nineteenth century to compensate for the lower quality of ores in eastern Bassar.

Later Iron Age technology

Considerable ethnohistorical and ethnographic evidence is available concerning traditional Bassar ironworking technology at the turn of the century, and the archaeological data suggest it has not changed significantly since the fourteenth century. Bassar hematite ore was mined from surface trenches or pits a few meters deep. Women (often Kabiye slaves) did the mining in the west, and men in the east, using wooden-handled iron picks. The ore was crushed into small nut-sized bits, and most impurities removed. Furnaces were of the induced draft type without bellows, ranging from two meters (6 ft 6 in; Bandjeli) to close to four meters (13 ft; Nangbani) in height (Figure 4.3). Furnaces were loaded with alternating layers of iron ore and wood charcoal fuel, and a typical smelt lasted two to three days at Bandjeli. Ironworking activities,

especially smelting, tended to be dominant during the dry season between the harvest and next year's planting. Bassar smiths then pulverized the bloom in bedrock mortars using spherical stone crushers and smaller pounders. Once freed from the slag, the resultant iron pellets were mixed with clay and vegetable fiber and reworked in a small smithy to improve its purity and working qualities (Dugast 1986; Goucher 1984:122–31). The iron was then made into hoes, axes/adzes, wedges, arrowheads, knives, spears, as well as bracelets, rings, fire strikers, slave irons, musical gongs, noise makers, and smelting and smithing tools. Smithing anvils and the larger forming hammers were made from stone, smaller finishing hammers from iron. Smithing bellows were made of animal skins fitted to a wooden frame. Air was forced into the semi-open smithy pit via a funnel-shaped tuyere made of clay and straw or kapok (de Barros 1986:152–4) (Figure 4.4). There were two types of smiths in Bassar: primary smiths who purified raw bloom and made such farming tools as hoes, axes, and machetes; and secondary smiths, who worked only with refined iron and made it into small items, such as jewelry and small knives (see Dugast 1986). The former were Bassar whereas the latter included both Bassar and other ethnic groups, such as the Kotokoli.

The rise of large-scale production

Beginning around AD 1300 the regional demand for iron increased substantially. Archaeological data suggest that induced-draft smelting furnaces were introduced to the region at this time. Such furnaces appear in Africa during the Later Iron Age and appear to be correlated with the need for higher levels of iron production to meet higher levels of demand (Kense 1983:155–7). The average Bassar region iron output from the early fourteenth through the late sixteenth centuries is estimated at about 10 to 20 metric tonnes per year, considerably beyond local needs (de Barros 1985:223–4, 295; 1986:168). It is therefore likely that Bassar iron and iron products were being traded to the neighboring Konkomba, Kabiye, and Kotokoli (Tem). Iron production was widespread as witnessed by slag heaps in the Bandjeli, Bitchabe, Kabu-Sara, Nababun, and Bassar areas, including near the sacred

Figure 4.4 Bassar smithing equipment: spherical stone for crushing iron bloom; two quartzite hammers for shaping iron; wood and skin bellows and clay tuyere (*umpolo*) for guiding air into smithy (not shown).

forest of Dikre and its permanent spring northwest of Bassar (Figure 4.2; see de Barros 1988: Figure 2).

The emergence of the neighboring political states of Dagomba, Mamprusi and Gonja (in modern Ghana) and their cavalry-based armies during the fifteenth and sixteenth centuries greatly increased the demand for iron for the production of weapons (spears and swords), horse paraphernalia (harnesses, stirrups), and even protective helmets and chain mail (Fage 1978:97–8; Goody 1971). These states, along with the rise of Bono-Mansu and its Asante successor state, helped stimulate the development of long-distance trade into the Middle Volta Basin (de Barros 1986: 164; Levtzion 1968:5–6) (Figure 4.1). Some have argued that the introduction of American food plants (cassava, corn) may have helped spur a general population increase (Hopkins 1973: 30–1; Van-

sina 1960:226–7), which would have increased demand for iron hoes (de Barros 1986:164). The Bassar region with its rich iron ores responded to this increased demand for iron with a vengeance. Between *c.* AD 1550/1600 and *c.* 1750/1800 Bassar iron production at the three major centers north of Bandjeli, north of Kabu, and near the recent Lamba settlement of Nababun is estimated to have increased between 400 and 600 percent, and that of the region between 300 and 450 percent (de Barros 1986:160–4) (see Figure 4.5).

Effects of large-scale production on Bassar society

This dramatic increase in iron production had important repercussions for Bassar society. There was a marked increase in the regional population—as much as 100–200 percent in the major ironworking centers (de Barros 1988:102). This was the result of three factors: natural population increase due to better living standards; the importation of slaves as domestic laborers (see below), made possible by increased wealth from the sale of iron and iron products; and the immigration of ironworkers, especially from the west and north, attracted to the growing Bassar iron industry (Cornevin 1962a:37–42; de Barros 1988:102; Martinelli 1982:26–37). Such immigration to major ironworking centers has also been documented at Sukur, Nigeria (David and Sterner 1995:10).

As the region's livelihood became increasingly tied to ironworking, the Bassar could spend less time on farming, obtaining a part of their foodstuffs through the trade of iron and iron products. Local farmland could thus support denser populations and villages would have to move less often in the face of declining soil fertility (de Barros 1988:103). As a result, the population became more sedentary and lived in increasingly more numerous and larger settlements. By the seventeenth century, ironworking so dominated Bassar economics and society that much of the Bassar population moved near the major ore deposits: Djowul near Bandjeli, Apetandjor north of Kabu, and the Bidjilib-Liba-Wawa hills near Nababun and the permanent spring of Tipabun (de Barros 1988:103–7) (Figure 4.5). Other major population centers included the vicinity of the sacred forest of Dikre and the Bitchabe smithing zone; however, little is known about the

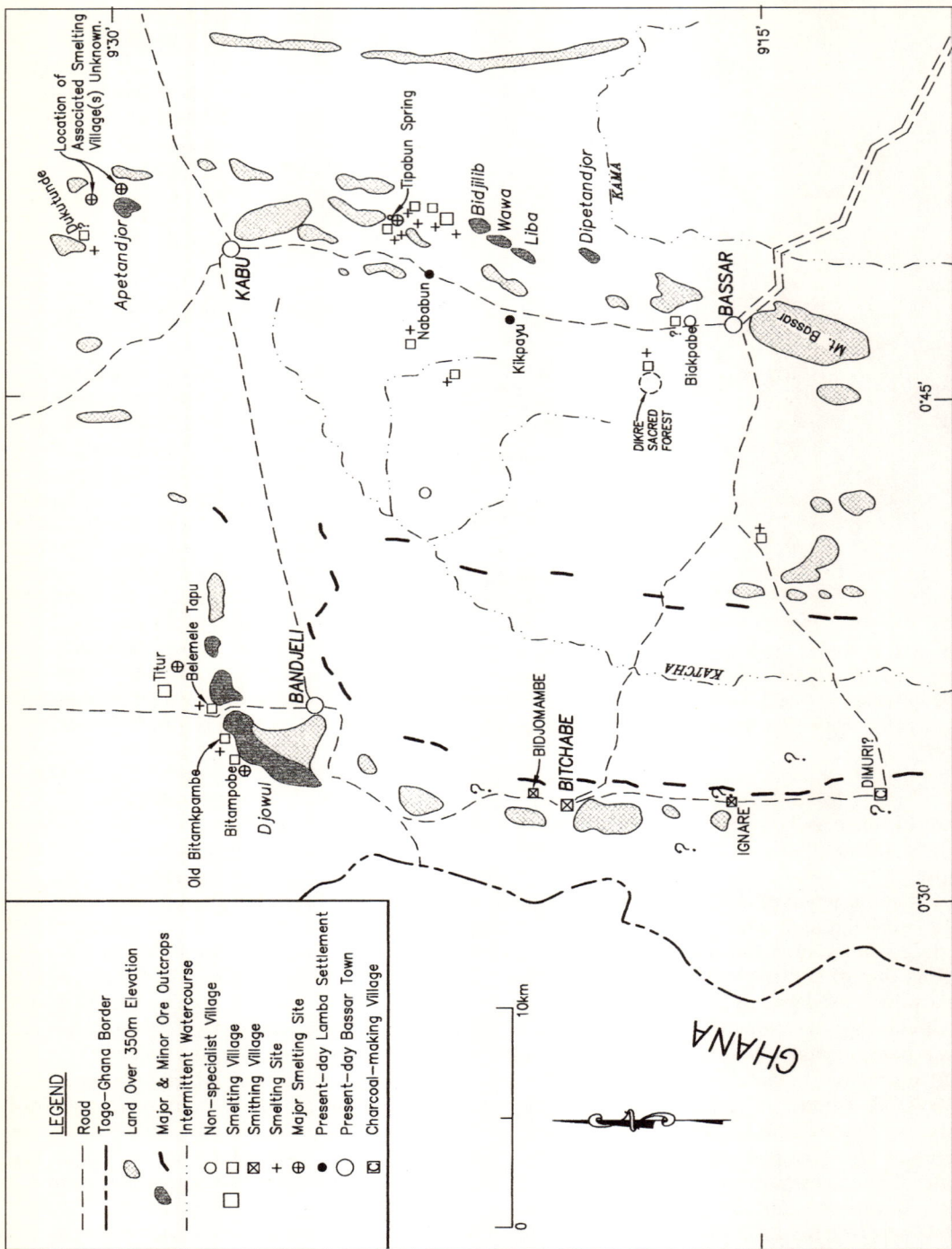

Figure 4.5 Bassar region *c.* AD 1600–1750. Major ironworking villages and sites shown for Bandjeli, Kabu, Nababun, and Bassar. Insufficient data are available for Bitchabe area.

details of settlement in the Bitchabe zone for this period, including whether Dimuri had as yet begun to specialize in charcoal making (see Figures 4.2 and 4.5). The rise of several iron-working centers may have resulted in regional competition, but the nature of that competition is poorly understood. As will be discussed below, the Bassar do not appear to have had a competitive 'big man' system, and the ethno-graphic record makes no mention of named chiefs prior to *c.* AD 1800.

Most villages, while still practicing farming, spent much of their time in ironworking activities. The archaeological evidence suggests that during the seventeenth century villages in the western region developed specialization within the iron industry itself: smelters centered around Bandjeli; smiths from Natchammba to Bitchabe to Ignare (areas rich in stone for anvils and hammers); and eventually charcoal makers at Dimuri as wood fuel supplies began to dwindle further north (de Barros 1985:218, 439; Kuevi 1975; Posnansky and de Barros 1980). Important smelting centers also existed in the eastern region north of Kabu and near Nababun (Figure 4.5). In the east, specialized activities were to become more varied with the rise of the Bassar and Kabu chiefdoms in *c.* AD 1800 and 1850, respectively. When the Germans arrived in the 1890s, the Bassar chief-dom included potting, smelting, and smithing villages and *ketemgban* specializing in tanning or leather-working and possibly weaving, as well as a few villages that concentrated purely on farming and cattle raising. The biggest cattle owners, however, tended to be the ironwork-ers as they could trade their iron products for food, slaves, cowrie shells, or cattle. In the Kabu chiefdom, Sara was composed of *kete-mgban* specializing in either smelting or smi-thing, while Kabu residents focused primarily on farming (Figure 4.2).

Major markets were located in Bassar, Bitchabe, Natchammba, Bandjeli, and Kabu (Figure 4.2). All were centers of both local and regional trade with neighboring peoples, such as the Gonja, Dagomba, Mamprusi, and Kon-komba to the southwest, west, and northwest; the Tyokossi, Lamba (Losso), and Kabiye to the north and northeast; and the Kotokoli (Tem) to the east (de Barros 1985:342–53; 1986). A wide range of products was traded, including iron and iron products. Cowrie shells served as a medium of exchange.

By the early to mid-nineteenth century, the slave trade with neighboring regions, par-ticularly with the overpopulated Kabiye to the northeast, was particularly active in Bassar because of the surplus wealth accumulated from the sale of iron and iron products. Young Kabiye were obtained in exchange for sor-ghum and/or cowrie shells. In addition, slaves obtained in war by other ethnic groups were sometimes sold at Bassar region markets. Slaves worked primarily as farm laborers and as domestic servants and their descend-ants were generally assimilated (Cornevin 1962a:88–98; de Barros 1985:64; Frobenius 1913:456–60; Klose 1964:166, 180–3; von Doering 1895).

The rise of large-scale iron production resulted in greater material wealth, particularly for ironworkers—who were most likely to become rich men (*okpli*) (de Barros 1997; Gbikpi-Benissan 1976:139–42). Ironworkers amassed wealth in the form of food, cowrie shells, cattle, slave labor in the mines and in the fields, and such sumptuary items as brass rings from the Dagomba, necklaces of flaked coral, agate beads from Kirotashi on the Niger, European glass beads, and native ground beads (Klose 1964:162–3).

Klose (1964:155, 162) uses the term 'big men' when referring to relatively rich family or lineage heads. While it is not unusual for African lineage heads to amass more wealth than more junior lineage members, the ques-tion is whether one can speak of 'big men' as it applies for example in Melanesia (Strathern 1969, 1971). Dugast (1986, 1988), a cultural anthropologist who has spent considerable time studying the Bassar, asserts that the Bas-sar have no equivalent to the 'big man' as described for Melanesian societies (Dugast, pers. com. 1996; see also Dugast 1992). Clearly wealthy lineage heads would have had more political and economic power arising out of their position as lineage heads. There does not appear to have been any formal political-economic competition between such lineage heads, such as competitive feasting.

The dramatic increase in iron production and exchange also resulted in the increased use of pottery vessels (as opposed to gourds), much of them obtained through trade. While Bassar archaeological ceramic assemblages show evidence of imported wares prior to the advent of ironworking, their dominance increases substantially after about AD 1400 and locally made Bassar wares become increasingly uncommon (de Barros 1985:541–93). Small, lightweight pottery bowls are so common in late sixteenth through eighteenth centuries that they appear to have replaced the small calabash bowls used for eating and drinking that are once again common in present-day Bassar. Shaped potsherds (circles, triangles, rectangles), which probably represent the remnants of potsherd pavements, make their appearance as early as the fourteenth century, when the Bassar first began to trade iron with neighboring populations (de Barros 1988:99).

The rise of long-distance trade

Levtzion (1968:17–18) argues that long-distance trade between Hausaland (northern Nigeria) and the Volta basin (modern Ghana) began before the end of the sixteenth century, and Dramini-Issifou (1981) suggests that such contacts date back to the late fourteenth or early fifteenth centuries. Three main routes developed (Levtzion 1968:24): one through present-day Niger and Burkina Faso (formerly Upper Volta), then southward to Yendi and Salaga; the second through Niger to Mango in northern Togo, and then to Yendi and Salaga; and the third through northern Dahomey (Nikki, Djugu), Kotokoli country (Dawude Mountains), and on to Yendi and Salaga. However, the oral traditions of the Bassar, Kotokoli, and Tyokossi make it clear that this third route also passed through Bassar and Bitchabe (Barbier 1982; de Barros 1985:325–9; Norris 1984) (Figure 4.1).

I have previously argued that the Hausa caravan route through the Bassar region probably did not become important until the mid-to-late eighteenth century. The development of this southern route corresponded with the development of the Gurma dynasty in Djugu (Benin), the Kotokoli chiefdoms in central Togo, and the rise of the Bassar chiefdom during this same period (de Barros 1985:331–7). This conclusion was based in part on the assumption that the development of long-distance trade routes and chiefdoms are mutually reinforcing. Caravans would prefer to pass through regions where local chiefdoms could provide some security for peoples and goods (in exchange for tolls or gifts), and the

rise of such trade routes tended to stimulate the development of centralized polities, which sought to take advantage of the economic benefits of their passage (de Barros 1988:107, 109; Hopkins 1973:62; Levtzion 1968:5–6, 22–5; Sundstrom 1974:5–13, 61–5). However, despite widely held beliefs about the symbiotic relationship between long-distance trade routes and the rise of centralized polities, it will be shown later that this assumption is highly problematical for the Bassar region.

By the nineteenth century, most of the trade between Hausaland and Salaga passed along the southern Hausa route through Bassar, with large caravans of upwards of 1,000 people and as many pack animals (Clapperton 1829:68 cited in Levtzion 1968:25). This southern route became popular because of a steep rise in the demand for kola nuts in Hausaland after Uthman dan Fodio's 1804 *jihad*, which banned alcoholic beverages. Kola became a key substitute, and, given it is a perishable commodity, the southern route was preferred as it was the shortest between Hausaland and Salaga (Martinelli 1982; Norris 1984).

There is conflicting evidence concerning whether the Hausa traded in iron and iron products from Bassar and aided in their distribution to other regions. Klose (1964:145, 1903b:341) observed Hausa buying iron tools in the smithing village of Binaparba. However, oral informants in Bitchabe, Bandjeli, Bassar, and Kabu insist that the Hausa did not trade in iron and iron products, but purchased only food (see also Dugast 1988:269–71). But oral and written sources do indicate that the Tyokossi and Kotokoli served as middlemen for the trade of iron products to the north and south (de Barros 1985:345, 352; Hupfeld 1899:191; von Doering 1895:263).

The advent of Dagomba and Tyokossi slave raiding

With the rise in the importance of the trans-Atlantic slave trade during the late sixteenth and especially the seventeenth and eighteenth centuries, a series of European forts and commercial outposts developed along the Ghanaian coast (Dutch, British, Swedes, Danes, and German Brandenbergers). With the growth of the Asante state in the seventeenth and eighteenth centuries, slaves flowed increasingly from Kumasi to the coast. The Asante obtained their slaves as a result of war, tribute from conquered peoples (including the states of Dagomba and Gonja), or from the sale of gold (Wilks 1993:77–8). However, Wilks (1993:76–8, 223–9) has shown that while the Asante used many of their slaves to help settle new agricultural lands as they expanded their kingdom, or used them as domestic servants and porters, surplus slaves, especially those captured in war, were sold to the coastal markets for trade to the Europeans.

Dagomba

During the period described above, the states of Dagomba and Gonja occasionally raided acephalous peoples for both slaves and cattle, including the Konkomba and Bassar (Tait 1961:9, 11). Tamakloe (1931:260) notes in his traditional history of the Dagomba that the great seventeenth-century Gonja warrior, Djakpa, raided the Bassar, 'who took refuge in their mountain passes but had to leave great herds of cattle for the raider to carry off' (de Barros 1985:654). This pattern of states and other centralized polities raiding acephalous peoples for slaves and booty (often livestock and/or iron) was common in the sixteenth through nineteenth centuries in several parts of West Africa (see Cohen 1974:165 and David and Sterner 1995:6 for northern Nigeria and Cameroon). Beginning in the late eighteenth century and continuing until the arrival of the Germans in the 1890s, however, the Bassar region was periodically subjected to intensive slave raiding by the cavalry-led armies of the Dagomba from the west and Tyokossi from the north. The Dagomba became an especially serious threat after they had to make regular tribute payments in slaves to the expanding Asante nation (Figure 4.1).

According to Wilks (1975:21–3), the Asante invaded Dagomba at Yendi in 1744–45, but did not actually regularize tribute relations until the reign of Asantehene Osei Kwadwo (1764–77). The tribute in slaves apparently began in the early 1770s and was set at 1,000 slaves per year. By the early nineteenth century, Bowdich (1819:320–1) reported that each major division of the Gonja and Dagomba states had to pay 200 cows, 400 sheep, 400 cotton cloths, 200 cotton and silk cloths, and 500 slaves annually, with minor divisions paying smaller amounts (Wilks 1975:66). Wilks (1975:431–2) estimates that the total annual tribute from Gonja and Dagomba was 'on the order of 5,000 slaves, 2,000 cows, and 4,000 sheep.' For Dagomba alone, the totals would have been 2,000 slaves, 800 cattle, and 1,600 sheep (Wilks 1975:432). Bassar, with its flourishing iron industry, growing population, and abundant cattle, was a natural place for the Dagomba to turn to meet their annual quota (de Barros 1985:654–5). During his travels at the turn of the century, Klose (1964:51, 80) described the presence of Bassar slaves in farming villages near Kete-Kratchi, and said that it was the Dagomba who provided most of the slaves sold at the kola market of Salaga. Von Doering (1895:260) also spoke of how the Dagomba had been warring against the Bassar for a long time.

Except for a short period during the reign of Ya Na Ya'qub (c. 1833 to c. 1864) when tribute payments to the Asante were suspended (see Wilks 1975:305), Dagomba slave raiding continued throughout much of the nineteenth century and is strongly embedded in Bassar oral traditions throughout the region. After 1867, the Dagomba under Ya Na 'Abdullah (c. 1864–76) led a series of expeditions against the Bassar, culminating in the Great Dagomba War of 1873–76 and the siege of the town of Bassar, which ended with the death of the Ya Na (Cornevin 1962a:57; de Barros 1985:655–6; Wilks 1975:67–8, 305–6). The siege of Bassar apparently had as its goal the incorporation of the agriculturally and iron-rich Bassar region into the Dagomba state. While the siege of Bassar failed, there is some evidence that the Bandjeli region paid tribute for a time.

Tyokossi

The Tyokossi (Anufo) originated from the present-day Ivory Coast. They consisted of a wandering group of Malinke (Mandingue) warriors led by the Ouattara of the royal family of the Kong kingdom, and a larger group of followers speaking Agni or Baoule (Cornevin 1962b:67). Their movements led them eventually to northern Togo where they established their war camp at Sansanne-Mango in about 1764 (Norris 1984:164). They first established their authority over the local Gangan population, and then spent about a decade destroying the former capital of the Gurma confederation in southern Burkina Faso. In the 1790s, they turned their attention to the south, attacking Djugu and Aledjo Kura in western Benin, and Bafilo, Dawude, and Bassar in north central Togo (de Barros 1985:656–7) (Figure 4.1).

The Tyokossi attacks usually had two goals: to obtain slaves, and to defeat the local population to make them pay tribute in the form of food (Norris 1984:164). Tyokossi oral traditions indicate that they succeeded in defeating the Bassar after a long siege, and some nineteenth-century German observers believed that Mango once held sway over the Bassar region (von Zech 1898:131). Tyokossi slave raiding appears to have abated somewhat during the second half of the nineteenth century, which may explain why the Bassar collective memory of Tyokossi raids is not as strong as it is for the Dagomba. However, according to Cornevin (1962a) and E. G. Norris (pers. com. 1984), the Tyokossi *ketemgban* (clan) of Kodjodumpu in the town of Bassar was founded in the 1870s or 1880s, primarily to keep an eye on an alternate trade route from Mango to Yendi (and Salaga) via Bassar owing to instability in Dagombaland after the defeat of the Asante by the British in 1874 (de Barros 1985:660–1; Wilks 1971:134–5). Finally, Klose (1903a:309) suggests, somewhat ambiguously, that Bandjeli and Bapure (Konkomba) were still paying tribute to the Dagomba or the Tyokossi in 1897.

While the link between Dagomba slave raiding and the Atlantic slave trade through the intermediary of the Asante has been established, it is legitimate to ask how Tyokossi slave raiding was related to the Atlantic trade. It is true the Tyokossi sought slaves for their own kingdom, but it can be argued that their departure from the Kong region in the Ivory Coast and their installation in northern Togo was a part of the dynamic movement of West African peoples that resulted from the slave raiding and the disruption and realignment of centers of power induced by the Atlantic slave trade.

The impact of the slave trade on Bassar society

The Bassar region was dramatically affected by the intense slave raiding of the late eighteenth and nineteenth centuries. While oral traditions have been an important source, these effects have been documented primarily with archaeological data.

A careful study of ethnographic and ethnohistoric data, including a list of chiefs, suggests that the Bassar chiefdom was created somewhere between AD 1780 and 1810 (de Barros 1985:723–9). This coincides rather well with the beginning of intensive slave raiding by the Dagomba and Tyokossi. It was previously suggested that the Gurma, Kotokoli, and Bassar chiefdoms rose in response to the increased importance of the southern Hausa kola route that passed through Bassar. In fact, Martinelli (1982:31, 36, 81–2) claims the Bassar chief levied tolls on caravans and taxes on market operations, and received iron products as tribute from local smelters and smiths. However, my own research of oral traditions failed to verify any of these points. More recent studies by Dugast (1988:269–73) have demonstrated that the Bassar chief did not benefit either directly or indirectly from the passage of the long-distance Hausa caravans. First, there is no evidence that anything other than symbolic gifts (millet beer, poultry) were offered to the Bassar chief by leaders of Hausa caravans. Second, the chief did not obtain tribute, taxes, or judgment fees in the form of sumptuary or other trade goods that could be commercialized via long-distance or regional trade. In fact, tribute was minimal and consisted of short, once-per-year labor requirements, contributions of food and a part of the hunt, and poultry when needed for ritual sacrifices (de Barros 1985:67–8; Dugast 1988:272). Judgment fees consisted of providing millet beer if the plaintiff was satisfied with the chief's verdict. Such tribute was primarily to help support the chief and indigent followers (including widows), and was more symbolic than economic in nature (Dugast 1988:272). Third, neither the chief nor his immediate subordinates exercised any control over iron production, which was under the control of local lineages or extended families. The iron trade was in the hands of Bassar primary smiths who either sold iron products at local markets or organized regional caravans to neighboring peoples; smelters sold their wares only at local markets (Dugast 1988:269–70). Finally, slavery was strictly a domestic institution in Bassar and this was true for the chief as well: slaves were not organized into separate work groups to produce a political surplus (Dugast 1988:269–73).

An alternative hypothesis is that the Bassar chiefdom developed as a defensive response to incessant slave raiding (de Barros 1986:166–7). If so, then one could argue that the Bassar chiefdom was itself a result of the slave trade. A number of authors (including myself) have also highlighted the military rivalry between the Bassar and Kabu chiefdoms (Cornevin 1962a:53–67, 109–13; see de Barros 1985: 65–8; Frobenius 1913:443; Gbikpi-Benissan 1976; Gnon 1967; Klose 1903a, 1903b; Martinelli 1982; von Zech 1898). However, cultural anthropologist Dugast (1988:273) has carefully studied this issue and has concluded that the Bassar chiefdom was not warlike and that it rarely engaged in anything more than raids where some minor pillaging took place. Early German observers assumed that the Bassar chiefdom once held sway over much of the Bassar region, but my own research and that of Dugast (1988) and Pawlik (1988) indicates it controlled primarily the area 5–10 km (3–6 miles) north and west of Bassar only.

Dugast (1988:274–9) argues that the Bassar chiefdom was, in fact, a reinvention and improvement upon an earlier, less centralized chiefdom, and that the primary goal was to eliminate previous factionalism and to create an institution that could deal with the huge influx of foreign refugees created by intense slave raiding (Dugast 1988:274–9). The chief was selected from the Nataka clan and ruled with the help of a council of elders from that clan. There was no organized police force and no hereditary titles. The Nataka clan was a political composite consisting of both indigenous and foreign elements and associated ritual leaders, including the earth priest for the local Bassar deity (*utandaan*) which resided in the sacred forest at Dikre, as well as ritual leaders associated with rain, wind, fertility, and the like. This grouping of ritual leaders within a single clan provided the spiritual legitimacy the chief needed to rule, but at the same time tightly circumscribed his authority (Dugast 1988:274–5). The Bassar chief's relative lack of political power resembles that of the chief of the Sukur ironworking society in northern Nigeria; however, it would appear that the Sukur chief had greater access to wealth through his participation in the iron industry

and export trade (David and Sterner 1995:10–11, 13).

If Dugast is correct, the primary motive for the creation of the Bassar chiefdom was not defensive, but political. The intensive slave raiding by the Tyokossi, and especially the Dagomba, led to population aggregation near Mount Bassar and an increasingly heterogeneous population. Horton (1971), Cohen (1974), and Vincent (1991) (see also David and Sterner 1995) have argued that increased settlement size and aggregation, primarily due to warfare, inevitably lead to increased clan (or lineage) heterogeneity. This increased heterogeneity, aggregation, and circumscription of the population inevitably calls forth the need for more centralized political institutions to deal with potential disputes. In Bassar, the local population was so concerned with the issue of disputes that the first chief was selected from a foreign group (possibly from Gonja) to ensure that he could be impartial in his decisions. Subsequently, the chief's office was to alternate between this foreign element of the Nataka clan and an indigenous element that had previously furnished the chief (Dugast 1988:277–8).

The rival Kabu chiefdom was founded in the late 1850s, during a lull in the slave raiding, by elements from Kalanga who had fled after losing a battle to the Bassar chiefdom. Its founding elements were influenced by Islamic models (such as the neighboring Kotokoli chiefdom), and it was clearly created to take advantage of the east–west trade of iron, food, and slaves between the Kabiye and Bassar (Gnon 1967). Here again, it appears that passing trading groups gave gifts to the Kabu chief, but there were no formal tolls or taxes.

Effect on settlement and demography

The combined effects of the Dagomba and Tyokossi raids in the late eighteenth century resulted in a massive settlement shift in the core of the Bassar ironworking region (see Figures 4.5 and 4.6). Populations rapidly abandoned unprotected open areas, moving to sites within easy reach of large mountains or hills that could be used as refuge areas during the cavalry attacks of the Dagomba and Tyokossi. Bassar oral traditions recount how the attacking horsemen could not easily make the climb uphill, and how the Bassar rolled large boul-

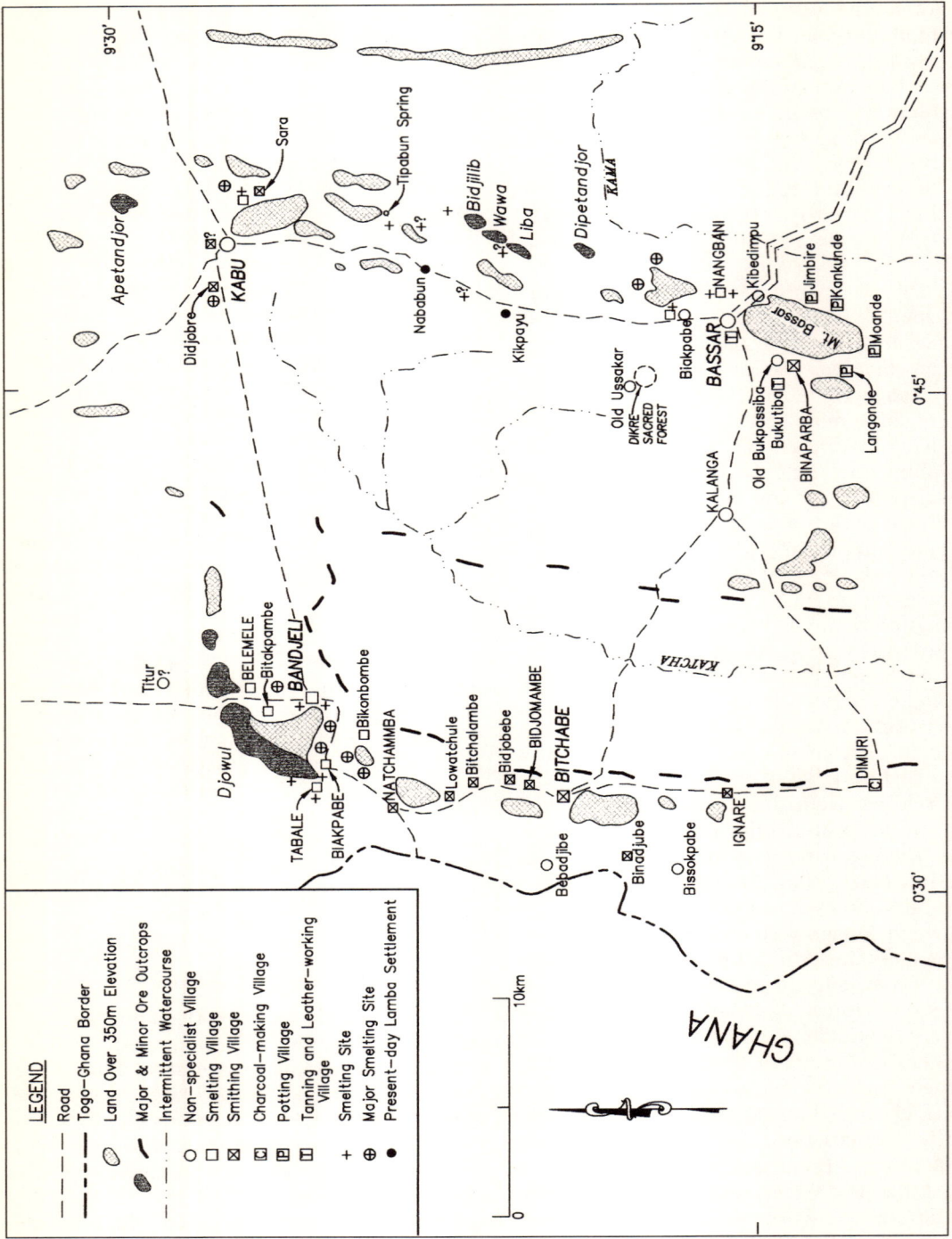

Figure 4.6 Bassar region c. AD 1825/1850. There has been a major shift in the distribution of smelting settlements south of Bandjeli and near the large mountains adjacent to Kabu and Bassar.

ders down upon them when they tried. The Bassar also recount with pride how they farmed on the top of Mount Bassar during the Dagomba siege of 1873–76 and archaeological evidence clearly indicates that they did in fact do this (Cornevin 1962a).

By *c.* AD 1825–50, the overall result was the abandonment of most of the Bassar peneplain and the concentration of population in the four centers known today: Bassar, Bandjeli, Bitchabe, and Kabu, though the actual town and chiefdom of Kabu-Sara was not founded until the 1850s (Figures 4.5 and 4.6). The siege of Bassar by the Dagomba in 1873–76 also led large numbers of people to flee the Bassar region entirely (Cornevin 1962a; Klose 1903a:309; Martinelli 1982).

In the Bandjeli area, Bassar ironworkers formerly lived and worked north of Djowul mountain. The major ironworking settlements of Bitampobe and Titur, which had been occupied for several centuries and had resulted in a combined 19,000 m³ of slag mounds, were mostly abandoned by *c.* AD 1800–25 (de Barros 1985:693–9, 741). Habitation and smelting sites were first moved closer to Djowul mountain, then finally south of the mountain as Dagomba (and Tyokossi) raids intensified (see Figures 4.5 and 4.6). Other ironworking populations fleeing Tyokossi expansion from the north also settled near Bandjeli (Kpandjal). To the south in the Bitchabe area, villages moved closer to the larger hills and some smiths founded Binaparba near Bassar, the location of the recently created Bassar chiefdom. North of Kabu, the settlements and smelting sites in the vicinity of Apetandjor were largely abandoned. Some population remnants remained, but most joined the growing refugee settlements near Bandjeli, and later Kabu.

In the Nababun area, the cluster of settlements near Bidjilib and the smelting center near Tipabun spring, as well as settlements in the Katcha Valley to the west, were also abandoned (Figures 4.5 and 4.6). Populations moved primarily to Bassar, with some later going to Kabu-Sara when this chiefdom was founded in the 1850s during a lull in the slave raiding. The populations living near the sacred forest of Dikre eventually took refuge beneath Mount Bassar (where some villages already existed), forming the nuclei of the future settlements of Bassar, Nangbani, and Bukpassiba. According to oral traditions, these villages were strategically placed to warn the local populations of impending Dagomba (and presumably Tyokossi) attacks, and to protect the chiefly residence set up at Kibedimpu. Other refugee groups eventually joined them.

Iron production and exchange

The massive population movements of the late eighteenth and early nineteenth centuries did not result in the destruction of the Bassar ironworking industry. While the Dagomba and Tyokossi may have exercised brief periods of hegemony or suzerainty over the Bassar region, the Bassar ironworkers continued to live and work at new locations. Smelting flourished south of Djowul in new settlements such as Tabale, Bitamkpambe, Belemele, and Kpandjal (Bandjeli). Smithing flourished near the hills and mountains between Natchammba and south of Bitchabe, while Dimuri developed into a charcoal-making center. The combined effects of slave raiding and the aggregation of population near Mount Bassar resulted in the development of a major iron production center in that vicinity for the first time in history. Two new, large smelting furnace centers (*m'pampu*) appeared in the early nineteenth century about 5 km (3 miles) north of Bassar. Smelters, living in Nangbani, Biakpabe, and possibly Bukutchabe, exploited the Dipetandjor ore source. Binaparba, founded by smiths from Bitchabe, became the major village of primary smiths. Finally, with the rise of the Kabu chiefdom in the 1850s, the nearby village of Sara was created as a smelting and smithing center under the protection of the Kabu chief (Gnon 1967).

For the Bassar region as a whole, iron production actually increased from *c.* 30 to 80 tons per year from the late sixteenth through eighteenth centuries to between 60 and 135 tons per year in the nineteenth century (de Barros 1986:168). The intensification of production, particularly near Bassar, is reflected not only in massive slag heaps, but also in a higher ratio of furnace emplacements to slag mounds and in larger groups of furnaces, suggesting a change in the organization of production with possible intergroup cooperation beyond the lineage or *ketemgban* level (de Barros 1985:235–9). Oral traditions from Bassar regarding the *m'pampu* sites north of Nangbani tend to confirm that larger work groups did

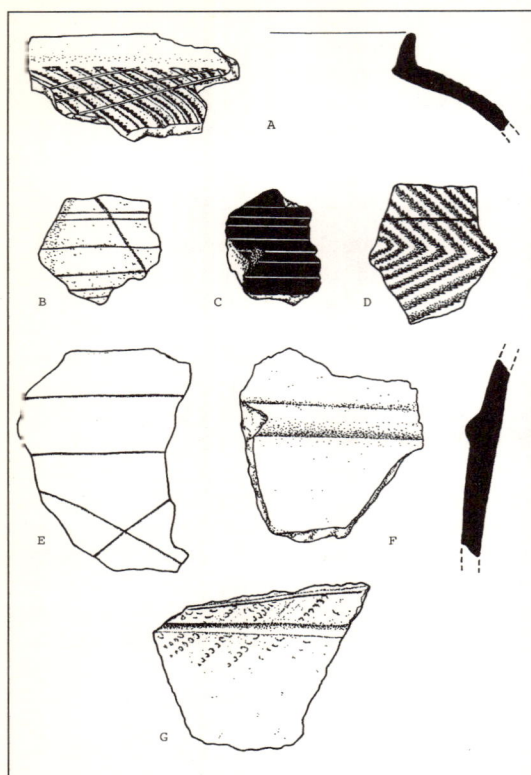

Figure 4.7 Bassar ceramics: A, B: Burnished Incised Thin Fine Micaceous Ware (jar rim, bowl sherd); C: Micaceous Wash Ware bowl sherd; D: Herringbone Roulette Ware sherd; E: Bassar Smoothed Ware bowl sherd; F, G: Bassar Protomodern jar sherds (F with appliqué).

exist and that they were linked to clan affiliations, which often cut across village ties (de Barros 2000b).

The intensified Dagomba raids and the siege of Bassar in the 1870s ultimately made the passage of Hausa caravans through Bassar very risky and most certainly disrupted ironworking activities. As a result, iron production and exchange declined in the late nineteenth century, and the Hausa caravans sought alternative routes to Salaga (and its successor town of Kete Kratchi), through Sokode and the Fasao Mountains to the south (de Barros 1985:328–30, 1986: Figure 8). This meant economic decline for Bassar from the early 1870s to the establishment of a German protectorate with Bassar chief Atakpa in 1894 von Doering 1895; de Barros 1985:304–5).

The dynamic and disruptive events of the late eighteenth and nineteenth centuries apparently did not have a major effect on ironworking technology. Induced draft furnaces without bellows continued to be used, and smelting and smithing tools apparently did not change. Archaeological evidence suggests, however, that the very large furnaces at the *m'pampu* sites north of Bassar-Nangbani are a late development associated with the rise of Bassar as a major production zone (Figure 4.3). To compete with the superior quality ores of the Bandjeli region, furnaces in the east were built to contain larger quantities of wood fuel and iron ore for a smelt lasting from three to five days (instead of the two days at Bandjeli). This allowed them to produce the standard 30-kg iron bloom weight as it was sold throughout the Bassar region. Even then, smiths from Binaparba would add Bandjeli iron to the locally produced iron before working it into tools (Hupfeld 1899:179, 191; de Barros 1986:153).

Pottery production and exchange

Pottery production and trade in the greater Bassar region were thriving in the seventeenth and eighteenth centuries prior to the Dagomba and Tyokossi slave raiding of the late eighteenth century. Garbage dumps (middens) at Bassar habitation sites from this period contain dense concentrations of pottery with sherd densities of more than $50/m^2$ (de Barros 1985:397). Except for the Bandjeli area, which was historically dominated by pottery made by the Konkomba to the north, Bassar region assemblages were dominated by three wares:

1) Burnished Incised Thin Fine Micaceous Ware, which is generally smudged and decorated with panels of knotted cord rouletting bordered or crossed by straight or curved grooves or incisions (upper portion of jars), and with fine, parallel incisions (lower portion of jars and on bowls) (Figure 4.7 A and B);
2) Micaceous Wash Ware, which is a well-smoothed, frequently smudged, relatively thin brown ware with decorations similar to those described above and usually coated with a micaceous wash, thereby mimicking the Burnished Incised Thin Fine Micaceous Ware (Figure 4.7 C); and

3) Bassar Smoothed Ware, a thicker ware ranging from yellow-orange, yellow-brown and orange to whitish-gray and light gray shades, with no evidence of smudging or micaceous wash, and decorated with broadly spaced linear and curvilinear incised lines (Figure 4.7 E).

The paste and surface treatment of the first two wares suggest manufacture to the east and north by the Kabiye and Losso, respectively. Bassar Smoothed Ware was almost certainly made within the Bassar region. The two imported wares dominate the ceramic assemblages, whereas the local Bassar ware is relatively uncommon.

With the advent of intensive slave raiding by the Dagomba and Tyokossi and the abandonment of the Bassar peneplain, major changes took place in both pottery production and trade. Burnished Incised Thin Fine Micaceous Ware was replaced by the less common Late Fine Micaceous – a mildly burnished, generally unsmudged micaceous ware that is decorated with knotted cord rouletting and often has a whitish sheen which may be a wash. Micaceous Wash Ware continues for a short while but its micaceous wash degenerates into a thin, almost unnoticeable film. In a short time, it is replaced by Herringbone Roulette Ware, a fully smudged ware characterized by knotted rouletting done in herringbone (fishbone) patterns (Figure 4.7 D). Bassar Smoothed Ware rapidly disappears and is replaced with an early type of Bassar Protomodern Pottery. Bassar Protomodern is characterized by buff, yellow, and yellow-orange and other earth tones, typical of open-hearth firing in an oxidized atmosphere. It is decorated with twisted cord rouletting which is sometimes overlain with horizontal grooves (Figure 4.7 G). An ancient characteristic of Bassar pottery not seen in centuries makes its reappearance in the form of an *appliqué* ridge around the center of large jars, marking where the lower and upper portions of the jars are attached during the production process (Figure 4.7 F).

In the Kabu region, the imported Herringbone Roulette and micaceous wares continue to dominate ceramic assemblages (e.g., at Dijobre and Dukutunde, Figures 4.5 and 4.6). In the vicinity of Bassar, however, the locally made Bassar Protomodern dominates and imported wares are relatively uncommon (e.g. at Old Bukpassiba, Figure 4.6). The regional instability created by the incessant slave raiding and the rise of the Bassar chiefdom resulted in the disruption of traditional patterns of pottery production and exchange. Losso and Kabiye pottery no longer arrived in the Mount Bassar region in significant quantities and local production became increasingly important. The development of the specialized potting villages of Kankunde, Jimbire, Moande, and Langonde beneath Mount Bassar may reflect both the difficulty of obtaining pottery sources from the north and east, as well as the growing importance of the Bassar chiefdom (Figures 4.2 and 4.6).

Changes in the paste between Bassar Smoothed Ware and Bassar Protomodern strongly indicate shifts in clay sources and production centers as a result of intensive slave raiding and the eventual abandonment of the Bassar peneplain. While it is not known where the makers of Bassar Smoothed Ware obtained their clays, studies of present-day potting villages such as Jimbire and Kankunde indicate that clay is mined to the east of Mount Bassar. Bassar Smoothed Ware paste is relatively fine-grained, with relatively small nonplastic (quartz) inclusions. Bassar Protomodern makes its first appearance prior to the complete abandonment of the Dikre sacred forest area. Ceramics associated with a small, c. AD 1800–25 hamlet directly adjacent to Dikre (Old Ussakar), consist almost entirely of a crude version of Bassar Protomodern. It is made of a relatively fine-grained paste, but it is not well smoothed or fired, and its clay is quite soft as a result. It is as if the potters were experimenting with a new clay source and had not yet worked out the best way to prepare and fire it. After the abandonment of Dikre, new clay sources were apparently identified, as specialist potting villages were established near Mount Bassar (Jimbire, Kankunde, Moande, Langonde). These later varieties of Bassar Protomodern paste contain important quantities of nonplastic inclusions made of greywacke and shale, giving it a chunky texture. Bassar Protomodern has since been refined into the relatively well-fired and well-burnished Bassar Modern Ware sold in Bassar region markets today.

Bassar under colonial rule

Somewhat belatedly, the Germans joined the European scramble for colonial territories in the late nineteenth century. German colonial history began in Togo in 1884 and was consolidated in the 1890s. In 1894, von Doering and the Bassar chief, Atakpa, signed the first protectorate treaty for the Bassar region. German Togoland was considerably larger than present-day Togo, as it included more lands east of the Volta and Oti rivers. The Germans worked rapidly to develop Togo into a self-sustaining colony and, using local labor, built a system of roads and most of the present-day railroad system.

The German period of colonial rule was, in fact, beneficial for Bassar iron production and exchange. The Germans encouraged local industries and trade. They also diligently recorded their output. German archival data indicate that Bassar iron production in the first decade of the twentieth century averaged 150 to 200 tons per year (de Barros 1985:Table 26; Togo National Archives 1911). Most of this production was at Bandjeli, whose pure hematite ores were best able to compete with increasing competition from cheap imported European iron, including that associated with the construction and repair of the colonial railroad (Goucher 1984:136–7). The iron production centers at Kabu-Sara and Bassar probably ceased operation around 1905 (de Barros 1986:168).

The Germans also encouraged traditional patterns of exchange in order to tax them (Norris 1984). As a result, Hausa caravans returned to their old route through Bafilo and the Bassar region. In 1900, 30,000 Hausa merchants passed through Bassar each dry season, and 80 percent of the kola reaching Hausaland passed along this route (Norris 1984:168). The Bassar iron trade may have reached its maximum extent during this period, covering most of Togo and much of eastern Ghana (Figure 4.1). At its peak the Bassar iron industry was providing iron hoes and other tools to as many as 600,000 people, covering an area of over 97,000 km² (38,000 square miles) (de Barros 1986:171) (see Figure 4.1). Goucher (1984) suggests that Bassar iron may have reached Kumasi (Ghana) and perhaps even the coast. On the other hand, recent studies of the Mam-purugu iron region (Gambaga escarpment) by Kense and Okoro (1993) suggest that the trade of Bassar iron into northeastern Ghana may not have been very important.

After World War I and the Treaty of Versailles of 1919, Togoland passed into French hands. The French did not actively encourage local industries, and Bassar iron production eventually succumbed to competition from locally available scrap iron. However, traditional iron smelting did not entirely cease until 1951 when the French outlawed it as a deforestation control measure. Traditional smithing technology continued to be practiced until the 1970s.

Conclusion

Until the late first millennium AD, the Bassar region was relatively isolated from mainstream events in West Africa. It was a simple horticultural society with a tribal level of political organization and no ironworking industry of its own. With the introduction of ironworking, a major smithing center developed at Dekpassanware, which may have been associated with a more hierarchical political system and regional trade, but by the early second millennium it had disappeared. It is only in the fourteenth century, with the appearance of the induced draft furnace (perhaps imported from the north), that Bassar began its rise to become one of the major ironworking centers of West Africa as it responded first to the regional demands of its neighbors, and then to the demands of the growing Gonja, Mamprusi, and Dagomba states of eastern Ghana. By the early seventeenth century, the growth of the iron industry and the immigrant ironworkers it attracted led to rapid population growth, population aggregation near the principal iron ores, and a low-level settlement hierarchy of large villages and satellite hamlets, which may have been associated with either a regionally competitive tribal system or nascent hereditary chiefdoms. By the eighteenth century, Bassar became integrated into a long-distance Hausa trade route between northern Nigeria and the Volta basin of Ghana. With its rich agricultural lands and iron and iron products, Bassar grew prosperous.

In the late eighteenth century, Bassar's involvement with the outside world took a negative turn. What previously had been an occasional raid for slaves and cattle by the neighboring Dagomba turned into a century of intensive slave raiding by both the Dagomba to the west, who sought slaves for tribute owed to the Asante, and the Tyokossi to the north. By the early nineteenth century, this raiding led to the depopulation of the Bassar peneplain and the concentration of refugee populations near large mountains like Mount Bassar. It led to a relocation of iron production centers and contributed to the rise of the Bassar chiefdom. A rival chiefdom at Kabu appeared in the 1850s. Contrary to commonly accepted beliefs, the Bassar chiefdom apparently did not arise as a response to the passage of the Hausa kola route, or as a result of control over iron production and exchange. The rise of intensified iron production near the town of Bassar resulted in the development of the larger Nangbani furnaces, capable of producing the standard-sized 30-kg (66-lb) iron bloom despite the relatively inferior quality of local ores. The regional instability created by slave raiding also resulted in a major reduction in the quantities of imported pottery reaching the town of Bassar and a concomitant rise in the importance of locally made Bassar wares, which required adapting to a new set of clay sources. Finally, the intensified Dagomba raids and the siege of Bassar in the 1870s led to a disruption in iron production and shift of the Hausa kola route to the south, resulting in a period of economic decline and depopulation. However, with the German colonial peace Bassar ironworking and exchange rebounded to new heights, despite stiff competition from European iron. In short, despite the major impact of the slave trade, the Bassar ironworking society demonstrated an amazing resilience and capacity for adaptation.

References

Anquandah, J. (1982) *Rediscovering Ghana's Past.* Accra: Sedco, and Harlow, Essex; Longman.

Barbier, J.-C. (1982) L'histoire présente, exemple du royaume Kotokoli du Togo. Bordeaux: Centre d'Etudes d'Afrique Noire. Mimeographed.

Bowdich, T. E. (1819) *Mission from Cape Coast Castle to Ashantee.* London: John Murray.

Calvocoressi, D. and David, N. (1979) A new survey of radiocarbon and thermolumines-

cence dates for West Africa. *Journal of African History*, 20:1–29.

Clapperton, H. (1829) *Journal of a Second Expedition into the Interior of Africa.* London: John Murray.

Clist, B. (1989) Archaeology in Gabon. *African Archaeological Review*, 7:59–95.

Cohen, R. (1974) The evolution of hierarchical institutions: a case study from Biu, Nigeria. *Savanna*, 3(2):153–74.

Cornevin, R. (1962a) *Les Bassari du Nord-Togo.* Paris: Berger-Levrault.

Cornevin, R. (1962b) *L'Histoire du Togo.* Paris: Berger-Levrault.

David, N. and Sterner, J. (1995) 'The wonderful society: the Burgess Shale creatures, Mandara polities and the nature of prehistory.' Paper presented at the Conference for Archaeology of Complex Societies, Complex Societies Group, California State University at San Bernardino. October 21, 1995.

Davies, O. (1964) *The Quaternary of the Coastlands of Guinea.* Glasgow: Jackson.

de Barros, P. (1983) A Kintampo rasp fragment from Bassar (Togo). *Nyame Akuma*, 23:35–6.

de Barros, P. (1985) 'The Bassar: large scale iron producers of the West African Savanna.' Ph.D. dissertation, Department of Anthropology, University of California, Los Angeles. Ann Arbor: University Microfilms.

de Barros, P. (1986) Bassar: a quantified, chronologically controlled, regional approach to a traditional iron production centre in West Africa. *Africa*, 56(2):148–74.

de Barros, P. (1988) Societal repercussions of the rise of large-scale traditional iron production: a West African example. *African Archaeological Review*, 6:91–113.

de Barros, P. (1992) 'Preliminary report on excavations at Agarade rockshelter, central Togo, West Africa, December 1988.' Paper presented at the 11th Biennial Conference of the Society of Africanist Archaeologists, University of California, Los Angeles. March 1992.

de Barros, P. (1997) Ironworking in its cultural context. In *The Encyclopedia of Precolonial Africa: Archaeology, History, Languages, Culture, and Environments*, edited by J. Vogel. Walnut Creek, CA: AltaMira Press, pp. 135–49.

de Barros, P. (1999) *Rapport sur les fouilles de l'abri d'Agaradé, aussi appelé Tchounbowou, entre Sokode et Bafilo dans la région centrale du Togo.* Report submitted to the Association Togolaise de Recherche Scientifique, Lome, Togo.

de Barros, P. (2000a) *Rapport sur le projet archéologique de la Vallée de l'Oti au nord Togo,*

1999–2000. Report submitted to the Association Togolaise de Recherche Scientifique, Lome, Togo.

de Barros, P. (2000b) Iron metallurgy in its sociocultural context. In *Ancient African Metallurgy*, edited by J. Vogel. Walnut Creek, Altamira Press, pp. 147–98.

Delord, J., Pasteur (1961) 'Notes et commentaires', on the translation of Leo Frobenius' 'Les Kabre', by I. Mury, A. Honegger and J. Pons. *Le Monde non chrétien* 59–60 (n.s.):101–73.

Dramini-Issifou, Z. (1981) Routes de commerce et mise en place des populations du nord du Bénin actuel. In *2000 Ans d'histoire africaine: le sol, la parola et l'ecrit; mélanges en hommage à Raymond Mauny*, Paris: Société Française d'Histoire d'Outre-Mer, pp. 655–72.

Dugast, S. (1986) La pince et le soufflet: deux techniques de forge traditionnelles au Nord-Togo. *Journal des Africanistes*, 56(2):29–53.

Dugast, S. (1988) Déterminations economiques *versus* fondements symboliques: la Chefferie de Bassar. *Cahiers d'Etudes Africaines*, 110, 28(2):265–80.

Dugast, S. (1992) 'Rites et organisation sociale: l'agglomération de Bassar au nord-Togo.' Doctoral thesis. EHESS, Paris.

Essomba, J. M. (1992) *Civilisation du fer et sociétés en Afrique centrale: le cas du Cameroun méridional*. Paris: L'Harmattan.

Fage, J. D. (1978) *A History of Africa*. New York: Alfred A. Knopf.

Flight, C. (1976) The Kintampo culture and its place in the economic prehistory of West Africa. In *Origins of African Plant Domestication*, edited by J. R. Harlan, M. J. De Wet and A. B. L. Stemler. The Hague: Mouton, pp. 211–21.

Fried, M. (1967) *The Evolution of Political Society*. New York: Random House.

Frobenius, L. (1913) *Und Africa Sprach, III (Unter den Unstraflichen Aethiopien)*. Berlin: Bita, Deutsches Verlagshaus.

Froelich, J. C. and Alexandre, P. (1960) Histoire traditionnelle des Kotokoli et des BiTchambi du nord-Togo. *Bulletin de l'Institut Fondamental d'Afrique Noire*, series B, 12, 1–2.

Gbikpi-Benissan, D. F. J. (1976) 'Pouvoirs politiques anciens et pouvoir politique moderne au Togo—la chefferie dans la nation contemporaine—essais de sociologie politique sur les chefferies en pays Bassari, Akposso et Mina.' Unpublished thèse de IIIème cycle, Université R. Descartes, Paris V.

Gbikpi-Benissan, D. F. J. (1978) Entretiens en pays Bassar. I. Origines, migrations, fondations de villages, conflits armés. *Etudes de Documents de Sciences Humaines*, series B, No. 1. L'Institut National des Sciences de l'Education, Université du Bénin, Lome, Togo.

Gbikpi-Benissan, D. F. J. (1979) Entretiens en pays Bassar. II. Organization politique, stratification sociale, période coloniale. *Etudes de Documents de Sciences Humaines*, series B, No. 2. L'Institut National des Sciences de l'Education, Université du Bénin, Lome, Togo.

Gnon, A. (1967) 'L'aménagement de l'espace en pays Bassari—Kabou et sa région.' Masters thesis. DES Géographie, Université de Caën.

Goody, J. (1971) *Technology, Tradition and the State in Africa*. London: Oxford University Press.

Goucher, C. (1984) 'The iron industry of Bassar, Togo: an interdisciplinary investigation of African technological history.' Ph.D. dissertation, Department of History, University of California, Los Angeles. Ann Arbor: University Microfilms.

Grébenart, D. (1983) Les métallurgies du cuivre et du fer autour d'Agadez (Niger) des origines au début de la période medièvale: vues générales. In *Métallurgies africaines: nouvelles contributions*, edited by N. Echard. Paris: Société des Africanistes, pp. 109–25.

Hopkins, A. G. (1973) *An Economic History of West Africa*. London: Longman.

Horton, R. (1971) Stateless societies in West Africa. In *History of West Africa, Vol. I*, edited by J. F. Ade Ajayi and M. Crowder. New York: Columbia University Press, pp. 73–119.

Hupfeld, v. F. (1899) Die Eisenindustrie in Togo. *Mitteilungen aus den deutschen Schutzgebieten*, 11:175–94.

Johnson, A. W. and Earle, T. (1987) *The Evolution of Human Societies: From Foraging Group to Agrarian State*. Stanford: Stanford University Press.

Kachinsky, V. (1933) Les gisements de fer au Togo. *Togo-Cameroun* (October). Agence Economique des Colonies Autonomes et des Territoires Africaines sous Mandat, Paris, pp. 179–85.

Kense, F. J. (1983) *Traditional African Iron Working*. African Occasional Papers 1, Department of Archaeology, University of Calgary, Calgary.

Kense, F. J. and Okoro, J. A. (1993) Changing perspectives on traditional iron production in West Africa. In *The Archaeology of Africa: Food, Metals, and Towns*, edited by T. Shaw, P. Sinclair, B. Andah and A. Okpoko. One World Archaeology, vol. 20, C. J. Ucko, series editor. New York: Routledge, pp. 449–58.

Klose, H. (1903a) Das Bassarivolk I. *Globus*, 83(20):309–14.

Klose, H. (1903b) Das Bassarivolk II. *Globus*, 83(22):341–4.

Klose, H. (1964) 'Klose's journey to northern Ghana, 1894.' Translated by Inge Killick. Institute of African Studies, University of Ghana, Legon. Mimeographed. Originally published (in 1899) as *Togo unter deutscher Flagge: Reisebilder und Betrachtungen*. Berlin: D. Reimer.

Koert, W. (1906) Das Eisenlager von Bangeli in Togo. *Mitteilungen aus den deutschen Schutzgebieten* 19:113–31.

Kouriatchy, N. (1933) Géologie du territoire du Togo. *Bulletin du Comité d'Etudes historiques et scientifiques de l'A.O.F.* (l'Afrique Occidentale Françoise). 16:493–629.

Kuevi, D. (1975) Le travail et le commerce du fer au Togo avant l'arrivée des Européens. *Etudes Togolaises*, 11–12 (n.s.):22–43.

Lawson, T. D. (1972) 'Géologie et perspectives economiques de la formation ferrifère de la cuvette du Buem au Togo.' Bureau National de Recherches Minières, Lome (Togo). Projet du Fond Spécial de l'ONU (L'Organisation des Nations Unies): Mines et Eaux. Mimeographed.

Levtzion, N. (1968) *Muslims and Chiefs in West Africa*. Oxford: Clarendon Press.

Martinelli, B. (1982) *Métallurgistes Bassar: techniques et formation sociale*. Etude et Documents de Sciences Humaines 5. INSE, Université du Bénin, Lome, Togo.

Norris, E. G. (1984) The Hausa kola trade through Togo, 1899–1912: some quantifications. *Paideuma*, 30:161–84.

Pawlik, J. (1988) 'La mort, expérience d'un peuple: étude des rites funéraires des Bassar du nord-Togo.' Doctoral thesis, University of Paris V, Paris. Mimeographed.

Phillipson, D. W. (1993) *African Archaeology*, 2nd edn. Cambridge: Cambridge University Press.

Posnansky, M. and de Barros, P. (1980) 'Archaeological reconnaissance of Togo, August 1979'. Submitted to the Ministry of Education and Scientific Research of the Republic of Togo. Mimeograph on file, Behavioral Sciences Department, Palomar College, San Marcos, California.

Schmidt, P. and Childs, S. T. (1985) Innovation and industry during the Early Iron Age in East Africa: the KM2 and KM3 Sites of northwest Tanzania. *African Archaeological Review*, 3:53–94.

Simpara, N. (1978) Etude géologique et structurelle des unités externes de la Chaîne Panafricaine (600 M.A.) des Dahomeyides dans la région de Bassar (Togo). *Travaux des Laboratoires des Sciences de la Terre*, series B, No. 13. St. Jérôme- Marseille.

Sprigade, P. (1905–1908) 'Karte von Togo, 1:200,000', Bismarckburg, Jendi, Bassari, Kete-Kratchi, Sokode and Sansanne-Mango sheets. *Mitteilungen aus den deutschen Schutzgebieten*, 19–21. Berlin: D. Reimer.

Stahl, A. B. (1985) Reinvestigation of Kintampo 6 rock shelter, Ghana: implications for the nature of culture change. *African Archaeological Review*, 3:117–50.

Stahl, A. B. (1994) Innovation, diffusion, and culture contact: the Holocene archaeology of Ghana. *Journal of World Prehistory*, 8(1):51–112.

Strathern, A. (1969) Finance and production: two strategies in New Guinea Highlands exchange systems. *Oceania*, 40:42–67.

Strathern, A. (1971) *The Rope of Moka*. Cambridge: Cambridge University Press.

Sundstrom, L. (1974) *The Exchange Economy of Pre-colonial Tropical Africa*. Introduction by A.G. Hopkins. London: C. Hurst.

Tait, D. (1961) *The Konkomba of Northern Ghana*. London: Oxford University Press, for the Institute of African Studies, University of Ghana at Legon.

Tamakloe, E. F. (1931) Which deals with matters of history. In *Tales Told in Togoland*, edited by A. W. Cardinali. London: Oxford University Press, pp. 230–79. (Originally published as 'A Brief History of the Dagbamba People', Accra.)

Togo National Archives (1911) FA1/217, General Report for the Sokode District, 1910/1911.

Van Grunderbeek, M.-C., Roche, E. and Doutrelepont, H. (1982) L'age du fer ancien au Ruanda et au Burundi: archéologie et environnement. *Journal de la Société des Africanistes*, 52:5–58.

Van Noten, F. (1979) The Early Iron Age in the interlacustrine region: the diffusion of iron technology. *Azania*, 14:61–80.

Vansina, J. (1960) Recording the oral history of the Bakuba, II, Results. *Journal of African History*, 1(2):266–7.

Vincent, J. F. (1991) *Princes montagnards du nord-Cameroun: les Mofu-Diamaré et le pouvoir politique*. Paris: L'Harmattan.

von Doering, H. G. (1895) Reiseberichte von Premierlieutenant v. Doering aus den Jahren 1893 bis 1895. *Mitteilungen aus den deutschen Schutzgebieten*, 8:231–75, Map 5.

von Zech, G., (1898) Vermischte Notizen über

Togo und das Togo Hinterlande. *Mitteilungen aus den deutschen Schutzgebieten*, 11:89–161.

Wilks, I. (1971) Asante policy towards the Hausa trade in the nineteenth century. In *The Development of Indigenous Trade and Markets in West Africa*, edited by C. Meillassoux. London: Oxford University Press, for the International African Institute, pp. 124–44.

Wilks, I. (1975) *Asante in the Nineteenth Century*. Cambridge: Cambridge University Press.

Wilks, I. (1993) *Forests of Gold*. Athens: Ohio University Press.

5 Change and Continuity in Coastal Bénin

KENNETH G. KELLY

Beginning in the seventeenth century, the coast of what is now the Republic of Bénin became one of the primary sources of enslaved Africans obtained for the Americas. Although Europeans were aware of the region prior to the advent of the Atlantic slave trade, there was little reason to establish contact as the region did not offer the significant amounts of gold and ivory then in demand. By the early eighteenth century merchants from England, France, Holland, and Portugal had established trade factories at Savi, capital of the coastal Hueda kingdom, and were doing a brisk business importing goods in exchange for slaves and other commodities. Using archaeological and historical data from the sites of Ouidah and Savi, this paper investigates the processes of cultural transformation that occurred from the early seventeenth century through the late nineteenth century, and the role European trade played in that transformation. Artifacts and activities identified archaeologically attest to the dynamic interaction of cultural traditions, by which no participating culture remained unaffected.

Introduction

Information gleaned from ethnographies, primary historic accounts, secondary histories and, most importantly, from archaeological research provides a more complete and coherent understanding of transformation and continuity in the material culture from the area of the historic 'Slave Coast' of southern Bénin and Togo. This discussion focuses primarily on archaeological and historical investigations conducted in the region of the town of Ouidah (Whydah) and its predecessor town of Savi, the capital of the Hueda kingdom from *c.* 1670 until its destruction in 1727, and summarizes research undertaken by others in the region (Figure 5.1).

The Slave Coast has a rich and important history, acquiring its notorious name in the sixteenth and seventeenth centuries as European traders began referring to reaches of the West African coast in terms of trading commodities. The Slave Coast is notable in West Africa, both for the extensive trade in humans and for the unique relationships that developed between European traders and African states. In contrast with other coastal trading nations, which generally maintained exclusive relations with traders from a single European nation (usually housed in a fort commanding the coastal trade center), the principal Hueda town and trading center lay over 10 km (6 miles) inland, beyond the support of European ships. Furthermore, the Hueda king expressly prohibited European traders from fortifying their accommodations, which

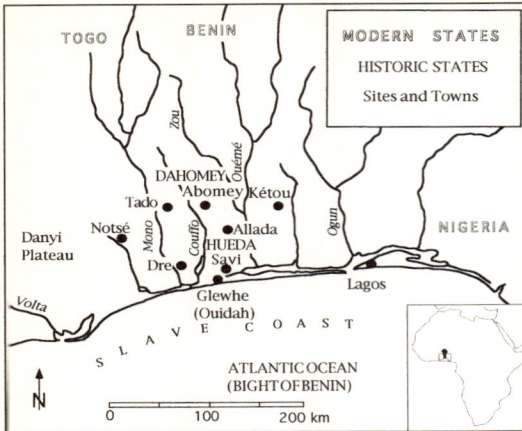

Figure 5.1 Map of the Bight of Benin indicating the sites and towns discussed in text, historic states mentioned in text, and the location of modern nations.

remained instead under the control of Hueda leaders.

The region is important for exploring political and institutional developments of the various states involved in European trade. The relationship between Allada, Hueda, and Dahomey and trading is particularly interesting. The Hueda achieved their independence from Allada by controlling European trade. Dahomey, in contrast, ultimately acquired its prominence by conquering Allada and Hueda, yet remained under the domination of Oyo cavalry to the north. The role of European trade within Hueda society and its significance in the region as a whole is of primary importance. Savi and the Slave Coast, as a primary point of departure for large numbers of enslaved Africans transported across the Atlantic to New World plantations, farms, households, and industries, has particular relevance to the history and development of African societies in the Americas. Despite this significant role played by the people of southern Bénin and Togo in the history of both the Old and New Worlds, the area has not hitherto been the subject of intensive archaeological study.

Physical setting

The Slave Coast's distinctive physical environment largely influences the history of human occupation of the area. Geography, geology, and vegetation combine to create a set of circumstances unique to the 300-km-wide (190-mile-wide) 'Dahomey Gap,' a comparatively flat and low-lying region characterized by the penetration of savanna vegetation through the rain forest to the coast. There are considerable isolated stands of trees (including possibly relict stands of species more frequently associated with the forest belt), yet these tall forest trees are almost exclusively preserved within the bounds of sacred forests associated with the spirit world, and they provide indication of human habitation from a considerable distance. Land clearance for agriculture is typically facilitated by burning at the end of the long dry season, which keeps the savanna grassy and prevents colonization by a variety of tree and shrub species (Christopher Lomer, pers. comm. 1993). The savanna habitat was easier to travel through, so trade and other relations tended to focus on the north rather than on the forest regions to the west and east. This topography also made some inhabitants of the gap, such as Dahomey, susceptible to raiding by horse-mounted troops from the state of Oyo to the north.

The Bight of Benin is characterized by a generally east–west coastline, without harbors or protected anchorages. The spread of savanna to the coast affects the sea off the coast of Bénin by creating regionally specific conditions that limit the wealth and variety of food resources available from the sea. Since the resources of the sea were not rich and sea travel was dangerous, the indigenous inhabitants of the region did not develop a maritime focus, tending instead to concentrate on the fresh and brackish water lagoon system that runs parallel to the shore from the mouth of the Volta River in the west, eastward to the mouth of the Niger, as a system of communication, transport, and as a source of food (Law 1989c).

Sources of information

European–African interactions during the fifteenth through nineteenth centuries are revealed through a variety of sources. These include letters, trading company reports, and travelers' accounts left by Europeans who were conducting business on the coast related to the slave trade during the period (Atkins 1737; Bosman 1705; Hair *et al.* 1992; Houstoun 1725; Labat 1731; Law 1989a, 1991a; Norris 1968; Smith 1744; Snelgrave 1734; Van Dantzig 1978; and others); ethnographies collected during the early portion of the twentieth century (Herskovits 1938; Le Hérissé 1911; Quénum [1936] 1983); oral traditions recorded during the twentieth century (de Medeiros 1984); historical analyses (Akinjogbin 1967; Argyle 1966; Djitrinou 1985; Kadja 1985; Karl-Augustt 1985; Law 1989b, 1991b; Manning 1982; Polanyi 1966); and archaeological and ethno-archaeological researches (Adandé 1984; Adandé and Kuevi 1990; Adandé and Metinhoué [n.d.]; Adedze 1990; Aguigah 1986, 1992a; Brunache 2001; Kelly 1994, 1995, 1997a, 1997b, Kelly *et al.* 1999, 2002; Norman 2000; Petrequin and Petrequin 1984).

Of all these potential sources of information about the cultures of the seventeenth- and eighteenth-century Slave Coast, only two— letters and travelers' accounts, and archaeological research—derive their data directly from the time period in question. Ethnographies and oral traditions, even those collected during the earliest days of colonialism in the late nineteenth and early twentieth centuries, still postdate the early slave trade by up to 200 years. These are a very significant 200 years, encompassing tremendous political and social changes in southern Bénin and Togo, with entire ethnic and language groups being either displaced or incorporated into other conquering groups. It is a reasonable supposition that political and social upheavals of this degree may also have had substantial transformative effects upon the material culture of the societies on the Slave Coast.

Historic documents: traders, captains, merchants, and administrators

The area of coastal Bénin was not visited by European traders and travelers as early or consistently as the neighboring Gold Coast and consequently suffers a lack of fifteenth-century through early-seventeenth-century eyewitness accounts. However, visitors' accounts from the late seventeenth and early eighteenth centuries are more numerous. This category of information is quite rich, as the Slave Coast was a destination frequented by Europeans of many nations who were engaged in the coastal trade.

These individuals often were relatively experienced observers, reporting back to their European directors about many matters that were of great importance to optimizing trade. Frequently they were participants in meetings with African political and economic leaders (e.g. Snelgrave in 1727 (1734); Van Dantzig 1978), and were able to move among Africans and visit towns and villages involved in trading. As traders, they often had contact with a variety of African cultures, acquired during stops at numerous ports of call along the coast. In these accounts, the level of detail recorded about many aspects of African life is striking (Kelly 1997b). However, the authors frequently neglected to record the kind of information that would be of greatest interest to archaeologists and anthropologists: information about settlement size, structure, and pattern, house construction, household organization, as well as material culture, to mention a few categories, was usually overlooked, or was mentioned only in relation to the high-status individuals with whom the traders were interacting.

Modern historians of the region have been able to extract a great deal of information regarding political events from these documents (see Law 1991b for an excellent example), but their potential for informing the more mundane aspects of life has limitations. There are, of course, exceptions to this rule; Captain William Snelgrave (1734) and others (e.g. Dalzel 1793; see Law 1991b) remarked on the populous countryside to be seen prior to the Dahomean conquest, and several authors occasionally remarked on the presence or absence of towns in the region. Despite any limitations they may have for directly answering questions of current interest, they remain a valuable source of information on a wide variety of subjects relating to commerce and culture along the Slave Coast. These sources must also be read critically, as the authors frequently wrote to present their opinions to specific audiences.

Ethnographic information

A number of ethnographies of southern Bénin and Togo exist, and several have been acclaimed as classics of the genre. An understanding of the Fon people (the founders of Dahomey) was an important goal for the

French colonial administrators, in their efforts to adapt the Fon to an administrative role in the new French colony. The works by the two Le Hérissés (R. Le Hérissé 1903; A. Le Hérissé 1911), published within two decades of the French victory over Dahomey and the exile of King Béhanzin to Martinique, are more clearly related to the goal of consolidating control over a recently vanquished population. Of the later works by Quénum (1983) and Herskovits (1938), the two-volume work written by Melville Herskovits is generally regarded as the most comprehensive account of Fon life. However, Blier (1989) reviewed the original 1931 field notes, and questioned to what degree the information Herskovits received was biased by having its source among the Dahomey élite, particularly from their translator, Prince René Aho. Additionally, Herskovits made little effort to identify aspects of Fon culture that were changing or differed from those in the past. In this regard, his view of timeless and unchanging African society differed little from British social anthropology of the colonial period (Ekeh 1990).

Recent histories

More recently, in the post-World War II period, and especially into the 1960s and 1970s, there has been an ever-increasing preoccupation with the societies of southern Bénin and Togo and their history and economy. Karl Polanyi (1966) viewed Dahomey as an ideal example of an archaic economy: one that was based on administrative redistribution and trade relations governed by the élite, yet without conflict with private marketing. Akinjogbin (1967) had as his thesis the view that Dahomey conquered the 'Slave Coast' in an effort to suppress the slave trade. Subsequent authors (especially Law 1977, 1986; Henige and Johnson 1976; Ross 1983) have disagreed, and have argued persuasively that Dahomey was in fact a predator state, and the conquest of the coast was merely one in a chain of predatory actions to secure access to firearms and other trade goods in order to further Dahomean political aspirations.

The cultural setting of the Slave Coast from 1500 to 1670

When Europeans first set eyes on the stretch of West African coast that would become known as the Slave Coast, they found a region that was inhabited by village agriculturists, organized into regional polities. The societies of the coastal area were characterized by numerous ethnic groups, each apparently localized, and speaking a number of closely related languages of the Aja-Ewe group. The Aja-Ewe were apparently rather recent arrivals in the area; most current groups trace their origins to the town of Tado in Togo and, before that, to western Nigeria. The earlier inhabitants who were present on the Slave Coast when the Aja-Ewe arrived are little known. The Houla or Pla were resident on the coast when European traders arrived, although there is considerable evidence indicating that they were themselves relatively recent arrivals (see Law 1989c). It is possible, but unlikely, that the Houla were the first to occupy the coastal zone, and that it had remained completely uninhabited until shortly before the arrival of Europeans.

A primary theme unifying historical, linguistic, and archaeological research in the Slave Coast region has been to trace the origin and movements of ethnic and linguistic groups present in the area. Prehistoric archaeological research in the region is virtually non-existent, with only limited finds associated with the Mono River Project (Adandé and Kuevi 1990). One of the greatest gaps in building culture history of the Bight of Benin is the absence of excavated stratified sites. As a result, regional ceramic sequences, tool technologies, and subsistence shifts are undocumented, and the timing of significant cultural evolutionary events, such as the origin of the first ceramics or the earliest reliance on agriculture or domesticated animals, is unknown. Indeed, the prehistory of the Dahomey Gap and its role in domestication and settled village life is one of the great unanswered questions of West African cultural evolution. In light of these lacunae, a reconstruction of the cultures of the Slave Coast at the time of European contact relies heavily on linguistic data and oral traditions to reconstruct the origins of the populations. It is certain that the indigenous inhabitants were agriculturists, probably raising crops of yams, millet, sorghum, and oil palm as dietary staples. The use of wild foods is highly probable, given the opportunistic provisioning strategy used by residents in the area today. Aquatic resources, including fish, wild fowl, and perhaps hippopotamus from the rivers and lakes, may have served a role in the pre-contact and early contact era diet.

Recently, there has been an expansion of historical research geared toward understanding the population movements in the pre-contact era, and reconstructing the dispersion of people throughout the region (de Medeiros 1984). These studies have taken linguistic evidence and oral traditions, coupled with shared ritual behavior, to attempt the recreation of the migration patterns of the Fon, Hueda, Ewe, and other language and ethnic groups. The consensus is that by about AD 1500, the coastal area was already settled with most of the groups encountered by early European traders, and that the origin of these Aja-Ewe groups should be traced to Tado and Notsé in Togo, and ultimately to Nigeria (Kadja 1985). The consensus regarding the Hueda is not so well formed, with a second opinion tracing an origin to Nigeria, based upon ritual behavior involving the python, and shared with the Bini (Karl-Augustt 1985). Nonetheless, there is a sizable body of evidence which suggests that the majority, if not all, of the coastal inhabitants present in historic times from the Volta River east to Lake Nokué and Cotonou, share a common ancestry and a divergence measured in, at most, hundreds of years (Kadja 1985; Karl-Augustt 1985; de Medeiros 1984). This relatively short period of separation, and a shared exploitation of a common environment, may result in a greater degree of cultural homogeneity than might otherwise be expected.

Little is known about the people, cultures, and settlement of the early historic period of the Slave Coast. Several factors influence this: the lack of wealthy urban centers such as Benin City (which lies deep in the Nigerian forest) or Loango in the Kongo Kingdom; no large states to pique the interest of traders; the lack of gold, which was the primary trade item of European interest until the mid-seventeenth century; and the complete absence of any suitable anchorages or large settlements visible from the sea. The economic focus of indigenous inhabitants toward the lagoon system, rather than toward the sea, limited opportunities for contact between European and African. This natural and cultural barrier to sustained contact may have insulated local populations from the transformations of the earliest European trade, but it also leaves us without any such detailed descriptions of African life in the area as have been left for other regions of the West African coast (for example Muller 1983; Ryder 1969; and De Marees 1987).

The prehistory of the Bight of Benin is poorly understood. However, the recently inaugurated joint Togolais/Béninois salvage project, *Archéologie de Sauvetage dans la Vallée du Mono*, will contribute the first comprehensive regional river valley survey in the Bight of Bénin (Adandé and Kuevi 1990). Archaeological research has proceeded in southern Togo following Posnansky and de Barros' (1980) inventory of archaeological sites and inaugural archaeological research at Notsé in 1981 (Posnansky 1981). It includes research by Aguigah (1986, 1989, 1992a, 1992b) and Quarcoopome (1993) at the towns of Notsé and Tado, which are considered to be ancestral towns for most Bight of Bénin groups, and Kuevi's (1989) research concerning agricultural settlements and features on the Danyi plateau adjacent to the Ghana–Togo border. Aguigah (1986, 1989, 1992a) has continued to work at Notsé, building on research conducted by Posnansky (1981, 1985), which traced the course of an earthen wall surrounding the town and estimated its initial height and breadth with a series of four sections. Initial archaeological interpretations of the wall suggest that it was not built for defensive purposes, but instead was built to symbolize or delimit territory under the authority of Notsé (Posnansky 1985). A similar interpretation has been put forth for the ditch system identified at Savi (Kelly 1997a).

Alternative interpretations, such as that presented by Quarcoopome (1993) based on oral traditions from Notsé, suggest that the wall was built to protect the town during the seventeenth century. Indeed, the labor mobilization by King Agokoli I to build the wall is remembered as the source of discontent that precipitated the dispersion of the Ewe people from Notsé. A potsherd found beneath the wall has been dated to the early sixteenth century, indicating that the wall was built post-fifteenth century, and not earlier as was once believed. Potsherd pavements have also been recorded in several locations at Notsé (Aguigah 1992a), and this trait, coupled with the town wall building tradition, has suggested ties to the east—to Oyo, Ife, and Benin City. This archaeological evidence may confirm the hypothesized origin and dispersal of the Aja-Ewe from a homeland in modern Nigeria (Quarcoopome 1993; Karl-Augustt 1985).

Complementing Aguigah's work is the project led by Alexis Adandé (1984), which was focused in and around Togudo-Awute, the site of the seat of the Allada kingdom (established at the beginning of the fifteenth century and destroyed by Dahomey in 1724), located a few kilometers from modern Allada (Adandé 1986–87, 1989). Adandé's research was concerned with identifying the origins of the Allada kingdom, its rise as pre-eminent power in the Bight of Benin, and with identifying its role in post-contact political developments and trade with Europeans.

The ramifications of post-contact population movements have also been investigated by the ethno-archaeological study of the lives of the lake dwellers of Lake Nokué conducted by Petrequin and Petrequin (1984). These lake villages are generally believed to have been founded in response to on-going warfare and raiding engendered by the Atlantic slave trade. Although their discussion provides a great deal of detail about the material aspects of life on the lake, it does not really address the issues that led to the establishment of the lake villages.

With the exception of the Atlantic slave trade, the economy of the Slave Coast region in the pre- and post-contact era is not fully understood. At present, most information concerning economic activities in the region comes from historic documents. Seventeenth- and eighteenth-century traders' accounts describe the manufacture and trade of salt, and the ethno-archaeological work of Rivallain (1977) has investigated present-day production of this commodity. The salt trade extended in excess of several hundred kilometers to the interior, reaching inland to the north of Allada, and including Oyo and Olukumi (Law 1989c: 220–1). This source was vital to the coast, forests, and savanna of southern Bénin and Togo, which lay at the far end of the Saharan salt trading routes (Rivallain 1977). It remains unclear whether the salt trade was well established prior to the development of coast-oriented trade, or whether it grew through its association with the slave trade (Law 1989a).

The rich fisheries of the lagoons were another source of economic opportunity, and fish were traded both along the coast and inland at least as far north as Abomey. Other economic activities of the Slave Coast included cloth manufacture of such quality and scale that 'Ardrah cloths' from Allada were in great demand for the early gold trade to the west (Law 1989c). Lastly, a cursory look at any site in the region occupied for even a short time demonstrates the importance of pottery in the local economies. Although the lack of excavated deeply stratified sites in the region has hampered the development of any regional ceramic chronology, ceramic production, distribution, and use have been the focus of considerable ethno-archaeological research in the Bight of Benin (Adandé and Kuevi 1990; Adandé and Metinhoué [n.d.]; Adedze 1990; Norman 2000; Rivallain 1981).

The historic setting of Savi

Savi, the capital and main town of the Hueda kingdom, enters the historic record nearly a century after the first trade contacts were established by Europeans on the Slave Coast. The first encounters by Portuguese traders in the area occurred possibly as early as 1472–73, and certainly by 1553. Slaves bearing ethnonyms indicating origin from the Allada region were in South America by the 1560s, and a Portuguese map dating to 1570 shows the coast of the Allada kingdom. By 1600 Allada had become the most important Slave Coast destination, and Dutch merchants began trading to supply the Brazilian demand for slaves. This trade grew, leading to the establishment of a permanent lodge staffed by several Europeans in 1660. Around this time, the Dutch were joined by Danes, Swedes, English, and French. The first English trade began in 1653, with a lodge following by about 1665. The French began their Allada trade in 1670. However, throughout this period (1620–70), the historic documents make no mention whatsoever of the Hueda area or the towns of Savi or Glewhe (modern Ouidah). (Unless noted otherwise, Law 1991b is the source for this historical overview.)

The first mention of permanent trading establishments in the Hueda kingdom refer to a French lodge at Glewhe inaugurated in 1671, in response to rebellion along the coastal area of Allada (Law 1991b: 127). The Hueda took advantage of this instability, and began cultivating ties with European trading partners, leading to Hueda independence from Allada (Law 1991b: 234). The English Royal African Company factory was established at Savi in 1681, with a warehouse built at Glewhe a few years later. The Dutch located their lodge at Savi in about 1692. In the mid-1690s both the French and Dutch presence in the Hueda kingdom lapsed temporarily, reviving again in 1697–98. By about 1700 the English, Dutch, and French were settled at lodges within the palace precinct at Savi, although the English and French also maintained fortified storehouses in Glewhe. The Portuguese presence at Savi was short lived in the seventeenth century, but grew in the early eighteenth century as Brazilian gold and tobacco became items in high demand at Savi. As the trade grew through the end of the seventeenth century and into the first decades of the eighteenth century, Savi and the Hueda kingdom became increasingly powerful and wealthy.

This prosperity proved to be a two-edged sword. In the early eighteenth century, the Fon kingdom of Dahomey began to expand from its center at Abomey; although the Fon people had been mentioned in documentary sources referring back as far as 1660, Dahomey is first mentioned by name only in 1716. Less than ten years later, in 1724, Dahomey had conquered Allada, and was becoming increasingly powerful as it controlled a greater part of the slave trade. However, possessing Allada was not fully satisfactory, and in 1727, Dahomey attacked and conquered the Hueda after a very short campaign, obtaining unfettered access to the sea. The palace at Savi, as well as the rest of the town, was sacked and burned on the day of the attack. Although a large number of Hueda escaped to the west with the Hueda King Huffon, casualties in excess of 5,000 dead were reported from the battle and subsequent terror.

Distracted by on-going cavalry campaigns by Oyo against their capital, Abomey, Dahomey was unable to defeat Huffon until 1734.

The continued threat of Hueda resurgence compelled the Dahomean army to prohibit any resettlement of Savi, and instead, the village of Glewhe, adjacent to the European forts, grew as the port of trade, becoming the second most important town in Dahomey after the capital at Abomey. As Savi faded from memory, and Glewhe's importance grew, it became known by the name of Ouidah—the name it holds today (Sinou 1995).

Current research

The remainder of this chapter will concentrate on archaeological materials recovered during the course of excavations at Savi and Ouidah conducted from 1991 through 1999 (Kelly 1994, 1995, 1997a, 1997b, 1998, 2001; Kelly *et al.* 1999). The Hueda Archaeological Project has been the only long-term and large-scale project underway in southern Bénin. Research at Savi and Ouidah was initiated as a cooperative project between UCLA and the Université Nationale du Bénin and is directed by the author. The goals of the project are several, including the identification and documentation of the site of the destroyed town of Savi, capital of the Hueda kingdom; mapping features to reconstruct the settlement pattern; and excavating a series of locations within the center of the abandoned site. These excavations were focused on recovering African and imported material culture from intact late-seventeenth- and early-eighteenth-century contexts, in an effort to characterize the life of the inhabitants of Savi. The recovered material allows the identification of the corpus of indigenous African culture, and the degree to which it had been modified or transformed by the introduction of foreign elements at that early period of the Atlantic trade. In spite of the difficulty inherent in recovering perishable materials from humid tropical conditions, both organic materials and the indications of structures have been identified from Savi. These artifacts and features complement the numerous more durable artifacts recovered from the site.

Excavations at Ouidah have been much more limited, owing to the greater difficulty of conducting excavations in a densely populated large town (*c.* 40,000 inhabitants). However, small-scale excavations conducted at several

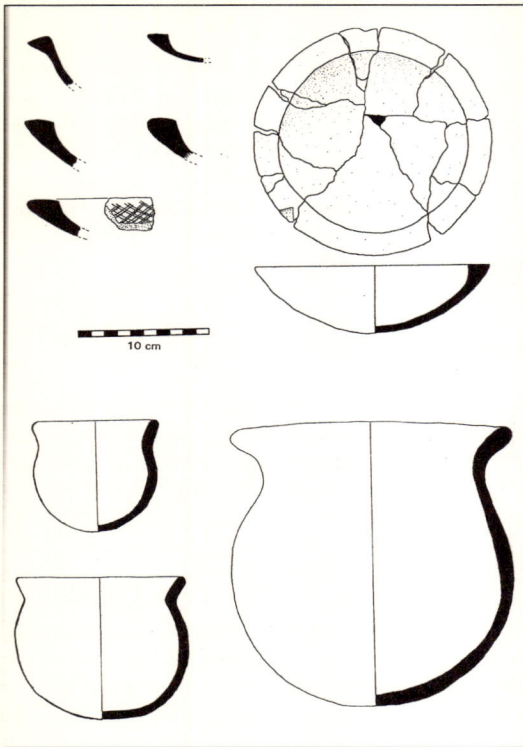

Figure 5.2 Complete locally manufactured cooking pots, bowl rims, and a complete bowl excavated at Savi. The bowl with the incised lines on the interior was probably used for grinding or processing soft foods.

locations in the town have provided a complementary collection of artifacts carrying the sequence from the destruction of Savi up through the late nineteenth century and early twentieth century, during which time Ouidah became the primary commercial center of the Dahomean state.

Material culture of Savi and Ouidah

Any characterization of continuity or transformation in the archaeological culture of southern Bénin will necessarily focus on the most durable of artifacts, and often on those that are most diagnostic. Changes in locally produced artifacts present an ideal framework to study the impact of new influences and trade. However, the lack of change does not necessarily represent continuity. The mere presence of imported materials need not imply profound cultural transformation: it is the use to which imported materials are put that is important for evaluating the impact of trade on a culture. Research at Savi and Ouidah has demonstrated that the centuries following European contact were characterized by both transformation *and* continuity in Hueda and Fon culture. Documentary and archaeological evidence suggests that the pattern of town settlement underwent at least two, and perhaps three significant stages of expansion and nucleation in the post-European contact period. The range and change in artifacts recovered at Savi and Ouidah indicate that innovation, adaptation, reinterpretation, and conservatism are all characteristics of the material culture of the Bight of Benin. Other aspects of Hueda and Fon life, including subsistence and architecture, demonstrate both continuity and change in the case of diet and remarkable conservatism in architecture.

Local ceramics

Excavations at Savi have yielded large numbers of ceramics; not only are they the most numerous artifact class, they are also the most common locally produced artifact. Despite their highly fragmentary state, preliminary analysis of the sherds has shown that a much wider range of ceramic forms was present during the heyday of ancient Savi than are currently used in the area. They include a wide range of size-differentiated cooking pots, occurring in both decorated and undecorated forms. The cooking pots are characterized by a moderate degree of incurving before the rim everts to a rounded lip (Figures 5.2 and 5.3). There are at least two broad varieties of bowl: one with a smooth interior, which was probably used for serving or condiment vessels; and an alternative interior treatment with a grid of intersecting lines deeply incised into the interior surface (Figure 5.2). Although these bowls are not present in the modern ceramic assemblage of the Savi region, it is clear that they were used to grind foods with a wooden pestle, as are similar examples still widely used in Ghana. They were probably used for grinding soft foods, such as pepper, tomato, and onion, usually ground today on a cement slab made especially for that purpose. The other, less common, bowl form is

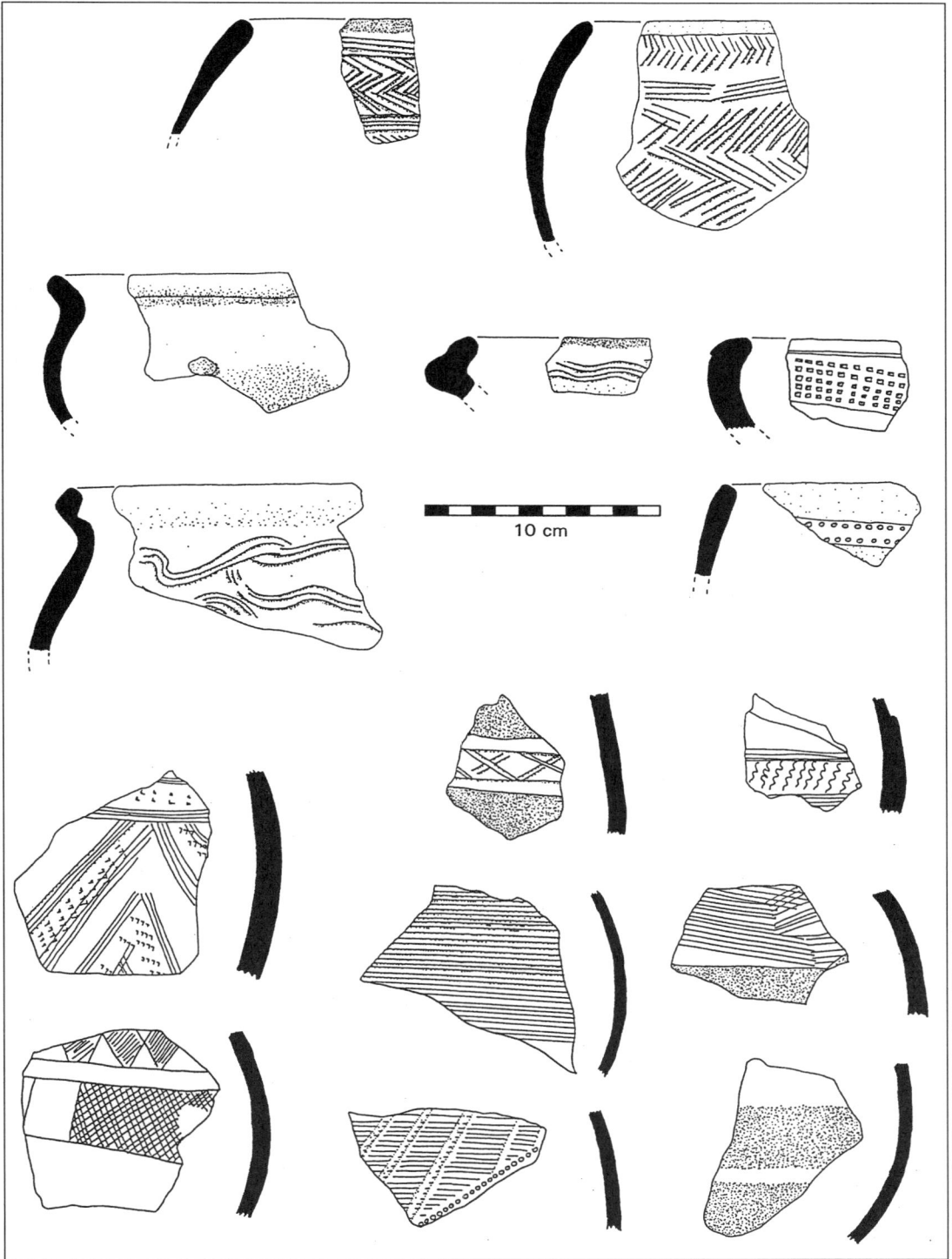

Figure 5.3 Decorated locally produced earthenware rims excavated at Savi. Stippling on sherds indicates the presence of red paint.

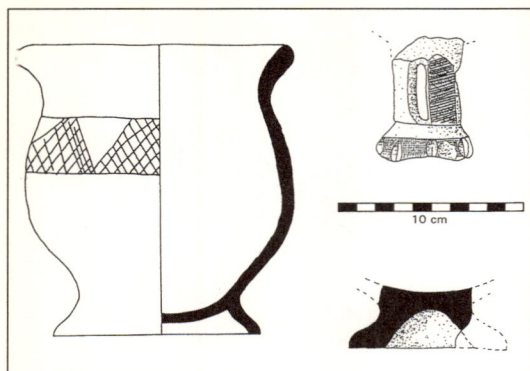

Figure 5.4 Complete urn-shaped vessel, an elaborate earthenware pedestal, and an earthenware foot, all excavated at Savi.

broadly hemispherical, with a thin, rounded, and slightly incurved rim.

In addition to serving and cooking forms, there are pierced 'colanders,' which may have also had a use as 'fetish' or ritual pots (Brunache 2001; Norman 2000), and several varieties of storage vessels. The storage wares, probably used both for liquids and solids, are present in two broadly differentiated varieties. One type exhibits a moderately constricted neck, opening to a flaring everted rim. These large jars may have served as storage or transport jars for water or grains. Another large-diameter vessel has a thickly buttressed incurved rim, and probably served as a water jar set partly into the ground, a use to which this form is put today. The other storage type is characterized by a thick everted rim and a great degree of constriction, possibly used for storing grains. When these necks have been recovered intact at Savi, they exhibit a purposeful grinding and smoothing of broken edges for use in another capacity, perhaps that of pot stand.

The last main type of ceramic present consists of an urn-shaped vessel with an applied foot ring (Figure 5.4). This type is often decorated, and may have been painted as well. In addition to these forms, a single elaborately formed pedestal base was recovered at Savi, as was a less elaborate base (Figure 5.4). Unfortunately, only the pedestal was recovered, leaving the complete shape of the vessel to conjecture. There are no similar vessels used in the area today. Excavations at Ouidah have yielded a similar range of ceramic forms,

although without the unusual pedestal and applied bases. However, the coal pot or brazier, a form entirely absent at Savi, is present in Ouidah, with a few fragments recovered from late-nineteenth-century contexts. This may reflect an increase in the use of charcoal, suggesting a greater reliance on cooking fuel transported longer distances as local supplies were exhausted. Other modern forms, such as the joined 'twin pots' and other similar small vessels important in ritual life, have not been recovered archaeologically at Savi and Ouidah, and this may be due to the context of their use.

The most noticeable difference between the ceramics at Savi and Ouidah lies in decoration. Decorated ceramics are present at Savi, although they are not common in the assemblage (Figure 5.3). The vast majority, over 90 percent, are undecorated. Decorative techniques present at Savi include red and white paint, fine line incision, broad line incision, and very limited examples of carved stamp impressions and cord rouletting. Also present are wavy line stamps and punctations. These elements are frequently combined to create abstract geometric designs, while figurative or representative decoration is absent from all pottery recovered at Savi. At Ouidah, the use of paint virtually disappears, and stamped and comb impressions predominate. At present there is no explanation for this, although further excavation may show this to be the result of the displacement of Hueda potters by Fon potters and trade networks following the Dahomey conquest of Savi. Modern ceramics, when decorated, are usually embellished with limited carved stamp impressions on the upper portions of the vessels.

There are no examples of locally manufactured ceramics either at Savi or Ouidah that appear to be imitating or inspired by items introduced via European trade, as the 'forowa' bowls of Ghana are influenced by imported brass bowls (DeCorse 1989). Additionally, no examples of corn-cob rouletted pottery have been recorded from excavations at Savi or Ouidah. These two behaviors, imitation or adaptation of new forms, and the use of new materials in internally consistent fashions, are frequently seen as hallmarks of extensive contact. That they are not seen in the Hueda region strongly suggests a firmly rooted tradition of ceramic manufacture and use.

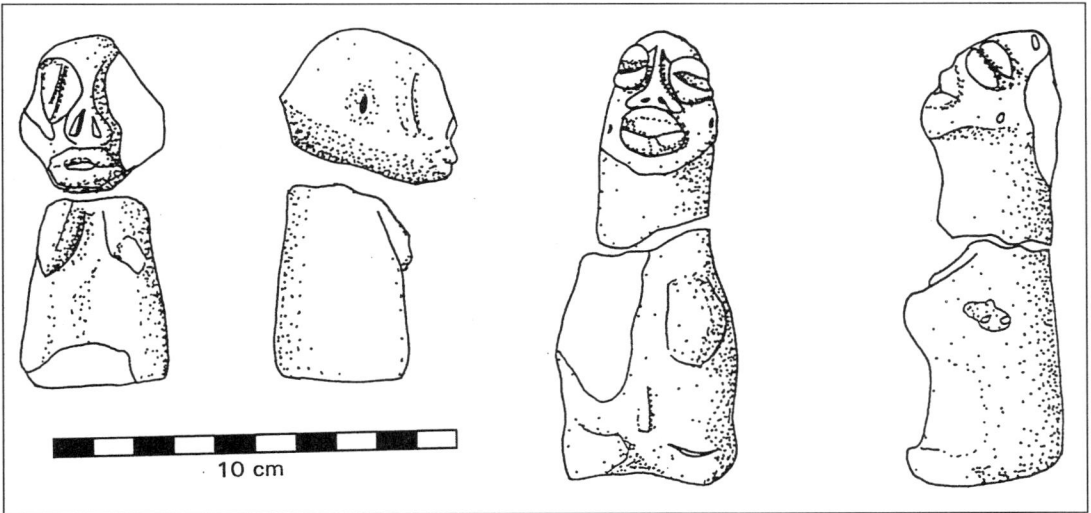

Figure 5.5   Terracotta or clay figurines excavated at Savi. The figure on the right may be hermaphrodite.

Imported European and Asian ceramics have been recovered from both sites. It is particularly notable that at Savi and Ouidah imported ceramics are comparatively rare—in stark contrast to other West African trade sites, such as Elmina, Ghana, where imported ceramics clearly outnumber locally produced wares. However, a more complete discussion of the imported ceramics is beyond the scope of this paper, and will be treated elsewhere.

Figurines

Several roughly shaped clay figurines were recovered from excavations at Savi (Figure 5.5). At least three figures are present, and there are also fired clay fragments that may represent one or more additional figurines. Although all three are broken, and some are missing parts, none appears to have ever measured more than 15 cm tall. The figurines apparently depict female figures, based upon the presence of breasts on the torsos, although one may be hermaphrodite. No similar figures have been reported from Bénin; however, several somewhat similar figures from Tado in Togo are depicted in Aguigah *et al.* (1990:16–17), and others have been identified in Ghana (Bellis 1982). The figures from Savi were all apparently broken prior to their deposition, as suggested by the refuse pit context from which they were recovered, and this may

be a result of the destruction of Savi in 1727. Local informants were quick to recognize the importance of the figures, although they had never seen any examples before, nor were they able to assign a function to them that was more specific than a general 'fetish' or ritual role.

Beads

Direct contact with European traders presented the opportunity to acquire glass beads in quantities previously unattainable. Beads were recovered from Savi in great numbers, and nearly all were of European trade origin. Beads of African origin were limited to several carnelian beads, one tube bead, and three disc beads, and two clay or terracotta beads (Figure 5.6). A workshop site, littered with the detritus of carnelian disc bead production, has been reported north of Timbuktu in Mali (Gaussen 1990). The presence of these stone beads provides an indication of Savi participation in long-distance African trade networks.

It is assumed that beads were used as decoration and as ornaments. However, all beads recovered from Savi and Ouidah were found in contexts of discard or accidental loss and little can be inferred about their uses, other than that glass beads were probably used in conjunction with, and as replacements for, locally available organic materials.

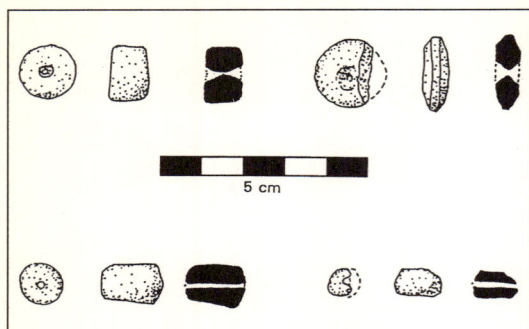

Figure 5.6 Stone and clay beads from Savi. The stone cylinder bead (upper left) and the stone disc bead (upper right) are manufactured from carnelian. The disc bead is similar to many reported from Mali. The clay beads (bottom left and right) are roughly manufactured.

Organics

Archaeological researchers in coastal West Africa are constantly reminded of the significant constraints the environment places on artifact and feature preservation. The high temperatures, coupled with high rainfall and acidic soils, promote rapid decomposition of organic materials, including bone and plant remains. The practice, current today (and also attested to by observers from the seventeenth century onward), of chopping bones into very small pieces and then cooking them for long periods of time, further compromises the preservation of faunal remains (Dalzel 1793:xxv). Today the small bones are also often cracked and chewed to extract the maximum nutritional value, leaving very little to be preserved in the archaeological record. Nevertheless, limited and fragmentary faunal remains were recovered at Savi. Identifiable mammalian species include cow, sheep, goat, and duiker or antelope (Kelly 1995). These remains do not indicate the presence of any identifiable species of European introduction, such as turkey or pig, although documentary sources indicate their presence at Savi by the beginning of the eighteenth century (Law 1991a). Faunal remains have yet to be recovered from Ouidah.

Carbonized plant food remains have also been recovered from Savi. This rare find of maize, beans, and millet grains demonstrates both that maize had been incorporated into the urban diet by the time of the town's destruction in 1727, and that millet remained a prominent food during the early historic period (Kelly 1995). However, in spite of the good fortune in recovering some food remains from the town site, these materials are very rarely preserved; none were found anywhere else at Savi. Further finds of carbonized organics would prove important in determining the timing of adoption of peppers and tomatoes—new world crops that are very important in the modern diet. Botanical remains may also help to clarify how the grinding bowls (discussed above) were used. Recovery of indigenous crops and cultigens could provide valuable information about the degree of dependence on less well documented foods, including sorghum and rice.

Architecture

Architectural remains along the coast of the Bight of Bénin are generally elusive. Structures of all sizes are built of earth, without the use of stone or wood in wall construction. Post molds, stone foundations, or foundation trenches containing artifacts are entirely absent. Despite the lack of foundations and pavements, locations of structures have been identified at Savi through the burned clay 'daub' that originally overlay the construction of ceilings. This daub was preserved at Savi by the fires that accompanied the destruction of the settlement. Soil was placed over a series of palm branches during ceiling construction, and the burning of the thatched roofs preserved the impressions of the palm wood, allowing its presence to be recognized today. This method of roof construction has been archaeologically identified in both élite and non-élite contexts at Savi, and is still employed in the modern village of Savi.

Structures associated with the palace complex of the Hueda leadership have also been identified at Savi. Élite structures are characterized by earthen walls, earthen floors, and thatched roofing, in much the same style as that used by non-élite residents. The primary feature differentiating palace structures from others is their imposing scale. In contrast to the one- and two-room structures believed to have been used by the bulk of the population, the palace structures are long, linear, multi-room buildings enclosing broad courtyard areas. Further setting several rooms of the palace complex apart from the rest of the town, floors of imported European brickwork have been excavated in at least seven presumed audience or public rooms (Kelly 1995, 1996, 1997a).

Potsherd pavements have been archaeologically identified at Notsé and Tado by Aguigah (1986, 1992a), but have yet to be recognized in other regions of coastal Togo and Bénin. The pavements identified by Aguigah, consisting of sherds set flat on the ground, contrast with the edgewise settings documented much earlier at Ife in Nigeria. Notsé and Ife pavements share similarities in other ways, however, including the integral setting of whole pots in the pavement design (Quarcoopome 1993:113–14). If potsherd pavements present at Notsé are associated with the early Ewe settlement and dispersal from Nigeria, then the potential exists that further finds of pavements will be made at other towns related to the dispersal from Notsé. However, even though brick flooring has been recovered at Savi, which may be in part influenced or inspired by potsherd pavings, no sherd pavements have yet been identified at Savi, and there are no pavements reported from Allada.

Stone artifacts

Stone resources at Savi are limited to two classes of artifact, milling stones and flaked stone artifacts. Reflecting difficult access to stone resources, all the milling stones and fragments recovered from Savi are extensively utilized. Even small pieces, less that 10 cm (4 inches) in their maximum direction, exhibit continued use after their breakage. Dalzel, in 1793, observed this conservation of stone resources, noting that 'cankey stones' came from an area 160 km (100 miles) distant (Dalzel 1793:iii). The source of the milling stones recovered from Savi is currently unknown; however the nearest sources of stone are at least 60 km (40 miles) distant.

Flaked stone artifacts from Savi are limited to chert or flint gunflints, and a few apparently reworked pieces of flint. The lack of cutting tools manufactured from lithics is strong evidence that iron had been in great enough supply to serve all the cutting needs of the Savi area from the very beginning of European trade. Bottle glass fragments found at Savi, originating in European trade, were carefully scrutinized for indications of modification or reuse as cutting tools, but no trace of flaking was present on any fragment. Overall, the lack of stone or glass cutting tools is a strong indicator of the degree to which the inhabitants of seventeenth- and eighteenth-century Savi relied on iron implements, and is indicative of a pre-European-trade iron supply sufficient to meet coastal needs.

Metals

Metals have been recovered from Savi, although in small numbers. Of the objects excavated, iron artifacts and fragments predominate. The iron suffers from environmental degradation, as do organics, with the result that the large majority of artifacts are corroded beyond recognition. Unfortunately it is impossible to determine visually whether the iron is of European or African origin or shaping, although the volume of iron imported by traders would suggest that raw European stock was extensively used by African smiths (Law 1991a). Research at Allada by Wantchecon (1983) recorded that there is no traditional memory of iron smelting in the region, and that European traders were the source of all iron used. Slag has been recovered archaeologically at Savi, but restricted to small amounts suggestive of smithing. No large-scale slag deposits of the size that are produced by iron smelting have ever been reported in the areas near Savi or Allada. The only iron-producing areas currently known in southern Togo and Bénin are the area surrounding Tado in Togo, and undated (although historic-era) slag heaps recently reported from the Abomey region by Iroko (1989). Tado, whence the Aja, ancestral to much of the region, have come, is attested to have been the iron-producing center of the region dating to even before the arrival of the Aja people (Pazzi 1977). Thus it appears that European iron supplemented, and perhaps replaced, an indigenous trade in raw iron produced north of the coastal region.

Several copper artifacts have been recovered from Savi (Figure 5.7). Of these, only a few can be assigned a definite African manufacture. These are several small bells manufactured by the 'lost wax' process of a style that is common on much of the West African coast. A copper alloy ring, formed from a bar of metal, triangular in cross section, was

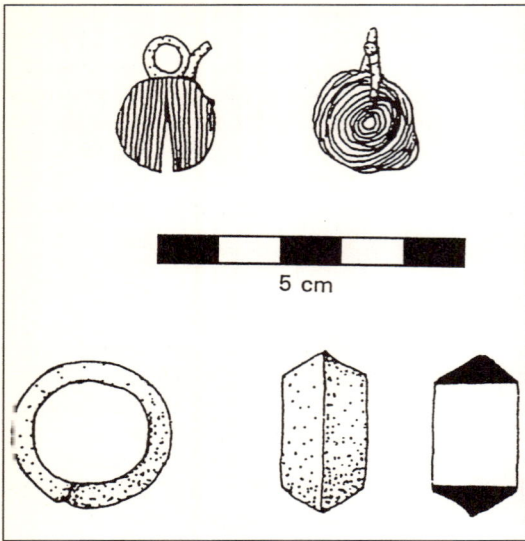

Figure 5.7 Copper bell and copper ring excavated at Savi.

recovered from a refuse pit context. This may be a finger ring, or it may have served another unknown purpose. It is not known whether the metal is of local, African, or European origin, although Dalzel (1793:xxv) referred to the presence of braziers and silversmiths in Dahomey, suggesting that the workmanship may be African. Other copper or copper alloy items are of European origin, and include no more than five buttons and button covers, pins, and several nest weights. The frequency of metal artifacts, when compared with ceramics, suggests that metal objects were comparatively rare in ancient Savi, and that the metal tools that certainly were present were used until there was little left to discard. Additionally, the environment may also play a strong role in limiting the preservation of discarded iron. Objects of copper alloy were probably considerably more limited in their presence among the residents of Savi, and also less likely to be discarded, as copper items were generally considered wealth objects in pre-colonial Africa (Herbert 1984).

Tobacco pipes

Following locally manufactured ceramics, the most common artifacts recovered at Savi were tobacco pipes. Both imported European white clay pipes and locally manufactured African

earthenware pipes were recovered in large numbers. The African pipes are of primary importance in the current work, demonstrating the rapid acceptance of tobacco smoking. Additionally, their form is unrelated to that of the pipes imported by Europeans, suggesting either indigenous antecedents for smoking, innovation upon the introduction of tobacco, or design influences originating from an as yet unidentified source (Philips 1983). The local pipe assemblage consists of more than 350 individual examples, many of which demonstrate a wide range of decorative treatments within a narrowly constrained range of sizes and shapes (Figure 5.8). Indeed, when comparing the pipes of Savi to those excavated in Ghana (Afeku 1976; Crossland 1989; Effah-Gyamfi 1985; Ozanne 1962, 1976; York 1973) or in the Sahel (Daget and Ligers 1962), one is struck by their extraordinary uniformity. The variation among the Savi pipes can virtually all be accounted for by variation in size, and a somewhat more elaborated variety of decorative treatments. The majority of the pipes are elaborately decorated with incised lines, molded and applied sprigs, and occasionally some rouletting, in addition to minimal red painting. Only a few examples showing little or no decoration were recovered. Virtually all of the Savi examples conform generally to Ozanne's (1976) type 2a, or flat, circular-based, short-stemmed pipes. The pipes have a circular base, which generally tapers inward and upward before the bowl sides begin to flare outward. In most cases the short pipe stems join the bowl above the base, creating what has been called a 'double-angled' pipe (Ozanne 1962).

The exception to the double-angled stem joints are found only on the largest of Savi pipes. In the large bowl cases, the bottom of the stem joins flush with the base, creating a single angle to the stem. In all cases the pipes are characterized by funnel- to cup-shaped flaring bowls that are angled slightly forward, or away from the smoker. The bowls are highly variable in size, very small pipe bowls having been found in the same stratigraphic deposits as pipes with large bowls. The co-occurrence of large and small pipe bowls indicates that the bowl volume cannot be used as a meaningful chronological indicator.

Ozanne's illustrated type 3a pipes from Accra and Shai exhibit decoration on the stem

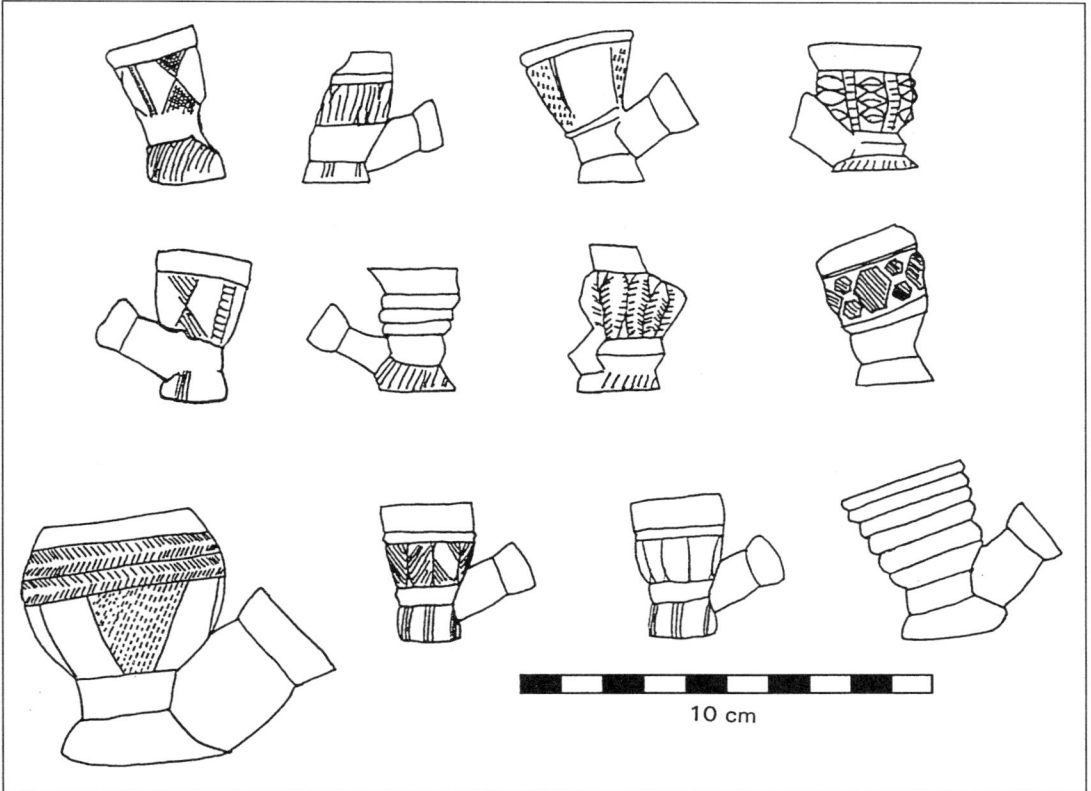

Figure 5.8 Sample of the variety of sizes and decorations present among locally manufactured tobacco pipes recovered at Savi. All pipes have round bases.

portion, as well as the bowl and base. This is in distinct contrast to the Savi pipe collection, where there is no example of a stem with any three-dimensional decoration; indeed, the only stem decoration identified on the Savi pipes is limited to red paint on the surface of the stem flange facing the smoker. Other decorative methods employed on the Savi pipes include the occasional use of red paint on the bowl rim, bowl exterior, and base. Many specimens from Savi had no traces of paint present, but this may represent post-depositional factors eroding or removing the paint, and not a lack of painting on the original surface. Impressed decorations include incisions, stamping, and rouletting. Relief decoration was also created through carving away some of the clay of the bowl, or by applying sprigs or pre-formed pieces to the bowl exterior. The decorations were all abstract, and typically involved repeated geometric design elements. In several

cases the bowl exteriors were burnished to achieve a glossy surface. The bases typically were decorated as well. The predominant motif was repeated diagonal incised lines encircling the base, although grouped clusters of incised diagonal lines were also present.

Eighteenth-century pipes excavated at Ouidah are not numerous, and generally conform to the Savi type. However, pipe fragments from nineteenth-century deposits in Ouidah exhibit a completely different form. In contrast to the earlier pipes, which do not resemble European forms despite their use alongside European pipes, the later pipes conform generally to the European shape of a bowl at approximately a right angle to a long thin stem. These bowls exhibit vertical grooves around the exterior, and are painted brown. The stems are clearly hand modeled. Pipes of this shape continue to be made, and are available in the local markets.

Settlement pattern

Excavation and survey data collected from Savi have demonstrated changes in the structure of the town settlement pattern, suggesting broad changes occurring in southern Bénin during the post-contact period. The survey and shovel testing program at Savi indicated that the historic town site was characterized by widespread, relatively dense occupation (Kelly 1995). Ceramic data recovered in the course of the testing regime provided continually high sherd densities for at least 2 km to the north, south, east, and west of the town center, indicative of town occupation covering an area considerably larger than that of the modern village of Savi (1 km, or about 1,000 yards, in maximum extent), or even the nearby town of Ouidah (population in excess of 40,000). The archaeological indicators of settlement extent, as well as contemporary observers' impressions, depict a town covering a considerably greater area than any modern towns of comparable population would today.

This lack of nucleation as identified at Savi, transitioning to much more nucleated settlements such as early Ouidah (Glewhe), can likely be attributed to the effects of political instabilities and warfare introduced in large part by the slave trade. As the frequency of predatory warfare and slave raiding by neighboring political groups increased, available protective measures included nucleation, flight to less accessible settings, and the construction of defensive walls or other mechanisms. All three of these options were exercised in southern Bénin and Togo, defensive walls having been identified at the Dahomean capital town of Abomey, the town of Kétou in eastern Bénin, Notsé, and at the village of Tinipé on the Danyi Plateau in Togo (Kelly 2001). The resettlement in safer and less accessible sites occurred in the coastal lakes of Bénin, where numerous lacustrine villages were founded by people fleeing slave raiding and warfare (Petrequin and Petrequin 1984). The effects of the predation of slave raiding continue to be visible in modern Bénin, where extensive areas of countryside north of Abomey, in the territory formerly between Dahomey and Oyo, continue to be underpopulated compared with the settlement density south of Abomey. Finally, nucleation was a strategy also practiced in the region, as visitors of the late eighteenth century and early nineteenth century remarked on the changes from a formerly broadly settled, park-like countryside to a landscape characterized by extensive unsettled regions between densely packed villages (Snelgrave 1734:19, 26; Dalzel 1793:5).

Conclusions

As this review demonstrates, the Bight of Bénin is an area of great archaeological potential. The region has witnessed the rise and fall of Allada, Hueda, and Dahomey—states of great importance in the social and political development of the area—and has been home to wide-ranging and significant population movements, both in the historic, post-contact period, and in the pre-contact era. Investigation of the role of the Dahomey gap, the belt of savanna woodland bisecting the coastal rain forest, in the development and collapse or decline of Dahomey, Oyo, and Notsé, among others, has yet to be initiated. There are many questions regarding pre-contact occupation, and most of these remain unanswered. The subsistence of the inhabitants, the degree to which agricultural resources or fish were relied upon along the coast, the role of trade in salt and cloth, the influence of Sahelian trade upon the coast, the timing of the introduction of iron- and brass-working, and the earliest domestication of plants and animals, are all questions of fundamental importance for improving our understanding of the evolution of human society in this part of coastal West Africa.

The post-contact period is equally important, as the limited research conducted thus far in the region has clearly indicated the wide range of variability in responses to trade and contact, with the pattern at Hueda expressing marked differences from that of the Gold Coast (DeCorse 1989, 1992, 1993, 1998). Coupled with the variation in trade responses, the changing nature of trade to the north and the political and social repercussions of the rise of coastal states played an important role in the transformations of coastal West African societies. The introduction of new food crops and the terrible depopulation of some areas resulting from the slave trade are two factors that manifested themselves in diametrically opposed ways. As new food resources were introduced, populations could grow beyond seasonal and other environmental limitations inherent in the indigenous repertoire of domesticated plants. At the same time, the impact of the slave trade depopulated huge areas of the Slave Coast, resulting in severely compromised economic growth (Manning 1982). Yet we know that these impacts were not felt universally in the same ways throughout West Africa. How did they differ, and what were the factors that allowed such drastically different manifestations of the same broad process?

The Slave Coast region can help to address these, and other questions. The historic period, though not documented as richly or as early as some other parts of West Africa, is still well recorded. The work at Savi discussed in this chapter draws on the records of visitors to Allada and Hueda, yet many other ports were visited by Europeans who recorded their impressions of life and commerce. These sources should be mined for additional information about the many sites they list.

Further archaeological contributions to the region should include the identification and excavation of some deeply stratified sites, permitting the kind of ceramic seriations and catalogs that would be of broad use in chronology building and intersite comparison. Sadly, studies of this kind are very rare in this region, with the resultant handicap that discussions of indigenous crafts (including pipes, ceramics, and other artifacts) are always site specific, and not comparable to other work conducted elsewhere. Related to this, of course, is the expense and difficulty of publishing comprehensive and elaborately illustrated site reports and regional syntheses so necessary to furthering of this kind of research.

These obstacles are much like those that face archaeologists in any region where researchers are just beginning to work. The advantages the Bight of Benin has in terms of historic documentation, fascinating questions, and, above all, dedicated and enthusiastic archaeologist citizens, are clear indications that we will only learn more about this important region as more archaeological research is completed on the many topics of interest.

References

Adandé, A. B. A. (1984) 'Togudo-Awute, capitale de l'ancien royaume d'Allada, étude d'une cité précoloniale d'après les sources orales, écrites et les données de l'archéologie'. Unpublished Ph.D. dissertation, Université de Paris I Panthéon-Sorbonne, Paris.

Adandé, A. B. A. (1986–87) Recherches à Togudo-Awute: le Grand Ardres retrouvé. *Cahiers des Archives du Sol*, 1:13–68.

Adandé, A. B. A. (1989) Recherche sur la capitale de l'ancien royaume d'Allada. In *Actes de la quinzaine de l'archéologie togolaise 10 janvier–4 Février*, edited by D. A. Kuevi and D. Aguigah. Lomé: L'Association Togolaise de la Recherche Scientifique, pp. 103–16.

Adandé, A. B. A. and Kuevi, D. A. (1990) *Archéologie de sauvetage dans la Vallée du Mono*. Equipe de Recherche Archéologique Béninoise/ Programme Archéologique Togolaise.

Adandé, A. B. A. and Metinhoué, H. [n. d.] *Potières et poterie de Sé*. Report prepared for the Ministère de l'Enseignement Supérieur et de la Recherche Scientifique.

Adedze, A. (1990) 'The ethnoarchaeology of Ewe pottery'. Unpublished Masters thesis, Archaeology Program, University of California, Los Angeles.

Afeku, I. K. (1976) 'A study of smoking pipes from Begho'. Unpublished Bachelor of Arts (Honors) thesis, Department of Archaeology, University of Ghana, Accra.

Aguigah, D. A. (1986) 'Le site de Notsé: contribution à l'archéologie du Togo'. Unpublished Ph.D. dissertation, Université de Paris I, Paris.

Aguigah, D. A. (1989) Recherches archéologiques & historiques à Notsé et Tado: résultats & perspectives. In *Actes de la quinzaine de l'archéologie togolaise 10 Janvier–4 février*, edited by D. A. Kuevi and D. A. Aguigah. Lome: L'Association Togolaise de la Recherche Scientifique, pp. 46–65.

Aguigah, D. A. (1992a) Les pavements en tessons de poterie, organisation de l'espace dans la région du Golfe du Bénin: le cas du Togo. *West African Journal of Archaeology*, 22:133–44.

Aguigah, D. A. (1992b) 'Iron-working at Tado.' Paper presented at the Society for Africanist Archaeology Meeting, UCLA, Los Angeles.

Aguigah, D. A., Tidjougouna, B. and Kuevi, D. A. (1990) *20e Anniversaire de l'Université du Bénin—Expo Archéologie*. Lome.

Akinjogbin, I. A. (1967) *Dahomey and Its Neighbours 1708–1818*. Cambridge: Cambridge University Press.

Argyle, W. J. (1966) *The Fon of Dahomey: A History and Ethnography of the Old Kingdom*. Oxford: Clarendon Press.

Atkins, J. (1737) *A Voyage to Guinea, Brasil, and the West Indies*. London: Ward and Chandler.

Bellis, J. O. (1982) *The Place of Pots in Akan Funerary Custom*. African Studies Program, Indiana University.

Blier, S. P. (1989) Field days: Melville J. Herskovits in Dahomey. *History in Africa*, 16:1–22.

Bosman, W. (1705) *A New and Accurate Description of the Coast of Guinea, Divided into the Gold, the Slave, and the Ivory Coasts*. London.

Brunache, P. L. (2001) 'Perspectives of African-European interaction through spatial dynamics and material culture on the coast of Bénin'. Unpublished MA Thesis, University of South Carolina.

Crossland, L. B. (1989) *Pottery from the Begho-B2 Site, Ghana*. Calgary: University of Calgary Press.

Daget, J. and Ligers, Z. (1962) Une ancienne industrie malienne: les pipes en terre. *Bulletin de l'Institut Fondamental d'Afrique Noire*, 24:12–53.

Dalzel, A. (1793) *The History of Dahomy, an Inland Kingdom of Africa*. London.

De Marees, P. (1987) *Description and Historical Account of the Gold Kingdom of Guinea (1602)*. Edited and translated by A. Van Dantzig and A. Jones. London: Oxford University Press.

DeCorse, C. R. (1989) 'An archaeological study of Elmina, Ghana: trade and culture change on the Gold Coast between the fifteenth and nineteenth centuries'. Unpublished Ph.D. dissertation, Archaeology Program, University of California, Los Angeles.

DeCorse, C. R. (1992) Culture contact, continuity, and change on the Gold Coast: AD 1400–1900. *African Archaeological Review*, 10:163–96.

DeCorse, C. R. (1993) The Danes on the Gold Coast: culture change and the European presence. *African Archaeological Review*, 11:149–73.

DeCorse, C. R. (1998) Culture contact and change in West Africa. In *Studies in Culture Contact: Interaction, Culture Change, and Archaeology*, edited by J. G. Cusick. Carbondale, IL: Center for Archaeological Investigations, Southern Illinois University, pp. 358–77.

Djitrinou, D. (1985) Ouidah dans la traite esclavagiste: passage de la traite à l'exportation de l'huile de palme. In *Les Voies de la renaissance de Ouidah*, edited by Union Générale pour le Développement de Ouidah (U.G.D.O.). Caen, France: Editions KANTA, pp. 83–96.

Effah-Gyamfi, K. (1985) *Bono Manso: An Archaeological Investigation into Early Akan Urbanism*. Calgary: University of Calgary Press.

Ekeh, P. P. (1990) Social anthropology and two contrasting uses of tribalism in Africa. *Comparative Studies in Society and History*, 32:660–700.

Gaussen, J. (1990) 'Perles néolithiques du Tilemsi et du pays Ioullemedene (ateliers et techniques)'. Paper presented in Milan, October, 1990.

Hair, P. E. H., Jones, A. and Law, R. (eds) (1992) *Barbot on Guinea: The Writings of Jean Barbot on West Africa 1678–1712*. London: Hakluyt Society.

Henige, D. and Johnson, M. (1976) Agaja and the slave trade: another look at the evidence. *History in Africa*, 3:91–126.

Herbert, E. W. (1984) *Red Gold of Africa: Copper in Precolonial History and Culture*. Madison: University of Wisconsin Press.

Herskovits, M. J. (1938) *Dahomey: An Ancient West African Kingdom*. New York.

Houstoun, J. (1725) *Some New and Accurate Observations Geographical, Natural, and Historical. Containing a True and Impartial Account of the Situation, Product, and Natural History of the Coast of Guinea, so Far as Relates to the Improvement of that Trade, for the Advantage of Great Britain in General, and the Royal African Company in Particular*. London: J. Peele.

Iroko, F. A. (1989) Les vestiges d'une ancienne industrie de métallurgie du fer dans la région d'Abomey. *West African Journal of Archaeology*, 19:1–20.

Kadja, G. (1985) Les grandes communautés de base de Ouidah: origines et apports. In *Les Voies de la renaissance de Ouidah*, edited by Union Générale pour le Développement de Ouidah (U.G.D.O.). Caen, France: Editions KANTA, pp. 49–60.

Karl-Augustt, E. (1985) Origine des Houéda. Problématique et essai de synthèse. In *Les Voies de la renaissance de Ouidah*, edited by Union Générale pour le Développement de Ouidah (U.G.D.O.). Caen, France: Editions KANTA, pp. 61–82.

Kelly, K. G. (1994) Recent excavations at Savi: an eighteenth century West African trade town. *Nyame Akuma*, 41:2–8.

Kelly, K. G. (1995) 'Transformation and continuity in Savi, a West African trade town: an archaeological investigation of culture change on the coast of Bénin during the seventeenth and eighteenth centuries'. Unpublished Ph.D. dissertation, Department of Anthropology, University of California, Los Angeles.

Kelly, K. G. (1996) Report on the 1996 field season, Savi, Republic of Bénin. *Nyame Akuma*, 46:2–5.

Kelly, K. G. (1997a) The archaeology of African-

European interaction: investigating the social roles of trade, traders, and the use of space in the seventeenth- and eighteenth-century Hueda kingdom, Republic of Bénin. *World Archaeology*, 28(3):77–95.

Kelly, K. G. (1997b) Using historically informed archaeology: seventeenth and eighteenth century Hueda/European interaction on the coast of Bénin. *Journal of Archaeological Method and Theory*, 4(3/4):353–66.

Kelly, K. G. (1998) 'Long distance trade and state formation: the archaeology of the Hueda state, Bénin, West Africa'. Paper presented at the 14th Biennial Conference of the Society for Africanist Archaeologists, Syracuse, NY.

Kelly, K. G. (2001) The African diaspora from the ground up: the importance of historical archaeology for diaspora studies. In *Papers from the Conference 'La Ruta del Esclavo en Hispanoamérica'*, edited by R. Caceres. San Jose, Costa Rica: University of Costa Rica. Forthcoming.

Kelly, K. G. (2002) Indigenous responses to colonial encounters on the West African coast: Hueda and Dahomey from the 17th through 19th centuries. In *The Archaeology of Colonialism*, edited by C. L. Lyons and J. Papadopoulos. Los Angeles: Getty Research Institute.

Kelly, K. G., Brunache, P. and Norman, N. L. (1999) Archaeological fieldwork at Savi, Republic of Bénin: the 1999 season. *Nyame Akuma* 52:2–10.

Kuevi, D. A. (1989) Vestiges et monuments anciens sur le Plateau de Danyi. In *Actes de la Quinzaine de l'Archéologie Togolaise 10 Janvier–4 Février*, edited by D. A. Kuevi and D. A. Aguigah. Lomé: L'Association Togolaise de la Recherche Scientifique, pp. 66–78.

Labat, J.-B. (1731) *Voyage du Chevalier des Marchais en Guinée, isles voisines et à Cayenne, fait en 1725, 1726 et 1727*. Amsterdam.

Law, R. (1977) Royal monopoly and private enterprise in the Atlantic trade: the case of Dahomey. *Journal of African History*, 28:555–77.

Law, R. (1986) Dahomey and the slave trade: reflections on the historiography of the rise of Dahomey. *Journal of African History*, 27:237–67.

Law, R. (1989a) *Correspondence from the Royal African Company's Factories at Offra and Whydah on the Slave Coast of West Africa in the Public Record Office, London, 1678–93*. Edinburgh: Centre of African Studies, Edinburgh University.

Law, R. (1989b) The slave-trader as historian: Robert Norris and the history of Dahomey. *History in Africa*, 16:219–35.

Law, R. (1989c) Between the sea and the lagoons: the interaction of maritime and inland navigation on the precolonial slave coast. *Cahiers d'Etudes Africaines*, 29:209–37.

Law, R. (1991a) *Correspondence of the Royal African Company's Chief Merchants at Cabo Corso Castle with William's Fort, Whydah, and the Little Popo Factory, 1727–1728: An Annotated Transcription of Ms. Francklin 1055/1 in the Bedfordshire County Record Office*. Madison: University of Wisconsin Press.

Law, R. (1991b) *The Slave Coast of West Africa, 1550–1750: The Impact of the Atlantic Slave Trade on an African Society*. Oxford: Clarendon Press.

Le Hérissé, A. (1911) *L'Ancien Royaume du Dahomey: moeurs, réligion, histoire*. Paris: LaRose.

Le Hérissé, R. (1903) *Voyage au Dahomey et à la Côte d'Ivoire*. Paris: Henri Charles-Lavauzelle.

Manning, P. (1982) *Slavery, Colonialism and Economic Growth in Dahomey, 1640–1960*. Cambridge: Cambridge University Press.

Medeiros de, F. (ed.) (1984) *Peuples du Golfe du Bénin*. Paris: Editions Karthala.

Muller, W. J. (1983) Description of the Petu Country, 1662–9, in German sources for West African history, 1599–1660. *Studien zur Kulturkunde*, 66:134–259.

Norman, N. L. (2000) 'Through the medium of the vessel: An ethnoarchaeological investigation of ritual earthenwares in Southern Bénin, West Africa'. Unpublished MA thesis, University of South Carolina.

Norris, R. (1968) *Memoirs of the Reign of Bossa Ahadee, King of Dahomy, an Inland Country of Guiney*. London: Frank Cass and Co. (First published 1789.)

Ozanne, P. C. (1962) Notes on the early historic archaeology of Accra. *Transactions of the Historical Society of Ghana*, 6:51–70.

Ozanne, P. C. (1976) Tobacco-pipes of Accra and Shai. Unpublished manuscript. Accra, Ghana.

Pazzi, R. (1977) Aperçu sur l'implémentation actuelle et les migrations anciennes des peuples de l'aire culturelle Aja-Tado. In *Peuples du Golfe du Bénin*, edited by F. de Medeiros, Cotonou, Bénin: Université Nationale du Bénin, pp. 5–16.

Petrequin, P. and Petrequin, A-M. (1984) *Habitat lacustre du Bénin: une approche ethnoarchéologique*. Paris: Editions Recherche sur les Civilisations.

Philips, J. E. (1983) African smoking pipes. *Journal of African History*, 24:303–19.

Polanyi, K. (1966) *Dahomey and the Slave Trade: An Analysis of an Archaic Economy*. Seattle: University of Washington Press.

Posnansky, M. (1981) Notsé town wall survey. *Nyame Akuma*, 18:56–7.

Posnansky, M. (1985) Togo and new directions in the Study of West Africa's Past. In *Actes du Séminaire UCLA – UB sur les Sciences Sociales*. Lome, Togo: Université du Bénin.

Posnansky, M. and de Barros, P. (1980) 'An Archaeological Reconnaissance of Togo, August 1979'. Prepared for H.E. The Minister of National Education for Scientific Research of the Republic of Togo under the sponsorship of the US International Communication Agency, Washington, D.C.

Quarcoopome, N. O. (1993) Notse's ancient kingship: some archaeological and art-historical considerations. *African Archaeological Review*, 11:109–28.

Quénum, M. (1983) *Au pays des Fons: us et coûtumes du Dahomey*. Paris: Editions Maisonneuve et LaRose. (First published 1936.)

Rivallain, J. (1977) Le sel dans les villages côtiers et lagunaires du Bas Dahomey: sa fabrication, sa place dans le circuit du sel africain. *West African Journal of Archaeology*, 7:143–69.

Rivallain, J. (1981) Un artisanat ancien: la poterie dans le sud du Bénin. In *Le Sol, la parole, et l'écrit: 2000 ans d'histoire Africaine*. Paris: Société Française d'Histoire d'Outre-Mer.

Ross, D. (1983) European models and West African history: further comments on the recent historiography of Dahomey. *History in Africa*, 10:293–305.

Ryder, A. F. C. (1969) *Benin and the Europeans: 1485–1897*. Harlow, England: Longman.

Sinou, A. (1995) *Le Comptoir de Ouidah: une ville africaine singulière*. Paris: Editions Karthala.

Smith, W. (1967) *A New Voyage to Guinea*. London: Frank Cass & Co. (First published 1774.)

Snelgrave, W. (1734) *A New Account of Some Parts of Guinea and the Slave Trade*. London: J. & J. Knapton.

Van Dantzig, A. (1978) *The Dutch and the Guinea Coast, 1674–1742: A Collection of Documents from the General State Archive at The Hague*. Accra: Ghana Academy of Arts and Sciences.

Wantchecon, A. M. (1983) 'Contribution à l'histoire des technologies anciennes du Bas-Bénin: L'exemple du travail du fer à Allada des origines du royaume à la conquête aboméene en 1724.' Unpublished Masters thesis, Université Nationale du Bénin, Cotonou, Bénin.

York, R. N. (1973) Excavations at New Buipe. *West African Journal of Archaeology*, 3:1–189.

6 Kanem-Borno: A Brief Summary of the History and Archaeology of an Empire of the Central *bilad al-sudan*

DETLEF GRONENBORN

This chapter examines the current state of historic and archaeological research on one of Africa's most powerful and enduring empires: Kanem-Borno. Originally emerging during the ninth century northeast of Lake Chad, it began to expand shortly after the adoption of Islam by the ruling élite during the eleventh century. By the sixteenth century the empire had reached its widest extension, from the central Sahara to the northern fringes of Central Africa, and from the Hausa city states to the eastern shores of Lake Chad. Although the empire resisted the Fulani *jihad* of the early nineteenth century, it was defeated by the invasion of a Sudanic warlord in 1893. Only with the help of incoming colonial forces was the old regime reinstalled. Over more than 1,000 years Kanem-Borno largely subsisted on the trans-Saharan trade, one of its major export goods being slaves. The empire thus constitutes one of the examples of West African political institutions that incorporated slavery not only economically but also politically long before the onset of the Atlantic slave trade and, in fact, continued to do so after the abolition of slavery in the Americas.

This paper is organized chronologically, dividing the more than 1,000 years of the empire's duration into four major epochs: the rise, the heyday, the decline, and the early colonial period. In each section historical sources are discussed first, followed by what is known about the archaeology. It will become evident that for extensive periods the archaeology of Kanem-Borno is still in its infancy, and most if not all the information has to be extracted from historical sources. In the final section the potential of future archaeological research is discussed.

The setting: the Central *bilad al-sudan*

The Kanem-Borno empire is one of the oldest polities in West Africa and its political heirs, the Emirates of Borno and Dikwa, still exist constitutionally beside the modern government institutions of Borno State in the Federal Republic of Nigeria. The roots of a state-level political system lay in the ninth century AD, when Arab sources first mention 'kings' for the

area today known as the 'Central *bilad al-sudan*.' By this term, meaning 'land of the black,' the Arab traders referred to the broad belt between the Atlantic Ocean and the Nile. Divisions into culture areas were first attempted by the expanding colonial powers at the end of the nineteenth century. The German geographer Meyer (1897: 1) summarized these early endeavors. According to him and others, the eastern Niger to the west and the eastern shores of Lake Chad to the east

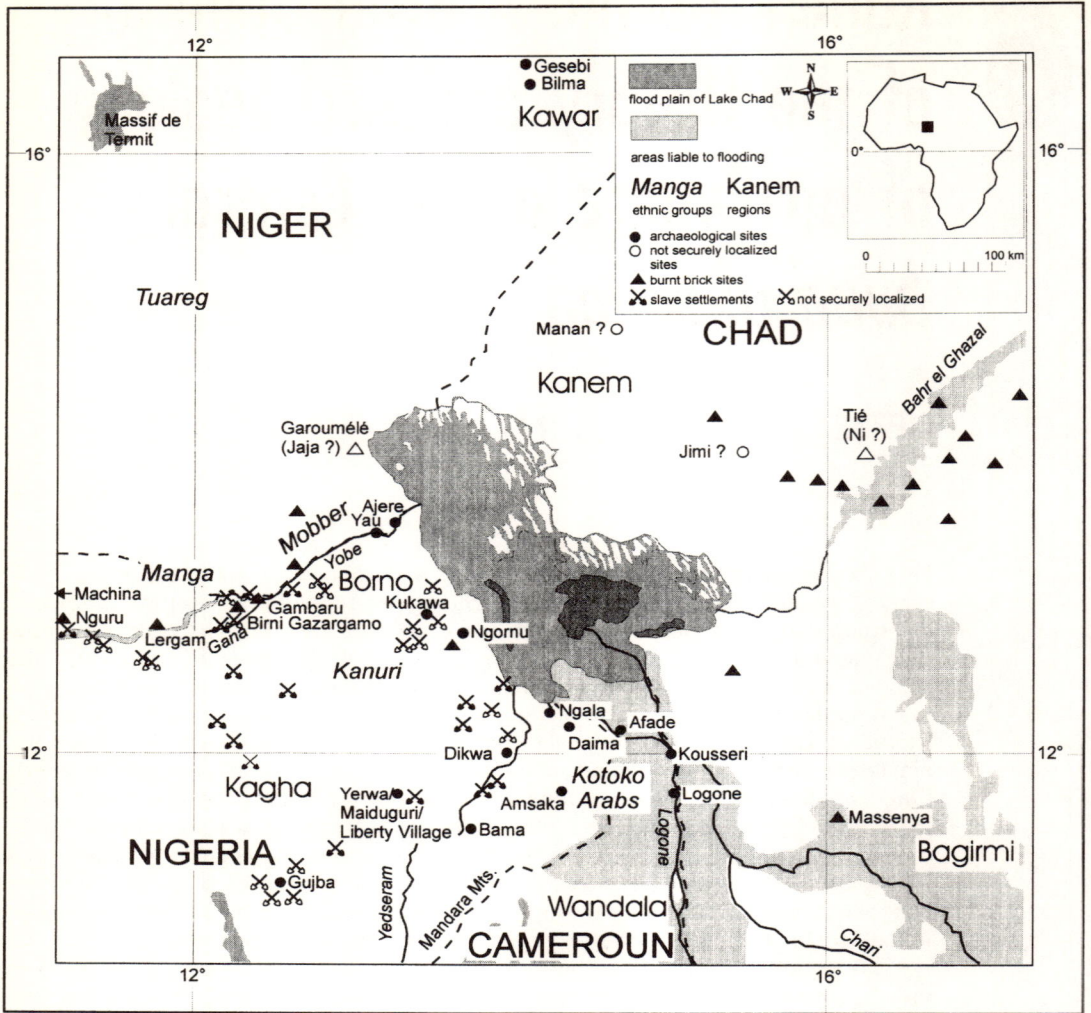

Figure 6.1 The Central *bilad al-sudan* with sites mentioned in the text. (Burnt brick sites in Chad mapped after Lebeuf 1972; slave settlements mapped after Mafama 1977.)

would delineate the 'Central Sudan.' Later Trimingham (1962: 104) defined the Central Sudan as the region between the middle Niger river and Waday—a territorial delineation which is still agreed upon up to this day (e.g. Reyna 1990: 15–26). To the north the Central Sudan is limited by the Sahara, toward the south by the thickets of the tropical forests. It thus largely encompasses territories in the modern states of northern Nigeria, southern Niger, Chad, and northern Cameroon (Figure 6.1).

A major geographical feature of the Central Sudan is the Chad Basin—a wide, almost completely flat landscape with Lake Chad at its center. The present lake is the remains of what once was one of the world's largest inland bodies of water, 'Mega Lake Chad', which extended over 300,000 square kilometers (116,000 square miles) during the early Holocene. Its size began to shrink about 6,000 years ago when the climate became gradually dryer (Maley 1981; Thiemeyer 1997). When waters receded, fertile grounds were left: sandy soils to the north and west of the lake, and heavy clays to the south.

The archaeological record shows that human occupation of the inner Chad Basin dates back to at least the sixth millennium BC. Hamlets with an agropastoral subsistence evolved west of the lake around 1000 BC (Breunig *et al.*, 1996; Gronenborn 1997). South of Lake Chad permanent villages seem to have emerged with the onset of the early Iron Age around 500 BC (MacEachern 1996). These villages persisted throughout the first half of the first millennium AD (Connah 1981; Gronenborn 1998).

It is unclear whether there had been contacts between the Chad Basin and the lands north of the Sahara during classical antiquity. No conclusive evidence exists apart from some vague Roman sources (Lacroix 1998: 17–42; Meyer, 1897: 1; Wheeler 1965: 110; Snowden 1970: 140–1). However, it is certain that trade became intensified after the domination of North Africa by the Arabs during the seventh and eighth centuries AD. From then on the Central Sudan was closely linked to the Muslim world (Barkindo 1985: 230) and the formation of the Kanem-Borno Empire was underway.

The rise of Kanem-Borno

The foundation of Kanem-Borno goes back to the eighth century AD. Arab writers mention various ethnic groups for the northern Chad Basin, some of which had developed hierarchically structured societies with aspects of divine kingship. Such can be taken from the work of the antiquarian Yaqut, dating to 1229. Although writing at the beginning of the thirteenth century he made use of earlier accounts. His narration probably reflects the situation of the tenth century, when he states:

> Their houses are all reed huts as is also the palace of their king, whom they exalt and worship instead of Allah. They imagine that he does not eat any food . . . He has unlimited authority over his subjects and he enslaves from among them anyone he wants . . . Their religion is the worship of their kings, for they believe that they bring life and death, sickness and health. (Yaqut in Levtzion and Hopkins 1981: 171)

This must have been the power base of the ruling élite that had established itself firmly over the territory of Kanem, the region north and east of Lake Chad (Barkindo 1985; 227;

Lange and Barkindo, 1988: 454–5). As the Sayfuwa dynasty they were to govern the Chad Basin for the next thousand years. Sayfuwa rulers were referred to as the *mai*, an ancient indigenous title related to the institution of divine kingship (Last 1985: 187), best translated into English as 'lord' (Smith 1987: 84). After the eleventh century the Sayfuwa began to incorporate Islamic principles into their political system, and soon afterward territorial expansion into areas north and west began. Historical information on those emerging years of the empire is dim and has to be carefully extracted from the accounts of Arab writers (Levtzion and Hopkins 1981), the scanty internal evidence in the Kanem-Borno king lists (Lange 1977), and the few fragments of internal scripts that have been recorded by the German traveler Heinrich Barth (1857–59; Lange 1987) and the British colonial officer Richmond Palmer (1967; 1970).

By the thirteenth century the political and territorial influence of the rulers of Kanem had expanded. The Arab historian Ibn Khaldun described a caravan with gifts arriving at Tunis in 1257 from 'the king of Kanem . . . ruler of Barnu' (Levtzion and Hopkins 1981: 337). It is from then on that the toponym 'Borno' appears in the text sources. This land of Borno would be of essential importance to the history of the empire since, shortly after Ibn Khaldun wrote his text, a long lingering conflict between the Sayfuwa and a neighboring nomadic ethnic group, the Bulala, broke out. This led to the collapse of the first Sayfuwa state and the abandonment of Kanem (Barth 1857–59 II: 33). The court left the old capital and migrated to a place variously called Jaja or Kaka, where a new political center was established. This Jaja/Kaka was situated in the land of Borno (Barkindo 1985: 240; Lange, 1993: 272). It seems, however, that on-going conflicts with the local population led to an abandonment of Jaja/Kaka and the Kanem-Borno *mais* were forced to move their seat frequently (Barkindo 1985: 245). In 1472 they established themselves permanently at the newly founded capital of Birni Gazargamo (Figure 6.3b).

Already at this early stage exports from Borno often consisted of slaves, which not only becomes evident from the above cited passage of Yaqut but also from the following note by the famous traveler Ibn Battuta, from the fourteenth century: 'From this country [Borno] they bring handsome slave girls and young men slaves and cloth dyed with saffron' (Ibn Battuta, in Levtzion and Hopkins 1981: 302). The preying grounds for these slaves would have been the newly conquered territories, but also lands south of Lake Chad, as is indicated in a text which survived from the Egyptian historian al-Maqrizi, where he writes: 'The King of Kanim made a raid on them [ethnic groups south of Lake Chad] from Aljama [the capital of Kanem] about 1252–53 and slaughtered and took prisoners' (Levtzion and Hopkins 1981: 354).

The riddle of the early capitals

While the historical sources provide a vague picture of the events of the first 500 years of the Kanem-Borno empire, archaeologically almost nothing is known. This paucity of archaeological data from the emerging years of the empire remains one of the most challenging research gaps in the Central Sudan (Bivar and Shinnie 1962: 1). Although the Arabic sources speak of several succeeding capitals in Kanem, none of them has been identified on the ground. Very helpful, however, in locating these early capitals might be a text on the Chad Basin compiled by the geographer Ibn Said. He wrote his *kitab al-jughrafiya*—'The Book of Geography'—shortly after 1269. Although he made use of earlier material, his description of the Chad Basin is based on a first-hand source from the early thirteenth century (Lange 1980: 150):

> To the east of the town of Badi, among the Muslim Kanim is Jaja. It is the seat of a separate Kingdom with towns and villages now belonging to the sultan of Kanim. It is characterized by fertility and abundance of the good things of life. There are peacocks there, and parrots, and speckled chickens, and piebald sheep of the size of small donkeys but shaped differently from our sheep. There are many giraffes in the land of Jaja. To the east of the town at the angle of the lake is al-Maghza where the sultan of Kanim's arsenal is situated. He often makes raids from there with his fleet on the lands of the pagans on the shores of this lake [Lake Chad] and attacks their ships and kills and takes prisoners . . . South-east of it is Jimi, the capital of Kanim . . . There resides the sultan of Kanim . . . The capital of his pagan ancestors

before they adopted Islam was the town of Manan . . . On a level with Jimi at the end of this section he possesses Ni where he has a garden and pleasure-ground and a boat. It lies on the west bank of the Egyptian Nile and is 40 miles from Jimi. Its fruits do not resemble ours. They have many pomegranates and peaches. They used to tend sugar-cane, but yielded little, and only the sultan concerns himself with it; the same applies to vines and wheat. (Levtzion and Hopkins 1981: 187–8)

Ibn Said's description contained a number of geographical coordinates referring to a map, now lost, but which has been tentatively reconstructed by Lange (1980) and myself (Figure 6.2a). If the medieval Arabic sources are brought into accordance with modern maps (Figure 6.2b) it becomes evident that most of the early towns were situated north of the lake. Manan, Jimi, and Jaja are mentioned as the successive capitals of the early Kanem-Borno empire before its shift to the location west of Lake Chad. The pre-Islamic capital of Manan should, according to the reconstructed map, be located well to the north of the lake. No archaeological remains have been discovered. It may be difficult to locate them on the ground since Yaqut's source only mentions reed huts as domestic structures. Such building construction is the major architectural type found in the areas north of Lake Chad (e.g. Barth 1857–59 III: 603–4). A settlement largely constituted by reed huts would leave little remains in the sandy territory, even if it was the focal point of a larger polity (Connah 1981: 70–3). Moreover, at the time of the capital Manan, during the tenth and eleventh centuries, a nomad component might still have persisted in the economy (Smith 1987: 85). Settlements by pastoralists are even more difficult to discern archaeologically.

The case of Jimi, the twelfth- and thirteenth-century capital, is equally unsolved. Although its presumed location appears on many historic maps of the Central Sudan (e.g. Ajayi and Crowder 1985: 63) it has never been securely located on the ground. Only one of the places mentioned by Ibn Said might have been identified with some certainty: Bivar and Shinnie (1962: 7–10), surveying for ruins related to the empire, discovered a site called Tié in the Chad Republic, east of the lake (Figure 6.1). Because of its small size they did

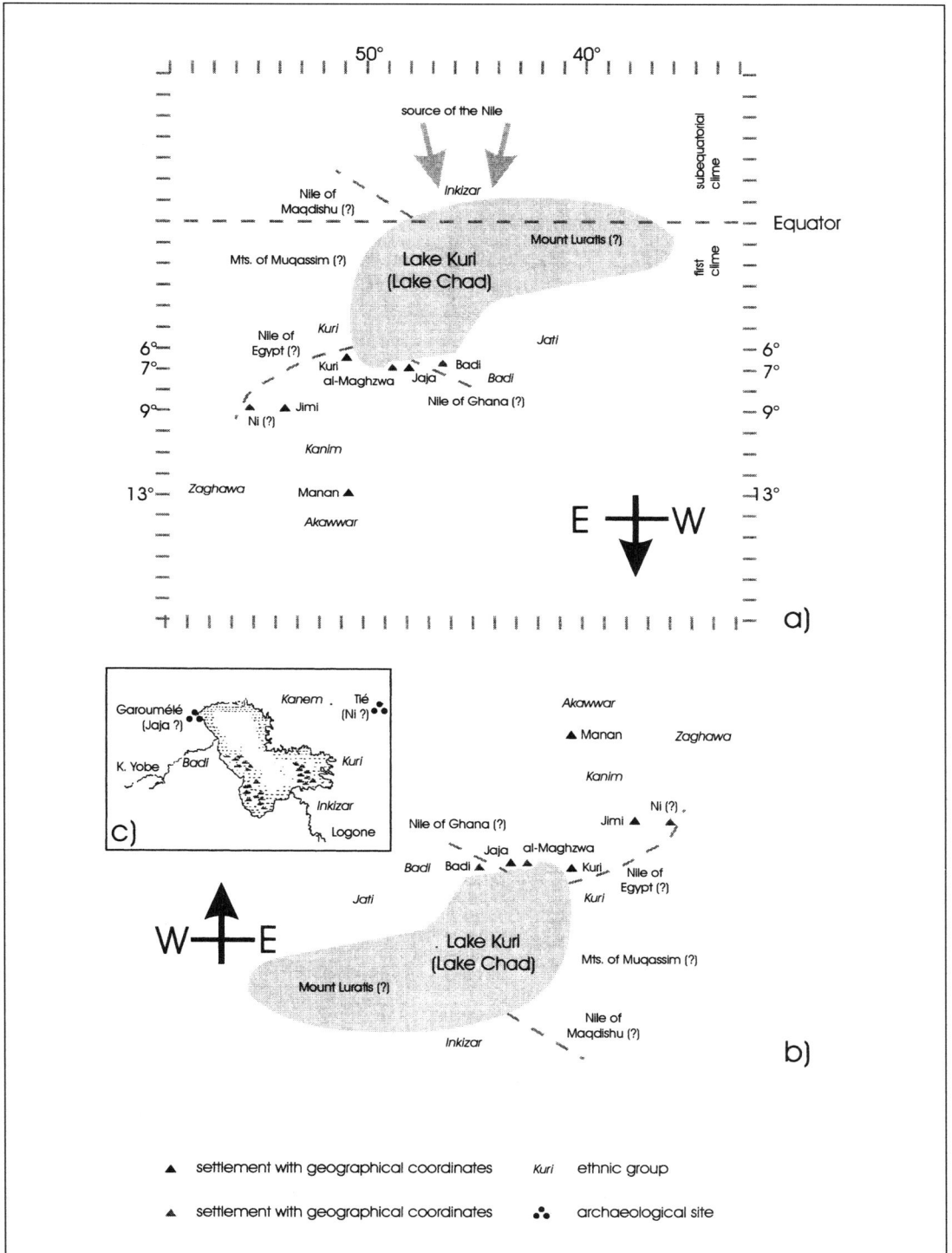

Figure 6.2 Map of the Chad Basin reconstructed after Ibn Said from the thirteenth century AD (source Lange 1980; Gronenborn 2000).

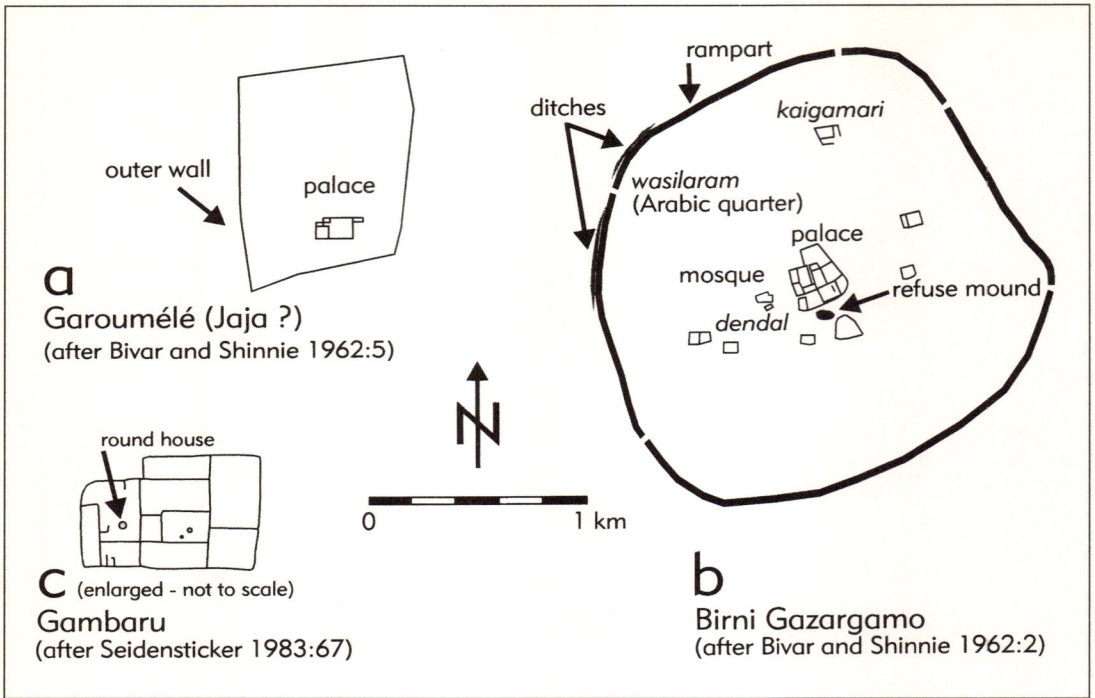

Figure 6.3 Plans of the capitals and palaces of the fourteenth to eighteenth centuries.

not consider it as one of the empire's former capitals. Judging from Ibn Said's description, however, it might have been the 'pleasure-ground' Ni of the sultan, being situated close to the Bahr-el-Ghazal which Lange (1980: 130–1) identifies as the 'Nile of Egypt' of the medieval sources. What is surprising about Ibn Said's passage is the description of lush vegetation and abundant agricultural products in a region where, today, annual precipitation does not exceed 50 to 100 mm (2–4 inches) and makes permanent residence impossible (Maley 1981: 65–8).

The place to which the Sayfuwa fled after the abandonment of their homeland in Kanem is called Jaja in Ibn Said's text. When the text was written in the thirteenth century, Jaja was described as a semi-independent kingdom, subordinate to the rulers of Kanem. During the fourteenth century the Egyptian writer al-Qalqashandi mentioned the new capital, and described it as being located in 'Barnu.' It was the seat of the sultan: 'The capital of the people of Barnu is Kaka ... It has already been mentioned that Kaka is the capital of the Sultan of al-Barnu. The distance between Kaka and Jimi

is 40 miles' (Levtzion and Hopkins 1981: 344–5).

There is little doubt among scholars that the Kaka of the fourteenth century is the Jaja of the thirteenth. Less agreed upon is the actual location. Various authors have suggested that Jaja/Kaka may have been located south or southwest of Lake Chad (Barkindo 1985: 246; Barth 1857–59 II: 587; Connah 1981: 225; Lange, 1993: 272). Yet a careful examination of Ibn Said's map and al-Qalqashandi's reference to the distance between Jimi and Kaka suggest the area northwest of the lake. It is tempting to associate the site of Garoumélé (Figure 6.3a), near the present settlement of Wudi in Niger (Bivar and Shinnie 1962: 4–6), with the seat of the Sayfuwa royal court. Here an elaborate structure of fired bricks and a rectangular enclosure of cone-shaped bricks are clear evidence that the site must have been at least a regional center. Interestingly, the construction of the wall with cone-shaped bricks is unusual for Borno and known only from Garoumélé. Such bricks, however, are still widely in use in areas outside of Borno, notably in Hausaland (Dmochowski

1990: 1.20–1.24) but also beyond (Denyer 1978: 160–3; Maas and Mommersteeg 1992: 36–40). Red fired bricks like those from the central court at Garoumélé are known from a number of sites in the Chad Basin (see below).

Unfortunately, as with the other sites, no archaeological work has been conducted at Garoumélé. Hence, the date of construction is unknown. A short passage in Barth (1857–59 II: 601) suggests that during the nineteenth century nearby Wudi was still remembered as a residence of 'several of the old Bornú kings'. Also Bivar and Shinnie (1962: 4), following Urvoy (1949: 45), promoted Garoumélé as a seat of the Sayfuwa after they had left Kanem, an assumption equally supported by Duyvesteyn (1973). A text fragment in Palmer (1967 III: 28) also refers to a site called Garu Kime (Kanuri 'red wall,' which in present-day Borno is a common denomination for burnt brick sites) near Wudi. However Zeltner (1980: 58–9) places Kaka near modern Geidam, closer to the later capital of Birni Gazargamo.

Nowadays the vicinity of Garoumélé is rather barren, but if one looks at the reports of the nineteenth-century travelers (Barth 1857–59 I: 575–7; Rohlfs 1868a: 49–50) vegetation was much richer, and Lake Chad was closer to the town. Thus, during the thirteenth century the region was likely to be much more attractive, and fertile enough to house the seat of a government with its court. Not too far distant from Garoumélé lies an area where vegetation is still lush today (Rohlfs 1868a: 50–1): the valleys of the River Yobe and its small tributary the River Gana (Figure 6.1). Considering the fertility and abundance of natural resources of the region, it is of no surprise that a number of Iron Age sites are found along the river banks. Two of these, the mounds of Yau and Ajere, have been tested by Connah (1981: 201–13). Both of them date between the eighth/ninth and thirteenth centuries AD. From the materials recovered Connah (1981: 208–13) was able to reconstruct an economy that relied mostly on the aquatic resources of the nearby River Yobe, but also encompassed cattle and sheep/goat rearing, as well as the growing of millet. A similar adaptation was still practiced in the area during the second half of the nineteenth century (Rohlfs 1868a: 50).

The pottery recovered at these sites is decorated with what Connah (1981: 58–9) called 'nodular roulette.' This decoration mode (see Figure 6.6, 10), otherwise called 'twisted strip roulette' (Gronenborn and Magnavita 2000), is typical for the Late Iron Age in the northwestern Chad Basin. It is associated with another decoration mode, termed *sgraffito* by Connah (1981: 207). This was created by scratching linear motifs through a burnished slip before firing. Sometimes the slip is covered with a glaze after incising and before firing (Rice 1987: 146). This particular decoration mode seems to have been practiced in the Yobe valley by the eighth or ninth centuries AD, and was later adopted into the pottery style that still characterizes ceramics of the fifteenth-century sites in the Yobe valley (see below). At what point in time this tradition evolved, and where, remains unclear as no early Iron Age sites have been tested. It is, however, quite likely that the lower Yobe valley and its surroundings could have constituted the location of the once independent kingdom of Jaja. Indeed, around the thirteenth century the region should have been fertile enough for peacocks, parrots, and giraffes to roam about, as is mentioned by Ibn Said. It is quite understandable that the rulers of Kanem gradually expanded their sphere of influence toward this direction and later, when forced to leave their homeland, decided to move there finally.

It is, however, notable, and has already been remarked by Connah (1981: 210), that neither carnelian nor glass beads or any metal artifacts except those of iron were found in the excavations. This poverty of material culture is quite surprising considering that the sites lay close to Kanem and thus should have participated in the external contacts, even more so as the above-cited text source by Ibn Khaldun indicates the domination of Kanem over these lands since the thirteenth century. Was the western Chad Basin excluded from the benefits of wide-reaching trade networks? Or were these two sites only the remains of poor fishing villages and would in no case have yielded exotic goods? Another unresolved question is whether the proposed date of abandonment of the mound of Yau around the thirteenth century (Connah 1981: 205) would have had anything to do with the increasing political pressure from Kanem. It certainly remains a worthwhile research topic for the future.

The upper layers of deeply stratified settlement mounds south of Lake Chad equally date to the end of the first millennium AD. The most famous of these sites is Daima, which was excavated by Connah (1976; 1981) during the 1960s. Since the beginning of human settlement in the area around 1000 cal. BC this region had been culturally distinct from the territories west of the lake, not only because the settlement system was different from that of the regions west of the lake—long-term occupied mounds as opposed to frequently moving villages or hamlets—but also because pottery styles have been quite dissimilar to those of the Yobe valley and its wider vicinity since the Late Neolithic and throughout the Early Iron Age (Breunig *et al.* 1996; Connah 1981; Gronenborn 1998; Holl 1995). By the sixth century AD complex villages had emerged in the south, and after the tenth century an increasing amount of iron and copper alloy goods in burials indicate widening exchange connections (Holl 1995; Gronenborn 2000). At Daima a ditch that might have surrounded the settlement could well date between the tenth and twelfth centuries, indicating not only the formation of formal settlements but also the necessity to defend them (Connah 1981: 167). Another old settlement in this very region, with roots in the late Early Iron Age, is the town of Ngala (Figure 6.1). Being situated on the route from Borno to Bagirmi it had been visited by most of the European travelers, beginning with Hugh Clapperton in 1823 (Lockhardt 1996: 111). The earlier accounts describe the city as quite remarkable in size, with an impressive palace on an elevation, surrounded by mighty walls. Oral tradition holds that it might have been a religious center during the sixteenth century (Forkl 1983: 167; Gronenborn 1998: 243–4). In 1996 the local ruler *mai* Ngalama Ibrahim Laminu initiated an excavation within the ruins of his palace. In total the sequence of archaeological layers reached a depth of 4.5m (14 ft 9 inches), beginning with the late Early Iron Age and continuing up to modern times (Figure 6.4). As will be explained further below, the pottery sequence of this site reflects the continuous expansion and increasing influence of the Kanem-Borno state in the region south of Lake Chad.

In many of the sites in the southern Chad Basin carnelian and glass beads make their appearance as grave goods by the fourteenth or fifteenth century. These beads might be interpreted as a reflection of the trans-Saharan trade (see discussion in Gronenborn 1998). It seems that while before the fourteenth century the region had been largely secluded from intensive contacts with the north, and had served the rulers of Kanem mostly as a preying ground for slaves, after that time interaction with the north increased. Moreover, a note by al-Maqrizi indicates that independent princedoms had evolved during the fourteenth century (Barth 1857–59 II: 436). It seems possible that part of the processes which led to the formation of these complex societies was the pressure from outside (Gronenborn 1998: 252). It also seems justified to interpret the archaeological indicators of northward contacts as a result of increasing economic and political exchange between the regions south of Lake Chad and the growing Kanem-Borno empire during and after the fourteenth century. That part of this exchange was violent in nature and involved enslavement of local populations is a pattern which persisted in the central *bilad al-sudan* until the end of the nineteenth century. It was, for instance, documented by Nachtigal (1971–87 III: 340–68) for slave raids of the sultan of Bagirmi (see also MacEachern, this volume). As described by Nachtigal so vividly, part of the local population might have assisted the incoming troops and might have been paid off with material goods. Or slaves were raided by local groups and then exchanged to Kanem-Borno merchants. That glass and stone beads served as currency in the Central Sudan during the fourteenth century is documented by al-Umari (Levtzion and Hopkins 1981: 260), and still during the nineteenth century glass and stone beads were used as currency on Adamawa slave markets (Passarge 1895: 433).

Also representing the early development of Kanem-Borno are some sites north of the Chad Basin, in areas that are desert today. These sites are not directly connected to the empire but were of central importance in the trans-Saharan trade between the Chad Basin and North Africa. The main trans-Saharan trade from the Chad Basin went directly northward, passing Bilma and Murzuk, and ended in Tripolis. Lange and Berthoud (1977) have surveyed several locations along this route that they connect to trading towns mentioned in the documentary sources. One of these to be mentioned here is Gesebi in Kawar, north of Bilma, which Lange and Berthoud (1977: 21)

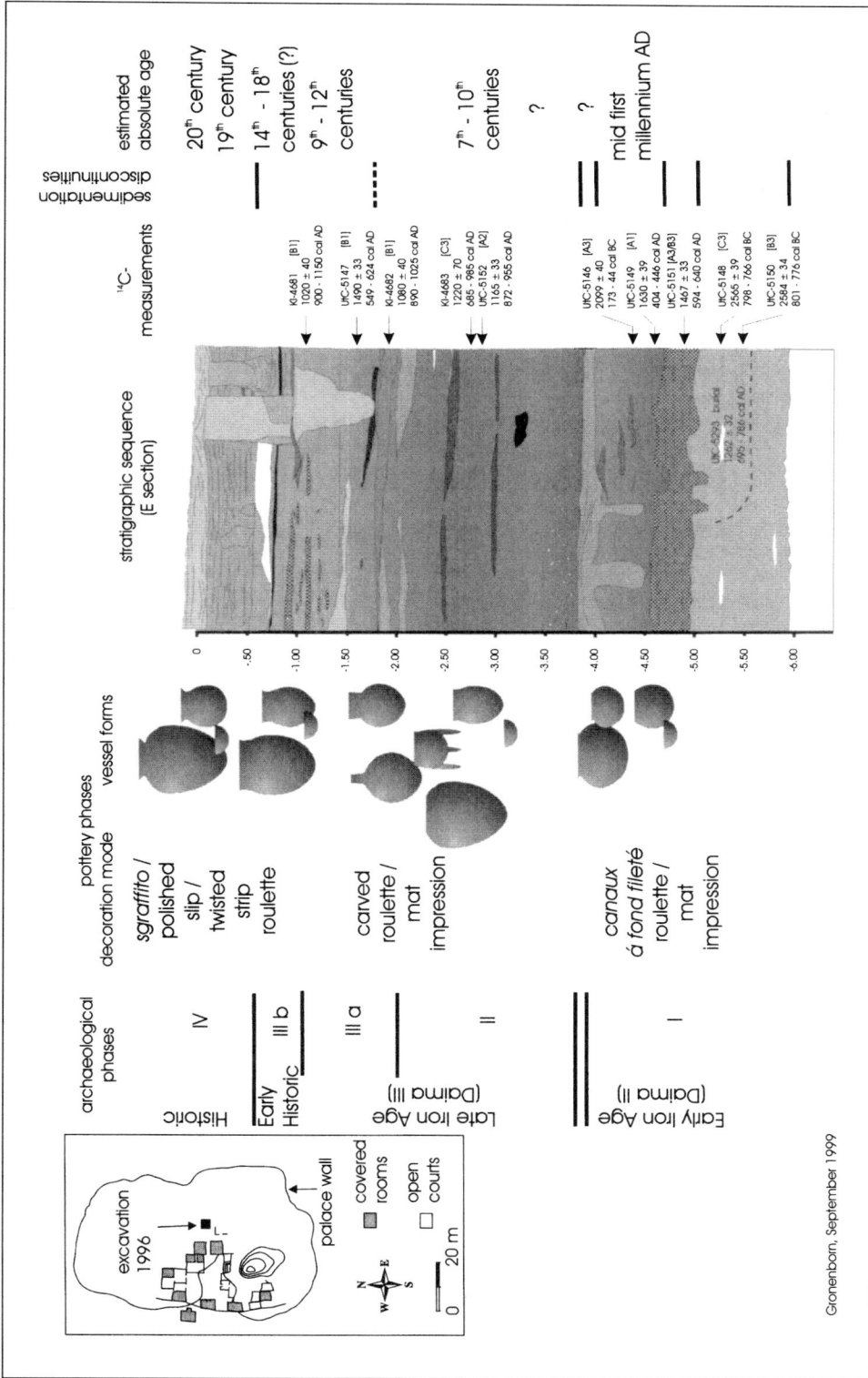

Figure 6.4 Ngala. Plan of the palace (inset) and stratigraphy (after Gronenborn, in press a).

identified as the al-Qasaba of the Arab writers. The earliest of these sources would be al-Idrisi, who wrote in the twelfth century: 'This [al-Qasaba] is a well built town, surrounded on all sides by date-palms and various kinds of wild trees.' (Levtzion and Hopkins 1981: 123). The source also describes the reason why the area was so attractive. Not only were there water wells in abundance, but by the twelfth century salt and alum were already being mined in Kawar and exported from there. The salt mines and the related trade remained important throughout the following centuries (Bovill 1970: 241–2). Regarding the long-term economic importance of the salt trade, Lange and Berthoud (1977: 22) propose an even-greater antiquity for the waystation at Gesebi, possibly going back to pre-Islamic times. They also describe settlement mounds near Bilma, the connecting point between the Tripolis–Borno route and the route to Fachi and Agadez, which is described as a minor settlement in the nineteenth century (Barth 1857–59 III: 613). Other trade stations have been identified further north, outside of the area considered here.

Summing up, very little is known about the capitals or towns of the early Kanem-Borno empire. The locations of the earliest sites have been obscured under the southwardly protruding sands of the Sahara, and none of the later locations can be identified with certainty. This lack of knowledge can only be overcome by surveys and further test excavations in the regions north and northeast of Lake Chad. Judging from the information available from Ibn Said and other sources, the location of the kingdom of Jaja/Kaka, and hence the seat of the kings of Kanem-Borno after their exodus from Kanem, should be sought in the vicinity of the River Yobe. It is nevertheless obvious that, already during the early years of the empire, slave raiding and trading constituted an important part of the economic activities, at least of the ruling élite. Archaeological indications of these slaving expeditions are indirect: materials possibly linked to the trans-Saharan trade make their appearance in regions which were cut off from these contacts before. Thus these raids may have opened new territories for exchange.

At the equinox of power: the fifteenth to eighteenth centuries

It was not until 1472 that a substantial and mighty capital was founded by the Sayfuwa dynasty, when *mai* Ali ibn Dunama (1465–97) had a city built that was to become the focal point of the Central *bilad al-sudan* for the next 300 years: Birni Gazargamo (Figure 6.3b). Situated at the southern terminus of the trans-Saharan trade routes and closer to the emerging trade centers in Hausaland than the previous locations in Kanem, the town had an ideal position in the trade routes of the Central Sudan. In contrast to the shifting capitals of earlier time periods, Gazargamo now served as a firm basis of political authority. With a focal point established, *mai* Ali Dunama reorganized the political structure and also the military force of the state (Barth 1857–59 III: 589; Lange 1993: 273–4; Nur Alkali 1983: 101–2).

Unfortunately we know very little about the political and administrative structure during these times. Most of the information has to be extracted from the notes of nineteenth-century travelers, primarily Barth and Nachtigal (Ben-isheikh 1983; Nur Alkali 1983b). One has to bear in mind that the internal structure was in constant transformation over the centuries as offices were created or adopted from subdued polities (Lange 1990; Nachtigal 1967 I: 708–31). Thus the situation of the nineteenth century might be rather different from that of the sixteenth. The basic principles are, however, clear. The political structure of Kanem–Borno was extremely hierarchical from its inception. At the center of the state stood the *mai*, a title going back to pre-Islamic times. After Islam became a state religion toward the end of the eleventh century, the rulers of Kanem-Borno were referred to as 'sultan' or 'emir,' both in external and internal sources. After the foundation of Gazargamo the rulers of Borno called themselves 'khalifas' (Barkindo 1985: 249; Lavers 1980: 193; Lavers 1993: 257). Nevertheless indigenous African beliefs and practices continued to persist (e.g. Tijani 1993). This becomes quite apparent in the custom of the public appearance of the *mai* behind a veil or a screen. Throughout medieval times Arab writers note this practice in connection with the sultans of Kanem-Borno. In 1352/53 the Arab traveler Ibn Battuta wrote, 'The people of

Burnu are Muslims having a king named Idris who does not appear to the people and does not address them except from behind a curtain' (Levtzion and Hopkins 1981: 302). Such relics of divine kingship have a wide distribution in many complex societies of sub-Saharan and tropical Africa that adhere to indigenous African religions (Lebeuf 1969: 123–252; Reyna 1990: 92–134; Vansina 1966: 32; 1992: 19–26). However, they certainly were not in accordance with the principles of Islam.

All the land was under control of the state and, whether acquired by conquest or submission, belonged to the *mai* (Benisheikh 1983: 79). They bore the title *kema lardema*, i.e., 'owner of the land.' This enabled them to secure their position by giving out fiefs and thus to balance the power of the members of the court. Acquiring a fief could mean enormous access to wealth and power within the empire, and most members of the *kogenawa*, a council formed by members of the nobility, were fief-holders (*cima kura*). They lived in or near the capital because of their active involvement in politics and administration. On their lands the *cima kura* were represented by subordinate officers (*cima gana*) who exercised immediate political and juridical authority and were responsible for tax collection. Power was extended to the local inhabitants through the village heads (*bulama*).

All taxes belonged to the *mai* (Benisheikh 1983; Nur Alkali 1983: 117). Apart from their share of this general income tax, fief-holders provided themselves with additional earnings through private plantations, which were farmed by either free individuals or slaves. Quite often it was members of this influential group of fief-holders who organized the many slave raids that made up the major source of income for the rich and powerful in Borno (Cohen 1967b).

The general social structure has been outlined by von Duisburg (1927; 1942: 56–64). Yet again, when consulting this information one has to bear in mind that it relates to the colonial situation in German Bornu at the beginning of the twentieth century. He distinguished three classes: the free (*kambe*), dependent (*susana*), and slaves (*kalia*). Of course societal structure in Borno was much more complicated than this coarse threefold scheme. For instance the slave class alone was divided into several subgroups (Cohen 1967b;

Mafama 1977). Particularly after the change of dynasty in the early nineteenth century, quite a number of slaves could rise to be powerful titleholders within the state's administration (Brenner, 1973). Most slaves, however, had a less favorable fate. If they were not incorporated into the households, they lived in separate settlements (*kaliari*). These were founded and maintained by the fief-holders and members of the *kogenawa*, and of course the *mai* himself. Many of these settlements surrounded the capital and were dispersed throughout the Yobe valley (Mafama 1977). Denham gives a description of such a slave settlement:

> At Belagana, the sheikh has a large inclosure of huts, within a wall, where he generally has from five hundred to eight hundred slaves of both sexes, under the charge of four eunuchs, who are employed in preparing cotton, and spinning the linen of which the tobes are made. (Denham *et al.* 1826 II: 88)

The free were also quite a diverse group. This is due to the complicated process of the ethnogenesis of the Saharan-speaking Kanuri people, nowadays the governing ethnic group of Borno (Cohen 1967a). While some researchers believe that a 'Kanuri identity' goes back as far as the thirteenth century (e.g. Barkindo 1985; Lange 1993), Seidensticker (1997) has recently stressed that during the nineteenth century still various Chadic and Saharan-speaking groups, although incorporated into the empire, nevertheless retained distinct ethnic identities. Despite this persistence of such distinct identities, the process of 'Kanurization' should have started with the foundation of Gazargamo in the fifteenth century. It was further fostered by the conquests of the rulers of the sixteenth century. Particularly significant for the consolidation of the Sayfuwa state and the 'Kanuri' at this time was the incorporation of the indigenous groups in the Yobe valley (Cohen 1970; Lange 1989; 1993). These appear in the sources as the 'So.' This term was applied to all indigenous groups in the western and southern Chad Basin (Ahmad ibn Furtu in Lange 1987), and probably relates to their custom of living in walled towns, a tradition uncommon in the regions north of the lake where the Sayfuwa came from (Lange 1989). Some of the groups south of Lake Chad were also called 'So' by Ibn Furtu (Lange 1987).

After the foundation of Gazargamo, the rulers of Borno were successful in consolidating the internal social and political structure of the empire. Nevertheless, threats from outside groups continued. Generally the fifteenth and sixteenth centuries can be taken as a time of expansion and on-going conflict with emerging neighboring polities, such as Wandala alongside the Mandara mountains (MacEachern, this volume), the Kotoko princedoms south of Lake Chad (Lebeuf 1969; Gronenborn in press a; Holl 1993; Holl, this volume), and the Hausa city states (Hunwick 1985: 355). Conflict also arose with other, more distant Sudanic states such as the Songhay empire. The latter posed a threat to Borno by extending its influence into Hausaland and occasionally raiding Borno territory (Lavers 1980: 195). This menace led the state to establish firmer relationships with the Turkish Ottoman empire, and thus secure a constant supply of firearms from North Africa (Hunwick 1985: 359).

The adoption of muskets and military training by Turkish instructors of the Bornoan army can be assigned to *mai* Idris Alauma (1564–1600), or maybe his immediate predecessors (Lavers 1980: 197). The achievements of this most ambitious ruler have been documented by Ahmad ibn Furtu (Lange 1987). The account gives a comprehensive description of the various campaigns against neighboring polities. Idris also led strikes against the non-Muslim groups of the 'So,' both in the vicinity of the capital and south of Lake Chad (Ahmad ibn Furtu in Lange 1987: 32–106). Another script (Palmer 1967 I) covers campaigns into Kanem, where Idris tried to re-establish the Sayfuwa domination.

Although actual territorial expansion under the reign of *mai* Idris Alauma seems to have been minor, the subjection of internal non-Muslim groups led to greater consolidation (Hunwick 1985: 354–5). He sought agreement with the southward-expanding Turkish empire in North Africa and with Morocco, by sending delegations to their courts (Lavers 1980: 198). Both attempts were not successful politically, but Idris was able to receive firearms from the Moroccans and was granted liberties for merchants and pilgrims coming from Borno. Under Idris Alauma, Borno was able to extend and secure its influence on the flourishing northward trade. At the end of the sixteenth century the Borno sphere of influence extended from the Fezzan to the south of Lake Chad, and from the Hausa states to the Bahr-el-Ghazal.

After the reign of *mai* Idris an era of stabilization followed, during which occasional invasions by the Tuareg occurred, mainly over control of the trans-Saharan trade (Lavers 1980: 200; 1993: 260). Later during the seventeenth century, conflicts with the Tuareg increased, which resulted in a more defensive military policy and the establishment of Bornoan frontier posts along the northern, eastern, and western borders (Nur Alkali 1978: 326). Between 1630 and 1645 the extensive territory of Kanem-Borno was partly put under the supervision of two provincial governors or viceroys, one for the western provinces with the seat at Nguru, and one for the eastern provinces with the seat at Gazargamo (Nur Alkali 1983: 111). This division was accompanied by the consolidation and incorporation of frontier polities, such as the Kotoko city states and the Manga and Mobber polities (Lavers 1980: 200–3). Economically the seventeenth century was a time of prosperity, as evidenced by the flourishing trans-Saharan trade (Lavers 1994a: 248–52; Nur Alkali 1978: 346–56). In the eighteenth century, however, expansion stagnated and Borno's power began to decline. This became most evident in the continuous quarrels with the neighboring Wandala state during the reign of *mai* Hamdum ibn Dunama (1717–31), and culminated in the invasion of the state under *mai* Ali ibn Dunama (1750–91) in 1781, and the subsequent defeat of the Borno troops (Adeleye 1985: 600; Lavers 1980: 209; MacEachern 1990: 55–7). However, before continuing with the history of the Borno empire and its changes in the turmoils of the early nineteenth century, the archaeological sites of the fifteenth to eighteenth centuries will be described.

Birni Gazargamo, Gambaru, and other sites in the Yobe valley

Impressive archaeological remains from the heyday of the empire have been preserved in the heartland of Borno, around the Yobe valley: the ruins of the metropolis Birni Gazargamo and the palace of Gambaru. (*Birni* means 'capital' or rather 'walled city' in Hausa and the term has been adopted into the Kanuri language (Lange 1987: 114).)

According to oral tradition, the town was built with the help of local rulers (Lange 1987: 115; Lavers 1980: 193). The location was wisely chosen as it lay on the connecting point between the routes to the north as well as to the west toward the Songhai empire (Lavers 1980: 194). The layout of the site becomes evident through aerial photography (Connah 1981: 228), from which a plan was drawn (Bivar and Shinnie, 1962: 2); it is the one reproduced here (Figure 6.3b). The surrounding rampart forms an irregular, elongated circle with a length of 6.7 km (4.2 miles). It mainly consists of loose sand and is heavily eroded. Lavers considers this to have been a local building tradition that was adopted by the Sayfuwa for their capital. However, the rampart has not been excavated and details about its construction are unknown. In some locations an exterior ditch is evident. In addition, shallow interior moats have been observed in the northwestern corner. These and the exterior ditches probably served as extraction pits for the rampart (Migeod 1924: 230). The site must have presented an impressive view:

> . . . but the capital is surrounded by a wall of fourteen feet in height, the foundations of which are from eight to ten feet deep, and which seems to be built with considerable strength. To this defence is given the additional security of a ditch, which encompasses the whole; and care is taken, that at sun-set the seven gates which form the communication with the country shall be shut . . . Bornoo [Birni Gazargamo] is surrounded by a wall, on which, however, there are no guards. (Lucas 1967: 146)

Another early nineteenth-century source was recorded by the German traveler Ulrich Jasper Seetzen (1995: 13) between 1807 and 1809 in Cairo. He recorded the accounts of an informant from Afade, an ancient Kotoko town south of Lake Chad: 'Burnu [Birni Gazargamo] has a number of town gates and is surrounded with a high, strong wall which has steps on the inner side and is built of stone and mud.' From this description one might infer a wall similar to the one at Kukawa (Figure 6.7), although it seems somewhat difficult to reconstruct the sandy ramparts of Gazargamo (Connah 1981: 229) in such manner. Other aspects of

Seetzen's account are also inconsistent with the archaeological record. Indeed, one wonders whether his informant had ever visited the town. Moreover, the account was doubted by Seetzen (1995: 13) himself.

The number of gates in the walls has been subject to continuing debate. While the chronicles recount seven gates (Lavers 1971a: 41), today about ten entrances may be discerned (Hambolu 1993: 6). It is known, however, that the Fulani, when attacking the city, destroyed portions of the wall (Lange 1987: 115), thus some of the modern openings might actually have been wall portions destroyed during the raid. Lucas' (1967: 146) account suggests that the entrances into the city must have had gates to close, whether with a clay gatehouse, as is reported for other towns (Abba 1992), or a wooden structure of yet unknown kind, is a question which remains to be solved, as the collapse of the ramparts and their erosion has completely obscured any possible remains of gatehouse construction. However, Walter Oudney, a member of the first British expedition into the Central Sudan in the years of 1822–25, and who visited the site 14 years after its abandonment, writes in a letter of 1823: 'The walls of the town are thick & high and partly formed of Clay & partly of brick' (Oudney 1966: 565). This might indicate more solid structures—possibly gatehouses—now completely collapsed.

The most figurative description of building interiors is provided by Lucas:

> . . . for even in the capital, the houses, straggling wide of each other, are placed without method or rule; and the obvious propriety of giving to the principal mosque, a central situation, exhibits the only proof of attention to general convenience . . . Bornoo [Birni Gazargamo] though a town of greater extent than Tripoli, consists of a multitude of houses, so irregularly placed that the spaces between them cannot be called streets. It is furnished with mosques, which are constructed of brick and of earth; and with schools, in which the Koran is taught, as in the principal towns of Barbary. (Lucas 1967: 144–5)

Hugh Clapperton, another member of the British expedition, described the ruins in his diary:

> [Monday, May 26th, 1823] After riding little better than a ¼ of an hour we arrived & entered at the eastern gate we rode down a

Figure 6.5 The ruins of Birni Gazargamo in 1854 (from Barth, 1857–59 III: 30). The circular feature is the partly overgrown wall, the central heap is the brick ruins of the palace. The conical tower in the distance might have been a mosque.

wide street which lies in a straight line and as broad as the best streets in London – we came to the ruins of the Sultan's palace which forms an immense mass of brick walls some of which are yet about 30 feet high which when inhabited had been plastered over. Omar Gana who had lived in the City when it was in its glory conducted us through the ruins pointing out to us the different apartments of the palace & the houses of the Sultan's head men – which were all built of brick – outside & cemented together with the same Materials viz cow dung & Clay mixed with straw [. . .], we ascended the Wall to the West and rode round the north side, here Omar had pointed out to us the quarters which the Arabs & Tibbos occupied, there had been no straw huts or coozies – all had been clay or bricks with excellent Squares & Shady trees [. . .] (Lockhart 1996: 141)

The interior of the site today is more or less plain, which already seems to have been the case by the mid-nineteenth century when the only prominent features were the palace walls and the surrounding compounds (Figure 6.5; Barth 1857–59 III: 31). According to Clapperton the interior buildings must have been clay wall and brick houses. These had completely eroded away within the 46 years that had passed between the abandonment of the city and Barth's visit. The *mai*'s palace and the compounds of other dignitaries incorporated fired bricks, but these were only used for courtyard walls (Connah 1981: 232). The palace building, or buildings, must have been constructed out of short-lived materials. The fired bricks were of high quality as Oudney's letter shows: '[. . .] the abode of the Sultan covers a great extent of ground and is entirely built of brick that is much superior to the brick of our country, its texture fine, and external surface has a fine gloss' (Oudney 1966: 565).

Fired bricks constitute a foreign element in the architecture of the Chad Basin and their origin has been subject to debate. Their first appearance in Borno seems to be at Garou-mélé. At Gazargamo, local oral traditions hold that craftsmen from Tripolis built the palace (Seidensticker 1983a: 65). Another version recounts that local builders had obtained the knowledge in the North African metropolis and applied it in Borno (Alexander 1912: 183). And indeed the late eighteenth-century description in Lucas (1967: 145) confirms the results of the excavation: 'The King's palace, surrounded by high walls, and forming a kind of citadel, is built, perhaps with a view to security, in a corner of the town.' The latter, of course, is not correct—as can be seen from the town plan (Figure 6.3b). Also in the accounts of relations of a certain Ali Eisami, we find a description of the palace as an elevated construction: 'he [the *mai*] and the Kanum priest [al-Kanemi] went to the Capital against the Pula [Fulani]; and when they saw the top of the Capital, all the Pula arose and met them on the way for an attack' (Koelle 1968: 223). The passage 'top of the Capital' certainly indicates that the palace could be seen from the far distance in the flat lands of northern Borno.

The central mosque was also constructed in fired clay bricks (Barth, 1857–59 III: 30; Lucas, 1967: 145; Seetzen, 1995: 13). The structure to the west of the central palace has been interpreted as being the remains of this very mosque (Lange 1987: 116). The *dendal* of Gazargamo, the central place common to all Kanuri towns (Abba 1992: 16), should then have been at the western side of the palace with the central mosque close to it (Figure 6.3b). A few other burnt brick clay foundations exist, the most impressive of which are the remains of the *kaigama*'s palace, the highest-ranking general and commander of the army. Here the respective ward (*kaigamari)* would have been located (Lavers 1971a: 42).

An approximation of the number of former inhabitants of Gazargamo is given by Dixon Denham, a third member of the British expedition. He writes that 'Old Birnie [Gazargamo] covered a space of five or six square miles, and is said to have had a population of two hundred thousand souls' (Denham in Denham *et al.* 1826 I: 211–12). However, this number appears exaggerated. More likely might be an estimate by Salih Isharku, who wrote about 1658:

> In Gazargamo there were four Friday mosques. Each of these had an Imam for Friday who led the Friday prayer with the people. At each mosque there were twelve thousand worshippers ... At Gazargamo there were six hundred and sixty roads cleared and widened called Le. Sixty of these roads were well known to the Amir, for he traversed them, but many of these roads were unknown to the Amir since he did not traverse them and so did not know them. (Salih Isharku in Palmer 1970: 34).

According to this text fragment the population should not have exceeded 50,000 people, a large but not impossible figure if seen in connection with other cities in the Sudan at this time.

So far the only archaeological work that has been conducted within the ruins of this once enormous metropolis is Connah's (1981: 220–3) excavation. He inserted a trench into an interior courtroom of the central palace up to a depth of 3.5m. From his excavation it seems quite possible that within the brick walls erosion has led to a deposit of about 2m of windblown sand. However, those layers might have already partly accumulated when the palace was still inhabited. The wall remains reach down almost 2m. The bricks were mortared with mud and the wall was reported to have been 1.19 meters wide at the present ground surface (Connah 1981: 232). This observation supports the impression one gets from the sources cited above. The palace of the Sayfuwa, when still erect, must have been an impressive sight: a symbol of the absolute power and authority of the rulers. Nowadays little of the former impressive remains has survived on the surface, as looting for the bricks at the beginning of the twentieth century (and possibly already during the nineteenth) has drastically accelerated the process of degradation (Migeod 1924: 229). Today the area inside the ramparts and the vicinity is uninhabited, except for temporary Fulani camps.

Another royal palace along the Yobe valley is Gambaru, which was also described by Denham (Denham *et al.* 1826 I: 213–14). The site of Gambaru has been mapped by Seidensticker

(1983a: 67) and the plan is reproduced here (Figure 6.3c). All walls are built out of fired bricks. According to information given to Migeod (1924: 226), Gambaru was built before Gazargamo but had to be abandoned because of repeated floods. In 1817 the traveler Ritchie collected oral histories from an informant from Borno, stating that Gambaru had been built by Christians who had lived there in former times (cited by Lavers 1971a: 45). It is very unlikely that the palace had been built by Christians. Nevertheless, the account may indicate that Europeans had lived at the court in Borno, probably as slaves. Gambaru was never a capital, but rather a refuge or part-time residence for the rulers of Gazargamo, possibly built by the *maira*, the king mother of Idris Alauma (Lavers 1971a: 44–45). The site has been investigated archaeologically by Hambolu (1993; 1996). He conducted excavations at a refuse mound immediately northeast of the palace structures, and unearthed several foundations of circular buildings constructed out of fired bricks. These foundations might offer a clue as to how the interior of the courtrooms once looked.

As already indicated above, the pottery recovered in Gambaru and Gazargamo is a further development of the style which was recovered by Connah at the Yobe valley mounds of Yau and Ajere, dating between the ninth and thirteenth centuries. Vessels from Gambaru are decorated with twisted strip rouletting on the body while the neck and shoulder are often covered by a red slip. Open bowls are often completely covered by red slip. This red slip is sometimes further decorated with zig-zag and triangular motifs in *sgraffito* technique (Figure 6.6, 1–2).

Gazargamo and Gambaru are not the only sites in the Yobe valley. In fact Oudney writes: 'There are marks of many large towns in the vicinity of these places [Gazargamo and Gambaru] and there can be no doubt the country was thickly inhabited [. . .]' (Oudney 1966: 565). Indeed, analyses of air photographs and satellite images have led to the discovery not only of abandoned walled settlements in the vicinity of Gazargamo, but also of wide areas with traces of abandoned field systems, which have been produced by wind erosion of intensively exploited soils (Thiemeyer 1997: 106–8). There are other sites in the Yobe valley where the fired brick technique was applied, the most

remarkable ones being Lergam, which is said to have been built in the eighteenth century (Lavers 1971a: 47; Seidensticker 1981: 242; 1991a: 18), and Nguru, after 1630 the seat of the governor of the western provinces (Lavers 1971a: 47). The most impressive building of fired brick, and in fact still inhabited, is the palace at Machina, the residence of a descendant of a Borno *mai* (Lavers 1971b: 3). The exact date of its foundation is not clear but oral traditions hold that it was built in the seventeenth or early eighteenth century (Migeod 1924: 278).

Of all the palaces built out of fired brick, Machina is the only structure which has survived to the present day; the others were given up before or by the beginning of the nineteenth century. Gambaru was abandoned at an unknown point in time (Lavers 1971a: 46; Seidensticker 1981), and Nguru and Gazargamo were violently destroyed by the invading Fulani in 1808 (see below).

The archaeological visibility of imperial expansion: the pottery sequences of the settlement mounds in the southern Chad Basin

A totally different group of sites are the mounds in the southern Chad Basin. Since all construction was done with molded clay, architectural remains are hard to discern. Nevertheless, the deeply stratigraphied sites contain good evidence of the increasing expansion of Kanem-Borno into these territories and the related change in material culture. As mentioned above, *mai* Idris Alauma moved against rebellious groups in this very region. The rulers of Kanem-Borno had attempted to expand into the area before: during and after the thirteenth century this region was continuously ravaged by slave raids. Possibly under this pressure local princedoms had evolved by the fourteenth century. By the fifteenth and sixteenth centuries these princedoms had accumulated considerable political, religious, and economic power. Such can be inferred from the writings of the Italian geographer Giovanni Lorenzo Anania who, in his *L'universale fabrica del mondo, overo cosmografia* of 1573, describes the southern Chad Basin in detail and specifically mentions the trade in iron that was smelted in the Mandara mountains and then traded northward, to

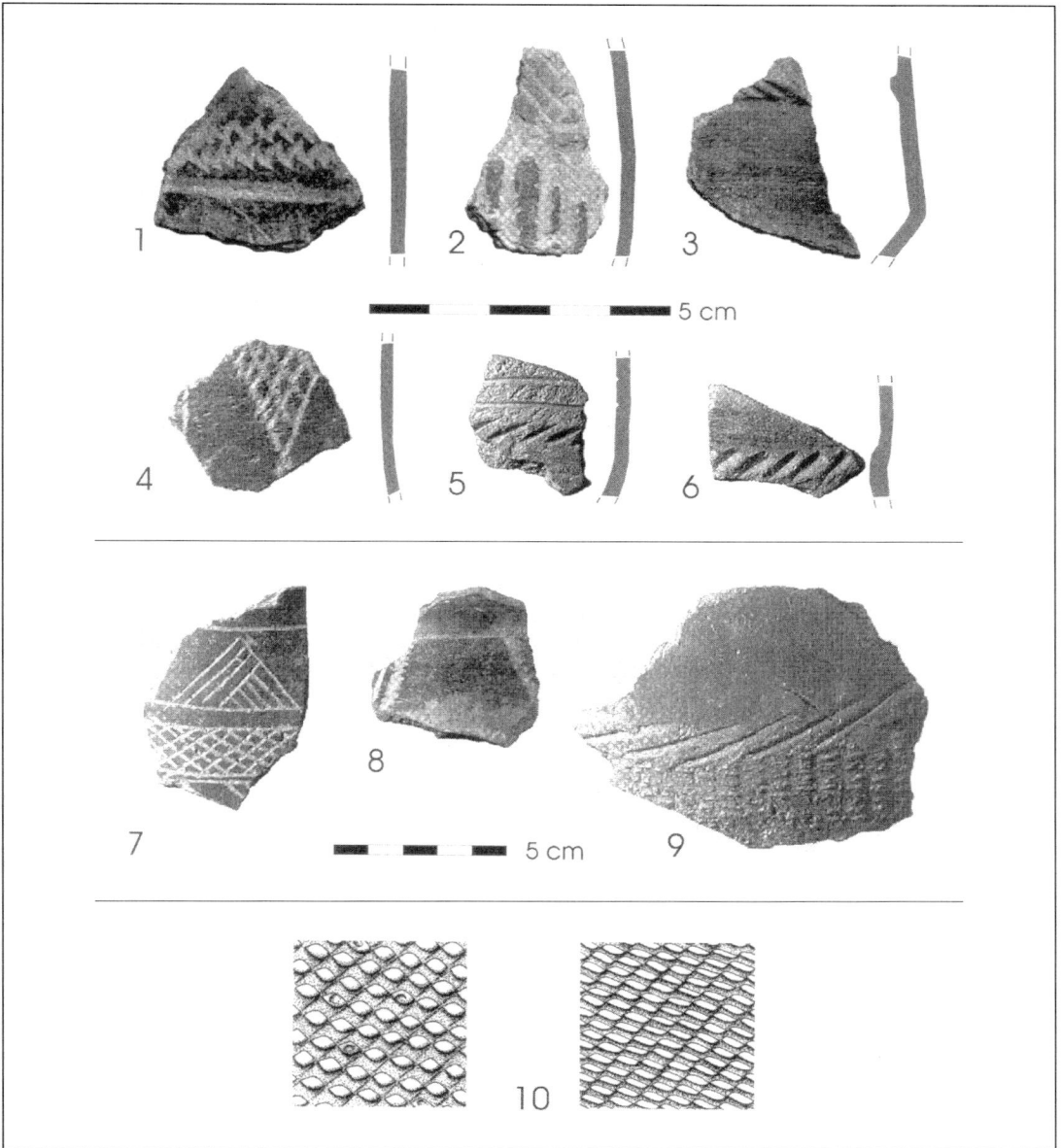

Figure 6.6 Pottery from site of Gambaru, Kukawa, and Dikwa. 1 and 2) Gambaru, *sgraffito* and burnished slip; 3) Gambaru, applied band with incisions and burnished slip; 4) Kukawa, *sgraffito* and burnished slip; 5) Kukawa, incisions; 6) Kukawa, applied band with incisions and burnished slip; 7 and 8) Dikwa, *sgraffito* and burnished slip; 9) Dikwa, incisions and twisted strip roulette; 10) pattern of twisted strip roulette. (Number 3 courtesy Musa Hambolu; numbers 7–9 after Gronenborn and Magnavita 2000.)

Borno (Lange and Berthoud 1972: 350). Up until then the polities had managed to remain largely independent, notwithstanding the slave plundering and military campaigns against them during the fourteenth century (Barth 1857–59 II: 33; Lange 1977: 75). This, however, changed when Idris Alauma advanced with his campaigns toward the lands south of Lake Chad. As Ahmad ibn Furtu's account of these attacks suggests, they must have had considerable consequences for the indigenous population. Villages were destroyed, the population decimated and led into slavery or driven away.

One of the towns specifically mentioned is Amsaka, which was besieged, subsequently destroyed, and the entire population either killed or led into slavery (ibn Furtu in Lange 1987: 58–65). Amsaka was never investigated archaeologically but these processes should have left traces in sites nearby too. Indeed, Connah (1976: 347) had suggested an abandonment of Daima in connection with the conquests of Idris Alauma. However, this hypothesis has to be slightly modified as the clay pipes found in the uppermost layers of Daima cannot have appeared before 1600, suggesting that the site must have been occupied until the beginning of the seventeenth century. Hence, the abandonment cannot be linked directly to the campaigns of *mai* Idris, but more likely to population movements after the territory became incorporated into Borno and local resistance was finally broken. Archaeologically the increasing dominance of Kanem-Borno can be observed in changes in pottery styles. In Daima as well as in Ngala, pottery with twisted strip roulette decoration, so typical for the eighth- and ninth-century Yobe sites and fifteenth-century Gazargamo and Gambaru (see above), appears in the uppermost layers (Connah 1981: 118–19; Gronenborn 1998: 236–8). At Ngala the earliest appearance of this ware can be dated after the fifteenth century (Figure 6.4), hence to the time of increasing pressure from Borno. The spread of twisted strip roulette decorated pottery into regions south of the lake is thus seen in connection with the extension of the power sphere of the Borno empire after the conquests of Idris Alauma. After this time the Sayfuwa began to found satellite towns in the newly acquired region, from which the territory was controlled. It is quite possible that from these centers Borno material culture spread out and was gradually received by the surrounding population. Nevertheless, they maintained a status of ethnic semi-independence up until the nineteenth century (Gronenborn 2000; Gronenborn and Magnavita 2000).

The dawn: The Fulani *jihad* and the nineteenth century

In the year of 1804 the Fulani Islamic scholar and teacher Usuman dan Fodio started a *jihad* against the 'pagan' polities in west central Sudan, a movement that resulted in the founding of the Sokoto Caliphate. After subjugating Hausaland, the Fulani marched toward Birni Gazargamo and the town was captured in 1808. The ruling *mai* fled and abdicated in favor of his son, who was able to reoccupy Gazargamo briefly, but was finally driven out of the ancient capital in 1809. After this date Gazargamo remained abandoned. During these years of agony, one man came to back the weakened Sayfuwa leaders: *mallam* (a religious scholar) al-Hajj Muhammad al-Amin ibn Muhammad al-Kanemi. It was he who reorganized the Borno army after their defeat and marched against the invaders. After defeating the Fulani troops, he requested the fief of Ngornu, which was granted him by the *mai* (Brenner 1973: 35). Al-Kanemi soon gained enormous power and managed to put himself at the top of the state (Cohen and Brenner 1984: 95–110). In 1814 al-Kanemi gathered his followers, founded his own town, Kukawa, and took the title *shehu* (Kanuri for sheikh). But still, although opposed by the Sayfuwa, he did not depose the *mai*. During the following years al-Kanemi began to reorganize the political system of Borno (Cohen and Brenner 1984: 105–6), strengthened its military organization, and secured its borders. One of the most noteworthy reforms in the administrative structure was the large-scale incorporation of slaves. The office of *khachalla*—slave army commander—stems from this reform (Brenner 1973: 58; Nur Alkali 1977: 257). With the death of al-Kanemi in 1837/38 tensions between the Sayfuwa *mai* and the successor of al-Kanemi, *shehu* Umar, rose again, and in 1846 (after the *mai* tried to overthrow the *shehu* with the help of invading forces from Wadai), he and his immediate successor were put to death. With this incident the reign of the Sayfuwa dynasty came to an end, after over 1,000 years.

During the reign of *shehu* Umar, Borno was visited by Heinrich Barth (1857–58; 1857–59). Barth traveled on behalf of the British government, together with the Englishman James

Richardson and the German astronomer Richard Overweg—both of whom did not survive the strenuous journey of five years' duration (1851–55). Also during Umar's regime two more German travelers visited Borno, Gerhard Rohlfs in 1866–67 and Gustav Nachtigal in 1870–73. Nachtigal traveled on behalf of the King of Prussia. He was to establish relations with Borno, which of course had profound economic implications as the expanding European powers sought trade partners in Africa.

The travelers' host, *shehu* Umar, governed Borno until his death in 1880/81 and, after two followers died within the next four years, was succeeded by his fourth son, *shehu* Hashemi, in 1885. During those years Borno's power and its influence on the neighboring polities was in the process of slow but steady decline, and the increasing European pressure to end the slave trade weakened the economic basis of the state. Moreover, alternative export goods such as ivory and ostrich feathers lost their value when Europe was struck by an economic crisis and the demand for luxury goods decreased (Cohen and Brenner 1984: 114). By that time the future colonial powers were beginning to expand inward from their coastal bases. Yet before opening the last chapter of Borno's pre-colonial history, we shall turn to the most remarkable archaeological site of the nineteenth century.

Kukawa

Al-Kanemi's reorganization of the empire and his centralization of power made his capital Kukawa, built in 1814, not only the focal point of the Borno empire but also, thanks to flourishing trade, one of the great metropolises of nineteenth-century sub-Saharan Africa. This fame attracted the European travelers who described the town extensively. So writes Barth about his entry into the city:

> Proceeding with some hesitation toward the white clay wall which encircles the town, and which, from a little distance, could scarcely be distinguished from the adjoining ground, I entered the gate, being gazed at by a number of people collected here, and who were still more surprised when I inquired for the residence of the sheikh. Then, passing the little daily market, which was crowded with people, I rode along the déndal, or promenade,

straight up to the palace, which borders the promenade towards the east. It is flanked by a very indifferent mosque, built likewise of clay with a tower at its N.W. corner, while houses of grandees inclose the place on the north and south sides. (Barth 1857–59 I: 591)

Nowadays the remains of the outer walls are almost completely eroded away, but a depiction from Monteil (1895) gives the nineteenth-century impression (Figure 6.7). The *dendal* described here was depicted by Barth (1857–59 I: 590) and later by Nachtigal (1967 I: 620).

Kukawa, at least from 1846 onwards, consisted of two parts—each with a *dendal*, a palace, and a mosque (Figure 6.8a; Seidensticker 1991b: 47). One was simply called the 'Western Town' (Kanuri: *bula futube*); here lived the foreign merchants and entrepreneurs and also the visiting Europeans. The 'Eastern Town' (Kanuri: *bula gedebe*) was mainly reserved for the *shehu* and his courtiers, state administrators, and dignitaries. After the eastern section was finally finished in 1846 the *shehus* seem to have resided mostly there. Figure 6.9 depicts the *dendal* of the Western Town. The palace in this part was smaller, consisting of two double-storey buildings with surrounding courts (Lenfant 1905: 253), whereas in the eastern part the palace consisted of three large buildings and several compounds with numerous small reed huts for the *shehu*'s women and slaves (Rohlfs 1868b: 1). Both parts were surrounded by walls which were precipitous and plain from the outside but stepped on the inside, with a wall walk on top (Rohlfs 1868a: 57), which is typical for Central Sudanic defense architecture. In between the two walled sections was a ward, or rather two, which were not fenced in; furthermore, several compounds or clusters of compounds existed in the immediate vicinity of the twin town. In the majority of cases the compounds (*fato*) were surrounded by clay walls and the interior buildings by reed huts (*ngim*), of which several belonged to one unit. Wealthier individuals owned compounds with one square clay building (*soro*), which in many cases had just one single room, surrounded by several reed huts which were usually inhabited by the women. Houses of rich traders or dignitaries were larger with several rooms and courtyards. The entire town was dominated by a large number of

Figure 6.7   View of the wall of Kukawa in 1892 (from Monteil 1895: 322).

trees and Rohlfs (1868a: 58) calls it a 'forest town.'

Nachtigal (1967 I: 613) and Rohlfs (1868a: 58) mention several markets. The largest and most important was held weekly on Mondays on the western edge of the town outside the walls (Rohlfs 1872: 5). Others were held daily and at various locations across the town, mainly on the *dendal* of the Western Town (Nachtigal 1967 I: 611). Products sold in these markets were cattle, sheep, and goats or crops such as millet and sorghum. Other noteworthy products were wild rice (Nachtigal 1967 I: 655), wheat, and barley. The latter were cultivated around the capital and seem to have been consumed only by wealthier individuals (Nachtigal 1967 I: 654). Maize was also part of the diet (Nachtigal 1967 I: 655). Cotton came from the lakeshore area (Nachtigal 1967 I: 683) and from the region south of Lake Chad around Dikwa (Rohlfs 1872: 60; Dominik 1908: 162), while butter and honey—traditional pastoralist products—were mostly traded by the Arab groups (Nachtigal 1967 I: 687).

The Europeans were quite interested in the commercial potential of Borno, and Rohlfs (1872: 61) lists the export goods. He particularly mentions horses, cattle, donkeys, sheep,

goats, game, ivory, ostrich feathers, indigo, cereals, groundnuts, leather, dried fish, skins, and slaves. Slaves, even at the end of the nineteenth century, were the main export article of Borno and Nachtigal gives an account of the slave market in Kukawa:

> In the eastern section of the south side of the market slave dealers have set up large stalls where, protected from the sun and rain, their wares, with or without chains, are displayed in long rows . . . Old men, tired of life, sit alongside small children snatched away from the tender care of a loving mother before they could retain any picture of her in their memories. Among repulsive-looking women, whose faded skin hangs loosely on their fleshless bones, and who have become apathetic through toil and misery, there are bright young girls, their well-rounded figures in the first bloom of youth, with coquettish headdress, washed clean and glistening with butter, who look hopefully into the future. (Nachtigal 1971–87 II: 215–16)

At the time of his visit in 1866/67 Rohlfs (1868a: 57) calculated the number of inhabitants of Kukawa at 60,000. In 1892 the town was visited again by a European traveler, the French Lieutenant-Colonel Monteil (1895:

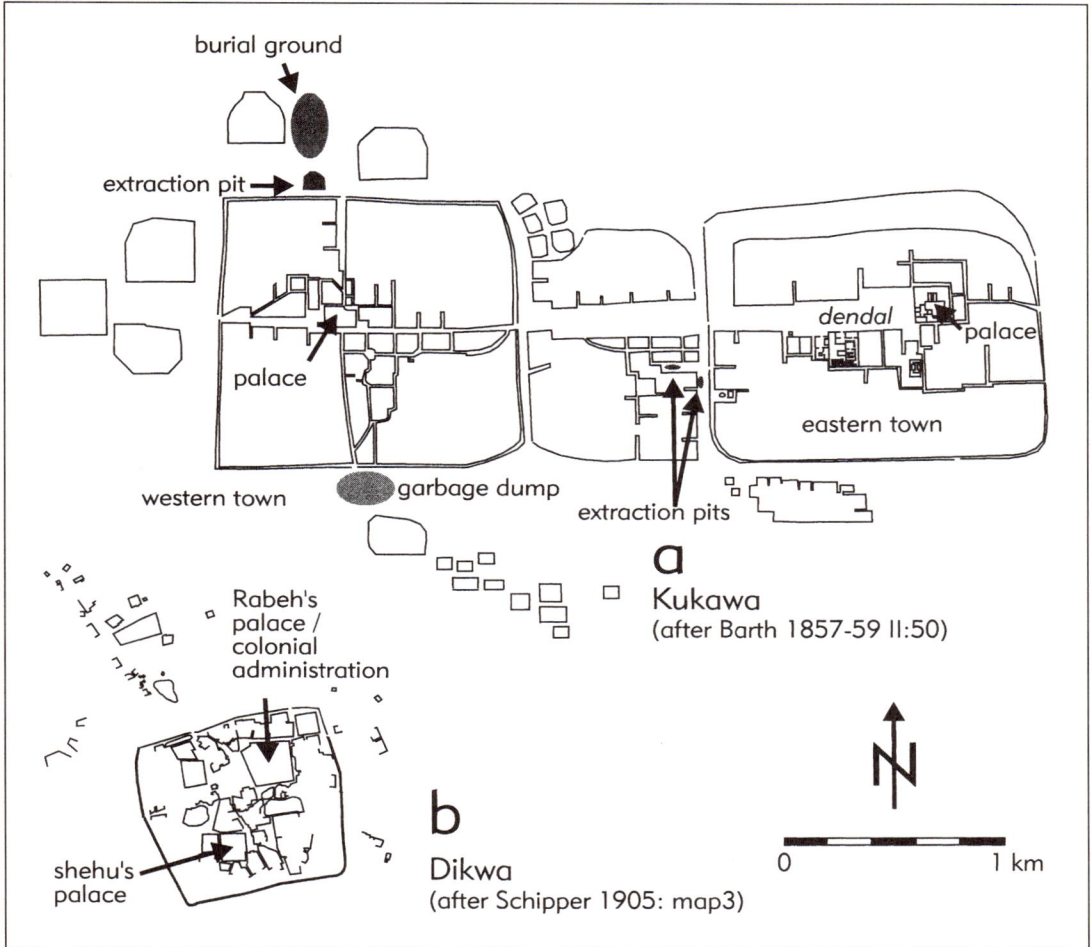

Figure 6.8 Plans of the capitals of the nineteenth and twentieth centuries.

318–58). He gave the last eyewitness account before Kukawa was destroyed by the troops of Rabeh in 1893 (see below). On this occasion the town was extensively ravaged, with books and records burned or looted (Migeod 1924: 177; Morland in Seidensticker 1992: 42). After 1902 *shehu* Garbai attempted to rebuild parts of the town, but soon realized that it would be an idle undertaking (Hogben and Kirk-Greene 1966: 338; Migeod 1924: 103; Morland in Seidensticker 1992: 41). In 1906 the *shehu* of Borno moved to Yerwa, close to Maiduguri where the British station was (Migeod 1924: 103; Seidensticker 1983b). Migeod (1924: 169–71) visited Kukawa in 1922 and gives a description of the remains; evidently the ruins

of the *shehu*'s palace in the Eastern Town were still partly in use.

Today Kukawa is a minor town and the seat of a local government administration. The Western Town is completely abandoned and leveled. Only with difficulty can the remains of the surrounding walls be made out. The only architectural remains that can be seen now are the tombs of the al-Kanemi *shehus* which stood inside the eastern palace compound (Migeod 1924: 11; Rohlfs 1868b: 1) and are nowadays protected by a concrete brick shelter. The entrance to the royal compound depicted in a 1963 photograph (Connah 1981: 242, Figure 10.11) has now eroded away. No archaeological work has been undertaken in

Figure 6.9 View of *dendal* in the western town of Kukawa around 1853 (from Barth 1857–59, vol. I: 590).

Kukawa or its vicinity, except for two brief surveys in 1993 and 1995 (Gronenborn and Magnavita 2000). Within the area of the *shehu*'s palace in the Eastern Town typical *sgraffito*-decorated pottery (Figure 6.6, 4–6) and some fragments of imported china were collected. The local pottery resembles that of Gambaru (Figure 6.6, 1–3). The site is worthy of investigation, not only to clarify the town layout, but also to get a deeper understanding of the metropolis' interaction with its environment. How did the agricultural slave settlements (*kaliari*) in its vicinity (Figure 6.1) contribute to the supply of the city? Can these slave settlements or quarters be differentiated archaeologically from hamlets of free farmers? One example of slave treatment, which should show archaeologically, is reported by Barth (1857–59 II: 50): on the town plan (Figure 6.8) he specifically mentions that before the southern gate 'all offal and dead bodies of camels and cattle and sometimes even of slaves' were thrown. Such unofficial 'burial grounds' might be much more widespread in the archaeological record and are not only a remarkable evidence of the treatment of some of the slaves in Borno, but could also serve as

an analogy for similar circumstances elsewhere (Gronenborn in press).

The aftermath: Rabeh and the colonial powers

Weakened by political instability and economic deterioration at the end of the nineteenth century, the empire faced the most serious attack since the Fulani invasion of 1804. What was to become the defeat of the al-Kanemi dynasty began in the Nilotic Sudan in 1879. The Egyptian army subdued the militias of several powerful slave traders who had built up state-like institutions in the Bahr-el-Ghazal and operated from Khartoum, one of their most successful leaders being Zubeir Pascha (von Oppenheim 1902: 9–14). One of his commanders, Rabeh, took advantage of the turmoil following the defeat of the slave traders. He gathered a force of soldiers around him and headed west. Still being chased by the Egyptian troops, the warlord nevertheless subdued several smaller polities, and finally challenged Wadai. This plan, however, failed and he was forced to move further southwest and threatened Bagirmi, the state immediately southeast of Borno (Lavers 1984; 1994b). *Shehu* Hashemi of Borno did not realize the danger and assisted Bagirmi only halfheartedly. The battle was won by Rabeh and he immediately set out for Borno, plundering and destroying towns on his way. Rabeh defeated one of the Borno generals who was sent against him, and then destroyed the hastily gathered and untrained troops of *shehu* Hashemi south of Kukawa. The court fled, leaving the capital. Early in the year 1893 Rabeh turned toward Kukawa, drove its inhabitants away, and destroyed the capital.

Rabeh abandoned the old capital and established himself in Dikwa, a town bordering the vast clay plains south of Lake Chad (von Oppenheim 1902: 48–50). In the same year, on November 15, 1893, this area had been assigned to Cameroon in a treaty between Germany and England. For a short period of time Rabeh was able to control a vast territory in the Sudan, reaching from the Sokoto empire to the Mahdist empire in Egypt, and from the Adamawa Emirate to the northern shores of Lake Chad. Yet his reign of terror, as it is still remembered by the Kanuri people in Borno, was not to last long. Too fragile were the bonds that he tried to tie to the neighboring states. Also, the major income of the former rulers of Borno, the trans-Saharan trade to Murzuk and Tripoli, became increasingly difficult because the slave trade with North Africa was continually threatened by the expansion of European influence in Algeria and Egypt. Furthermore the loss of control of the northern territories of Borno enabled the Tuareg to intervene in the trade (von Oppenheim 1902: 67). Rabeh's attempt to survive economically by linking up with the expanding Royal Niger Company was unsuccessful (von Oppenheim 1902: 69).

French troops finally put an end to Rabeh's regime in a dreadful campaign, resulting in the death of the French commander Lamy, as well as Rabeh during the final battle in 1900 (Gentil 1902). One of Rabeh's sons, Fadl Allah, managed to continue a guerrilla war until he also was defeated and killed in 1901. The French reinstalled the old al-Kanemi dynasty and put Omar Sanda, *shehu* Hashemi's eldest son, into power (von Oppenheim 1902: 186; Gentil 1902: 250). He was overthrown shortly afterwards, also because he did not meet the French indemnity payment requirements, and his brother Garbai became *shehu* in Dikwa. In 1902 the British moved to Borno in order to establish their authority that they felt was threatened by the French presence, and installed themselves at Maiduguri. Soon afterwards Garbai left Dikwa for the British territory, with a large body of former Rabeh troops, and was appointed *shehu* of Borno (Dominik 1908: 152). In Dikwa, the French enthroned a cousin of *shehu* Garbai, Sanda Mandarama, and by doing so initiated the separation of the al-Kanemi dynasty. Borno was now divided into two traditional political entities, the Dikwa Emirate and the Borno Emirate (Hogben and Kirk-Greene 1966: 307–9). Afterwards, in 1902 the Germans established their garrison in Dikwa (Dominik 1908, von Oppenheim 1902: 155) and French troops retreated to their fort in Kousseri. The region remained under German control until 1915 when the French reconquered northernmost Cameroon (Ferrandi 1928; Surén 1934).

The Dikwa Emirate was handed over to the British in 1916 and became a mandated territory under the League of Nations in 1922. Later, in 1942 the seat of the Emir of Dikwa was moved to Bama, but the old colonial borders still survive in the delineation of the Dikwa Emirate as a part of today's Borno State of Nigeria (Hogben and Kirk-Greene 1966: 352; Map 15).

Dikwa

The sources which might hint at the roots of Dikwa are discussed by Adam (1990). He gives most credit to a local oral tradition that claims that the town was founded by one of the Sayfuwa rulers because of the fertility of the area and as an extension of power into the lands south of the lake. The list of rulers of Dikwa (*dikwama*) seems to go back to the sixteenth century. According to Adam the *dikwama* were able to rule relatively independently and develop their own political structures (Adam 1990: 4). With the general decline of the Borno Empire and the heavy taxes imposed on the inhabitants at the end of the nineteenth century, the loyalty of the small 'states' bordering Borno's heartland weakened, and Dikwa broke away with the advent of Rabeh when *dikwama* Adam submitted to the warlord and joined the invading troops with his followers.

Denham (Denham *et al*. 1826: 144) saw

Dikwa as a large walled town, governed by a sultan subject to the *shehu* of Borno, with 'a population of thirty thousand.' At the time of Barth, who visited Dikwa in 1851, it was a town of some 25,000 inhabitants, and surrounded by an impressive, 10-m-high wall in good condition (Barth, 1857–59 II: 329–34). Rohlfs (1872: 23) later described Dikwa as a town of minor importance and completely controlled by Kukawa. The town walls were still standing at that time but obviously were in a state of decay. The sultan inhabited a palace structure larger than the other buildings. This was probably the palace later rebuilt by Rabeh, which was described as a most impressive sight by various early colonial writers (Dominik 1908: 148; Gentil 1902: 246). Although the French campaign against Dikwa resulted in the partial destruction of the stronghold, large areas of the town remained intact (Figure 6.8b). The palace was occupied by the colonial troops and the Germans used many of the old buildings and fortifications to build their barracks (Dominik 1908: 151). The *shehu* took quarters in one of the palaces of Rabeh's son (Figure 6.8b). The German garrison was abandoned without a fight during the French conquest of northern Cameroon in 1915 (Ferrandi 1928; Surén 1934). Dikwa soon came under British domination and the district officer installed himself in Rabeh's palace. The other remains of Rabeh's town were left to decay. In 1921 when Migeod (1924: 117) visited Dikwa, he described the surrounding wall as being almost leveled. Dikwa today is a medium-sized town northeast of Maiduguri, on the border of the vast *firki* plains south of Lake Chad. The site of the old palace is now under the protection of the National Commission of Museums and Monuments, and parts of the buildings have been re-erected (Adam 1990; Seidensticker 1990). A museum has recently been opened at the site. Other remains of Rabeh's times have mostly disappeared, and modern Dikwa has expanded to the northwest of the former town (Seidensticker 1990).

In 1996 a test excavation was conducted near Rabeh's palace (Gronenborn and Magnavita 2000). Extensive ash layers and several pits were found. The ash layers are interpreted as indicators of the partial destruction of the palace during the French campaign of 1900–02. The pits may relate to the French looting of the site: the usurper was thought to have hidden treasure under his palace (Gronenborn and Magnavita, 2000). No evidence for buildings predating Rabeh's palace was discernible. The pottery assemblage has a strong stylistic and typological resemblance to the pottery tradition in the area today. Again, vessels with twisted strip rouletting and *sgraffito* decoration resemble those of Kukawa and Gambaru (Figure 6.6, 7–9). But, as in Ngala, there are notable stylistic differences from earlier pottery traditions in the region (Gronenborn 2000; Gronenborn and Magnavita, 2000). Equally, as in Ngala, the massive appearance of the new style should date to the later nineteenth century (Gronenborn and Magnavita 2000). By that time the local population had begun to adopt the Kanuri language and the ethnic self-identification of the local population gradually began to change (Gronenborn 2000). Indeed, the incorporation of outside ethnic groups into the empire and their 'Kanurization' is a continuous process in the wider region up to this day (Cyffer *et al.* 1996). Therefore, as already explained, the spread of the ceramic tradition from the Yobe valley southward into the lands south of Lake Chad is interpreted as an archaeologically visible expression of ethnic change interrelated with the expansion of the power sphere of Borno (Connah 1978: 21; Gronenborn and Magnavita 2000). While at first Yobe-style pottery appears only gradually and in small amounts aside from local ware, it dominates the spectrum during the nineteenth century and thereafter. The local population had adopted aspects of Kanuri material culture associated with an ethnic identity that seemed politically more promising in the Kanem-Borno empire.

Dikwa was the last pre-colonial capital of Borno. In the twentieth century the importance of the town has been reduced. Maiduguri became the seat of the British colonial administration for the Borno Province and, much later after independence, the government of Borno State. As before, historically a good deal of information is available (e.g. Kirk-Greene 1958; Mukhtar 1992; Seidensticker 1983b) but archaeologically no research has been undertaken at all. Again, the potential would be there: Liberty Village, for instance, where freed slaves without family ties were settled, is located in the vicinity of the city (Seidensticker 1978).

An outlook: possibilities and prospects for Historical Archaeology in the central *bilad al-sudan*

In this paper I have attempted to summarize what is presently known about the history and archaeology of one of Africa's oldest and longest-lasting empires. Over the centuries its economic basis had been the trans-Saharan trade, the main export good being slaves, which were acquired through raids against the surrounding non-Muslim groups. Often territorial expansion began with such slave raids, and when the local population was weakened their political and social institutions were incorporated into the state system. A reasonably well-researched example is the southern Chad Basin. Through a combination of historical and archaeological research it was possible to link the gradual change in the local ceramic tradition to the expansion of the empire into this region. This change in pottery style is also paralleled by the appearance of beads of possible North African or Mediterranean origin, and it may well be that some of these beads were exchanged for local slaves. After the region became dominated politically, migrations of small groups from the Borno heartland in the Yobe valley resulted in an increasing dominance of Kanuri culture. In the end, this led to a transformation of the ethnic identity of the local population.

However, elsewhere within the empire's realm the archaeology of the late prehistoric and historic periods is still in its infancy and our picture about the general history is still very much incomplete and largely restricted to rulers' genealogies, their conquests, and defeats. The situation becomes worse, the deeper in time we go. Almost nothing is known about the early capitals between the eighth and fifteenth centuries—they have still not been located. Information on these should, for instance, result in a more varied picture of urbanization and state formation in the Sudanic and Sahelian zones. Equally unanswered remain many questions regarding the economic basis, internal organization, social structure, and regional trade before the Denham and Clapperton expedition reached the country. But also quite clearly the sites of the nineteenth century require further detailed attention as far as, for instance, their layout is concerned, or simply basic questions of building traditions.

Another worthwhile research aspect would be the interrelation between the economy and the changing climate in the Central Sudan. Already at this point certain patterns are visible, like the southward movement of the empire's capitals over the past 1,000 years. It would be interesting to investigate how various political events were linked to environmental change. So the conflicts with the Bulala and the subsequent exodus from Kanem in the thirteenth and fourteenth centuries might be connected to a dry period observed elsewhere in the *bilad al-sudan* (Brooks 1998: 149–52; Reichelt *et al.* 1992: 74–5). Equally, the increasing Tuareg conflicts during the seventeenth and eighteenth centuries, and the resulting migration of Kanuri to southeastern Borno, might have been fostered by the desiccation of the desert (Gronenborn 2000; Lovejoy and Baier 1975). And lastly there are many sites, completely unexplored so far, which will reveal valuable information about the treatment of slaves and the conditions under which they lived (Mafama 1977; Seidensticker 1978). Indeed, information about these unfortunates is almost completely absent from the written sources. The potential for Historical Archaeology is immense in the Central *bilad al-sudan*.

Acknowledgments

I would like to thank Christopher DeCorse and several anonymous reviewers for their useful recommendations for improvements of this paper. Then, over the years many people have contributed their invaluable knowledge. First and foremost my gratitude goes to the many friends and colleagues at the University of Maiduguri, namely Kyari Tijani, Wilhelm 'William' Seidensticker (†), Gisela Seidensticker, Abubakar Garba, Yakubu Mukhtar, David Koroma, Mohammed Adam, and many more for which room here is too limited. Also of great help and support were Musa Hambolu of the Nigerian National Commission of Museums and Monuments, now at Kano, as well as Alhaji Mohammed Adam, chairman of the Borno Museum Society, Maiduguri. Holger Kirscht, University of Frankfurt, gave helpful advice for the latest version of the manuscript. I am also very much indebted to the German Research Foundation (DFG) for their continuous support of our and my research in Nigeria (SFB 268–1, C1, C7; Gr 1643 1–1/2/3). Last but not least, mention must be made of the gracious support and interest of Alhaji Kyari ibn Umar El-Kanemi, the Shehu of Dikwa, and Alhaji Mustafa ibn Umar El-Kanemi, the Shehu of Borno.

References

Abba, S. B. (1992) Borno towns and their gates. *Borno Museum Society Newsletter*, 11/12:15–26.

Adam, M. (1990) The historical importance of the Old City of Dikwa. *Borno Museum Society Newsletter*, 2:3–12.

Adeleye, R. A. (1985) Hausaland and Borno 1600–1800. In *History of West Africa*, Vol. 1, edited by J. F. A. Ajayi and M. Crowder. Harlow, Essex: Longman, pp. 577–623.

Ajayi, J. F. and Crowder, M. (1985) *Historical Atlas of Africa*. Cambridge: Cambridge University Press.

Alexander, H. (1912) *Boyd Alexander's Last Journey*. London: Arnold.

Barkindo, B. (1985) Early states of the central Sudan: Kanem, Borno and some of their neighbours to *c.* 1500 AD. In *History of West Africa*, Vol. 1, edited by J. F. A. Ajayi and M. Crowder. Harlow, Essex: Longman, pp. 225–54.

Barth, H. (1857–58) *Travels and Discoveries in North and Central Africa: Being a Journal of an Expedition Undertaken under the Auspices of H.B.M.'s Government, in the Years 1849–1855*. London: Longmans.

Barth, H. (1857–59) *Travels and Discoveries in North and Central Africa*, Vols I–III. New York: Harper & Brothers.

Benisheikh, A. (1983) The revenue system of the government of Borno in the nineteenth century. In *Studies in the History of Pre-Colonial Borno*, edited by B. Usman and M. Nur Alkali. Zaria: Northern Nigerian Publishing Company, pp. 78–100.

Bivar, A. D. H. and Shinnie, P. L. (1962) Old Kanuri capitals. *Journal of African History*, 3(1):1–10.

Brenner, L. (1973) *The Shehus of Kukawa: A History of the Al Kanemi Dynasty of Bornu*. Oxford: Clarendon Press.

Breunig, P., Neumann, K. and Van Neer, W. (1996) New research on the Holocene settlement and environment of the Chad Basin in Nigeria. *African Archaeological Revue*, 13/2:111–45.

Brooks, G. E. (1998) Climate and history in West Africa. In *Essays on Africa's Later Past*, edited by G. Connah. London: Leicester University Press, pp. 139–59.

Bovill, E. W. (1970) *The Golden Trade of the Moors*, 2nd edn. London: Oxford University Press.

Cohen, R. (1967a) *The Kanuri of Bornu*. New York: Holt, Rinehart and Winston.

Cohen, R. (1967b) Slavery among the Kanuri. Special Supplement—Slavery in Africa. *Transaction*, January/February.

Cohen, R. (1970) Incorporation in Bornu. In *From Tribe to Nation in Africa*, edited by R. Cohen and J. Middleton. San Francisco: Chandler, pp. 150–74.

Cohen, R. and Brenner, L. (1984) Bornu in the nineteenth century. In *History of West Africa*, Vol. 2, edited by J. F. A. Ajayi and M. Crowder. Harlow, Essex: Longman, pp. 93–128.

Connah, G. (1976) The Daima sequence and the prehistoric chronology of the Lake Chad region of Nigeria. *Journal of African History*, 17(3):321–52.

Connah, G. (1978) Borno revisited: ethnographic and archaeological fieldwork in 1978. *Zaria Archaeological Paper*, 3(6):2–24.

Connah, G. (1981) *Three Thousand Years in Africa: Man and His Environment in the Lake Chad Region of Nigeria*. Cambridge: Cambridge University Press.

Cyffer, N., Löhr, D., Platte, E. and Tijani, A. I. (1996) Adaptation and delimination. Some thoughts about the Kanurization of the Gamergu. In *Vorträge Internationales Symposium – SFB 268 – Frankfurt/Main 13–16.12.*, edited by G. Nagel. Frankfurt am Main: Berichte des Sonderforschungsbereichs 268, Vol. 8, pp. 49–66.

Denham, D. (1826) Supplemental chapter on Bornou. In *Narrative of Travels and Discoveries in Northern and Central Africa, in the Years 1822, 1823, and 1824*, Vol. II, edited by D. Denham, H. Clapperton and W. Oudney. London: John Murray, pp. 138–77.

Denham, D., Clapperton, H. and Oudney, W. (1826) *Narrative of Travels and Discoveries in Northern and Central Africa, in the Years 1822, 1823, and 1824*, Vol. I. London: John Murray.

Denyer, S. (1978) *African Traditional Architecture*. New York: Africana Publishing Company.

Dmochowski, Z. R. (1990) *An Introduction to Nigerian Traditional Architecture. Vol. I: Northern Nigeria*. Lagos: Ethnographica, National Commission of Museums and Monuments.

Dominik, H. (1908) *Vom Atlantik zum Tschadsee.*

Kriegs- und Forschungsfahrten in Kamerun. Berlin: Ernst Siegfried Mittler.

Duyvesteyn, H. (1973) 'Architecture of the western Sudan: a study of the development of building and planning in the caliphate of Borno'. MS. on file, Portsmouth Polytechnic School of Architecture, Portsmouth.

Ferrandi, J. (1928) *Conquête du Cameroun-Nord (1914–1915).* Paris: Charles Lavauzelle.

Forkl, H. (1983) 'Die Beziehungen der zentralsudanischen Reiche Bornu, Mandara und Bagirmi sowie der Kotoko-Staaten zu ihren südlichen Nachbarn unter Berücksichtigung des Sao-Problems'. *Münchner Ethnologische Abhandlungen* 3. Munich: Minerva.

Gentil, E. (1902) *La Chute de l'empire de Rabah.* Paris: Hachette.

Gronenborn, D. (1997) An ancient storage pit in the SW Chad Basin. *Journal of Field Archaeology,* 24:431–9.

Gronenborn, D. (1998) Archaeological and ethnohistorical investigations along the southern fringes of Lake Chad, 1993–1996. *African Archaeological Review,* 15(4):225–59.

Gronenborn, D. (2000) *Mai-mbauji. Eine Studie über Entstehung und Wandel eisenzeitlich-historischer Fürstentümer im südlichen Tschadbecken (neuntes Jahrhundert n. Chr. bis ca. 1925).* Habilitation thesis, University of Frankfurt.

Gronenborn, D. (in press a) Princedoms along the lakeshore. Historical–archaeological investigations on the development of complex societies in the southern Chad Basin. In *Berichte des Sonderforschungsbereichs 268,* Frankfurt am Main.

Gronenborn, D. (in press b) Zum (möglichen) Nachweis von Sklaven/Unfreien in prähistorischen Gesellschaften Mitteleuropas. *Ethnographisch-Archäologische Zeitschrift.*

Gronenborn, D. and Magnavita, C. (2000) Imperial expansion, ethnic change, and ceramic traditions in the southern Chad Basin: a terminal nineteenth century pottery assemblage from Dikwa, Borno State, Nigeria. *International Journal of Historical Archaeology,* 4/1:35–70.

Hambolu, M. O. (1993) 'The resource base of Birnin Gazargamo the *C.*15th–*C.*19th capital of Borno empire'. Paper presented at the 12th Archaeological Association of Nigeria Conference Maiduguri, 28th November to 3rd December, Maiduguri.

Hambolu, M. O. (1996) Recent excavations along the Yobe valley. In *Vorträge Internationales Symposium – SFB 268 – Frankfurt/Main 13–16.12,* edited by G. Nagel. Frankfurt am

Main: Berichte des Sonderforschungsbereichs 268, Vol. 8, pp. 215–30.

Hogben, S. J. and Kirk-Greene, A. H. M. (1966) *The Emirates of Northern Nigeria: A Preliminary Survey of Their Historical Traditions.* London: Oxford University Press.

Holl, A. F. C. (1993) Community interaction and settlement patterning in northern Cameroon. In *Spatial Boundaries and Social Dynamics: Case Studies from Food-producing Societies,* edited by A. Holl and T. E. Levy. Ann Arbor: International Monographs of Prehistory and Ethnoarchaeology Series 2, pp. 39–62.

Holl, A. F. C. (1995) Réseaux d'échanges préhistoriques dans la plaine tchadienne. *Sahara,* 7:17–28.

Hunwick, J. O. (1985) Songhay, Borno and the Hausa States, 1450–1600. In *History of West Africa,* Vol. 1, edited by J. F. A. Ajayi and M. Crowder. Harlow, Essex: Longman, pp. 323–71.

Kirk-Greene, A. H. M. (1958) *Maiduguri and the Capitals of Borno.* Zaria: Norla.

Koelle, S. W. (1968) *African Native Literature.* Graz: Akademische Druck- und Verlagsanstalt. (First published in 1854.)

Lacroix, W.F.G (1998) *Africa in Antiquity: A Linguistic and Toponymic Analysis of Ptolemy's Map of Africa, Together with a Discussion of Ophir, Punt and Hanno's Voyage.* Saarbrücken: Verlag für Entwicklungspolitik.

Lange, D. (1977) *Chronologie et histoire d'un royaume Africain (de la fin du Xe siècle jusqu'à 1808).* Wiesbaden: Franz Steiner.

Lange, D. (1980) La région du Lac Tchad d'après la géographie d'Ibn Sa'id: textes et cartes. *Annales Islamologiques,* 16:149–81.

Lange, D. (1987) *A Sudanic Chronicle: The Borno Expeditions of Idris Alauma (1564–1576) According to the Account of Ahmad b. Furtu.* Studien zur Kulturkunde 86. Wiesbaden: Franz Steiner.

Lange, D. (1989) Préliminaires pour une histoire des Sao. *Journal of African History,* 30:189–210.

Lange, D. (1990) Das Amt der Königinmutter im Tschadseegebiet. Historische Betrachtungen. *Paideuma,* 36:139–56.

Lange, D. (1993) Ethnogenesis from within the Chadic state. Some thoughts on the history of Kanem-Borno. *Paideuma,* 39:261–77.

Lange, D. and Barkindo, B. W. (1988) The Chad region as a crossroads. In *General History of Africa III: Africa from the Seventh to the Eleventh Century,* edited by M. Elfasi and I. Hrbek. UNESCO International Scientific Committee for the Drafting of a General History of Africa. London: Heinemann, pp. 436–60.

Lange, D. and Berthoud, B. W. (1977) Al-Qasaba et d'autres villes de la route centrale du Sahara. *Paideuma*, 23:19–40.

Lange, D. and Berthoud, S. (1972) L'intérieur de l'Afrique occidentale d'après Giovanni Lorenzo Anania (XVIe siècle). *Cahiers d'Histoire Mondiale*, 14/2:299–351.

Last, M. (1985) The early kingdoms of the Nigerian savanna. In *History of West Africa*, Vol. 1, edited by J. F. A. Ajayi and M. Crowder. Harlow, Essex: Longman, pp. 167–224.

Lavers, J. E. (1971a) A note on Birni Gazargamu and 'burnt brick' sites in the Bornu caliphate. In *Papers Presented to the IV Conference of West African Archaeologists*, edited by A. Fagg. pp. 39–57. Jos. MS. on file, Lavers collection, Arewa House, Kaduna, Nigeria.

Lavers, J. E. (1971b) 'A report of a visit to the "burnt brick" sites of Nguru and Machena (Aug. '71)'. MS. on file, Lavers collection, Arewa House, Kaduna, Nigeria.

Lavers, J. E. (1980) Kanem and Borno to 1808. In *Groundwork of Nigerian History*, edited by O. Ikime. Ibadan: Heinemann, pp. 187–209.

Lavers, J. E. (1984) An introduction to the history of Bagirmi *c.* 1500–1800. *Annals of Borno*, 1:29–44.

Lavers, J. E. (1993) Adventures in the chronology of the states of the Chad Basin. In *Datations et chronologie dans le bassin du Lac Tchad. Séminaire du réseau Méga-Tchad ORSTOM Bondy, 11 et 12 septembre 1989*, edited by D. Barreteau and C. von Graffenried. Paris: Éditions ORSTOM Colloques et Séminaires, pp. 255–67.

Lavers, J. E. (1994a) Trans-Saharan trade before 1800: towards quantification. *Paideuma*, 40:243–78.

Lavers, J. E. (1994b) The Awlad Rabih 22 April 1900–23 August 1901. *Paideuma*, 40:215–42.

Lebeuf, A. M. D. (1969) *Les Principautés Kotoko: essai sur le caractère sacré de l'autorité.* Paris: Editions du Centre National de la Recherche Scientifique.

Lebeuf, A. M. D. (1972) *Atlas pratique du Tchad.* N'djamena: Institut National Tchadien des Sciences Humaines.

Lenfant, Commandant. (1905) *La Grande Route du Tchad.* Mission de la Société de Géographie. Paris: Hachette.

Levtzion, N. and Hopkins, J. F. F. (1981) *Corpus of Early Arabic Sources for West African History.* Cambridge: Cambridge University Press.

Lockhart, J. R. B. (1996) Clapperton in Borno. Journal of the travels in Borno of Lieutenant Hugh Clapperton, RN, from January 1823 to September 1824. *Frankfurter Westafrikanische Studien*, 12. Cologne: Rüdiger Köppe.

Lovejoy, P. E. and Baier, S. (1975) The desertside economy of the central Sudan. *International Journal of African Historical Studies*, 8(1):551–81.

Lucas, S. (1967) *Mr. Lucas's Communications.* Proceedings of the Association for Promoting the Discovery of the Interior Parts of Africa. London: Dawsons of Pall Mall. (First published 1810.)

Maas, P. and Mommersteeg, G. (1992) *Djenne – chef-d'Œuvre architectural.* Eindhoven: Université de Technologie.

MacEachern, S. (1990) 'Du Kunde: Process of montagnard ethnogenesis in the northern Mandara Mountains of Cameroon'. Unpublished Ph. D. dissertation, Department of Anthropology, University of Calgary, Alberta.

MacEachern, S. (1996) Iron Age beginnings north of the Mandara Mountains, Cameroon and Nigeria. In *Aspects of African Archaeology: Papers from the 10th Congress of the Pan African Association for Prehistory and Related Studies*, edited by G. Pwiti and R. Soper. Harare: University of Zimbabwe, pp. 489–96.

Mafama, A. T. (1977) 'Some aspects of slavery in Borno'. B. A. thesis. Kano: Department of History, Bayero University, Kano.

Maley, J. (1981) *Etudes palynologiques dans le bassin du Tchad et paléoclimatologie de l'Afrique nord-tropicale de 30,000 ans à l'époque actuelle.* Travaux et documents de l'ORSTOM 129. Paris: Editions de l'ORSTOM.

Meyer, P. C. (1897) *Erforschungsgeschichte und Staatenbildungen des Westsudan mit Berücksichtigung seiner historischen, ethnologischen und wirtschaftlichen Verhältnisse.* Petermanns Mitteilungen Ergänzungsheft Vol. 121, Gotha.

Migeod, F. W. H. (1924) *Through Nigeria to Lake Chad.* London: Heath Cranton.

Monteil, P.-L. (1895) *De Saint-Louis à Tripoli par le lac Tchad.* Paris: Germer Baillière.

Mukhtar, Y. (1992) 'Trade, merchants and the state in Borno, *c.* 1893–1939'. Unpublished Ph.D. dissertation, School of Oriental and African Studies, London.

Nachtigal, G. (1967) *Sahara und Sudan: Ergebnisse sechsjähriger Reisen in Afrika.* 3 vols. Graz: Akademische Druck- und Verlagsanstalt. (First published 1879–81.)

Nachtigal, G. (1971–87) *Sahara and Sudan: Translated from the Original German with New Introduction and Notes by A. G. B. Fisher and H. J. Fisher.* 4 vols. London: Hurst.

Nur Alkali, M. (1977) Factors in the economic development of Borno under the Seifuwa dynasty, 1500–1800 AD. In *The Central Bilad Al-Sudan: Tradition and Adaptation*, edited by Y. Fadl Hassan and P. Doornbos. Khartoum: Sudanese Library Series, Vol. 11, pp. 245–61.

Nur Alkali, M. (1978) 'Kanem – Borno under the Sayfawa (a study of origin, growth and collapse of a dynasty)'. Unpublished Ph.D. dissertation, History Department, University of Maiduguri, Borno State, Nigeria.

Nur Alkali, M. (1983) The political system and administrative structure of Borno under the Seifuwa Mais. In *Studies in the History of Pre-Colonial Borno*, edited by B. Usman and M. N. Alkali. Zaria: Northern Nigerian Publishing Company, pp. 101–26.

Oudney, W. (1966) Dr. W. Oudney to R. Wilmot. In *Missions to the Niger, III. The Bornu Mission, 1822–25. Part 2*, edited by E. W. Bovill. The Hakluyt Society Second Series No. 79. London: Cambridge University Press, pp. 564–9.

Palmer, H. R. (1967) *Sudanese Memoirs*. London: Frank Cass. (First published 1928.)

Palmer, H. R. (1970) *The Bornu, Sahara and Sudan*. New York: Negro Universities Press. (First published 1936.)

Passarge, S. (1895) *Adamaua: Bericht über die Expedition des Deutschen Kamerun-Komitees in den Jahren 1893/94*. Berlin: Dietrich Reimer.

Reichelt, R., Faure, H. and Maley, J. (1992) Die Entwicklung des Klimas im randtropischen Sahara-Sahelbereich während des Jungquartärs – ein Beitrag zur angewandten Klimakunde. *Petermanns Geographische Mitteilungen*, 136:69–79.

Reyna, S. P. (1990) *Wars without End: The Political Economy of a Precolonial African State*. Hanover, NH: University Press of New England.

Rice, P. M. (1987) *Pottery Analysis: A Sourcebook*. Chicago: University of Chicago Press.

Rohlfs, G. (1868a) *Reise durch Nord-Afrika vom Mittelländischen Meere bis zum Busen von Guinea 1865 bis 1867*. Ergänzungsheft No. 24 zu Petermann's 'Geographische Mitteilungen', Gotha.

Rohlfs, G. (1868b) Die Stadt Kuka in Bornu. *Globus*, 13:1–6

Rohlfs, G. (1872) *Reise durch Nord-Afrika vom Mittelländischen Meere bis zum Busen von Guinea 1865 bis 1867*. Ergänzungsheft No. 25 zu Petermann's 'Geographische Mitteilungen', Gotha.

Schipper, Lt. (1905) Bemerkungen zu den Plänen von Dikoa. *Mitteilungen von Forschungsreisenden und Gelehrten aus den Deutschen Schutzgebieten*, 18:192–3.

Seetzen, U. J. (1995) About the great African empire Bornu and its tributary countries and about the language of Affadeh. U. J. Seetzen in Kahira. November 1808. Zach'sche Monatliche Korrespondenz 22 B, 1810. Translated by Gisela Seidensticker-Brikay. *Borno Museum Society Newsletter*, 25:9–16.

Seidensticker, W. (1978) Four archaeological sites in Borno. *Zaria Archaeological Papers*, 3:1–5.

Seidensticker, W. (1981) Borno and the East. Notes and hypotheses on the technology of burnt bricks. In *Proceedings of the Nilo-Saharan Conference – Leiden 1980*, edited by T. Schadeberg and M. L. Bender. Dordrecht: Foris, pp. 239–50.

Seidensticker, W. (1983a) A note on the site of Gambaru, Borno State. *Zaria Archaeological Papers*, 5:65–7.

Seidensticker, W. (1983b) Notes on the history of Yerwa (Maiduguri). *Annals of Borno*, 1:5–15.

Seidensticker, W. (1990) Historical sites of Dikwa, Ngala, and Ndufu. *Borno Museum Society Newsletter*, 2:29–31.

Seidensticker, W. (1991a) Report on the first voyage of the Janaga. *Borno Museum Society Newsletter*, 8–9:11–24.

Seidensticker, W. (1991b) Kukawa: chronicle of events in the 19th century. *Borno Museum Society Newsletter*, 6–7:44–8.

Seidensticker, W. (1992) Beginning of colonialism in Borno – Morland's report. *Borno Museum Society Newsletter* 11/12:38–50.

Smith, A. (1987) The early states of the central Sudan. In *A Little New Light: Selected Historical Writings of Professor Abdullahi Smith*, Vol. I. The Abdullahi Smith Centre for Historical Research, Zaria, Nigeria. Zaria: Gaskia Corporation, pp. 80–130.

Snowden, F. M. (1970) *Blacks in Antiquity: Ethiopians in the Graeco-Roman Experience*. Cambridge, MA: Belknap Press.

Surén, H. (1934) *Kampf um Kamerun*. Berlin: Scherl.

Thiemeyer, H. (1997) *Untersuchungen zur Spätpleistozänen und holozänen Landschaftsentwicklung im südwestlichen Tschadbecken. (N. East Nigeria)*. Jenaer Geographische Schriften 5, Jena.

Tijani, K. (1993) The Mune in pre-colonial Borno. In *Vorträge Internationales Symposium – SFB 268 – Frankfurt/Main 16.12. – 19.12. 1992*, edited by G. Nagel. Frankfurt am Main: Berichte des Sonderforschungsbereichs 268, Vol. 2, pp. 227–54.

Trimingham, J. S. (1962) *A History of Islam in West Africa*. London: Oxford University Press.

Urvoy, Y. (1949) *Histoire de l'empire du Bornou*. Paris: Mémoirs de l'Institut Français d'Afrique Noire.

Vansina, J. (1966) *Kingdoms of the Savanna*. Madison: University of Wisconsin Press.

Vansina, J. (1992) Kings in tropical Africa. In *Kings of Africa*, edited by E. Beumers and H.-J. Koloss. Utrecht: Foundation Kings of Africa, pp. 19–26.

von Duisburg, A. (1927) Zur Geschichte der Sultanat Bornu und Wándala (Mándara). *Anthropos*, 22:187–96.

von Duisburg, A. (1942) *Im Lande des Cheghu von Bornu: Despoten und Völker südlich des Tschad*. Berlin: Dietrich Reimer.

von Oppenheim, M. (1902) *Rabeh und das Tschadseegebiet*. Berlin: Dietrich Reimer.

Wheeler, M. (1955) *Rome Beyond the Imperial Frontiers*. London: Bell.

Zeltner, J. C. (1980) *Pages d'histoire du Kanem*. Paris: L'Harmattan.

7 State Formation and Enslavement in the Southern Lake Chad Basin

SCOTT MACEACHERN

Archaeological and historical data indicate that drastic changes in settlement patterning and in power relationships between ethnic groups took place in the southern Lake Chad Basin over the last thousand years. At the beginning of this period, this region appears to have been inhabited by independent agrarian communities, linked by local trading relations. By colonial times at the beginning of this century, centralized, and primarily Islamic, polities had become the norm throughout this area. The genesis of this situation appears to date to the first half of the present millennium, when the states of Kanem, Bornu, and Baghirmi progressively extended their influence south of Lake Chad. These states engaged in predatory expansion at the expense of indigenous communities, financing their growth through the sale of slaves and natural resources as they exploited their superior access to wider African trading systems. This led to important social and ethnic developments in 'peripheral' areas like the Mandara Mountains and the islands of Lake Chad, and to the establishment of a Muslim/'pagan', state/non-state dichotomy that dominates the cultural landscape of the region today.

Introduction

There existed, in the territories south of Lake Chad, a somewhat different relationship between regional political developments and enslavement from the one that held in many of the lands closer to the Atlantic shores of Africa. In this area, direct European contact and colonialism came late. Isolated, relatively powerless European travelers ventured into the region after the beginning of the nineteenth century; some died there (Hair 1967:32 n. 4). Articulation of the region directly into continental economic systems occurred slowly over the next 150 years. The extension of colonial control was gradual, and only by the early twentieth century were European pow-ers—England, Germany, and France—able to impose structures of administration and domination over indigenous societies. Europeans in these regions are associated with the suppression of the slave trade through the first half of this century, albeit often in a context of omission, prevarication, and vacillation on the part of European governments and of the colonial officials themselves (Beauvilain 1989; Lovejoy and Hogendorn 1993).

At the same time, two points should be made. Slave taking, slave trading and slave holding had been significant elements of the cultural and political milieu of this area since at least the sixteenth century AD. The consequences of that trade will be examined later in this paper. Suffice it to say that those consequences were important, both for the states that used the slave trade to increase their wealth and competitive advantage and for the 'peripheral' populations, the targets of slave-taking operations, that were forced to modify their traditional life in response to external attack. We may thus be able to use this Central Sudan case as an appropriate comparison to the social and cultural effects of the Atlantic slave trade on African populations.

In the second place, we cannot assume lack of influence in both directions from lack of physical contacts between Europeans and the peoples of the area around Lake Chad. As has been made clear by a number of studies (see, for example, Wolf 1982), economic, social, and political networks ramify, and important cultural consequences can occur at great distances from their sources. The articulation of Central Sudanic slave systems with Euroamerican slave systems on the African Atlantic coast has not received comprehensive historical treatment, but there is no doubt that such an articulation existed by the end of the eighteenth century, and most likely before that time as well. The consequences of enslavement for a certain (though certainly small) proportion of captives from the southern Lake Chad Basin was sale to Euroamerican slave traders and movement to the New World.

In this paper, I will first examine available data on the Iron Age cultural milieu in the area south of Lake Chad. I will then examine the processes by which slavery became an important part of the human environment, and the relationship between slavery and state formation in this area. The geographical scope of this inquiry runs from the Komadugu Yobe in the west to the Chari in the east, and from Lake Chad in the north to the Mandara Mountains and the Biu Plateau in the south. It thus includes varying parts of the traditional territories of the Bornu, Wandala, and Baghirmi polities, and part of what would eventually become the Sokoto Caliphate (Figure 7.1). The temporal scope will be the period from AD 300 to AD 1900, the time during which indigenous states capable of marshaling slave trades and incorporating alienated slave labor probably developed in this region. I will examine the archaeological consequences of slavery in this area, as the transformation of an entire human landscape in response to the pressures of the slave trade.

The southern Lake Chad Basin to the sixteenth century

Archaeological data

The territory south of Lake Chad includes the *firki* clay plains of Holocene Lake Mega-Chad; the sand and clay plains, punctuated by relict dune fields and depressions, that surround the *firki* plains to the west, south, and east; permanent and seasonal watercourses, including particularly the Logone/Chari, Ngadda, Yedseram, and Komadugu Yobe river systems, all of which have striking effects on local environments; and the highland areas to the south of the lake, including most especially the Mandara Mountains and the Biu Plateau, along with outlying inselbergs and uplands (Figures 7.1 and 7.2). These environments are not, of course, always easily demarcated on a local level; they grade into and affect one another to varying degrees. Their importance for humans lies fundamentally in the possibilities that they open up: the options that they allow and the resources to which they give access.

Today, this area is occupied by a bewildering constellation of different ethnic, linguistic, religious and economic groups, exploiting different natural and cultural environments and interacting with one another in a multitude of different ways. At the broadest level, we find speakers of three of the four African language families (Nilo-Saharan, Niger-Congo, and Afroasiatic) interacting locally on a daily basis, in a situation where multilinguality is often essential to social exchange (Barreteau *et al.* 1984:177–80; MacEachern 1990:255–62). The presence of many 'ethnic groups' may well understate the cultural and ethnic variability of the southern Lake Chad Basin, since a large number of these groups are artificial conglomerations, created for the convenience of colonial administrators and the edification of an anthropological audience (MacEachern 1990: 46–53, 233–54; 2000a). This is certainly the case for many of the small, non-Muslim societies living in and around the area's highlands. At the other end of the scale, obvious problems exist in treating large groups like the Hausa, Fulbe, or Kanuri as unitary ethnic entities. (For an excellent illustration of this, see the relevant sections in Wente-Lukas 1985.) A similar level of variability exists in the economic adapta-

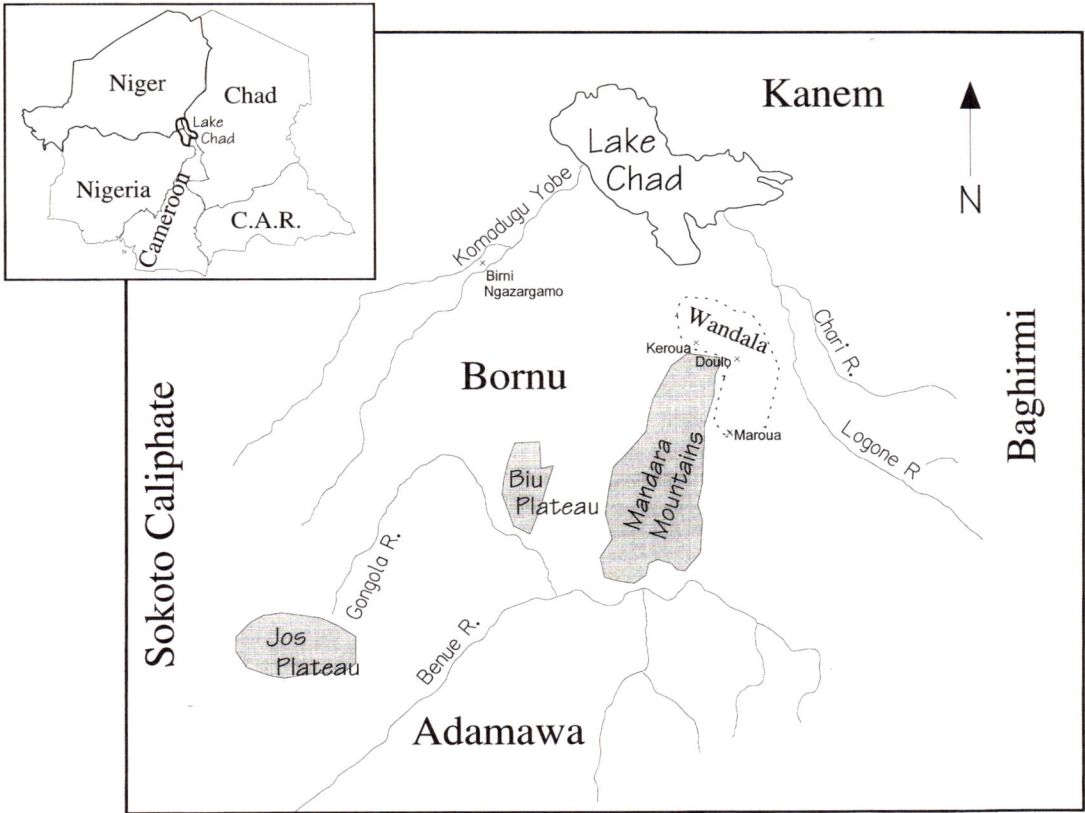

Figure 7.1   Traditional states of the Lake Chad Basin.

tions pursued throughout the area (Boutrais and others 1984; de Leeuw 1972).

We can probably say with some confidence that the present-day social and cultural differentiation has existed in this area for the last 200 years, but our archaeological reconstructions beyond that point remain, at the moment, relatively impoverished. The various investigations into the Iron Age prehistory of this area to date (Bourges *et al.* 1999; Connah 1981, 1984; David and MacEachern 1988; Holl 1988; Lebeuf 1962, 1969; Lebeuf *et al.* 1980; MacEachern 1993b, 1996; Marliac 1985, 1991; Marliac and Delneuf 1984) have established that the plains environments at least have been foci of settlement over the last 2,000 years. We have, as yet, no evidence that the Mandara Mountains have been intensively occupied for more than perhaps the last 500 years; they would probably be quite heavily forested, without the high population densities and intense terrace farming that exist there today.

Reasons for the occupation of such forbidding terrain will be examined below.

The scale and intensity of our archaeological endeavors to date, though significant, allow us only the most general picture of cultural variation in the southern Lake Chad Basin. Available data indicate that there have been general similarities in settlement patterning and economies throughout this area during the period between AD 300 and AD 1200. The earliest Iron Age, before AD 300, is not well documented to date, but probably involves a transitional Neolithic-to-Iron Age occupation in many areas. The degree of continuity between Neolithic and Iron Age populations in this area is not well understood, although such continuity certainly existed at Daima and at sites along the edge of the Mandara massif (Connah 1981; MacEachern 1996). After AD 300, we find a more visible Iron Age occupation throughout the plains, and along the inselbergs and massif-edges to the south of

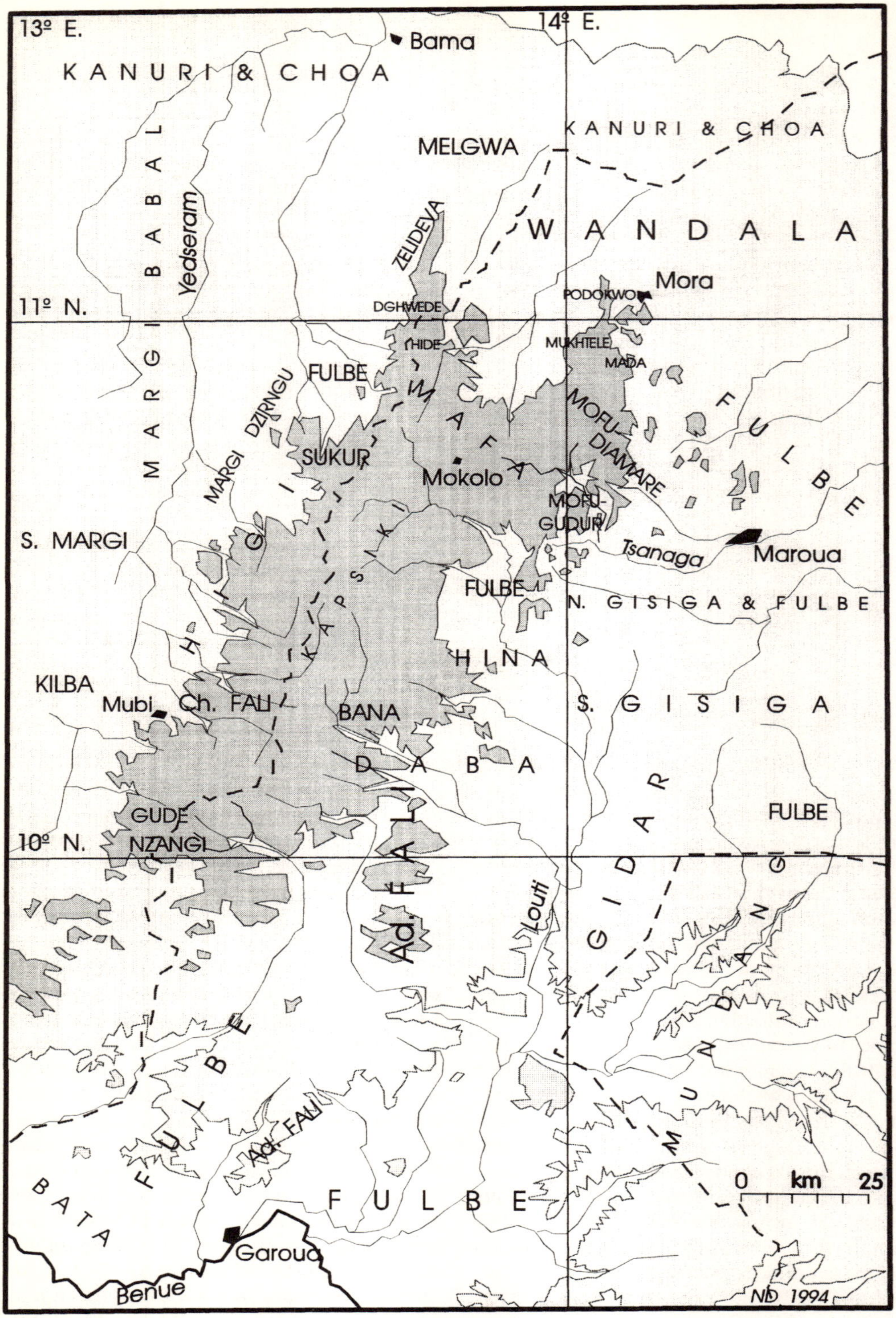

Figure 7.2 Major ethnic groups in and around the Mandara Mountains.

Lake Chad. Population densities in the plains through this period seem to have been relatively high, and it is evident that Iron Age peoples were well adapted to life on both the *firki* plains to the north and on the sand and clay plains further away from the lake.

There is, within this area, little archaeological evidence of site hierarchies over the period AD 300–1200, except those associated with everyday task differentiation in agrarian societies. The largest sites located to date appear to be large villages. During the later part of this period, it seems that walls and/or ditches were added to some of these communities (Connah 1981:167; Lebeuf 1969:12, 19–22; Lebeuf *et al.* 1980). These features might obviously be important in identifying the period when external defense became important, but none are well dated. Defensive features may also have played an increasing role in site placement near the Mandara Mountains through the Iron Age (MacEachern 1993c), although this requires more investigation.

Iron smelting seems to have been carried out at various locations in the plains and near the mountains to the south, where most of the iron ore probably originated. Quarrying of stone for grindstones, blacksmith's hammers, and possibly for ground stone axes was mostly restricted to the southern highland areas. There is, therefore, evidence for intra-regional trade, in stone and iron, and probably salt, at least. Trade with more distant areas seems to become increasingly important through this AD 300–1200 period in the northern part of the area (as at Daima and Mdaga), while remaining relatively unimportant further to the south (MacEachern 1990). There are regional differences in ceramic assemblages (in rouletting and other decoration types, in vessel morphologies), but these exist within a context of general stylistic (and utilitarian?) similarities.

The historical milieu

An enforced regional approach can have advantages, since it does compel archaeologists to take note of large-scale cultural patterning. Ethnographers, working locally and usually overwhelmed by a flood of difficult-to-assimilate data from their informants, often restrict their analysis to a micro-level—typically, a particular community or ethnic group.

Linguistic demands reinforce this habit, which results in bounded ethnographies and less information about regional cultural patterning. Detection and description of such patterning has frequently been left to historians and geographers, and it is, of course, one of the stocks-in-trade of archaeologists. In this case, the regional differentiation that we detect archaeologically may be similar to the agrarian patterning that we see in the area under investigation today—not the neat lines that supposedly delineate 'ethnic groups' on maps, but the more complex gradations of artifacts, habits, and identifications that make up the geography of everyday life. Regional variability in the archaeological record may be the prehistoric equivalent of the gross cultural patterning, on the level of the linguistic (Chadic or West Atlantic, for example), or large-scale 'ethnic' (Hausa, Kanuri) groups that exist today.

There are a number of possible reasons for our failure to detect smaller, more local ethnic units, of the sort that appear to be most significant in the day-to-day lives of people. In the first place, our research may simply not be fine-grained enough to detect local ethnic groups—a general archaeological problem (MacEachern 1992; Sackett 1990). In the second place, it is possible that local, self-conscious ethnicities did not exist in the area south of Lake Chad in the early Iron Age. It has been argued that the construction of such ethnic units is not an act intrinsic to human culture, but rather 'a consciously crafted ideological creation' (Vail 1991; see also Comaroff 1987), with origins usually to be found in relations of domination and mystification of some communities by more powerful ones. In reality, this question is almost always phrased in terms of European colonial domination, but there is no reason that such processes should not have occurred among pre-European communities, as when states dominate 'peripheral' groups (Reyna 1990). If this is the case, then localized ethnicities as we today understand them may not have existed south of Lake Chad before the development of at least small states in that region.

Questions of this sort will be very difficult to approach archaeologically, but they are more amenable to historical analysis. The first direct attestation to states around Lake Chad comes in the ninth century AD, when al-Yakubi and ibn Kutayba stated that Kanem was ruled by the Zaghawa (Lange 1988), although the long-standing geographical focus of that state was to the north and east of the lake. There was certainly an expansion from Kanem around both sides of Lake Chad after that time, but we do not know when the Kanem state would have started to have an impact on the way of life of the agrarian communities in the study area—AD 1200 may be an appropriate approximation (see below). It is possible that the evidence for increased trade and for the beginning of fortification detected at sites south of the lake date from this period. States can be both lucrative and dangerous neighbors.

The impact of Kanem upon the people living in the southern Lake Chad Basin may well have been indirect and limited at first, but states also spawn imitators, with the generation of secondary polities in peripheral areas (Kopytoff 1987: 49–75). It is likely that the states of Bornu and Baghirmi were at first such successor polities, originating in regions where access to Kanem was possible but not too easy, allowing some autonomy. Before the thirteenth century an independent, indigenous polity probably existed in Bornu to the west of the lake (Lange 1988: 456). Such a polity would have had much easier access to the southern plains than did Kanem, which could only achieve a fluctuating suzerainty over Bornu until the fifteenth century. At that time, pressure from Bulala (and possibly Arab) pastoralists to the east forced the reigning Sefuwa (or Sayfuwa) dynasty of Kanem to abandon the heartland of that state and transfer their capital to Bornu in the southwest. Baghirmi probably came into existence at roughly the same time (Reyna 1990: 49–51). There was some contemporary migration of populations from Kanem into the southern plains as well. Over this period, from AD 1200 or before to AD 1500, communities south of Lake Chad would have found themselves occupying the interface between, first, the states of Kanem and its sometime vassals Bornu and Baghirmi and, later, between Bornu, Baghirmi, and Bulala.

Almost no historical data exist concerning autochthonous populations in this area before the thirteenth century. At that time, Ibn Said gave a short description of the peoples of the area in his *Geography* (Lange 1980), and the groups identified are, for the most part,

recognizable as ethnic units in the area today. Later, al-Maqrizi's *Description of the Races of the Sudan* supplemented Ibn Said's list. Most of the groups identified are today quite large (Hausa, Kotoko, Baghirmi), but others (Kuri) are much smaller. We see somewhat later the appearance of the term 'Sao' (or 'Saw') to denote the indigenous inhabitants of the plains south of Lake Chad—the first time that the communities living south of the lake appear in an historical source (Lange 1989). Interestingly enough, the term 'Sao' appears to be an outside, Kanembu/Kanuri name for indigenous groups, and not a local ethnonym. We have in this case, then, not the creation of ethnicity where none before existed, but rather the obscuration of pre-existing cultural differentiation by external terms (Lange 1988; 1989).

Despite abundant confusion connected with the term 'Sao,' I will continue to use it to signify the indigenous, pre-Islamic inhabitants of the plains south of Lake Chad, because original ethnonyms no longer exist. One exception is the area just north of the Mandara Mountains, where the term 'Maya' denotes similar populations at a local level. The relationship between Sao and Maya populations remains unclear, and there is no good reason to think that it indicates a particularly important ethnic distinction. Later internal and external sources, between the fourteenth and the sixteenth centuries (and including Fra Mauro, Leo Africanus, Giovanni Lorenzo Anania, and ibn Fartwa (MacEachern 1990)), offer valuable supplementary data on the area, and identify a number of other ethnic groups. Of these, the most important are probably the Wandala (whom the Kanuri call the Mandara) and the Marghi, plains groups today occupying the peripheries of the Mandara Mountains.

Cultural formations in the southern Lake Chad Basin

Our archaeological and historical data are thus in all cases fragmentary. A number of conclusions can nevertheless be drawn. In the first place, our knowledge of this region drops dramatically as we move from north to south, from the *firki* plains to the Mandara Mountains and their peripheries, and then to the plains and highlands even further to the south and west. In the latter areas, data are incomplete in the extreme, and it is nearly impossible to derive even a gross picture of cultural changes during the Iron Age. Thus, the Jukun polity, or polities, may well have played a role comparable to that of Kanem with the small ethnic groups around the Biu Plateau between the thirteenth and the seventeenth centuries, but virtually no data exist on relations between the Jukun and those groups (see Isichei 1982). This difference can be traced back to the political and economic relationships extant in the study area before the sixteenth century. The *firki* and sand plains were a jousting-ground for rival Sudanic polities from well before that period, and this led to cultural responses by local peoples themselves and attracted the attentions of indigenous and foreign chroniclers. Much of the archaeology done in this area has, in turn, been a response to the data available in these historical sources.

Between AD 300 and AD 1200, the southern plains were occupied by small, agrarian, iron-using communities, probably in part descended from earlier stone-tool-using populations. Economic spheres of interaction were probably quite localized during this period, and there is little evidence for organized inter-community conflict. Centralized states had grown up in the lands around Lake Chad by the end of the first millennium AD, the probable culmination of a process that had begun some hundreds of years earlier. However, the centers of those states were to the east, north, and west of that body of water, because one of the economic bases of state power was the trans-Saharan trade. Under those circumstances, the area south of the lake continued to be a backwater in a number of senses, its populations living in a frontier territory on the fringes of larger polities whose attentions were often focused past them. The names of groups identified in these areas by early external and internal sources are often still found in the area today. It is probably impossible to identify any period after AD 300 when ethnic identifications and interactions would not have played a part in conditioning the social and cultural milieu south of Lake Chad, especially since on the *firki* plains settled community life would from the beginning have been centered on the relatively rare high ground. Population growth, inter-regional trade and the advent of state-level societies would, of course, be expected to affect the relationships between different ethnic groups: in all cases by bringing increasing numbers of people from different cultures into contact and making self- and group identification more important.

Some of the changes in economies and political systems between *c.* AD 1200 and 1500 can be ascribed to the successful nature of human adaptations to the environments of the southern plains, but increased contact with neighboring states was also vital. External influences derived from the increase in power of Kanem in the region, the development of a polity in Bornu, and most importantly the movement of the Sefuwa from Kanem to Bornu in the fifteenth century and the establishment of the Kanuri capital at Birni Gazargamo. Trade items increase in frequency in the north, defensive features become more common on plains sites, and we see references to Sao 'towns' like Ghaliwa (Lange 1987). Indigenous polities probably began to develop in the southern plains during this period, but these were almost certainly small units, developed in reaction to these external pressures and thriving especially when the larger states to the east and west were weakened by war and dynastic struggles.

The area from the plains of Bornu to the Logone River, and south to the Mandara Mountains and Biu Plateau, served as the predation zones of regional 'fields of empire,' to use Reyna's (1990:10, 39–40) evocative term. They were the areas where resources were extracted to support outside states. It is absolutely essential that we remain conscious of the intimate connection between trade and war in these circumstances. Sudanic states traded in order to gain the revenues necessary to support the state apparatus, including and often notably its military arm, and they went to war to gain tradable resources and to gain or defend access to trade systems. The closeness of this relationship is reinforced by the fact that one of the most important trade goods produced in the Central Sudan over the last thousand years has often itself been a by-product of war, or at least of armed conflict. That trade good is, of course, slaves.

The slave trade south of Lake Chad and its consequences

The beginnings of the trade

We know little about the beginnings of the slave trade in the study area. We do not find the remains of fetters on Iron Age sites south of Lake Chad, and the slave communities of Baghirmi, Wandala, and Bornu are known only from historical sources. A slave trade is closely related to transformations in the social systems of slave-owning societies, since commerce in humans will exist only when a significant demand for slaves exists. Such a demand may be 'internal,' when slaves are obtained for local use, or 'external,' when slaves are obtained for trade to foreign markets. One need not imply the other (Beauvilain 1989: 245–9; MacEachern 1990: 68), but in practice slavers often satisfy both internal and external markets. Data exist on the sale of slaves from the Lake Chad Basin across the Sahara to external markets, and on the actual slave raiding, but very little is known of the origins of slavery as an economic and social institution among Central Sudanic societies themselves. An important question here is: did slavery as a central social institution (Lovejoy 1983:8–11) evolve around Lake Chad as a response to a Mediterranean slave market, or did it begin as a local development, only later supplying a trans-Saharan trade?

A trans-Saharan slave trade in the Central Sudan existed from the ninth century AD, when al-Yakubi states that the Berber inhabitants of Zawila in the Kawar region were slave traders, and that 'the kings of the Sudan sell the Sudan [blacks] for no reason, and quite apart from any wars' (Lange 1988: 451). It is unlikely that this refers to anything but the area around Lake Chad. Significantly, this is also the first source to mention Kanem as an important state. A century later, al-Muhallabi states explicitly that the king of Kanem had the power to reduce to slavery whomsoever he wished (Lange 1988:449). Slave raiding remains a constant element in the literature of the Lake Chad Basin over the next 900 years.

It thus appears that the origins of Kanem were closely bound up with that of a regular trans-Saharan trade in slaves and that slavery was also an important economic and social

institution within the state. This does not mean that a slave trade to the north, and thus contact with Berbers and/or Arabs, were the engines driving Kanem's development as a centralized polity. *Ex borealis lux* has ceased to be a viable explanation for events in sub-Saharan Africa. Rather, political expansionism, the evolution of external political relations, and the development of lucrative sources of state income should be conceived of as interacting mechanisms in a process of state development and competition with other societies. Military tactics (as determined by the import of horses, firearms, and armor) and, later, the adoption of Islam (as a means of increasing external ties and prestige for élites, and of avoiding capture by Muslim slave raiders for common people) would also be drawn into this dynamic. As Lange (1984:250–1) and others have pointed out, the slave trade would never have been the economic basis of the Kanem state. Agriculture, pastoralism, metallurgy, and other such economic activities were always far more important, and the trade in salt and natron may well have been more valuable. But slaves were high-value exports that could be traded for exotic products. Their pursuit and possession were, in addition, prerogatives of kingship and power.

We do not know where these first slaves raided by Kanem came from. Presumably, they would have mostly been drawn from peripheral populations, since it would do no good for a leader to decimate his own people in a quest for slaves, and at first they probably came from around the Bahr-el-Ghazal. The zone of peripheral communities would have expanded as Kanem increased its territory and its reach, and the later development of states like Bornu and Baghirmi (see above) would also have an effect. Slave raiding, as well as the migration and political changes that would eventually see the complete transfer of the state to south-west of the lake, were probably the most important mechanisms by which Kanem first came into contact with populations south of Lake Chad. This contact may well have been responsible for the construction of defensive features around these communities, and archaeologists may examine the proliferation of defensive architecture and changes in regional settlement patterning as responses to an economic and political system within which enslavement played a central part (Figures 7.3 and 7.4a).

Kanuri slave raids south of Lake Chad to AD 1600

Four rulers of the Sefuwa dynasty of Kanem were killed in rapid succession in wars against the Sao in the fourteenth century, as Kanem attempted to expand its influence over the plains to the south of the lake. Pressure against local populations continued, first from Kanem and then from Bornu, into the sixteenth century and, more sporadically, later (Lange and Berthoud 1972; Leo Africanus 1896). These attempts at control of the southern plains culminated in the campaigns of *mai* Idris Alauma of Bornu between 1571 and 1583. *Mai* Idris Alauma conducted an extended series of raids and battles against the populations living to the south of Lake Chad over this period, forcing such groups to accept the suzerainty of Bornu or driving them out of the area entirely (Lange 1987).

These campaigns were, as before, heavily resisted by local communities, and it is clear, despite ibn Fartwa's panegyrics, that the Kanuri forces often had no easy time defeating the Sao and neighboring groups. Local mud and wood fortifications were often quite strong, and *mai* Idris appears to have made a scorched earth policy the center of many of his campaigns. Ibn Fartwa (Lange 1987: 46) states that Idris Alauma 'cut down their trees in the summer, their crops in the autumn, and raided them in the winter.' There are also references to the cutting of trees inside towns, and the Sao populations may have sometimes taken refuge in large trees when their communities were attacked, as was the case in the Marghi settlement of Isge-Nguru (MacEachern, field notes 1993), and as is attested by Nachtigal (1987:340–6).

It is clear from ibn Fartwa's account that two engines drove this set of campaigns. In the first place, *mai* Idris Alauma was interested in stabilizing the frontiers of the state of Bornu, securing tribute payments from Sao and other communities, and eliminating particularly troublesome groups. In the second place, ibn Fartwa's accounts are full of defeated populations being sold into slavery. *Mai* Idris Alauma and his predecessors had been responsible for a number of military innovations during this period, including the reorganization and expansion of the Kanuri cavalry force, the acquisition of camels, the import of firearms, and the recruitment of a corps of Turkish gunners (Barkindo 1989; Lange 1987). Such innovations would have given his forces important advantages against non-centralized, agrarian populations like the Sao (and, probably more significantly, against more powerful polities like that of the Bulala). However, the introduction of horses, camels, guns, and gunners would demand corresponding exports—and slaves were one of the only major exports from this area saleable in North Africa. Leo Africanus (1896:3:832–4) describes the avidity of an earlier ruler of Bornu for horses, and notes that slaves were traded for them.

The situation southeast of Lake Chad, after the defeat of the Sefuwa dynasty by the Bulala and their retreat into Bornu, is considerably less clear. Certainly the Bulala built up an effective state apparatus in that area, but the Kanuri attempted, with varying degrees of success, to retake the region in the fifteenth and sixteenth centuries, so it was being fought over continuously. Reyna's (1990:35–8) account of Baghirmi and the putative states of Kuka, Medogo, and Babelyia make it plain that slave raiding and slave trading were fundamental elements of nation building east of the Logone-Chari river system, as they were to the west. The plains south of Lake Chad were thus, by the sixteenth century, an area that produced revenue, in the form of tribute and captives, for Bornu and the states to the east. No doubt the playing out of such dramas of state upon their territories contributed to the conversion to Islam and to the cultures of Islamic groups of many Sao populations, as noted by Barkindo (1989) and Connah (1981:38).

It is particularly important to note that by the sixteenth century, *mai* Idris Alauma was caught up in local politics and slave raiding around the northern and western margins of the Mandara Mountains, in a context which implies that his predecessors had been similarly involved for some time (Lange 1987: 76–8). This is, however, the first mention of military campaigns this far to the south of Lake Chad. Although the horse-borne mobility of the Kanuri raiders was probably effective against local populations unaccustomed to cavalry attacks, the Kanuri had some difficulties conducting operations away from the heartland of their

Figure 7.3 Defensive wall at the Iron Age site of Manaouatchi-Gréa, northern Cameroon.

Figure 7.4 Landscape of defense and domestication in the Mandara Mountains of northern Cameroon.

state. Those difficulties were exacerbated by the propensity for populations living near the Mandara Mountains to use the outlying insel-bergs as defensive positions. Certainly both the Marghi and the Wandala, theoretically Kanuri vassals, did so, and an initial attack on Keroua, then the capital of the Wandala state, was frustrated when the Wandala retreated to the top of Keroua inselberg and *mai* Idris Alauma could not starve them out.

Although the Kanuri raided around the northwestern edges of the massif, they appar-ently did not do so in the northeast, around the second and third Wandala capitals of Doulo and Mora. Local communities in that area seem to have remained unmolested for the time being (see, for example, David and MacEachern 1988). Similarly, there are no mentions in ibn Fartwa's work of raids south of Marghi territory, and it appears that the peoples of the Biu Plateau were safe from Kanuri depredations. The northwestern edges of the massif and the plains immediately sur-rounding it seem to have been the boundaries of Kanuri raiding, at least in the middle of the sixteenth century. This was probably due to an increase in logistical difficulty for forces oper-ating that far away from their bases, and to the defensive potential of the massifs and of the inselbergs around them—as the British and French found, to their cost, as late as World War I (Ferrandi 1928). The islands of Lake Chad and the banks of the Logone and Chari rivers appear to have offered some protection to more eastern populations over the same period (but see Forkl 1983: 386–7). Ibn Fartwa does not speak of slave raids into the Mandara massif itself. Indeed, montagnard groups do not figure in his accounts at all. According to Palmer, the 'people of the hills of Zajadu and the hills of N'gasara' (ibn Fartwa 1926:12) were populations living to the west of the massif, partly in what is now Marghi territory, and like the Marghi and the Wandala they used inselbergs as defensive positions.

Sub-contractors: the involvement of the Wandala and other groups, 1600–1800

It is probable that slave raiding would become steadily more difficult and less profitable for the Kanuri throughout this area over this period. As Lovejoy (1983: 83–4) and Meillas-soux (1982: 81) have pointed out, such cam-paigns resulted in the stripping of target populations from slaving frontiers, as people were captured or killed, fled to less vulnerable areas (the margins of Lake Chad or highland areas, for example), or otherwise tried to put themselves beyond the reach of the slavers. A number of possible solutions to this problem existed. In the first place, the slave require-ments of the Kanuri state could be met by exploiting untouched target territories. Slaves could also be generated through alternate methods—through kidnapping or criminal prosecutions, for example. Alternatively, the Kanuri could pass the function of actually enslaving people on to peripheral groups—'sub-contracting' it, so to speak. As a large and complex state, no doubt all three options were exploited, but it is the last that is of concern here. Between the sixteenth and the eight-eenth centuries the Wandala state began to trade slaves to the Kanuri.

It is difficult to ascertain the origins of the Wandala polity. Archaeologically, a single car-bon sample from excavations in an inselberg-foot terrace system at Keroua, the first well-attested Wandala capital, yielded a cali-brated radiocarbon date of *c.* AD 900–960 (TO-4425; 1120 +/- 50 b.p.). The sample was associated with sparse ceramics. This may be evidence of occupation, although more testing is needed, but it is certainly no proof of political complexity. The Wandala *tlikse* (king) list, derived from various sources (Forkl 1993), might offer some indication of the time-depth of Wandala's political development; Forkl places this event at *c.* 1250 AD. However, the dangers of assuming that such chronologies are accurate accounts of past events are well known (Henige 1974; Vansina 1985), and in any event the proposed 34-year average reign for Wandala *tlikse* (Forkl 1993:216) seems very high.

The Wandala first enter written histories in the 1440s to 1450s, in a map completed by Fra Mauro, an Italian monk known for his geo-graphical expertise (Garparrini Leporace 1956). The work incorporates a good deal of imagin-ary detail on the African interior, but 'Man-dera' (Wandala) and 'Mergi' (Marghi) are placed in approximately their correct positions, along with 'Bolaglia' (Bulala?) and a number of places not, as yet, identified. 'Mergi' appears to have been thought of as a more important locality than 'Mandera' on Fra Mauro's map; it is treated as the name of a region, and that term and 'Mandera' are also given as the names of towns. Over a hundred years later, the Wandala state appears again in *L'Universale fabrica del mondo, overo cosmografia*, published by Giovanni Lorenzo Anania (in Lange and Berthoud 1972). The text is in the form of four chapters dealing with different areas of the world, the third of which concerns Africa. This consists of a list of place-names and comments upon them, and the information concerning the Chad Basin is quite accurate and detailed (Lange and Berthoud 1972:342–3, 346, 348). From the same period, the Wandala also appear in ibn Fartwa's work.

There is, in these fifteenth- and sixteenth-century sources, no real evidence that the Wandala were differentiated from other non-Muslim groups living south of Lake Chad—groups like the Marghi and the Sao (MacEachern 1990: 261–5). We should not place too much emphasis on the subordination of 'Mandera' to 'Mergi' in Fra Mauro's map, but the two polities are also not treated particularly differently in ibn Fartwa's accounts of 120 years later. Anania's work does mention the Wandala, as one of a constellation of groups/communities to the south of Lake Chad. Particular attention is given to the export of iron and 'pierres Nicoli' (possibly a sort of onyx) from the Mandara area (Lange and Berthoud 1972: 342). None of these written sources mentions Wandala involvement in a slave trade, and to ibn Fartwa they were a target population, as were other indigenous groups in the study area.

It is possible that the origins of a Wandala predatory, slave-trading state lie in the development of commercial and political links between Wandala and Bornu between the sixteenth and the eighteenth centuries. The position of the Wandala homeland around Keroua *vis-à-vis* the new Kanuri capital at Birni Gazargamo may have allowed the Wandala to dominate the important export trade in Mandara iron to Bornu from the sixteenth century. The concentration of Iron Age sites in this area (MacEachern 1994) may support this proposal. The profits from such an export were then used to acquire foreign goods, which were then used to increase further Wandala power. Such goods would have included guns and armor, as well as other sorts of goods useful in increasing the prestige of the Wandala élite.

(An hypothesis that horses would have been important in this trade (MacEachern 1990) has been cast into doubt by the discovery of horse remains in pre-Wandala contexts north of the Mandara Mountains (Bourges *et al.* 1999).) The development of Wandala slave taking meant that populations further to the east and south of the Mandara Mountains came under threat, as they had not been from Kanuri slave raids. Wandala 'sub-contractors' exploited these 'resources' to fulfill internal demands, as well as to supply the external markets of Bornu and the continental trading networks (Morrissey 1984).

The transformation of the Wandala state between the sixteenth and the eighteenth centuries was quite startling. The leader described by ibn Fartwa in the mid-sixteenth century, haring up to a mountain redoubt for defense against *mai* Idris Alauma, commanded a very different state from that of the *tlikse* who ordered his army out on the plains west of Doulo to defeat a Kanuri invasion in the 1780s (Mohammadou 1982). Changes in Wandala political and social organization have been documented by Morrissey (1984) and especially by Forkl (1988, 1993), but for present purposes the most important changes over the period *c.* 1550–1800 were:

1) a movement of the state's political and economic centre of gravity to the east;
2) increasing political centralization;
3) the adoption of Islam in the early eighteenth century, first by élites and only gradually (and still incompletely) by commoners;
4) the increasing importance of slaves, both in domestic economies and politics and as an export item; and
5) the incorporation of large numbers of people from other groups (as slaves or through assimilation) into Wandala society.

These changes evolve to some extent as a package, produced by external and internal demands upon the state (*cf.* Reyna 1990). The slave trade and related events moved the Wandala into a very different trajectory from that taken by the Marghi, their erstwhile compatriots to the west, who remained only weakly centralized and largely non-Muslim until recent times.

There were other 'sub-contracting' groups

in the region beside the Wandala. Reyna (1990:37) posits the same set of processes for an important Kuka polity (which Reyna refers to as 'Magna Kuka'), southeast of Lake Chad during the fifteenth century, using the accounts of Leo Africanus as data. The Kuka slave trade presumably articulated with the trans-Saharan trade via Kanem. The Wandala themselves employed Giziga vassals (Figure 7.2) to take slaves in the Diamaré plains south of Wandala territory from the late eighteenth century onward, again gaining access to territories beyond their own logistical and military reach. These processes progressively moved the slaving frontier into areas earlier untouched, including the Biu Plateau, the regions west, east, and south of the Mandara Mountains, and the more southerly reaches of the Logone-Chari flood plains. Again, in these cases slave raiding cannot easily be separated from influences similar to those described for the Wandala above. Slave-taking, via raids, kidnapping, or other means, was never in this area a purely commercial undertaking; it existed in an environment of competition between different groups, and probably often played a role in political centralization and the assimilation of cultural elements from 'contracting' groups (see also Forkl 1983).

Responses by target groups

The effects of these processes upon local target peoples were drastic. Indigenous populations south of Lake Chad—the Sao, Maya and others—were faced with a number of alternatives, some less palatable than others. They could, in the first place, resist incursions by the slavers, but the advantages conferred by horses, firearms, and military organization would make that a dangerous tactic. Although some larger communities, like the Kotoko towns, were more or less successful in resisting *mai* Idris Alauma and his successors over the short term, few were able to do so for any prolonged period. The same process existed within Wandala territory; the small communities scattered over the plains north of the Mandara massif are most often abandoned now, the Muslim descendants of their inhabitants usually living near by (MacEachern 1993b, 1994). Submission and eventually some degree of assimilation were probably the response of most such plains-dwelling peoples, and the memory of

such assimilation persists today among populations that now call themselves Kanuri, Wandala, Kotoko, and Baghirmi (Connah 1981:38–9; Lange 1984:255; MacEachern 1990:186–7, field notes 1993–96; Migeod 1924:205–6; Reyna 1990). Conflict between state and village usually ends in the defeat of the village.

A third tactic involved the retreat of target populations to areas where natural defenses would tend to negate the advantages given to the slavers by horses and guns. These should not be thought of as mass migrations by coherent ethnic units. Rather, it would involve displacement of individuals, families, and small groups over a timespan of decades and centuries, and the gradual formation of new ethnic units from the amalgamation of such refugees with groups already inhabiting safer regions (MacEachern 1990:239–62, 311–16). A number of such environments exist within the study area. The Buduma/Yedina population of the Lake Chad islands is probably descended from such groups, and probably especially from the 'Sao Tatala' who earlier lived along the southwest edge of the lake (Lange 1984:256; 1989). They, along with the Kuri and sections of other groups (Nachtigal 1987: 3:1 07), have used the lake environment as a refuge since that time. The banks of the Logone and Chari rivers provided refuge for other peoples (see, for example, de Garine 1964). To the south, the area around the Biu Plateau may have been a haven to people moving from the north, although this remains to be further investigated (Adelberger 1992; Berns 1993).

Work in and around the Mandara Mountains strongly suggests that a similar process occurred there as well. Available evidence (David 1998; MacEachern 1990; 1993a; 1993b; 1996) suggests that the northern Mandara massif was only minimally occupied before perhaps 500 years ago, although occupation at the foot of the mountains and around inselbergs in the surrounding plains probably dates to the Late Stone Age at least. The mountains themselves have probably been covered with a fairly dense Sudanic forest through much of the Holocene, and thus would provide an unattractive environment for habitation by Neolithic or Iron Age farmers. A small proportion (about a dozen) of the hundreds of lineages occupying the northern Mandara Mountains today claim autochthonous origins there, and even then most seem traditionally to have lived along the edges of the massif. The massif/inselberg edges provide resources—stone, iron ore, sometimes good soils—that make them considerably more attractive than the mountains themselves as places to live and/or work.

Mountainous environments appear to have been used as refuges from the sixteenth century onward. Oral traditions from a number of montagnard lineages living in both Cameroon and Nigeria speak of immigration into the mountains from the plains around the massif, and particularly the plains to the north (MacEachern 1990: 213–22), where the isolated inselberg of Waza is often used as a reference point. Pressure from plains groups, and especially the Kanuri and Shuwa Arabs, is often given as an explanation for that movement. Another important group of lineages claim origins near the Wandala homeland around Keroua, and their explanation for the general antipathy between Wandala and montagnards (although not specifically for their own movement into the mountains) ascribes this relationship to the Wandala adoption of Islam and of slave raiding (MacEachern 1991, 1993a). It appears that these refugees were at first accommodated into the scattered autochthonous communities on the flanks of the Mandara massif without much trouble, although problems set in as more immigrants arrived. Such migrations would probably date to the sixteenth century onward, although some concentration of population around the mountains may have occurred somewhat earlier.

The effects of the slave trade on the southern Lake Chad Basin, 1200–1800

The effects of these population movements upon the physical and cultural landscapes of the southern Lake Chad Basin have been very drastic indeed. The consequences of these processes are obvious in the *firki* and sand plains to the south of the lake. Sao and Maya communities have disappeared, although individuals and groups retain a memory of their ancestral ethnic affiliations. Plains people now call themselves Kanuri, Wandala, Kotoko, Hausa, and Shuwa, although in these cases there are probably few who do not have Sao and/or Maya forebears. It is very probable that

an homogenization of plains ethnicity and culture has occurred over this time period. As noted, the very term 'Sao' is a Kanuri ascription (Lange 1989) that probably conceals considerable ethnic and cultural variation. The amalgamation of communities into 'ethnic groups' by European colonial administrators in this region has similarly concealed a good deal of such diversity in the twentieth century. Élites from different polities within the region progressively adopted elements of social and political systems of dominant groups—the widespread adoption of Kanuri court titles and functions is a striking example. The progressive embracement of Islam by élites and commoners in this region over the last thousand years would contribute to such an homogenization of local culture. Archaeological research provides some support for these positions, given the long-standing differentiation in ceramics between communities near the Mandara Mountains that are now all referred to as 'Wandala' (MacEachern 1993b, 1993c).

Perhaps the most striking change in the landscape of this region involved the occupation of more peripheral areas by populations seeking refuge from Kanuri, Wandala, Bulala, Baghirmi, and other raids. Given the great fluctuations in lake levels that Lake Chad displays, its margins and islands are probably not promising places for archaeological research, and indeed we do not know if those areas were occupied before the coming of the Kuri and Yedina/Buduma. It is probable, however, that occupation of the lacustrine environment increased considerably with the coming of refugee populations.

In the same way, the northern Mandara Mountains have been transformed, physically as well as culturally, through their occupation by expanding groups, reinforced by immigrants. This area of the massif is now entirely a cultural landscape, consisting of a web of ground surfaces that are continuously modified and renewed by their occupiers. The Sudanic woodland that would have covered massif slopes before the coming of humans has disappeared, except for a few relict stands at the highest elevations (Boutrais 1984; Hallaire 1976; White 1983). The mountains have in many areas been virtually denuded of trees, those remaining being carefully protected by local people for their wood and other useful products. The intensive agriculture that is carried out in many parts of the Mandara Mountains has resulted in the construction of innumerable small, stone-built terraces, sometimes watered by hand and often covering entire hillsides; these are necessary to support population densities that frequently exceed 100 people per square kilometer, and in the northern massif may attain 250 people per square kilometer (Figure 7.4a,b,c). Similar processes probably occurred on and around the Biu Plateau, but at present archaeological and ethnohistorical data do not allow us to say this with certainty.

In many areas, the massif gives the impression of being completely domesticated, as much a human artifact as Euroamerican parkland, albeit considerably more intensively exploited. These conditions must have been created relatively quickly, because these terrace systems cannot exist without high population densities for their construction and maintenance, and without terracing of large areas for the prevention of up-slope erosion and the elimination of animal pests in peripheral woodlands (Hallaire 1976: 16). This points to a comparatively rapid, and quite massive, increase in massif population densities and exploitation, probably to be ascribed to the needs of defense and labor. This increase was probably stimulated by the depredations of the Wandala and other slaving groups, and so in the northern massif at least probably dated to the seventeenth century. The physical consequences of this occupation are, for the purposes of the present study, perhaps the least important. The establishment of a large, agrarian, non-Muslim montagnard population in the highlands south of Lake Chad, and the accompanying dislocation of the pre-existing Iron Age plains communities, were events of the greatest importance in the history of the southern Lake Chad Basin. These highland populations evolved a complicated, and intensely ambiguous, relationship with the Wandala and other plains-dwellers living below them, one based on complementary and conflicting resource requirements and social ties, that has persisted until the present day (MacEachern 1993a). Archaeological investigations in this area have not yet progressed to the point where we have discovered physical evidence of the slave trade itself. That will come, and may profitably involve examination of known slave-trading markets, such as that at Wakwirsa inselberg near Doulo (MacEachern, field notes 1996) and of known slave villages (Morrissey 1984:166–73). However, many of the cultural, economic, and material configurations of human life in this area can be traced to the evolving relationship between mountains and plains peoples, and that relationship is itself to a great extent due to the slave trade.

Slave destinations and the continuation of the trade, 1800–1900

Magnitudes and destinations

As noted above, markets for slaves can be internal or external to the societies of the slave raiders. In the 'sub-contracting' situation that I have identified for the Wandala and other groups, the initial market would be external; slaves were sold to the Kanuri to buy other items. However, an internal market undoubtedly developed very quickly, since slaves were very far from being a mere commercial good—the possession of other humans being a potent sign of wealth and power. By one estimate, slaves made up 50 percent of the population of the Wandala state at the end of the nineteenth century, out of a total population of probably 20,000 to 30,000 people (Hallaire 1965:58). Certainly not all of these slaves were taken in raids—many would have been born into slavery—but this does imply a continuing, and substantial, input of captives. There are no data on the proportion of slaves among the other societies of the study area, although the data for the Wandala seem to be generally comparable to proportions found in other states in the Western and Central Sudan over the same time period (Lovejoy 1983:185–202). This indicates a total slave population for the study area of some scores of thousands of individuals, although this is really a guess dignified as an estimate. We also have no data on changes in the proportion of slaves through time in Wandala or other states, although the numbers of slaves held probably expanded somewhat during the nineteenth century, for external and internal reasons (Lovejoy 1983; Manning 1990: 75–6; Morrissey 1984: 212–18).

The number of slaves exported annually from Wandala territory to Bornu was some

1,000 to 3,000 during the eighteenth century (Morrissey 1984: 43); of these, a small and varying number were sent as tribute, but most moved through commercial networks. Exports climbed during the nineteenth century, although sales in external markets were hampered by the 'capture' of some target societies by the Fulbe of Adamawa, and probably by an increased demand for slaves within the Wandala state itself. It is likely that the figure of 1,000 to 3,000 slave exports/year is a good approximation for the total volume of the Wandala trade through the seventeenth and eighteenth centuries, when target communities were still quite available, the Kanuri were the Wandala's main competitors in the plains, and slaves were not as economically and politically central to Wandala as they would later become (Morrissey 1984). We may compare this to Reyna's (1990:129–30) estimate of an annual *intake* of *c.* 6,000 slaves in Baghirmi in the early twentieth century, about 1,000 of whom were obtained as tribute, and the rest captured in raids. This, of course, does not take into account slave trade and employment within the study area, or mortality rates in slave taking, which could be very high.

Throughout the entire period of slave taking and slave trading south of Lake Chad, the primary external market for slaves from the study area lay in North Africa, with captives shipped across the Sahara via the trade route that ran through Bilma. Rather fewer captives were shipped from Kanem and Baghirmi east through Darfur to Egypt. Lovejoy (1983) and Austin (1992) give rough estimates of total exports of perhaps 1,000–2,000 people/year on the trans-Saharan trade routes through Bilma and Darfur between the tenth and nineteenth centuries, rising to perhaps 3,000 from Bornu through the mid-nineteenth century, and then falling again. It is probable that a very large proportion of these slaves came from within the study area. The trade in slaves toward the south (i.e., to the Fulbe communities of Adamawa and so further south) appears never to have been very important. The southern Diamaré was an important source of Mandara slaves, before being taken over by the Fulbe in the early nineteenth century, and so was hardly an inviting area for slave sales; trade routes through Cameroon to the Gulf of Guinea did not develop until the early twentieth century (Roupsard 1991).

There was, however, articulation with other slave trade systems through Bornu and the Hausa states. Bornu was always the greatest market for slaves from the survey area, and there was some trade in slaves from the Kanuri capitals at Birni Gazargamo and Kukawa to the markets in Kano and Katsina. Those markets in turn sold slaves south to the Gulf of Guinea and Bight of Bénin by the late eighteenth century, and there were also a certain number of slaves exported from Hausa territory to Asante (Adamu 1979; Lovejoy 1983: 26, 72, Table 7.8; Manning 1990: 75). A number of Europeans collected Hausa and Kanuri vocabularies along the West African coast and in the New World in the early to mid-nineteenth century, showing some involvement of slaves from the Central Sudan in the Atlantic trade at that time (Hair 1967: 34–6).

The slaves from the study area who were eventually incorporated within the Atlantic slave trade reached the Atlantic coast via these routes, and most especially the former one. The trade in slaves was not the primary engine behind this trade to the coast. Rather, most of the slaves who passed through this route did so as domestic slaves, specialized craftsmen or porters, and were then sold to Asante or Yoruba owners, to be resold at a later time. There is almost no information available on the origins and numbers of slaves from the study area incorporated into the Atlantic slave trade over time. Origins are, in most cases, subsumed under the labels 'Bornu'/'Kanuri' or, even more generally, 'Hausa' (Lovejoy 1983:Table 7.8), although it is likely that by the end of the eighteenth century most slaves from Bornu would actually be from 'peripheral' populations like those in the study area. Most sources (see especially Adamu 1979) agree that the magnitude of the Central Sudan–Atlantic coast trade was comparatively small, probably no more than a few hundred people annually, and that there were often significant time lags between local sale by the Central Sudanic traders and later sale to Europeans. These slaves moved along trade routes of some antiquity in the area. Their sale was the continuing expression of regional exchanges that saw, for example, Islam and cultural and political systems associated with Islam become more influential along the northern forest belt of West Africa, and Euroamerican trade goods and cultigens move in the opposite direction, northeast to Lake Chad. They are thus indicators of social changes that were of central importance in the history of West and Central Africa.

The end of the trade, 1800–1940

I have concentrated upon the period before AD 1800 in this discussion of slavery and the slave trade, and their cultural consequences, in the southern Lake Chad Basin. This may appear somewhat perverse, given that most of the data on slavery from this area dates to the nineteenth century. However, by 1800 much of the study area had been incorporated within the ambit of Muslim states, large segments of the populations of those states were at least nominally Muslim, and target populations had been restricted to fragmented, 'peripheral' communities. In some cases, these latter populations were probably the objects of attempts at destabilization by slavers anxious to prevent the development of competing centers of economic and political power (MacEachern, 2000). In any case, there was relatively little scope at that point for such 'peripheral' populations to become serious competitors to the large Sudanic states. Incipient centralization in small montagnard polities like Sukur, Gudur, and the Mofu 'princedoms' (David and Sterner 1993; Jouaux 1991; Seignobos 1991; Vincent 1991) was confined to limited territories, while the Kotoko communities were becoming Islamized and more open to cultural and political influences from their larger neighbors.

The slave trade continued through the nineteenth century, and well into the twentieth, in the study area. There had been an increase in the number of slaves exported from Bornu in the mid-nineteenth century, and around Bornu, Wandala, and Baghirmi that period probably saw an increase in slave taking for external and internal markets (see above). After that time, the demand for slaves declined quite quickly, while central political authorities lost control of the trade to merchants and adventurers (Morrissey 1984: 174–210). It was only at the end of the nineteenth century that outsiders like Rabeh Zubair could take advantage of new military technologies and the disorganization associated with European colonialism, to establish temporary suzerainty over large parts of the territory south of Lake Chad. By that time, of course, new factors had entered the equation, and both the local slave trade and relations between Central Sudanic communities were becoming more and more subject to decisions made in London, Paris, and Berlin. The fundamental characteristics of the slave trade did not change until the European powers established control over what had become Nigeria, Kamerun and Tchad, when colonial officers began to force it underground with varying degrees of enthusiasm and competence.

Conclusions

I have argued in this paper that slavery and slave taking became important in the southern Lake Chad Basin only after c. 1200, and that from then until AD 1600 at least there were some differences in the vulnerability of various indigenous groups to slave raids. These distinctions were related to the proximity of different areas to the political centers from which slave raiders emanated, and to local environmental features that might offer some protection against raiders. This difficulty was eventually overcome by the involvement of new, 'subcontracting' groups, living in close proximity to target populations, in the slave trade. Bornu may well have started out as such a 'subcontractor' to Kanem. The Wandala and Baghirmi were also such groups, although they eventually attained varying degrees of freedom of action. Wandala went from being one of a number of small agrarian societies located near the northwestern extremity of the Mandara Mountains to being a dominant state on the plains south of Lake Chad, as slave trading supplemented, and eventually exceeded in value, the iron trade north from the massif.

This incorporation of new societies into the trade happened continuously in the Central Sudan. This resulted in the uninterrupted development of a slaving frontier, a frontier on which 'peripheral' populations were under threat of enslavement and behind which adoption of dominant cultural and religious forms allowed people at least a theoretical immunity to such enslavement. The development of the slaving frontier had important effects on local cultural systems; it erased a number of pre-existing ethnic groups in the area and led to the establishment of new sorts of communities in defensible regions. The archaeological signatures of those processes remain to be sorted out; indeed, archaeological testing of such a model, built primarily on historical and ethno-historical data, is very greatly needed and is only just beginning.

Within the southern Lake Chad Basin, slave taking and slave possession were never exclusively the sports of kings and nobles. People were captured by their neighbors, in disputes over lands and property; children were sold by their parents in times of famine; merchants became steadily more involved in what was rightly seen as a lucrative commerce. Slavery existed within a ubiquitous social context, and it drew all manner of people into its realm. However, there seems to have been an intimate relationship between states and slavery throughout the last thousand years in this area. We have very little data (archaeological or otherwise) on the earliest states around Lake Chad; it may turn out that politically complex communities existed in this area earlier in the first millennium AD, presumably before slave taking and slave holding became economically and socially important. At present, there is no evidence that that was the case, and state-level societies and slavery appear virtually simultaneously in historical sources.

This relation is relatively easy to understand in more recent periods. As Reyna (1990:39) says, 'States . . . warred to trade and traded to war.' Commodities and populations had to be controlled to guarantee that consumable and tradable resources could be produced. This was especially the case when valuable natural products, like the gold of West Africa, were not available, and when human populations thus themselves became commodities. Sources of slaves had to be acquired; trade routes had to be protected. It may, however, be dangerous to give too much privilege to economic structures in this argument. While organized warfare and the capture and owner-ship of slaves served the economic interests of states, these activities were also among the defining pursuits of élites in those states, and it is likely that the spread of slave taking and slave holding had as much to do with efforts by nascent élites to become established and accepted as it did with economic circumstance. Unsurprisingly, the adoption of a slave-taking system caused intense alienation between raiding cores and raided peripheries (MacEachern

1993a; Reyna 1990). The adoption of Islam became a means for élites in raiding societies £to differentiate themselves socially and culturally from raided neighbors, as well as allowing them to enter into closer economic and political relations with Muslim societies further afield; while its acceptance by common people theoretically furnished them with a measure of security against slave raids. As seems to be the case with the Wandala, slavery could penetrate pre-existing trading systems, where it then had a catalytic effect upon the external and internal sociopolitical relations of the society.

The slave trade in the southern Lake Chad Basin was central to the creation of local societies as we know them today. There is, however, a tendency to view the African slave trade through the glass of states, literate people, and the production of Great Traditions, European and Muslim. Using the texts of such a tradition, people become demographic data, as we see them move from the possession of raiding parties, to intermediate traders, to eventual owners, some in the New World, some in the Old. It would probably be a good thing to examine somewhat more closely the stories of 'peripheral' populations in this region, because—as was the case in many parts of Africa—it was among the small, mute, agrarian populations that the most strenuous opposition to the slave trade often took place. In a perverse way, historians and ethnohistorians working in the Lake Chad Basin are fortunate, because the slave trade there is so recent that the voices of experience can still be heard. It would be better had it been otherwise.

Acknowledgments

I would like to thank Chris DeCorse for his editorial efforts with this work, and Nicholas David and Genevieve LeMoine for perceptive criticisms of earlier versions of the paper. I would also like to thank Raymond Asombang (Université de Yaoundé), for all of his help during work in Cameroon. This research was carried out through grants from the Social Sciences and Humanities Research Council of Canada (Mandara Archaeological Project grants 410–83–0819, 410–85–1040 and 410–88–0361, and Project Maya-Wandala grants 410–92–1860 and 410–95–0379), the

National Geographic Society, Bowdoin College, the Alberta Heritage Fund, and the Department of Research Services of the University of Calgary.

References

Adamu, M. (1979) The delivery of slaves from Central Africa to the Bight of Benin in the eighteenth and nineteenth centuries. In *The Uncommon Market: Essays in the Economic History of the Atlantic Slave Trade*, edited by H. Gemery and J. Hogendorn. New York: Academic Press, pp. 163–80.

Adelberger, J. (1992) The Muri Mountains of northeastern Nigeria—an outline of the ethnographic and linguistic situation. *Nigerian Field*, 57 (1–2):35–48.

Austin, R. (1992) The Mediterranean Islamic slave trade out of Africa: a tentative census. In *The Human Commodity: Perspectives on the Trans-Saharan Slave Trade*, edited by E. Savage. London: Frank Cass, pp. 216–48.

Barkindo, M. B. (1989) *The Sultanate of Mandara to 1902*. Stuttgart: Franz Steiner Verlag.

Barreteau, D., Breton, R. and Dieu, M. (1984) Les langues. In *Le Nord du Cameroun: des hommes, une région*, edited by J. Boutrais and others. Collection mémoires 102. Paris: Editions de l'ORSTOM, pp. 159–80.

Beauvilain, A. (1989) *Nord-Cameroun: crises et peuplement*. Paris: published privately by the author.

Berns, M. (1993) Art, history and gender: women and clay in West Africa. *African Archaeological Review*, 11:129–48.

Bourges, C., MacEachern, S. and Reeves, M. (1999) Excavations at Aissa Hardé, 1995 and 1996. *Nyame Akuma*, 51:6–13.

Boutrais, J. (1984) Les milieux naturels et l'occupation du sol. In *Le Nord du Cameroun: des hommes, une région*, edited by J. Boutrais and others. Collections mémoires 102. Paris: Editions de l'ORSTOM, pp. 63–100.

Boutrais, J. and others (1984) *Le Nord du Cameroun: des hommes, une région* Collections mémoires 102. Paris: Editions de l'ORSTOM.

Comaroff, J. (1987) Of totemism and ethnicity: consciousness, practice and the signs of inequality. *Ethnos*, 52 (3–4):301–22.

Connah, G. (1981) *Three Thousand Years in Africa: Man and His Environment in the Lake Chad Region of Nigeria*. Cambridge: Cambridge University Press.

Connah, G. (1984) An archaeological exploration in southern Bornu. *African Archaeological Review*, 2:153–71.

David, N. (1998) The ethnoarchaeology and field archaeology of grinding at Sukur, Adamawa State, Nigeria. *African Archaeological Review*, 15(1):13–64.

David, N. and MacEachern, S. (1988) The Mandara Archaeological Project: preliminary results of the 1984 season. In *Le Milieu et les hommes: recherches comparatives et historiques dans le bassin du Lac Tchad*, edited by D. Barreteau and H. Tourneux. Collection colloques et séminaires. Paris: Editions de l'ORSTOM, pp. 51–80.

David, N. and Sterner, J. (1993) 'Water and iron: phases in the history of Sukur'. Paper presented at the 1993 Mega-Chad Conference, Frankfurt May.

de Garine, I. (1964) *Les Massa du Cameroun*. Paris: P.U.F. (Presses Universitaires de France).

de Leeuw, P. N. (1972) Present and potential land use. In *The Land Resources of North East Nigeria*, edited by P. Tuley. Surbiton: Directorate of Overseas Surveys, pp. 183–97.

Ferrandi, J. (1928) *La conquête du Nord-Cameroun*. Paris: Lavanzelle, Paris.

Forkl, H. (1983) *Die Beziehungen der zentralsudanischen Reiche Bornu, Mandara und Bagirmi sowie der Kotoko-Staaten zu ihren südlichen Nachbarn unter besonderer Berücksichtigung des Sao-Problems*. Münchner Ethnologische Abhandlungen 3. Munich: Minerva-Publikation.

Forkl, H. (1988) Innerafrikanische Akkulturation bei den Wadela, einem Stamm der Kerdi-Mura (Nordkamerun). *Münchner Beiträge zur Völkerkunde*, 1:63–77.

Forkl, H. (1993) La chronologie et le problème de la succession légitime des rois Wandala dans les manuscrits arabes. In *Datation et chronologie dans le bassin du Lac Tchad*, edited by D. Barreteau and C. von Graffenried. Paris: Editions de l'ORSTOM, pp. 209–27.

Garparrini Leporace, T. (1956) *Il Mappamondo di Fra Mauro*. (with reproductions of the Fra Mauro map of 1459). Rome: Istituto Poligrafico dello Stato.

Hair, P. E. (1967) *The Early Study of Nigerian Languages: Essays and Bibliographies*. Cambridge: Cambridge University Press.

Hallaire, A. (1965) *Les Monts du Mandara au Nord de Mokolo et la plaine de Mora: étude géographique régionale*. Yaoundé ORSTOM/IRCAM.

Hallaire, A. (1976) Problèmes de développement au nord des monts Mandara. *Cahiers ORSTOM, Série Sciences Humaines*, 13 (1):3–22.

Henige, D. (1974) *The Chronology of Oral Tradition:*

Quest for a Chimera. London: Oxford University Press.

Holl, A. (1988) Transition du Néolithique à l'Age du Fer dans la plaine péritchadienne: le cas de Mdaga. In *Le Milieu et les hommes: recherches comparatives et historiques dans le bassin du Lac Tchad,* edited by D. Barreteau and H. Tourneux. Collection colloques et séminaires. Paris: Editions de l'ORSTOM, pp. 81–109.

ibn Fartwa, A. (1926) *Kirgam Ghazawat Barnu.* (Translated by H. R. Palmer as *History of the First Twelve Years of the Reign of Mai Idris Alooma of Bornu.*) Lagos: Government Printer. (First published 1582/3.)

Isichei, E. (ed.) (1982) *Studies in the History of Plateau State, Nigeria.* London: Macmillan.

Jouaux, C. (1991) La chefferie de Gudur et sa politique expansionniste. In *Du politique à l'économique: études historiques dans le bassin du Lac Tchad,* edited by J. Boutrais. Paris: Editions de l'ORSTOM, pp. 193–224.

Kopytoff, I. (1987) The internal African frontier: the making of African political culture. In *The African Frontier: The Reproduction of Traditional African Societies,* edited by I. Kopytoff. Bloomington: Indiana University Press, pp. 3–84.

Lange, D. (1980) La région du lac Tchad d'après la géographie d'ibn Said. Texts et cartes. *Annales Islamologiques,* 16:149–81.

Lange, D. (1984) The kingdoms and peoples of Chad. In *General History of Africa, IV. Africa from the Twelfth to the Sixteenth Century,* edited by D. T. Niane. Paris and London: UNESCO and Heinemann Educational Books, pp. 238–65.

Lange, D. (1987) *A Sudanic Chronicle: The Borno Expeditions of Idris Alauma (1564–1576).* Wiesbaden: Franz Steiner.

Lange, D. (1988) The Chad region as a crossroads. In *General History of Africa, III. Africa from the Seventh to the Eleventh Century,* edited by M. el Fasi. Paris and London: UNESCO and Heinemann Educational Books, pp. 436–60.

Lange, D. (1989) Préliminaires pour une histoire des Sao. *Journal of African History,* 30 (2):189–210.

Lange, D. and Berthoud, S. (1972) L'interieur de l'Afrique Occidentale d'apres Giovanni Lorenzo Anania (XVIIème siècle). *Cahiers d'Histoire Mondiale,* 16 (2):299–351.

Lebeuf, J.-P. (1962) *Archéologie tchadienne: les Sao du Cameroun et du Tchad.* Paris: Hermann.

Lebeuf, J.-P. (1969) *Carte archéologique des abords du Lac Tchad (Cameroun, Nigérie, Tchad).* Paris: Editions du CNRS.

Lebeuf, J.-P., Lebeuf, A. M. D., Treinen-Claustre, F. and Courtin, J. (1980) *Le Gisement Sao de Mdaga (Tchad): fouilles 1960–1968.* Paris: Société d'Ethnographie.

Leo Africanus (1896) *The History and Description of Africa and of the Notable Things Therein Contained.* Translated by John Pory. New York: Hakluyt Society. (First published 1526.)

Lovejoy, P. (1983) *Transformations in Slavery: A History of Slavery in Africa.* Cambridge: Cambridge University Press.

Lovejoy, P. and Hogendorn, J. (1993) *Slow Death for Slavery: The Course of Abolition in Northern Nigeria, 1897–1936.* Cambridge: Cambridge University Press.

MacEachern, S. (1990) 'Du Kunde': processes of montagnard ethnogenesis in the northern Mandara mountains of Cameroon. Ph.D. thesis, University of Calgary, Calgary.

MacEachern, S. (1991) Les gens de Ngolélé: an examination of prehistoric ethnic relations in the northern Mandara Mountains. In *Du politique a l'économique: études historiques dans le bassin du Lac Tchad,* edited by J. Boutrais. Paris: Editions de l'ORSTOM, pp. 165–92.

MacEachern, S. (1992) 'Defining ethnicity: the Mandara example'. Paper presented at the annual conference of the Canadian Archaeological Association, London, May.

MacEachern, S. (1993a) Selling the iron for their shackles: Wandala – montagnard interactions in northern Cameroon. *Journal of African History,* 33(2):241–70.

MacEachern, S. (1993b) The Projet Maya-Wandala: preliminary results of the 1992 field season. *Nyame Akuma,* 39:7–13.

MacEachern, S. (1993c) 'Iron Age and recent settlement patterning in northern Cameroon'. Paper presented at the annual conference of the Society for American Archaeology, St. Louis, April.

MacEachern, S. (1994) The Projet Maya-Wandala: preliminary results of the 1993 field season. *Nyame Akuma,* 41:48–55.

MacEachern, S. (1996) Iron Age beginnings north of the Mandara Mountains, Cameroon and Nigeria. In *Aspects of African Archaeology: Proceedings of the Tenth Pan-African Congress,* edited by G. Pwiti and R. Soper. Harare: University of Zimbabwe Press.

MacEachern, S. (2000 a) Setting the boundaries: linguistics, ethnicity, colonialism and archaeology south of Lake Chad. In *Archaeology, Language, and History: Essays on the Prehistory of Ethnicity,* edited by John Terrell. New York: Greenwood Publishing Company.

MacEachern, S. (2000 b) Blacksmiths, castes and

state societies in the northern Mandara Mountains. Special volume of *Iowa Studies in African Arts*.

Manning, P. (1990) *Slavery and African Life: Occidental, Oriental and African Slave Trades*. Cambridge: Cambridge University Press.

Marliac, A. (1985) *L'Age du fer au Cameroun septentrional: rapport préliminaire sur le site du Salak au Diamaré*. Paris: Editions de l'ORSTOM.

Marliac, A. (1991) *De la préhistoire à l'histoire au Cameroun septentrional*. Paris: Editions de l'ORSTOM.

Marliac, A. and Delneuf, M. (1984) *Reconnaissances archéologiques au Cameroun septentrional*. Paris: ORSTOM-MESRES Cameroon.

Meillassoux, C. (1982) The role of slavery in the economic and social history of Sahelo-Sudanic Africa. In *Forced Migration: The Impact of the Export Slave Trade on African Societies*, edited by J. E. Inikori. London: Hutchinson University Library, pp. 74–99.

Migeod, F. W. H. (1924) *Through Nigeria to Lake Chad*. London: Heath Cranton.

Mohammadou, E. (1982) *Le Royaume du Wandala ou Mandara au XIXe siècle*. Tokyo: Institute for the Study of Languages and Cultures of Asia and Africa.

Morrissey, S. R. (1984) 'Clients and slaves in the development of the Mandara élite: northern Cameroon in the nineteenth century'. Ph.D. dissertation, Boston University. Ann Arbor: University Microfilms International.

Nachtigal, G. (1987) *Sahara and Sudan*. London: C. Hurst. (First published 1881.)

Reyna, S. P. (1990) *Wars Without End*. Hanover, NH, and London: University Press of New England.

Roupsard, M. (1991) Evolution des échanges entre le bassin tchadien (Tchad, Nord-Cameroun) et la côte du Golfe de Guinée pendant la période coloniale. In *Du politique a l'économique: études historiques dans le bassin du Lac Tchad*, edited by J. Boutrais. Paris: Editions de l'ORSTOM, pp. 107–17.

Sackett, J. (1990) Style and ethnicity in archaeology: the case for isochrestism. In *The Uses of Style in Archaeology*, edited by M. W. Conkey and C. A. Hastorf. Cambridge: Cambridge University Press, pp. 32–43.

Seignobos, C. (1991) Le rayonnement de la chefferie théocratique de Gudur (Nord-Cameroun). In *Du politique à l'économique: études historiques dans le bassin du Lac Tchad*, edited by J. Boutrais. Paris: Editions de l'ORSTOM, pp. 225–316.

Vail, L. (1991) Introduction: Ethnicity in southern African history. In *The Creation of Tribalism in Southern Africa*, edited by L. Vail. Berkeley: University of California Press, pp. 1–19.

Vansina, J. (1985) *Oral Tradition as History*. Madison: University of Wisconsin Press.

Vincent, J.-F. (1991) *Princes montagnards du Nord-Cameroun: les Mofu-Diamaré et le pouvoir politique*. Paris: L'Harmattan.

Wente-Lukas, R. (1985) *Handbook of Ethnic Units in Nigeria*. Studien zur Kulturkunde 74. Stuttgart: Franz Steiner.

White, F. (1983) *The Vegetation of Africa: A Descriptive Memoir to Accompany the Unesco/AETFAT/UNSO Vegetation Map of Africa*. Paris: UNESCO.

Wolf, E. (1982) *Europe and the People Without History*. Berkeley: University of California Press.

8 500 Years in the Cameroons: Making Sense of the Archaeological Record

AUGUSTIN F. C. HOLL

This paper explores implications of the recent archaeological research and their relevance to a deeper understanding of the history of the Cameroons from AD 1500 to 1900. The archaeological data available have been collected in five major areas of the country: the Grassfields Plateau in the southwest, the Yaoundé Plateau in the south, the Adamaoua Plateau further north, the Upper Benue Basin, and the Chadian plain in the Northern Province. It can be argued that southern Cameroon was involved in the slave trade and the Atlantic commercial network, while the north was more connected with the trans-Saharan trade. Both exchange systems were, however, intimately connected. The involvement of communities in long-distance exchange networks resulted in social transformations that generated different evolutionary trajectories in a 'domino-like' chain reaction from cores to peripheries.

Introduction: aims and purposes

This paper aims to explore the implications and societal meanings of the archaeological record of Cameroon. It integrates, within a social and historical framework, different kinds of material evidence in order to provide a deeper understanding of the recent past of peoples and cultures of this part of Africa, from the sixteenth to the end of the nineteenth century. Owing to differences in coverage and intensity of fieldwork and the nature of published material, our discussion will focus on the best documented cases: the Western Grassfields, the Yaoundé Plateau, the Adamaoua Plateau, the Upper Benue Basin, and the Chadian plain (Figure 8.1).

Chronological boundaries are always partly arbitrary and debatable, but they are also very useful. It depends on the researchers to demonstrate the utility of each chronological construct. In this regard, our chronological boundaries, AD 1500 to c. AD 1900, which witnessed the onset and the development of the Atlantic slave trade, may have different meanings depending on the area under consideration. In the southern part of the country, approximately from southern Adamaoua to the Atlantic coast, including the forested areas of the southeast, the lower boundary (AD 1500) is demarcated by the advent of Europeans on the coast. In the Chadian Basin, the dominant feature is the development of the Kanuri kingdom of Bornu, which may have generated a long-term cycle of social and political reorganization among neighboring societies.

It is not claimed that these 'events' are the ultimate explanation of everything that happened in the whole country during the 400 to 500 years to come. It is, however, considered that these phenomena, which may

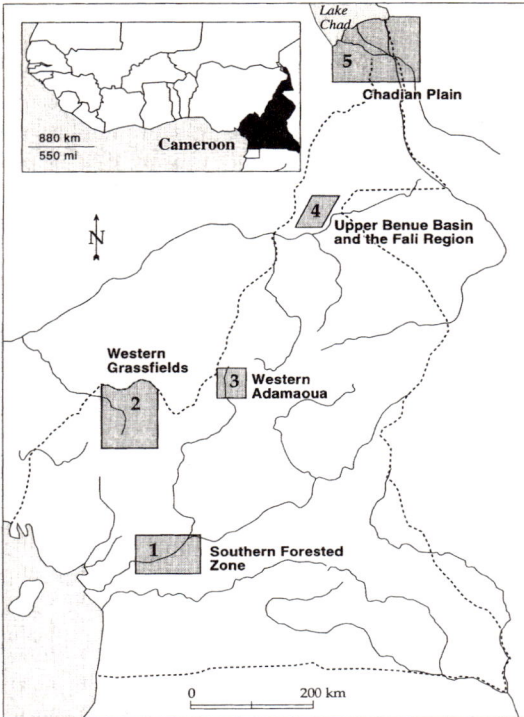

Figure 8.1 Location map of the selected regional cases studied: 1) The Lékié-Yaoundé region in the southern forested zone; 2) The Western Grassfields; 3) The Western Adamaoua; 4) The Upper Benue Basin and the Fali region; 5) The Chadian plain.

seem at first glance relatively independent of each other, can be used as appropriate chronological boundaries for our discussion. The upper boundary is, theoretically, easier to formulate, as it coincides with a radical change in the relations between European powers and Africa—being characterized by competition for colonies or 'scramble' for territories, followed by the implementation of European colonial systems during the second half of the nineteenth and the twentieth centuries. In the case of the Cameroons, German colonization officially began on July 14th, 1884, with the treaty signed by G. Nachtigal in the name of Kaiser Wilhelm II with King Akwa and King Bell at Duala (Pakenham 1991: 214). Colonial authority was extended over the rest of the country in the following decades.

The Cameroons cover an area of 475,000 square kilometers, (183,000 square miles) stretching from the equatorial forest in the

south to the Sahelian margins in the Lake Chad basin. This vast area is characterized by a diversity of linguistic, ethnic, and cultural groups with a diversity of socio-political organizations ranging from dispersed kin-based groups in the south to highly centralized chiefdoms and states in the west and the north. These various groupings have followed different evolutionary pathways. Some disappeared from the historical records, subsumed by dominant groups, while some new societies may have emerged through the combination of formerly distinct groups. The emphasis on these different trajectories underscores the difficulties involved in the uncritical use of present-day ethnic and linguistic labels in attempts to reconstruct the past (Tardits 1981). Social groups, be they characterized by shared world-views, language, or ethnic ascription, are products of historical processes. They are not permanent 'essences' which last for ever.

Keeping these issues in mind, it can be argued that the southern part of the country has been differentially involved in the slave trade and the Atlantic commercial network, while the north was more connected—through Hausa, Kanuri, and Arab traders—with the trans-Saharan trade and its own important slave trade (Lewis 1993). Both exchange systems were, however, intimately connected (Rowlands 1986, Tardits 1981, Von Morgen 1982, Warnier 1985). In all the cases, intra- and inter-group social dynamics, the differential involvement of native communities into local and long-distance exchange networks, and the social and demographic consequences of the slave trade have resulted in deep and radical transformations of the region's social systems, and have probably generated different evolutionary trajectories in a 'domino-like' chain reaction.

The archaeological data available will be integrated into a wider sociohistorical context of the transformations of the past Cameroonian societies. Documentary sources, ethnohistories, oral sources, and archaeological data will be considered within a regional framework. Each category of data poses its own theoretical and methodological problems and refers to a specific part of the historical process under investigation (Vansina 1984, 1990). In this regard, it would be a better research strategy to treat each of them separately. Such a work, however, is beyond the scope of this paper. The major issue under investigation may be framed as follows: what do archaeological data tell us about Cameroonian societies during the last 500 years?

A search for patterns: the archaeological record in regional perspective

For a variety of reasons, archaeological research has focused on some areas while others have been neglected. The northern part of the country has been studied more intensively (David 1981; Gauthier 1981, 1992; A. Lebeuf 1981; J. P. Lebeuf 1992; Marliac 1981). In contrast, it is only during the last two decades that sustained archaeological investigations have been conducted in the south, in the forested zone and the Grassfields highlands (Essomba 1992, 1993; de Maret 1982, 1985, 1992). Hurault (1979, 1986, 1988, 1993), a geographer, has studied the dynamics of pre-Fulani settlements in western Adamaoua, and has thus provided important information on an 'archaeological no man's land.' More recently, some younger Cameroonian archaeologists, working in very difficult conditions, often with limited funding, have initiated surveys in order to map settlement distributions in the forest zone and Grassfields highlands (Asombang et al 1990; Atangana 1989, 1992; Mbida 1992a, 1992b; Ossah-Mvondo 1990, 1992a, 1992b).

For the purpose of this work five main regional clusters of sites will be considered: the Yaoundé-Lékié on the left bank of the Sanaga river in the Central Province; the northern part of the Grassfields highlands in the west; the territory of the Banyo *lamidat* or polity in western Adamaoua; the Upper Benue Basin and the Fali region in the north of Garoua; and the mounds sites of the Chadian plain in the extreme north (Figure 8.1). The Mandara Mountains (a sixth cluster) was examined by MacEachern in the previous paper.

The forested zone and the Sanaga–Lékié settlements

From the Sanaga river valley to the Cameroon–Gabon boundary in the south, archaeological surveys and small-scale excavations carried out during the last decade are changing the older picture of the equatorial forest area as an environment unsuitable for human settlement. The recorded sites are not yet securely dated, and detailed publications of the excavated material are not available. It is, therefore, far from certain which settlements were inhabited during the last 500 years. Even with these limits in mind, the data attest to a wide extension of iron production; the patterns of intensification observed in the Matomb and Babimbi regions are an archaeological testimony of changing socio-economic circumstances between the sixteenth and nineteenth centuries.

Recent archaeological research has shown that portions of the Yaoundé were inhabited by food-producing communities from 4000 BC (de Maret 1992). The presence of iron technology is attested to between 600 and 400 BC, and much research has been focused on the emergence of this technology. Even if the available data are far from complete, recent surveys have widened the range of settled areas within the southern forested zone and suggest the existence of a more complex situation (Asombang et al. 1991; Atangana 1989, 1992; Mbida 1992a, 1992b; Ossah Mvondo 1990, 1991, 1992a, 1992b, 1993). Surveys conducted by Ossah-Mvondo (1992) in the southeastern part of the forest zone, in the regions of Djoum and Mintom, have allowed the discovery of six new settlements, not yet securely dated. According to informants, Alat Makay, one of the newly discovered sites, was an important nexus of exchange of local and European goods at the time of German control. It may have involved all of the surrounding territory within 100 km (60 miles) (Ossah-Mvondo 1992: 18).

In the Southern Province, two new clusters of sites have been discovered; the first one is close to the small town of Zoetélé (Asombang et al. 1990), and the second one, with five recorded sites (Avebe, Benelabot, Ngomessane, Ngulemelong, and Mengong), exposed by road construction and therefore located along the main road between Sangmélima and Ebolowa (Mbida 1992a, 1992b).

More intensive research has been conducted in the Sanaga-Lékié zone, which is inhabited today by the Beti and Bassa. Surveys, excavations, and interviews have been used to reconstruct the patterns of settlement and the history of present-day ethnic groups (Essomba 1985, 1986, 1987, 1992, 1993; de Maret 1992; Mbida 1992a, 1992b). On the southern bank of the Sanaga river, in the *département* of Lékié, a relatively dense cluster of 16 settlements has been mapped in an area measuring approximately 600 square kilometers (230 square miles) and situated between the modern cities of Monatélé in the northwest, Saa in the north, Obala in the east, and Evodoula in the west (Figure 8.2).

Iron production seems to have been a widespread socio-economic activity. Unfortunately very little is known about the diversity and the range of iron artifacts manufactured, partly because of their general scarcity in recorded archaeological assemblages and the small extent of archaeological excavations. The recorded evidence and the localities mapped seem to be organized according to functional differences between sites, in integrated aggregates with distinct habitation, smelting, and smithing sites. According to informants, in pre-German times, iron ore was collected in the area of Mebomo, where numerous mining pits have been found, and then smelted within the territory of each settlement. One furnace excavated at Pongsolo has been dated to 220 ± 70 b.p. (Beta 15800) and another one, discovered at a depth of 0.60 m at Nkometou, was dated to 100 ± 07 b.p. (Beta 23586) and calibrated to AD 1694–1728. The uncalibrated date of Pongsolo probably ranges from *c.* AD 1500 to 1750. The site of Nkometou was the focus of an excavation program carried out by Essomba (1985, 1987, 1992, 1993) during the last decade. This settlement is claimed by oral tradition to have been the Beti's point of convergence after the epic crossing of the Sanaga River (Essomba 1992; Laburthe-Tolra 1981a, 1981b; Ngoa 1981).

According to Ngoa (1981), the toponym *Nkometou* results from the combination of two lexemes: *Nkom* meaning hill-rock, and *Otu* from the name of the founding ancestor of the present-day Beti lineages (Mvog Ada, Mvog Betsi, Mvog Dzu, Mvog Ntigi), Otu Tamba. Otu Tamba's genealogy suggests that his grandfather Essomba Nagbana settled at Nkometou after crossing the Sanaga River in AD 1770–72. For Laburthe-Tolra (1981a, 1981b), the same set of events took place earlier, in *c.* AD 1730, with different individuals belonging to another lineage. Finally, from another series of oral

information collected by the excavator of the site during his fieldwork (Essomba 1986: 105–12), it is considered that Nkometou was settled much earlier, in 1689, by another set of individuals. These differences, which may appear at first glance puzzling, are quite normal after a closer examination of the data at hand. Each researcher has relied on a different informant belonging to a different lineage.

The archaeological section of Nkometou, exposed by road construction, revealed a series of pits in a profile measuring approximately 7m (23ft) in depth. The locality appears to have been settled as early as 500–400 BC by food-producing communities with iron technology. Discussions of the relevance of the Beti migration hypothesis focused on the latter occupation phase, which produced a smithing furnace dated to the late seventeenth or early eighteenth century. The single radiocarbon date from the latter occupation phase of Nkometou matches the chronology obtained through oral information. Yet, even if this makes sense from the point of view of the present-day inhabitants, the history of the site, with its 2,500 years of archaeological sequence, is obfuscated instead of being clarified. From the archaeological viewpoint, the generalization and spatial patterning of iron production appear to be the most important aspect of the history of peoples from the *département* of Lékié. Iron artifacts probably circulated in various exchange networks and were used for social transactions, as well as in warfare and subsistence activities.

In the south forested zone, in areas settled by the Bassa (Figure 8.2), surveys were facilitated by oral sources. The data suggest an interesting and unexpected picture of the intensification of iron production. Two main clusters of sites have been investigated, one in the southwest within the administrative division of Matomb, and another in the northwest in the area of Babimbi within the district of Ndom (Essomba 1985, 1986, 1987, 1993). More recently, a new but undated site, which can be included in the Matomb sites cluster, has been discovered and tested at Mandoumba (Ossah-Mvondo 1992).

Ten kilometers (6 miles) to the north of Matomb, four sites have been recorded and two of them excavated. A large stone anvil was found at Mangwen I at what appears to have been a smithing site. At Nkongteck, a locality

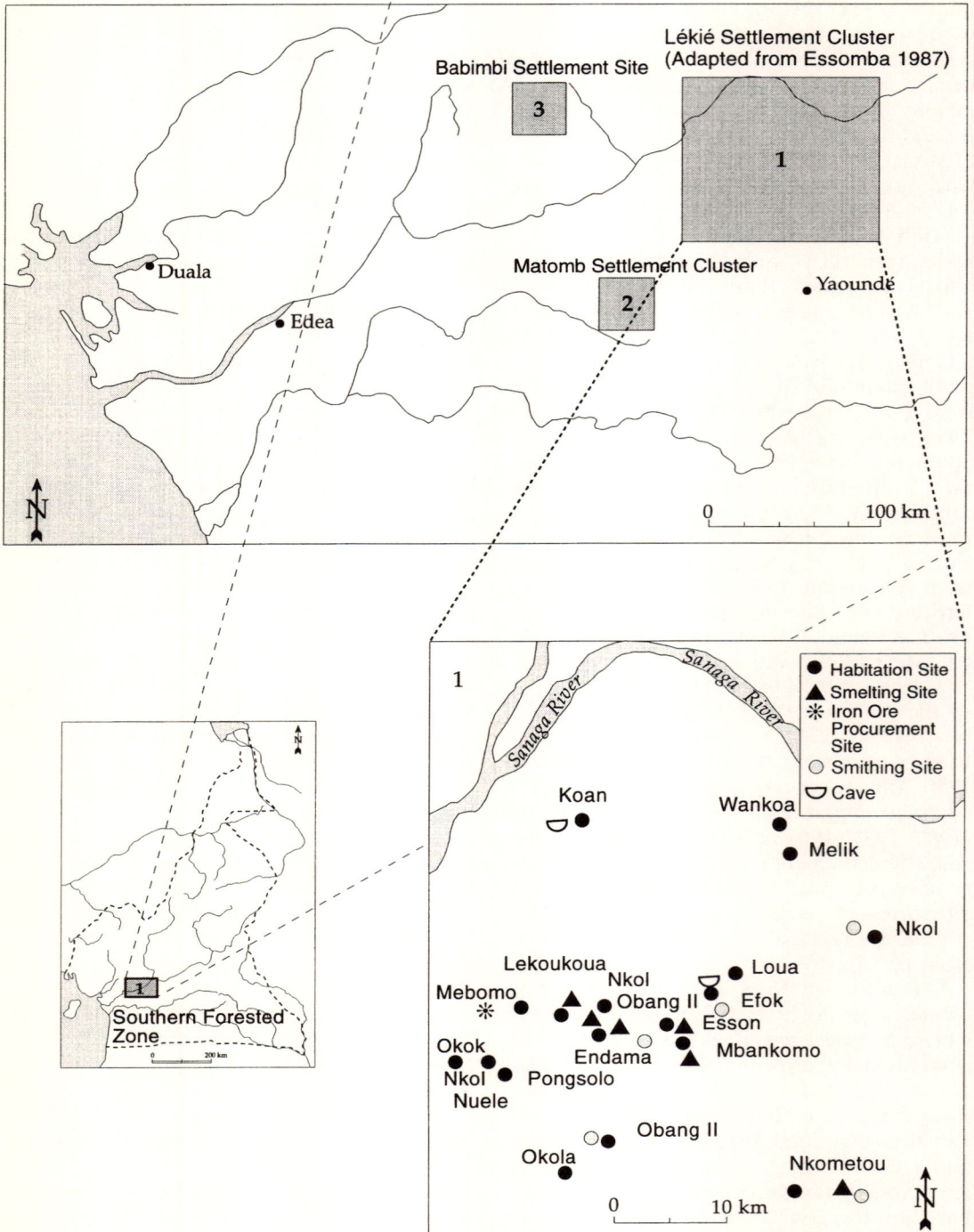

Figure 8.2 The southern forested zone: 1) The Lékié settlement cluster (adapted from Essomba 1987); 2) Location of the Matomb settlement cluster; 3) Location of the Babimbi settlement cluster.

Table 8.1 Major smelting sites from the southern forested regions

Cluster site	Matomb		Babimbi	
	Pan Manguenda	Pan Nsas	Nguilumlend	Massangui II
Surface (m²)	775	1,572	?	?
Number of features	4	4	1	1
Smelting furnace	1	1	1	1
Height (m)	3.80	3.65	?	3.00
Diameter (m)	1.15	1.25	?	1.25
Rectangular pit	1	1	1	1
Length (m)	3.00	2.80	?	?
Width (m)	2.00	1.60	?	?
Depth (m)	1.20	2.00	?	?
Houses	2	2	?	?
Slag heaps	15 m³	Present	Present	Present
Chronology	1440–1750	1450–1700	1600–1700	1600–1800

informants say was an important iron-ore procurement site, 25 pits have been exposed by road construction. Two important smelting sites, 10 km (6 miles) apart, were excavated at Pan-Nsas and Pan-Manguenda. In both sites there are three classes of structures: two rectangular habitation features; heaps of smelting debris; and a large furnace (Table 8.1, Fig. 3). The furnaces are cylindrical, measuring 1.15 to 1.25 m in diameter and 3.65 to 3.80 m high, inserted in a rectangular pit dug to depth between 1.2 and 2.0 m. The walls of the furnaces were built with superimposed layers of clay coated with thin fire-hardened red bricks, which were also used as pavement for the pits' floors. At Pan-Nsas, a 'medicine pot' was found in the floor of the rectangular pit. These natural draft furnaces were built for intensive production and long-term use. They were situated at the highest point of the site and the rectangular pit was oriented toward the northeast so that air was forced to go through the furnace from its mouth at the bottom to the chimney at the top. Radiocarbon dates for the construction of these impressive structures include dates of AD 1450–1680 (LY 4027) and AD 1500–1700 (LY 4028) for charcoal samples collected at Pan-Nsas, and dates from Pan-Manguenda of AD 1440–1690 (LY 4026) to AD 1650 -1750 (LY 4025). These ages strangely coincide with the onset of the Atlantic trade network.

In the northwest, in the Babimbi cluster surrounding Ndom, no site has been excavated. Surveys have been carried out with the help of former blacksmiths and dating extends only to the pre-German time. The archaeological sites share strong similarities with those of the Matomb cluster. Similar large-scale smelting furnaces have been discovered at Nguilumlend, Nyeng, and Massangui II, located 35 to 40 km (21–25 miles) north of Ndom, in what appears to have been the iron ore procurement area (Essomba 1985: 3–4). Blacksmiths' workshops were located at Ngock and Nindje further south. According to informants, in pre-German times, blacksmiths from Ngock and Nindje were provided with iron by smelters from Nguilumlend and Massangui. Production was distributed in 'the whole region of Babimbi, from Ndom to Ngambe and Edea' (Essomba 1987: 57), along the valley of the Sanaga River in the direction of the Atlantic coast. Owing to the presence of falls, the locality of Edea had played the role of an important exchange center between the hinterland and the coast.

The archaeological record from the Matomb and Ndom regions indicate an intensification of iron production from the sixteenth to the eighteenth century. This intensification is probably due to a higher demand, which may have resulted from the combination of

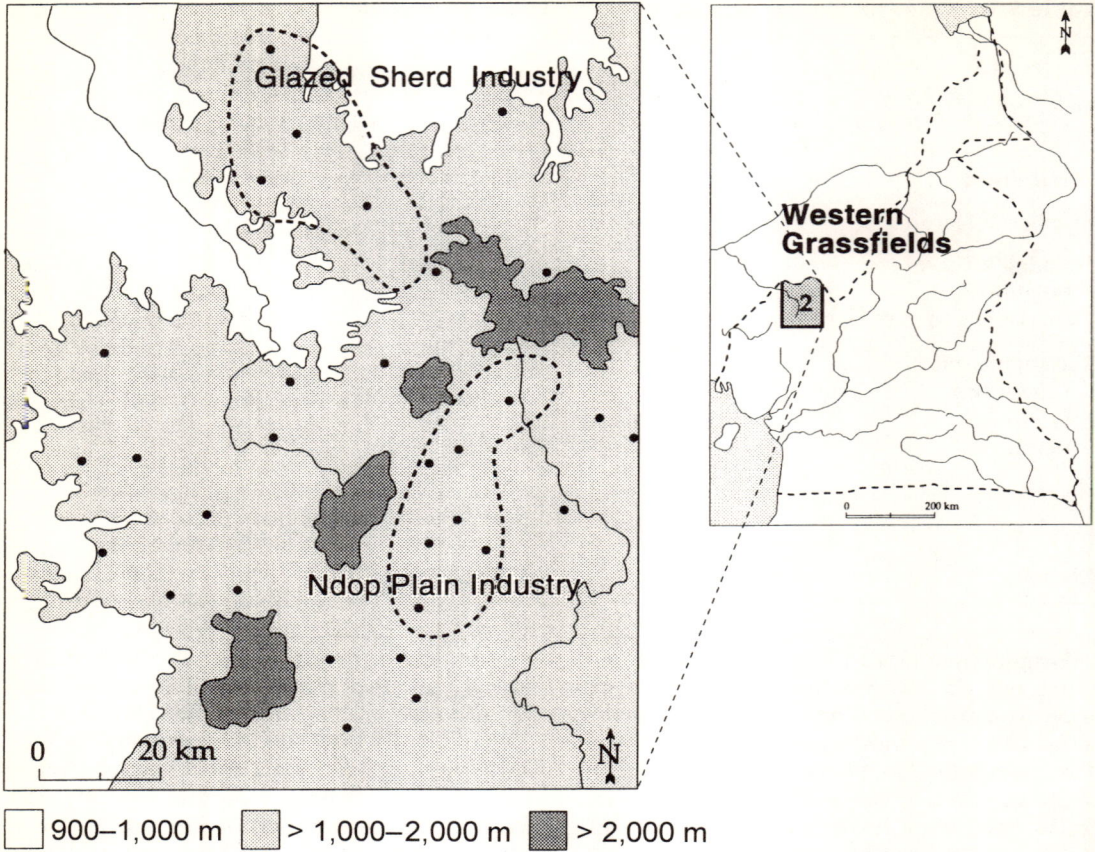

Figure 8.3 Distribution of settlements in the Western Grassfields (from Rowlands and Warnier 1993: 515): 1) Glazed Sherd Industry (GSI) settlement cluster; 2) Ndop Plateau Industry (NPI) settlement cluster.

several factors, both internal and external. Iron artifacts were used as currency, as tools for subsistence activities, as weapons in warfare, and as payment of bride prices. As such, they were inserted in networks of local, regional, and pan-regional systems of exchange in which European goods had played an important role with the onset of the Atlantic trade.

The Western Grassfields

The Grassfields region is situated between the 4th and 7th parallels (Figure 8.3). It is a high lava plateau with altitudes varying from 500 to 2 000 m above sea level, broken by volcanic peaks and flanked on its peripheries by a series of lower plains and valleys (Goheen 1992; Warnier 1984, 1985; Warnier and Fowler 1979). The earliest archaeological evidence

suggests that this area was formerly forested, as shown by the remains of African buffalo, bushbuck, duiker, giant forest hog, bush pig, wart hog, and monkey from Late Stone Age sites like Mbi Crater, Fiye Nkwi, and Shum Laka (Asombang 1992). Today the vegetation consists of high-altitude savanna, a consequence of long-term human exploitation (Warnier 1984).

Recent archaeological surveys have identified new sites, like Banock in the *département* of Menoua (de Crits 1992), Mandja near Bagangté (Mbida 1992a, 1992b), and 16 localities in the Kom culture area (Ossah-Mvondo 1990; Schmidt and Asombang 1990). These new sites are not yet dated or published in detail, but they are considered to belong to the early ceramic phase by the authors of the survey on the basis of the decorative tech-

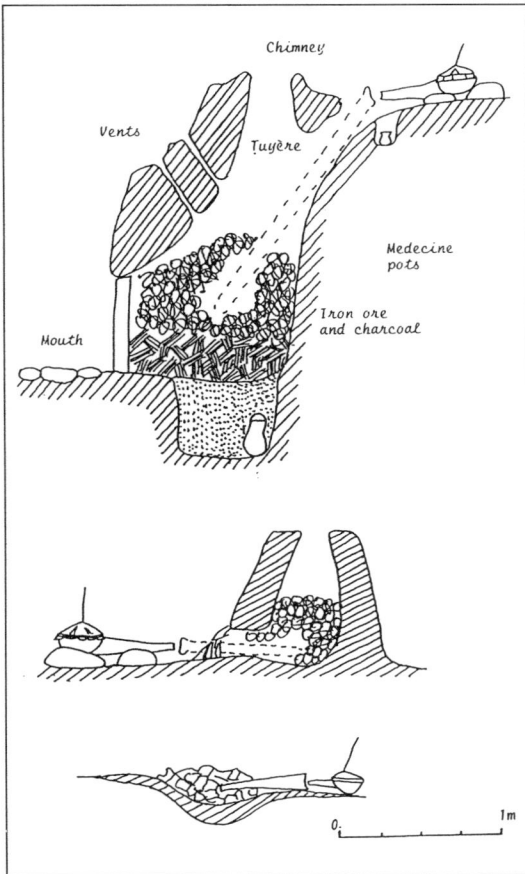

Figure 8.4 Furnace types recorded in the Western Grassfields: top, clump furnace from the Ndop Plateau Industry; middle, cylindrical furnace; bottom, bowl furnace.

niques represented (Schmidt and Asombang 1990b: 13). The focus on iron production, therefore, presents a biased picture of the development of Western Grassfields societies during the last 500 years. Even with these limitations, the archaeological data available from the northern part of the Western Grassfields seem to be congruent with the timing of the Atlantic trade system, a pattern already highlighted in the discussion of the southern forested zone.

More intensive research on the transformation of iron metallurgy has been carried out on the Bamenda Plateau, where earliest evidence of iron production has been dated to AD 300 (Ossah-Mvondo 1990; Rowlands 1986; Rowlands and Warnier 1993; Warnier 1984,

1985, 1992; Warnier and Fowler 1979). The chronology of this industrial tradition is not fully understood, but three main types of furnaces have been recorded. Oral information, supported by few radiocarbon dates, suggests that the low cylindrical furnaces were the earliest and the most widespread, continuing up until the 1940s in the most northern part of the Grassfields (Figure 8.4 middle; Rowlands 1986: 6). The intensification of iron production, with the invention of the 'clump furnace,' may have occurred in the seventeenth century, and reached its peak in the second half of the eighteenth and the first decades of the nineteenth centuries, within the context of long-distance exchange networks (Figure 8.4 top). Finally, during the last decades of the nineteenth century, a 'small bowl furnace' appears (Figure 8.4 bottom).

Hundreds of iron-producing sites have been discovered as a result of several 'judgmental' surveys based on information from interviews (Rowlands and Warnier 1993; Warnier 1992). The archaeological data recorded have been partitioned into two major industrial traditions: the Ndop Plateau Industry (NPI), located in the southern part of the study area, and the Glazed Sherd Industry (GSI) in the north (Figure 8.5).

The Ndop Plateau Industry (NPI)

Within the NPI area, more than 274 smelting sites have been mapped holding more than 228,000 cubic meters of iron production debris (Table 8.2). Some of the most important chiefdoms such as Babungo, Bamessing, Bafanji, and Bamenyan were turned into dominant providers of iron artifacts for the whole Grassfields and neighboring regions down to the Atlantic coast at Duala and Calabar (Rowlands 1986; Warnier 1985). The 'clump furnace' technology was labor-intensive and fuel-minimizing: smelting installations could be in permanent operation for months with alternating work crews. Although there are minor differences such as the number and position of vents and size, all of the furnaces share basic patterns (Fig 8.4 top, Warnier and Fowler 1979: 334). First, a rectangular pit was dug to a depth of 1.5 to 2.0 m. A small pit for medicine was then dug in the floor and the walls of the furnace were built leaning on one side of the pit. Ducts for *tuyères* were built opposite vents half-way up

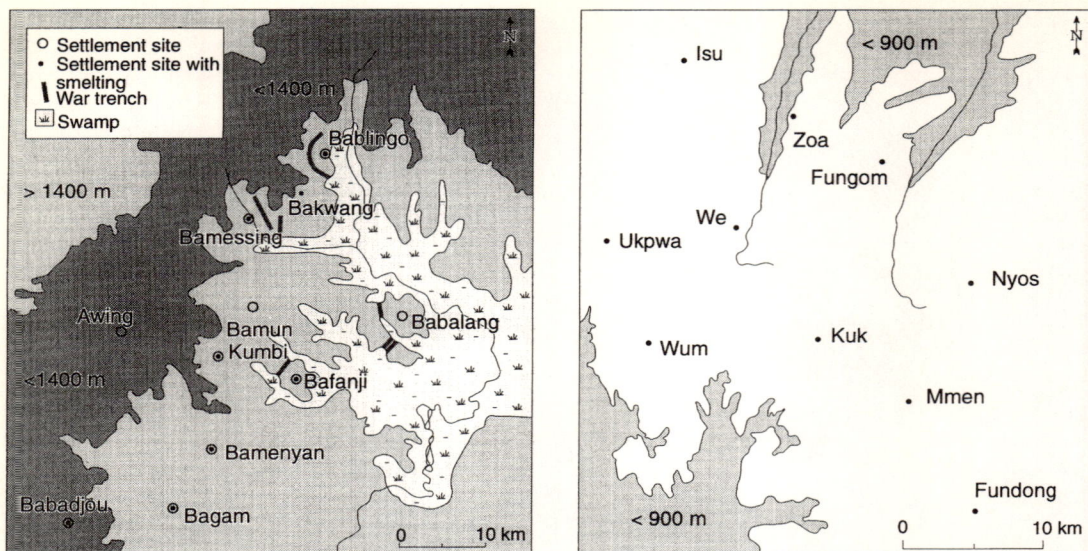

Figure 8.5 *Left:* settlement patterns at the climax of the Ndop Plateau Industry (adapted from Warnier and Fowler 1979: 332); *Right:* settlement pattern in the Glazed Sherd Industry cluster (adapted from Rowlands and Warnier 1993: 516).

the furnace, with the chimney at the top. The smelting furnaces were always protected by a shelter and production debris was scattered around, generating sub-circular to horse-shoe-shaped slag heaps (Warnier and Fowler 1979).

The development of clump furnace technology occurred after an important shift in settlement patterns, from a system of widely dispersed small villages to densely packed settlements, protected by 'war trenches.' The regional distribution of smelting sites was dependent upon the availability of raw material: high quality kaolin that had to be resistant enough to sustain high furnace temperatures. Three chiefdom centers along the east–west axis of the study area (Figure 8.5: Bambalang, Bali-Kumbat, and Awing) are devoid of iron-smelting centers and may only have had smithing workshops. From this axis of central villages without smelting sites, the study area may be divided into two groups of central settlements: the northern one, with Babungo, Bakwang, and Bamessing, and the southern one, with Bamunkumbit, Bafanji, Bamenyan, Bagam, and Babadjou. In both groups, it is striking that the most important iron-smelting chiefdoms are almost equidistant from each other, about 10 km (6 miles) apart: Babungo and Bamessing in the northern group

with 125 and 54 recorded smelting sites; and Bafanji (25 smelting sites) and Bamenyan (more than 70 sites) in the southern group (Table 8.2). The spatial organization of the NPI, supported by differences in scales of production and variants in the types of 'clump furnaces,' shed some light on the dynamics of socio-economic systems of that part of the Bamenda Plateau during the last 500 years.

Table 8.2 Iron production sites in the Ndop Plateau Industry (NPI)

Village chiefdoms	Volume of slag (m³)	Number of smelting sites
Babungo	163,000	125
Bamessing	40,000	54
Bafanji	>15,000	25
Bamenyan	>10,000	>70
Babadjou	Traces	?
Bamenkumbit	Traces	?
Bagam	?	?
Total	>228,000	>274

Source: Warnier and Fowler 1979: 331.

Table 8.3   Iron production sites of the Glazed Sherd Industry (GSI)

Village chiefdoms	Volume of slag (m³)	Number of smelting sites	Number of smithing sites
Fundong	135	21	–
Mmen	783	15	11
Nyos	?	3	1
Kuk	20	1	2
Fungom	25	2	5
Wum	3,960	12	6
We	538	12	13
Zoa	150	2	1
Ukpwa	3,152	19	–
Isu	902	11	9
Total	9,665	98	48

Source: Rowlands and Warnier 1993: 517.

The Glazed Sherd Industry (GSI)

While the NPI is highly concentrated, the GSI is characterized by its dispersion between smaller chiefdoms (Rowlands and Warnier 1993; Warnier 1992). This industrial tradition has been recorded in an area extending from Fundong in the south to Isu in the north (Figure 8.5); smelting sites are fairly evenly distributed over the whole area with some concentrations. Rowlands and Warnier note:

> The 98 smelting sites fall into two broad categories: small, scattered sites around Fundong – 21 sites, each averaging 6.44 m³ of smelting debris – and rather bigger sites concentrated within clustered settlements – 77 sites with 12 to 330 m³ of smelting debris each . . . Yet the volume of smelting debris is heavily concentrated in the Northwest, where two settlements – Wum and Ukpwa – possess 75 per cent of the smelting debris of the whole industry. Only in Fundong, to the southeast, are small sites found, scattered in the countryside. Everywhere else, they are concentrated in clustered settlements. (Rowlands and Warnier 1993: 515–16)

The Glazed Sherd Industry owes its name to the presence of vitrified sherds on smelting sites. Two radiocarbon dates from charcoal samples collected in smelting debris at Fundong suggest that GSI may date as early as AD 610–1260 (LY 3067) and AD 1305–1669 (LY 3066), extending up to modern times in terms of radiocarbon timescales (Rowlands and Warnier 1993: 518, Table 32.2). Cylindrical furnaces measuring 0.7 to 1.5 m in diameter at the bottom and 1 to 1.5 m high were used (Figure 8.4 top). Although many of them have been destroyed, the furnaces appear to have been built in pairs. Thirteen sites with twin furnaces have been recorded out of a total of 98. Within living memory, only one site had a single furnace, a feature due to the lack of labor force, according to informants (Rowlands and Warnier 1993). *Tuyères* were passed through the mouth of the furnace, which was closed during the smelting of iron ore. Owing to very high temperatures, sherds in direct contact with iron bloom were vitrified.

It is difficult to assess the magnitude of iron metallurgy within the GSI. At first glance, the quantity of smelting debris may seem impressive and interpreted as an indication of large-scale production for export. Such an interpretation, partly supported by oral tradition, does not consider the fact that evidence of GSI iron production spans one and a half millennia, from *c.* AD 610 to 1900. The smelting debris may have resulted from long-term accumulation by generations of iron producers in some areas, or from genuine intensification for shorter periods in others, or a combination. Lack of more accurate chronological data precludes thorough evaluation. Analysis of the distribution of settlements (Figure 8.5, Table 8.3) shows that chiefdoms with higher concentrations of smelting debris (Wum, Ukpwa, and Isu) are located in the northwestern part of the study area, while those with lower concentrations of debris (900 to 700 cubic meters), but

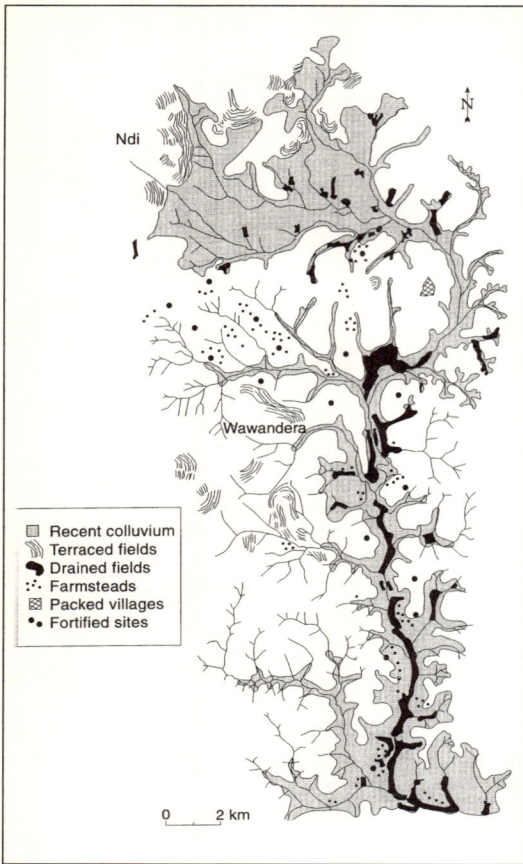

Figure 8.6 The Mayo Wodeo and Mayo Oumiare catchment basins, in the Western Adamaoua: distribution of settlements and land-use patterns (adapted from Hurault 1979 and 1986).

with a higher number of smithing sites (Mmen, We, and Isu) are situated along a central northwest–southeast axis (Fundong to Isu). Finally, chiefdoms like Fungom, Zoa, and Nyos, with the smallest volumes of debris and only a handful of smelting and smithing sites, are confined to the northeast. It can also be observed that each of the recorded axes of chiefdoms—1) Ukpwa–Wum; 2) Isu–We–Kuk–Mmen–Fundong; and 3) Zoa–Fungom–Nyos—is composed of almost equidistant settlements, with distances between neighboring centers varying from 10 to 12 km (6 to 8 miles).

The dispersed nature of archaeological evidence of the GSI suggests that iron production may have been based on household labor force and primarily geared to meet the local demand. This does not rule out the possibility of episodes of intensification to satisfy higher demands generated by the development of long-distance trade, including the Atlantic trade and the interior Hausa-dominated exchange system (Dillon 1981; Kopytoff 1981; Wilhelm 1981).

The Western Adamaoua

The Adamaoua mountain range is oriented east–west, with altitudes ranging from 1,000 to 2,000 m above sea level. The landscape is broken with steep narrow valleys, the vegetation sudano-guinean savanna, with gallery forest along the water courses. The present-day inhabitants belong to five ethnic groups: the Niem-Niem in the northeast; the Voute in the east; the Wawa in the center; the Kondja in the south; and the Mambila in the west. This area is, in a sense, archaeological *terra incognita* even if some features, such as megaliths, iron smelting furnaces, and samples of potsherds have been recorded (Marliac 1981).

Insights into past socio-cultural transformations are offered by historical geography. From 1976 to 1982, Hurault (1979, 1986, 1988, 1993) carried out an intensive survey (Figures 8.1; 8.6), focusing on the investigation of patterns of land-use and distribution of settlements prior to the Fulani conquest at the beginning of the nineteenth century. His research was aimed at explaining the sharp contrast between the large number of abandoned settlements and the low population density of today. According to Hurault (1979: 12–14, 1986: 121), pre-Fulani agricultural systems, ranked in terms of labor intensification, were distributed according to altitudes. Slash-and-burn agricultural practice, associated with low-density populations in dispersed homesteads (less than 15 inhabitants per square kilometer), characterized the forest galleries between 900 and 1,000 m above sea level in the Tibati–Tignere area. Higher densities of population (60–120 inhabitants per square kilometer) occur between 1,100 and 1,500 m, in the Banyo region, with the implementation of more intensive agricultural techniques based on the drainage of marshy alluvium and colluvium at the bottom of relatively wide valleys. Finally, above 1,500 meters, in the Mambila Plateau, the highest densities of population (200–250 inhabitants per square kilometer)

Table 8.4 Distribution of archaeological features in the Western Adamaoua

	Wawa[a] Mayo Wodeo—Mayo Oumiare[b]			Kondja[a] Mayo Darlé[b]		
	Number	Density (per km²)	Theoretical territory (km²)	Number	Density (per km²)	Theoretical territory (km²)
Settlements						
Large villages	2	0.01	52.50	1	0.0008	1,120.00
Nucleated villages	1	0.09	105.00	9	0.008	124.00
Farmsteads	92	0.87	1.14	?	?	?
Fortified villages	—	—	—	2	0.001	560.00
Fortified camps	17	0.16	6.17	66	0.05	16.96
Total	112	1.13	0.93	78	0.06	14.35
Fields						
Terraced fields	16	0.15	6.56	4	0.003	280.00
Drained fields	53	0.50	1.98	29	0.02	38.62
Total	69	0.65	1.52	33	0.02	33.93
Total of features	181	1.78	0.58	100	0.08	11.20

[a] Ethnic group
[b] Drainage

were characterized by extensive evidence of terraced fields on the steeper mountain slopes.

Hurault used both aerial photography and field surveys, while oral traditions were collected to help identify former ethnic associations. No archaeological excavations were carried out and the chronological resolution is, therefore, relatively loose, based on a few thermoluminescence and radiocarbon dates (Hurault 1979: 20, 1988: 4). Parts of the area seem to have been settled from the end of the first millennium AD up to the onset of the Fulani conquests in the 1800s. Different kinds of settlements have been recorded, including dispersed homesteads without terraced fields; fortified camps; clustered villages with and without terraced fields; and semi-subterranean compounds associated with terraced fields.

Two smaller areas situated in the region of Banyo at 1,100 to 1,400 m above sea level have been studied in more detail: the Mayo Wodeo–Mayo Oumiare drainage basin in the former territory of the Wawa, located 30 km (14 miles) northwest of the central Fulani settlement of Banyo (Figure 8.6); and the Mayo Darlé valley, the territory of the Kondja ethnic group, 50 km (30 miles) southwest of the same town.

One hundred and twelve settlements have been mapped in the Mayo Wodeo–Mayo Oumiare drainage basin. Large villages with terraced fields are located in the western and northwestern part of the territory beyond a line of fortified camps. Ndi and Wawandera are the largest recorded settlements, measuring 82 and 25 hectares. According to Hurault (1979), (203 and 62 acres) such large settlements were already abandoned prior to the Fulani conquest following a shift toward a pattern of dispersed family homesteads within river valleys. This conclusion, based only on surface features, seems highly unreliable if we consider the distribution of archaeological features as a socio-political map in which dispersed homesteads, fortified camps, villages, and terraced and drained fields are parts of an overall settlement system. In this regard, it is clear that large villages and terraced fields are organized into two main clusters: one in the north and another in the center, protected by a line of fortified camps (Figure 8.6, Table 8.4).

Fortified camps are not habitation sites. They are typically composed of a circular ditch 3–5 m deep and 4–6 m wide, complemented by an earth embankment 3–4 m high, their surface extent varying from 0.5 to 2 hectares.

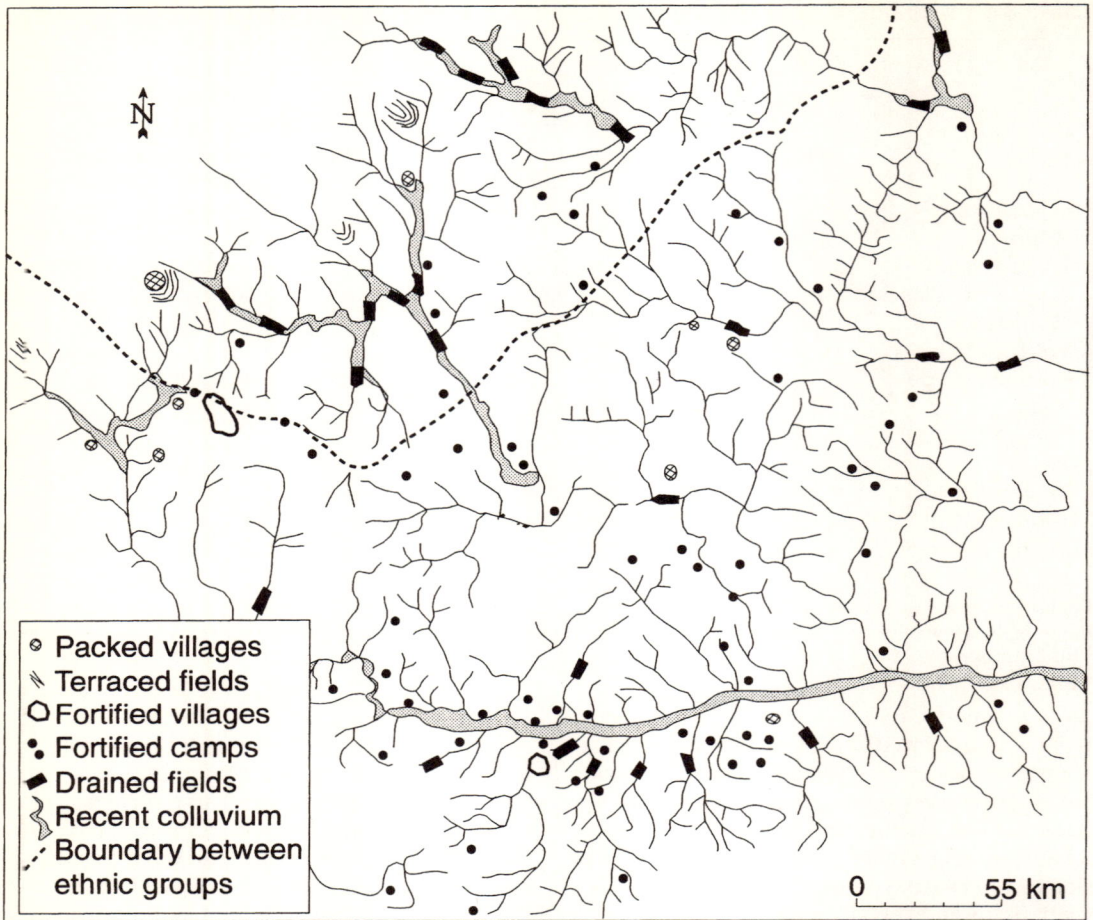

Figure 8.7 The Mayo Darlé catchment basin in the Western Adamaoua: distribution of settlements and land-use patterns (adapted from Hurault 1986).

These features were probably used in cases of inter-ethnic warfare between neighboring local groups, as defense against Fulani, and refuge against slave raiders. The virtual absence of such fortified camps along the Mayo Wodeo in the northern part of the territory and their concentration along the Mayo Oumiare suggest that there was a threat from the southeast in the direction of Banyo and Vouté territories. Drained fields are distributed in almost all river valleys and dispersed easily built homesteads were probably used as field houses. Depending on circumstances—peace or war—they may have been abandoned or inhabited for longer periods.

Seventy-eight settlements have been mapped in the Mayo Darlé valley in the Kondja territory (Figure 8.7, Table 8.4), with two fortified and nine nucleated villages. There is a settlement pattern similar to that noted in the Mayo Wodeo–Mayo Oumiare drainage basin. The largest habitation sites are situated in the northwest of the studied area, behind a dense network of fortified camps, which are more numerous along the major river valley, the principal passage through the tortuous mountain landscape. The major threat clearly seems to have been situated in the east, in the territories of Banyo and the Vouté. In both drainages, the density of settlements varies from 1.06 to 0.06 sites per square kilometer (Table 8.4). With the average theoretical territory per settlement varying from 0.93 to 14.35 square kilometers. If village sizes are con-

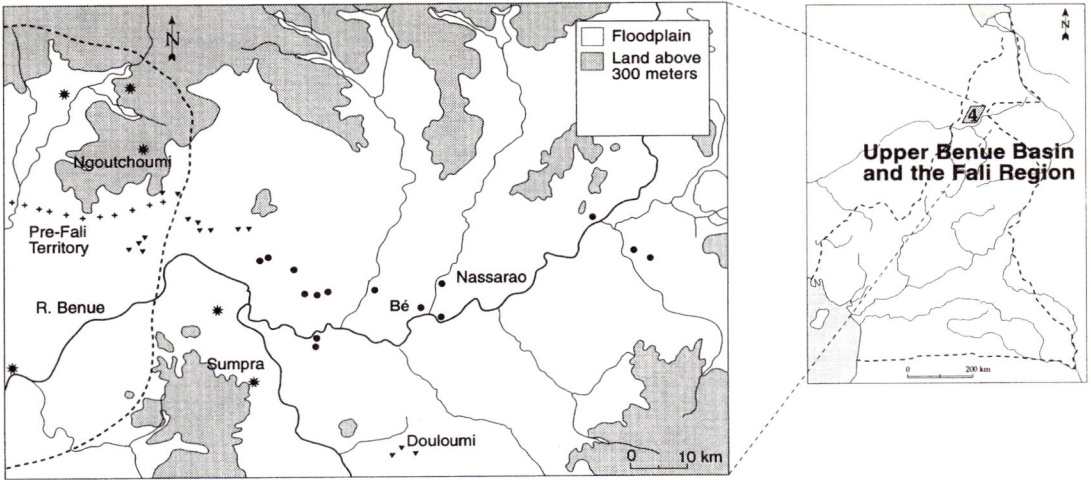

Figure 8.8 The Upper Benue Basin and the Fali region: general distribution of recorded archaeological sites (adapted from David 1981 and Gauthier 1981).

sidered, excluding dispersed homesteads which may have shifted from place to place, the average theoretical territory per village then varies from 35 square kilometers in the Mayo Wodeo–Mayo Oumiare drainage basin to 93.33 square kilometers in the Mayo Darlé valley. The average territory of fortified camps, which were not used as habitation sites but mostly for short-term protection in case of emergency, varies from 6.17 to 16.96 square kilometers (Table 8.4). These later figures suggest that the average radius of territories protected by a fortified camp varies from 1.5 to 2.5 km, a distance which could be covered within an hour, depending on the topography.

The distribution of archaeological sites suggests a settlement hierarchy with dispersed homesteads and fortified camps, fortified villages, and larger villages measuring 25 to 60 hectares in surface extent. This hierarchy is partially supported by the distribution of recorded grinding slabs. Small slabs were predominant at dispersed homesteads and, according to Hurault (1986: 136–7), they were moved from site to site. Heavier specimens (200 to 300 kg), used for communal grinding, were found in large villages. All of them are made from granito-gneissic outcrops up to 10 km from settlements. The organization of labor, as well as transport of heavy loads clearly beyond those needed by an individual household unit, may be linked to the rise of prestigious village headmen. Such individuals may have acquired the capacity to attract followers, mobilize labor forces, and supervise community affairs.

According to Hurault (1986, 1988), the Fulani conquest at the beginning of the nineteenth century disrupted earlier social systems of the Western Adamaoua as the area was plagued with warfare, slave raiding, venereal diseases, and the destruction of former agricultural systems. Free-range Fulani cattle pastoralism and the development of Fulani *lamidat* (towns) at Banyo, Tibati, and Tignere generated the migrations and conquests partly known in the Western Grassfields as the Chamba Migration. It is worth noting that central settlements of the three recorded Fulani *lamidat* are situated 100 km (60 miles) from each other, suggesting that the average territorial range of Fulani polities extended over a radius of 50 km (30 miles), with a total land area of approximately 7,854 square kilometers.

The Upper Benue Basin

Situated in the Sudanic savanna, the Upper Benue Basin comprises both hilly and flat landscapes (Figure 8.8). Archaeological research has been conducted in the Benue–Mayo Kebbi drainage and the neighboring area of the Fali in the north of Garoua (David 1972, 1980, 1981; Gauthier 1969, 1979, 1981, 1990, 1992). In the former area, one cave and 39 mounds

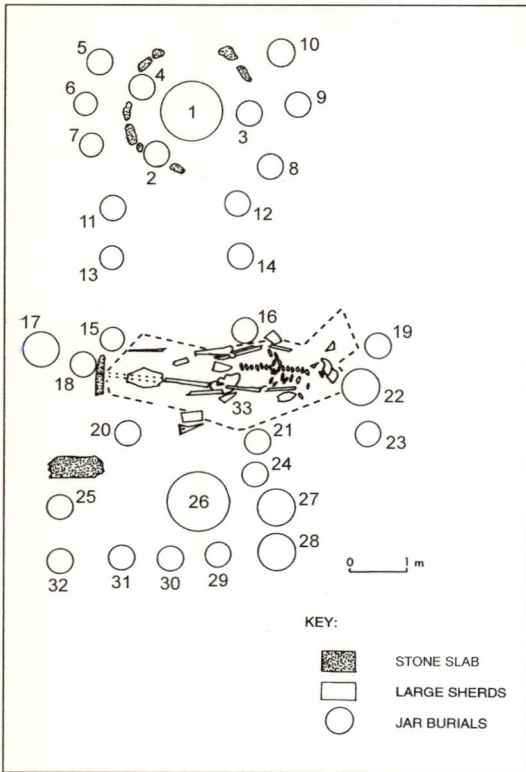

Figure 8.9 Spatial organization of the cemetery of Barki-Ngoutchoumi in the Fali region (adapted from Gauthier 1990: 208).

and mound complexes have been mapped, and some of them tested. The former inhabitants subsisted by fishing, cereal agriculture based on the cultivation of sorghum and *eleusine*, and cattle and sheep/goat husbandry. A few iron artifacts have been uncovered, but no evidence of smelting. With the exception of occasional beads, exotic trade items are almost entirely absent.

Four of the tested sites—Pouss, Nassarao, Sumpra Cave, and Bé (Figure 8.8)—were settled during the last 500 years. Sumpra Cave, with its upper three levels dated to AD 1600, may have been settled on a seasonal basis. Nassarao, with its upper levels dated to AD 1490, may have been abandoned at the end of the fifteenth century. In general, however, the Benue–Mayo Kebbi drainage basin was settled by sedentary mixed farming societies from the first half of the first millennium AD. The archaeological data available show a con-

tinuity in material culture and building techniques that does not support the migration accounts of the ethnohistorical record. These are more likely movements associated with the Fulani conquests at the beginning of the nineteenth century, which have been pushed back in time in the oral traditions.

The settlement of Pouss, composed of two mounds, is located on the shore of the Logone River in the northeastern part of the study area. The archaeological deposits are 5.20 m thick, with the earliest occupation dated to the eleventh century (David 1981). The settlement was continuously inhabited from that time and then abandoned at the time of German colonization, with the four upper levels dating between AD 1400 and 1700. David (1981: 88) notes:

> the continuity of material culture throughout a sequence lasting over a millennium is quite striking. In the absence of any identifiable stratigraphic or cultural breaks, we would, while denying the relative recency of the peopling of this region, concur with the view . . . that over the period covered by the Pouss sequence, the region has been inhabited continuously by closely related Chadic-speaking groups classified generically as Massa, Mousgoum, Mouloui, Mousouk, Mouskoum, etc.

The site of Bé has been more intensively studied. It consists of three large mounds extending over 3.25 hectares, with a 7.25-m-deep archaeological deposit, and several smaller mounds. According to informants, the locality of Bé was conquered in 1839 by a Fulani war leader named Ardo Jamhuura (David 1981: 90). The upper 2.5 m of the archaeological sequence dates between 1500 and 1900. Two circular huts with a potsherd-paved courtyard were exposed. The dwelling units thus seem to have been composed of small compounds with tightly clustered huts, a pattern in contrast with the more widely spaced Fulani system.

In the Tinguelin hills north of Garoua, Gauthier has concentrated on mortuary evidence (Figure 8.9; Gauthier 1969, 1979, 1981, 1990, 1992). In the absence of secure radiocarbon dates, the chronology of the Fali area is based on oral traditions and archaeological seriation (Gauthier 1981: 193). Settlement before the sixteenth-century societies is attested by rare and isolated burials attributed to the Ngomna people by Fali informants. The dead were buried in an extended position on their right side, their faces oriented toward the west. In general, tombs are devoid of grave goods, but some undecorated potsherds, clay beads, and a few local stone beads have been found.

The area seems to have been more densely settled at the end of the sixteenth century by immigrants from the Benue–Mayo Kebbi basin. The formative period of Fali cultural identity (AD 1500–1800) is attested by the presence of densely packed cemeteries at Bibemi, Nassarao, and Guebaké in the Benue valley and Beri, Toro, Mpogma, Hou, and Ngoutchoumi in the Tinguelin Hills (Gauthier 1969, 1981, 1990, 1992). Two hundred and twelve tombs, ranging from low stone tumuli to burials in large jars, have been excavated. Each clan had, and still has, its own burial ground in which all kin were supposed to be buried, regardless of their residence at death. Tombs are typically composed of two superimposed jars containing the remains of the deceased. It is not unusual to find two or three individuals in the same burial. At Ngoutchoumi-Barki, a single-level cemetery, there is a relatively neat distribution of burials according to age and sex. The burial ground covers a surface of about 250 square meters, out of which 72 square meters (12 × 6 m) have been excavated (Figure 8.9). Thirty-three tombs in jars and one extended burial were recorded. Four of the deceased are adults, five teenagers, nineteen children, and six undetermined. Two burials, one male (Number 1) and one female (Number 26), are situated at the center of the most significant clusters. It is tempting to consider tomb Numbers 1 and 26 to be burials of a father/husband and mother/wife, the founding members of a lineage segment, if interpreted according to Fali cultural standards (Gauthier 1969, 1990), and the remaining burials to be those of their descendants down to their grandchildren.

Grave goods associated with burials in this period are much more diverse and informative. They include zoomorphic and anthropomorphic figurines, some metal items, a handful of small iron beads, arm-rings of copper alloy, and glass and stone beads from both local and exotic origins. Carnelian beads are more numerous, but their distribution is highly skewed. They were probably obtained through trade along the Benue valley, as was certainly the case for glass beads from European origins, which are more abundant after 1700 (Gauthier

1981:194–5). Carnelian beads, ranked at the top of the currency system by Fali informants, were obtained through the Atlantic and interior trade. Glass beads from Venice beginning in the sixteenth century and the Netherlands and Bohemia later (Gauthier 1981: 195), were obtained through links with the European trade on the coast.

According to informants, stone and glass beads were not used in direct trade transactions but mostly as repositories of wealth and prestige. One carnelian bead was the equivalent of two white, or three black, or ten blue glass beads, while three carnelian beads were the price of a slave. The quantity and diversity of beads present in each burial may provide us with a picture of the social and economic status of the deceased. It is, however, important to be cautious in extending the ethnographic present into the past. It is doubtful that values of material items remained unchanged for centuries. Depending on demand, the relative socio-economic value of beads may have fluctuated. Unfortunately, the absence of chronological and contextual information does not allow clarification. The most important point concerning the formative period of Fali cultural identity is the development of localized burial grounds, processes congruent with the build-up of a socio-cultural landscape integrating large parts of the Benue floodplain around Garoua and the Tinguelin Hills.

In the middle of the eighteenth century different ethnic groups, probably connected with the infiltration of Fulani pastoral groups in the Benue valley, started to move into the Tinguelin Hills and the Kangou Plateau. This resettlement process probably reached its climax during the first half of the nineteenth century with the foundation of the Fulani *lamidat* of Garoua, Bibémi, Tchéboa, Demsa, Bachéo, Bembo, and Bé, and their ensuing conquest of the whole Benue floodplain (Gauthier 1969: 19–30). Many of the informants from the Tinguelin Hills traced their lineage origins to settlements in the floodplain, an area conquered by the Fulani between 1750 and 1820. The Tinguelin Hills and the Kangou Plateau can thus be considered as places of refuge for different social groups that coalesced as the 'Wopti-Tshalo culture,' a new cultural order which tried (with varying degrees of success) to escape Fulani and, later, German domination.

Archaeological data on the 'Wopti-Tshalo

culture' are confined to burial evidence distributed throughout the mountain landscape. They include secondary burials in rock-shelters and caves, as well as clustered and dispersed tombs. Erected stones, sanctuaries, cultic sites, and habitation features such as abandoned huts and compounds, stone walls, and granaries also occur, but they are not yet published in detail (Gauthier 1992). Long-term use of burial grounds seems to have been abandoned: the pattern of settlement consists of dispersed compounds, and tombs are located within the territory of each household unit. The deceased are wrapped in special clothes and buried in a sitting position in a deep cylindrical pit. Grave goods are composed almost exclusively of pottery vessels, sometimes associated with zoomorphic and anthropomorphic clay figurines. The tombs are characteristically low stone and earth mounds.

As far as the whole Upper Benue Basin is concerned, the archaeological record suggests two major settlement patterns: one system with mound sites situated in or on the edge of the floodplain, and inhabited at least from the middle of the first millennium AD to the present; and another one in the Tinguelin Hills and Kangou Plateau. Both settlement systems were disrupted by Fulani expansion and conquest. During the first half of the sequence considered in this chapter, evidence of long-distance trade and patterns of accumulation of wealth were confined to the western part of the Upper Benue Basin, on the meridian of Garoua, while settlements upstream were almost devoid of trade items. Social groups of the Fali formative period may have successfully monopolized long-distance trade from both the Atlantic and the Sahara. During the more recent past, Fulani domination initiated extensive movements of peoples and the emergence of new cultural identities.

Mound sites of the Chadian plain

The Chadian plain, abutting Lake Chad, is a flat land in the northernmost part of the country. The vegetation is the sudano-sahelian savanna type with thorny trees. The major part of the landscape is flooded during the rainy season. Mound sites and walled cities in the region, first mentioned by d'Anania in 1582, have attracted archaeologists and ethnographers from the beginning of the twentieth

century (Griaule and Lebeuf 1948, 1950, 1951; A. Lebeuf 1969, 1992; J.-P. Lebeuf 1962, 1969, 1981a, 1981b, 1992; Lebeuf and Lebeuf 1977; Lebeuf and Masson Detourbet 1950; Lebeuf et al. 1980; Wulsin 1932). Archaeological research has focused on the decipherment and the chronological ordering of the Soa Civilization with heavy reliance on migration models. The Sao Civilization is characterized by the presence of a wide range of zoomorphic and anthropomorphic clay figurines, copper alloy objects, and jar burials. Recent research provides new and complementary evidence (Connah 1981, 1985; Holl 1987a, 1987b, 1988, 1989, 1990, 1992, 1993; Holl and Levy 1993; Holl et al. 1991).

As far as the last 500 years are concerned, we will focus on walled settlements, centers of former polities (Figures 8.10). Some of these walled cities, Makari (*Macari*), Gulfey (*Calfe*), Afade (*Afadena*), Wulki (*Ulchi*), Kusseri (*Uncusciuri*), Sao (*Sauo*), and Logone (*Lagone*), were described at the end of the sixteenth century as chiefdom centers in which rulers were buried in mounds with several of their sacrificed subjects (d'Anania 1582: 350). Many of these settlements were visited and described by nineteenth-century European explorers: Major Denham, Captain Clapperton and Dr Oudney (1828) in the 1820s; Heinrich Barth (1965) in the 1850s; and Gustav Nachtigal (1980) in the 1870s. Later ethnographic research provided additional information on political systems of the Chad plain polities (A. Lebeuf 1969). We will, therefore, focus our discussion on categories of material evidence pertaining to social ranking and settlement patterns.

Cemeteries emerged during the fifteenth and sixteenth centuries during a period of resettlement that took place after the abandonment of the area around AD 1350–1450 owing to adverse climatic conditions (Holl 1987b; Maley 1993). Occupation hiatuses have been recorded in all mound sequences. At the end of the fourteenth century (AD 1380), groups of Arab pastoralists started to move into the Chad Basin and may have been present in the plain c. AD 1500–50 (Levtzion and Hopkins 1981). The neighboring Kanuri state had also started to expand (Holl 1993; Holl and Levy 1993; Lange 1977, 1987). The combination of these events may have been crucial in the development of ranked societies in the Chadian plain.

The development of cemeteries was an

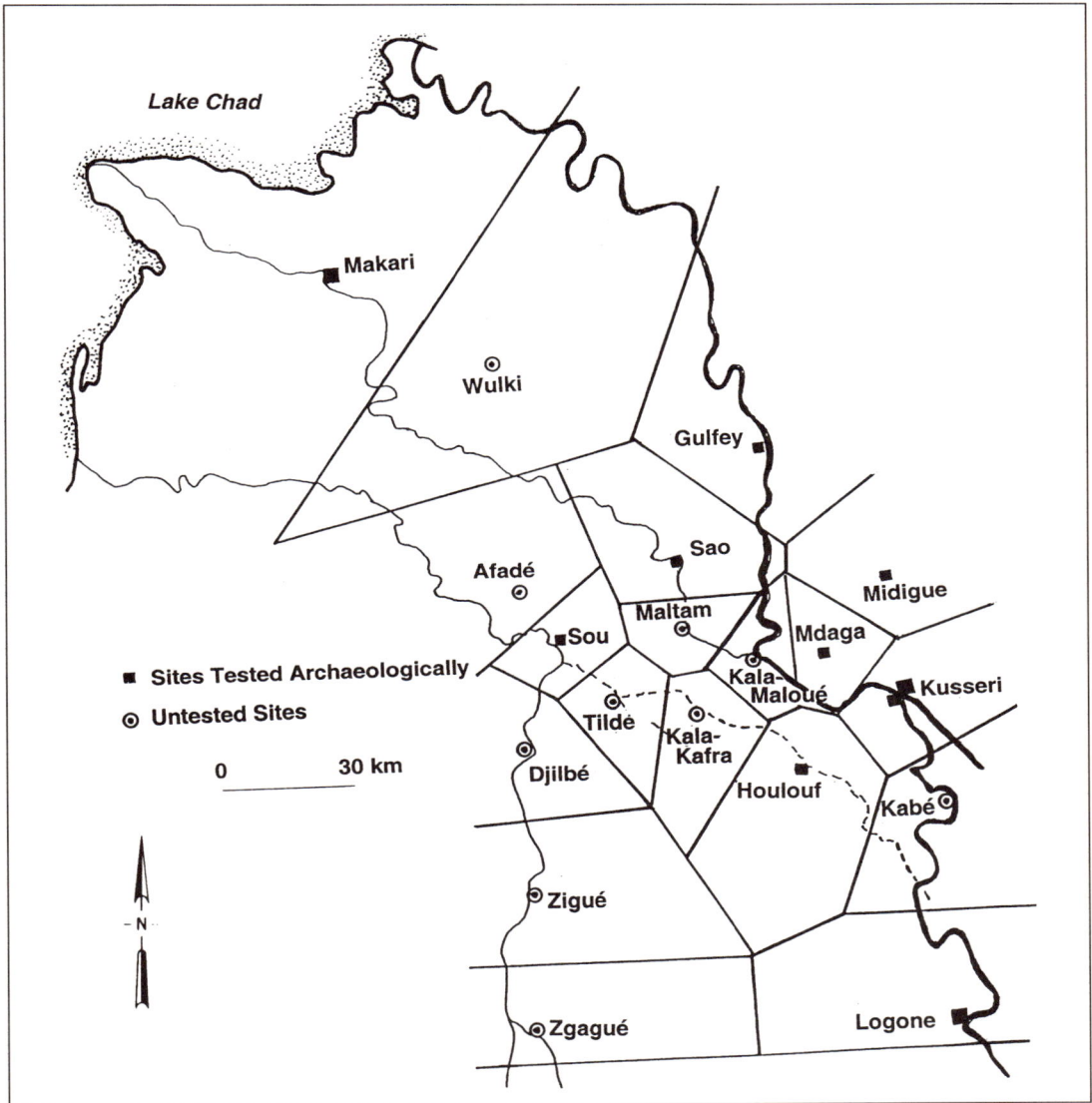

Figure 8.10 Walled cities of the Chadian plain and inferred territorial organization based on Thiessen polygons.

ideological and symbolic device aimed at exclusive control of the land, while earthen ramparts may have strengthened the unity of the communities in their attempts to face border encroachments. In the Houlouf region, 12 mound sites out of a total of 14 tested in an area measuring 400 square kilometers (150 square miles) were abandoned during the 1500–1600 period. Habitation was concentrated at the walled village of Houlouf and the nearby site of Hamei, situated 2 km northeast (Holl 1988, 1994). During the same time, with the rise to paramountcy of Logone-Birni, all the walled cities on the borders with the Bornu and Bagirmi kingdoms were integrated within a larger political system—the Lagwan kingdom—through matrimonial alliance, clientship, and, in some cases (mostly in the south), conquest (A. Lebeuf 1969, Sultan Mahamat Bahr Maruf of Logone-Birni: pers. comm.).

Table 8.5 Some Chadian plain sites: walled cities with studied cemeteries

Site	Sao	Mdaga	Midigué intra-muros	Midigué extra-muros	Houlouf
Settlement size					
Length (m)	580	350	350	350	450
Width (m)	350	200	200	200	400
Surface (ha)	20.30	7.00	7.50	7.50	15.90
Shape	ellipsoidal	ellipsoidal	ellipsoidal	ellipsoidal	sub-circular
Cemeteries					
Surface (m²)	69	109	180	47.50	38.50
No. of tombs	11	22	30	13	26
Density/m²	0.15	0.20	0.16	0.27	0.67
Average space per tomb (m²)	6.27	4.90	6.00	3.65	1.48

With a tight network of fortified settlements along its borders, the Logone kingdom remained relatively independent up to the colonial conquest.

Makari and Kusseri followed different pathways. The former, an early ally of Kanuri rulers, was a part of the Bornu kingdom, while the ruler of the latter was captured by Bornu troops, led by King Idris Alauma, between 1564 and 1592 (Lange 1987: 97). The Kusseri polity thus became a dependent territory with a Kanuri consul or *Khalifa*. Before the end of the nineteenth century the whole area was devastated by Rabeh's troops. Colonial domination started with Rabeh's defeat at Kusseri in 1900, in a battle against French troops (Zeltner 1980).

Graveyards and burials in jars are almost exclusively associated with walled settlements (Holl 1988, 1989, 1990, 1994). This is the case at Kabe, Kala-Kafra, Maltam, Kala-Maloue, and Logone-Birni in Cameroon, and at Ngala in Nigeria. Some isolated jar burials have been excavated at Afade, Sou, Makari, Gulfey, Kusseri, and Logone-Birni, and more substantial cemeteries have been studied at Sao and Houlouf in Cameroon, and Midigue and Mdaga in the Chad Republic. Located on rivers, these sites vary in size from seven (Mdaga) to over twenty (Sao) hectares (20–49 acres) (Table 8.5). The regional distribution of walled settlements in this flat landscape can be studied using locational models: Thiessen polygons suggest that each site was a political center (Figure 8.10). The smaller territorial units are situated in the middle of the study area and

larger ones at each end. We may dare consider that walled cities, cemeteries, and competition for territories were different facets of the same socio-political process.

Archaeological data from cemeteries can be used to evaluate the accuracy of the above hypothesis. With the exception of one extended burial from the cemetery of Mdaga, all the recorded tombs are jar-burials. It is, however, important to specify that these jars were not always used for the same purpose. At Houlouf, jars were used as 'tombstones': placed above the body and always situated at 0.30 to 0.50 m above the head (Holl 1988, 1994). In this cemetery, the dead were buried in a sitting position, oriented southwest, with their feet in a pot. In contrast, at Sao, Mdaga, and Midigué, jars were used as coffins. In all cases, the number of jars per tomb varies from one to three. Graveyards vary from 38.50 (Houlouf) to 180 square meters (Midigue Intra-muros), and the number of burials in each, from 11 (Sao) to 30 (Midigué intra-muros). Two of the cemeteries (Mdaga and Midigué extra-muros) are situated outside of the settlement. According to informants (Lebeuf *et al.* 1980: 96, note 51), graveyards situated out of the ramparts were those of blacksmiths. It is, therefore, not surprising that most of the excavated burials from these cemeteries were devoid of grave goods. In terms of spatial patterning, the density of burials varies from 0.15 (Sao) to 0.67 (Houlouf) per square meter, and average space per tomb from 1.48 (Houlouf) to 6.27 (Sao) square meters (Table 8.5). At cemeteries within the walls, burials are distrib-

Table 8.6 General aspects of the distribution of grave goods in tested mound sites

Site	Sao	Mdaga	Midigué intra-muros	Midigué extra-muros	Houlouf
Number of tombs	11	51	30	13	26
Tombs with grave goods	10	26	30	—	23
Burial facilities (jars)	17	28	57	13	32
Raw materials					
Carnelian	449	11	255	—	914
Glass	162	10	22	—	1
Alloyed copper	130	7	43	—	71
Pots	6	11	9	—	22
Others	6	1,613	17	—	25

uted in clusters, which suggests different social fractions.

Grave goods can be partitioned into two broad categories: local and exotic (Table 8.6). Locally made items, such as clay beads, smoking pipes, pottery, and figurines are recurrent, but in very small amounts. Exotic goods such as carnelian and glass beads (long, cylindrical, and opaque blue) and copper alloy artifacts are relatively abundant, but their distribution between settlements and burials is highly skewed. At Houlouf, for example, the frequency of carnelian beads varies from 1 to 174, and the number of copper alloy artifacts from 1 to 12 (Holl 1994). Exotic items were obtained through long-distance trade and used as symbols of prestige and power. In the Chadian basin, in AD 1600–1900, trade networks linked slave procurement areas on the southern margins of the study area to market places of the Bornu kingdom and Hausa polities in the north/northwest, the Bagirmi kingdom and the Dar Fur in the east, and, ultimately, North Africa and the Nile Valley, via the Sahara.

Conclusion: process and transformation

Different patterns have emerged from our discussion. These patterns can be subsumed under two major headings: 1) population movements and settlement relocation; and 2) patterns of exchange, craft specialization, and social ranking. Depending on the resolution and diversity of the archaeological data at hand, it is possible to highlight differences or similarities in evolutionary pathways.

Population movement and settlement relocation

Population movement and settlement relocation are among the most recurrent themes in ethnohistorical narratives (Tardits 1981a). In some cases, these oral accounts are supported by archaeological investigation and the documentary record. This is the case in the Chadian plain, the Fali domain in the Tinguelin Plateau, and the Adamaoua Plateau. In the Upper Benue flood plain, the ethnohistorical record is at variance with archaeological evidence. Elsewhere, in the Western Grassfields, the western Adamaoua Plateau, and the southern forested zone, the situation is far from clear. However, these last three study areas seem to have witnessed grand-scale population movements during the eighteenth and the beginning of the nineteenth centuries. It is not known if these events were interconnected, but some information suggests that this is the case. The Chamba migration, which may have started from the Tikar plain in the southern part of the western Adamaoua Plateau and culminated with the formation of the Bamun kingdom and the development of major village-kingdoms of the Western Grassfields (Tardits 1981b; Warnier 1985), is partly contemporary with the Beti migration and the epic of crossing the Sanaga river in the forested zone to the southwest (Essomba 1993; Laburthe-Tolra 1981; Ngwa 1981). During the nineteenth century, the expansion of the Vouté, from the Adamoua Plateau toward the Sanaga River valley in the south, was probably another facet of the same sequence of events (Von Morgen 1982). It appears as if all these groups were rushing toward the Atlantic coast in order to take advantage of the new opportunities of trade.

In the northern part of the country, the rise of Fulani generated a radical transformation of relations between ethnic groups. From the fifteenth century, the presence of Fulani pastoralists is reported in the historical record of Bornu and the southern part of the Chadian plain (Seignobos 1993). The Fulani *jihad* at the end of the eighteenth century resulted in a dramatic expansion of Fulani cultural identity, with a transformation from an exclusively nomadic pastoral way of life to that of a sedentary nobility residing in towns—*lamidats*. These *lamidats* were polities of various size, centered on localities such as Maroua, Garoua, and Ngaoundéré (Mahammadou 1981). The Fulani expansion probably instigated the movement of peoples in a domino-like chain reaction.

Different settlement patterns are represented in our regional samples: a system of dispersed homesteads in the southern forested area and the Tinguelin Plateau; central villages protected by ditches and earth embankments or walls in the Western Grassfields and the Chadian plain; and a combination of both types in the western Adamaoua. In general, population movements and relocation of settlements have produced complex interaction spheres, with overlapping social, economic, political, and ideological networks.

Patterns of exchange, craft specialization, and social ranking

Historical and ethnographic research shows that a wide range of goods, foodstuffs, drinks, and crafts items were involved in trade in various parts of the Cameroons (Barth 1965; Denham *et al.* 1828; Dillon 1981; Kopytoff 1981; Nachtigal 1980; Tardits 1981b; Von Morgen 1982; Warnier 1981, 1985). Depending on the area, different goods were involved in interregional and long-distance trade transactions. The situation can be subdivided into three main forms: the trans-Saharan long-distance trade in the north, the Atlantic trade system in the south, and a wide area of overlap between both

systems extending from the Upper Benue Basin in the north to the Adamaoua Plateau, the Western Grassfields and the savanna zone situated on the north of the Sanaga valley.

Archaeological trade items are extremely rare in the southern forest and the Western Grassfields, perhaps partly because of the research emphasis on iron technology. Elsewhere, in the Fali area of the Tinguelin Plateau, and the Chadian plain, carnelian and glass beads and copper alloy artifacts shed some light on long-distance trade. It can be inferred from ethnohistorical information that iron ore and artifacts were an important part of local exchange in the southern forested area (Essomba 1993). In the northern trade system, exotic goods like carnelian and glass beads, copper alloy artifacts, horses, books, special kinds of Saharan salts, and textiles were obtained through Hausa and Kanuri traders or from central market places in Bornu in exchange for grain, smoked or dried fish, local cotton cloth, ostrich feathers, and (especially) slaves (Lovejoy 1986).

The slave trade was monopolized by members of ruling families (Barth 1965; Nachtigal 1980). Slaves were mostly captured among the neighboring southern groups in purposeful expeditions, and acquired as war captives. It was also common to enslave those unable to pay their debts. The pressure exerted by slave raiding and warfare on target ethnic groups resulted in two kinds of settlement pattern. One was characterized by highly dispersed and relatively mobile kin groups, as seen from the settlement patterns of the Fali on the Tinguelin Plateau—a system which probably increased the cost of slave procurement. Another consisted of densely packed and fortified settlements able to fight and defeat slave raiders, as shown by evidence from the western Adamaoua.

In the Atlantic trade zone, sea salt, brass manillas, glass beads, firearms, alcohol, tobacco, and clothes were obtained in exchange for ivory, wild animal skins, and, mostly, slaves. The inland part of the Atlantic trade network was organized by a chain of middlemen with two kinds of procurement systems (Rowlands 1986; Tardits 1981; Warnier 1985). The first one, present in the centralized societies of the Western Grassfields, was in the hands of appointed officials—slave dealers with the hereditary privilege to manage

Table 8.7   Slave trade on the Cameroonian coast as known from British Parliamentary Papers

Ship name	Nation	Capacity (tons)	Number of slaves	Departure	Arrival	Date
Governor Parry	United Kingdom	180	279	?Cameroon	Martinico	4–01–1797
Anne	United Kingdom	206	277	Bimbia	Martinico	13–05–1797
Resource	United Kingdom	236	363	Malimba	Jamaica	6–12–1798
Louisa	United Kingdom	331	455	Malimba	Jamaica	13–12–1798
Swift	United Kingdom	263	388	Malimba	Jamaica	21–12–1799
Expedition	United Kingdom	220	232	Malimba	Jamaica	9–10–1800
Brooks	United Kingdom	352	336	Malimba	Jamaica	15–11–1800
Eagle	United Kingdom	284	287	Malimba	Grenada	1–04–1801
Commerciante	Portugal	?	167	Wouri	(captured)	7–09–1822
Ana	Spain	?	130	Wouri	(captured)	11–10–1825
Invincible	Brazil	?	440	Wouri	(captured)	26–12–1825
Clementine	Brazil	?	156	Wouri	(captured)	5–08–1828
Voadore	Brazil	?	(empty)	Bimbia	(captured)	20–08–1828
Arcenia	Brazil	?	269	Wouri	(captured)	30–10–1828
Estrella do Mar	Brazil	?	(empty)	Wouri	(captured)	30–10–1828
Repita	Spain	?	179	Wouri	(captured)	30–06–1834

Source: E. and S. Ardener 1981.

transactions with middlemen in the coastal trade entrepôts of Calabar, Bimbia, Duala, and Malimba (Table 8.7). The second was less tightly organized and was probably controlled by community leaders. Each ethnic group involved had its own traders and transactions took place in border areas between neighbors, as was the case at Edea near Sanaga Falls, which is located between the Bassa and the Malimba (Von Morgen 1982).

Published accounts of the slave trade are limited as not all shipments were reported. Nevertheless, the account of the Cameroon coast by E. and S. Ardener (1981, Table 8.7) in the eighteenth century demonstrates that the shipment of slaves was routine at Malimba, Wouri (Duala) and, probably, Bimbia during the heyday of the trade. Owing to competition between these trade entrepôts 'trade was slack, and trade at Malimba ... has stopped altogether because of an attack on a trading ship' (E. and S. Ardener 1981:565). The attack probably refers to events of 1787–88. Conflicts between the Duala and Bassa at the beginning of the nineteenth century, related to trade competition, are recounted in the epic poem *Les Fils de Hitong*, recorded by Ngijol (1980). The increasing pressure toward abolition and the foundation of a new factory at Kribi on the southern part of the Cameroonian coast in 1828

were probably reasons for the movement of Beti groups toward the southwest (Laburthe-Tolra 1981; Von Morgen 1982).

By the nineteenth century, the Atlantic trade had generated peculiar regional patterns of exchange from the coast to the hinterland. Factories were located according to preferential relations between trade partners. Coastal leaders from Duala, Malimba, and Batanga ethnic groups offered security and peace. Some of them became landlords with large farms of maize and cassava worked by slaves, which produced food for slave populations and ships' crews. Farther inland, the Mbo toward the Bamiléké Plateau, the Bassa in the center, along the Sanaga valley, and the Ngumba in the south, toward the land of the Beti, played the role of intermediaries between the coast and the hinterland communities. With abolition, new opportunities offered by the foundation of the factory of Kribi on the one hand, and the demographic and social consequences of more than three centuries of the slave trade on the other, generated intensive warfare and technological setbacks almost everywhere in the Cameroons, particularly in areas situated between the Adamaoua mountain range and the southern forested area (Von Morgen 1982).

The lack of archaeological evidence precludes any discussion of exchange patterns in the western Adamaoua mountain range. However, information provided by German explorers at the end of the nineteenth century and ethnographic records can be used to document some of the aspects of trade and the associated socio-political dynamics (Mohammadou 1981; Von Morgen 1982). The land conquered by the Fulani was divided into competing chiefdoms such as Banyo, Tibati, Tignéré, and Ngaoundéré. This process opened new opportunities for trade and intensified slave raiding on the northern shore of the Sanaga River. The Vouté had expanded southward in the search for slaves and ivory. Slave labor was used for farming and intensive iron production.

According to Von Morgen (1982: 252), in the village of Ngila there were 12 blacksmith workshops, with 5–7 craftsmen working every day from morning to night. The exclusive purpose was the production of weapons. Numerous Hausa traders were present during the sojourn of Von Morgen. In exchange for cotton cloth, glass beads, and horse equipment they received slaves and ivory. There was, however, some competition between the inland side of the Atlantic trade network, represented this time by the Germans, and the Hausa continental trade system. The village headman, named Ngilla, solved the problem and provided the Germans with the needed ivory and the Hausa with slaves. In his speech at the reception ceremony for the German officer, Ngilla said:

> You, white king, Allah lead you to my home, to make me much more powerful than I am. Now that you are my friend, I am not afraid of anyone, even among the most powerful; I will defeat all of them, even the overlord of Tibati; from now, I will cease to pay a tribute. (Von Morgen 1982: 252)

This address sheds some light on the relations between Fulani overlords and their dependants from the periphery and the annual tribute, which mostly consisted of slaves. It can be considered that the emergence of Fulani domination generated long cycles of predatory expansion and accumulation (Reyna 1990).

Social ranking can be inferred from settlement hierarchy and mortuary data. Western Adamaoua settlement systems, with central villages, smaller hamlets, and homesteads, suggest the existence of leading individuals with managerial capacities. In the Western Grassfields and the Chadian plain the relocation of populations and the reorganization of settlements resulted in the emergence of competing peer-polities. Intensified iron production in the Western Grassfields, including the development of clump furnace technology and, in the Matomb and Ndom areas, with large natural draft furnaces, seems to be congruent with radical social changes and the emergence of chiefship and 'great men'-like features (Godelier 1982; Vansina 1990). Access to exotic goods may have played a crucial role in the rise and fall of some leaders, families, lineages, clans, and even whole ethnic groups. In the southern forested area, settlement types range from dispersed homesteads to large villages. Along the Atlantic coast, communities of agriculturists and fishermen belonging to the Duala, Malimba, Bassa, and Batanga ethnic groups were organized into competing lineages led by 'entrepreneurs,' and some of them became wealthy and prestigious 'great men.' Some of the latter were called 'kings,' though they were not strictly speaking rulers of kingdoms (Beckombo-Priso 1981). Such an evolution was also observed in sixteenth- to nineteenth-century Congo and Loango (Vansina 1990), with brokers who profited the most from the trade owning no invested 'capital' at all, and therefore avoiding any commercial risk, but playing an indispensable role of intermediaries in the trade system.

References

d'Anania, Giovanni Lorenzo (1582) *L'universale fabrica del Mondo*. Venice.

Ardener, E. and Ardener, S. (1981) Preliminary chronological notes for the south. In *Contribution de la recherche ethnologique à l'histoire des civilisations du Cameroun*, edited by C. Tardits. Paris: Editions du CNRS, pp. 563–77.

Asombang, R., Essomba, J. M. and Ossah-Mvondo, J. P. (1991) Reconnaissance archéologique dans l'arrondissement de Zoétélé, province du sud, Cameroun méridional. *Nyame Akuma*, 35:17–21.

Atangana, C. (1989) 'Archéologie du Cameroun méridional: étude du site d'Okolo'. Doctoral thesis, University of Paris I-Sorbonne.

Atangana, C. (1992) Les fosses d'Okolo (sud du Cameroun): fouilles et axes de recherches. *Nyame Akuma*, 38:7–13.

Barth, H. (1965) *Travels and Discoveries in North and Central Africa 1849–1855*. London: Frank Cass.

Beckombo-Priso, M. (1981) Essai sur le peuplement de la région côtière du Cameroun: les populations dites Dwala. In *Contribution de la recherche ethnologique à l'histoire des civilisations du Cameroun*, edited by C. Tardits. Paris: Editions du CNRS, pp. 503–10.

Connah, G. (1969) Archaeological work in Bornu 1964–1966 with particular reference to the excavations at Daïma mound. In *Actes du premier colloque international d'archéologie africaine*, edited by J.-P. Lebeuf. Fort-Lamy. pp. 116–24.

Connah, G. (1981) *Three Thousand Years in Africa*. Cambridge: Cambridge University Press.

Connah, G. (1985) Agricultural intensification and sedentarism in the Firki of N.E. Nigeria. In *Prehistoric Intensive Agriculture in the Tropics*, edited by I. S. Farrington. Oxford: British Archaeological Reports, pp. 765–85.

Crits, E. de. (1992) Excavations at Banock, Grassfields, Cameroon. *Nyame Akuma*, 38:13–17.

David, N. (1972) An archaeological reconnaissance in Cameroon and the Iron Age site of Nassarao I, near Garoua. In *VI Congrès panafricain de préhistoire et d'études du quaternaire*, edited by H. J. Hugot. Chambery. pp. 307–8.

David, N. (1980) History of crops and peoples in north Cameroon to AD 1900. In *West African Culture Dynamics*, edited by B. K. Swartz and R. A. Dumett. The Hague: Mouton Publishers, pp. 139–82.

David, N. (1981) The archaeological background of Cameroonian history. In *Contribution de la recherche ethnologique à l'histoire des civilisations du Cameroun*, edited by C. Tardits. Paris: Editions du CNRS, pp. 79–100.

Denham, D., Clapperton, H. and Oudney, W. (1828) *Narrative of Travels and Discoveries in Northern and Central Africa in the Years 1822, 1823 and 1824*. London: John Murray.

Dillon, R. G. (1981) Notes on the pre-colonial history and ethnography of the Meta. In *Contribution de la recherche ethnologique à l'histoire des civilisations du Cameroun*, edited by C. Tardits. Paris: Editions du CNRS, pp. 361–70.

Essomba, J. M. (1985) Archéologie et histoire au sud du Cameroun: découverte de hauts fourneaux en pays Bassa. *Nyame Akuma*, 26:2–4.

Essomba, J. M. (1986) *Bibliographie critique de l'archéologie camerounaise*. Yaoundé: Librairie Universitaire.

Essomba, J. M. (1987) Le fer dans le développement des sociétés traditionnelles du sud Cameroun. *Annales de la faculté des lettres et sciences humaines*, 3(2):33–65.

Essomba, J. M. (1992) Archéologie du sud du Cameroun: notes préliminaires de recherches au site de Nkometou (Mfomakap). In *L'Archéologie au Cameroun*, edited by J. M. Essomba. Paris: Karthala, pp. 229–46.

Essomba, J. M. (1993) *Le Fer dans le passé des sociétés du sud Cameroun*. Paris: L'Harmattan.

Gauthier, J. G. (1969) *Les Fali de Ngoutchoumi: montagnards du nord-Cameroun*. Oosterhout: Anthropological Publications.

Gauthier, J. G. (1979) *Archéologie du pays Fali: Nord-Cameroun*. Paris: Editions du CNRS.

Gauthier, J. G. (1981) Les Fali du Cameroun septentrional. In *Contribution de la recherche ethnologique à l'histoire des civilisations du Cameroun*, edited by C. Tardits. Paris: Editions du CNRS, pp. 187–203.

Gauthier, J. G. (1990) Organisation des nécropoles et tradition orale: l'exemple du pays Fali Nord-Cameroun. *Bulletin et Mémoire de la Société d'anthropologie de Paris*, 2(3–4):201–18.

Gauthier, J. G. (1992) Sites et gisements archéologiques en pays Fali. In *L'Archéologie au Cameroun*, edited by J. M. Essomba. Paris: Khartala, pp. 41–50.

Goheen, M. (1992) Chiefs, sub-chiefs and local control: negotiations over land, struggles over meaning. *Africa*, 62(3):389–412.

Griaule, M. and Lebeuf, J.-P. (1948) Fouilles dans la région du lac Tchad. *Journal de la Société des Africanistes*, 18(1):1–116.

Griaule, M. and Lebeuf, J.-P. (1950) Fouilles dans la région du lac Tchad. *Journal de la Société des Africanistes*, 20(1):1–152.

Griaule, M. and Lebeuf, J.-P. (1951) Fouilles dans la région du lac Tchad. *Journal de la Société des Africanistes*, 21(1):1–95.

Holl, A. (1987a) Mound formation processes and societal transformations: a case study from the perichadian plain. *Journal of Anthropological Archaeology*, 6:122–58.

Holl, A. (1987b) Le projet archéologique de Houlouf: campagne 1987. *Nyame Akuma*, 29: 10–13.

Holl, A. (1988) *Houlouf I: Archéologie des sociétés protohistoriques du nord-Cameroun*. Oxford: British Archaeological Reports.

Holl, A. (1989) Individus et statuts: variabilité mortuaire dans la plaine tchadienne préhistorique. In *Singularités: les voies d'émergence individuelles*. (Collectif). Paris: Plon, pp. 351–67.

Holl, A. (1990) Variabilité mortuaire et transformations culturelles dans la plaine péritchadienne. In *Relations interethniques et culture matérielle dans le bassin du lac Tchad*, edited by D. Barreteaux and H. Tourneux. Paris: Editions de l'ORSTOM, pp. 13–31.

Holl, A. (1992) Systématique archéologique et étude des processus culturels: l'exemple de la région de Houlouf. In *L'Archéologie au Cameroun*, edited J. M. Essomba. Paris: Karthala, pp. 51–78.

Holl, A. (1993) Community interaction and settlement patterning in northern Cameroon. In *Spatial Boundaries and Social Dynamics*, edited by A. Holl and T. E. Levy. Ann Arbor: International monographs in prehistory, pp. 39–61.

Holl, A. (1994) The cemetery of Houlouf in northern Cameroon (AD 1500–1600): fragments of a past social system. *R.A.A.* 12:133–70.

Holl, A. and Levy, T. E. (1993) From the Nile valley to the Chad basin: ethnoarchaeology of Shuwa Arab settlements. *Biblical Archaeologist*, 56(4):166–79.

Holl, A., Levy, T. E., Lechevalier, C. and Bridault, A. (1991) Of cattle, mounds and men: archaeology and ethnoarchaeology in the Houlouf region (northern Cameroon). *West African Journal of Archaeology*, 21:7–37.

Hurault, J. (1979) Une application de la photo-interprétation à l'archéologie de l'Afrique tropicale: la reconstitution des modes de peuplement et des systèmes agraires disparus. Exemple de l'Adamaoua Occidental (Cameroun-Nigérie). *Bulletin de la Société française de photogrammetrie et de télédétection*, 75 (3): 7–47.

Hurault, J. (1986) Les anciens peuplements de cultivateurs de l'Adamaoua Occidental (Cameroun-Nigérie): méthodologie d'une approche spatiale. *Cahiers ORSTOM: Sciences Humaines* 22(1):115–45.

Hurault, J. (1988) 'Evolution récente des vallées de l'Adamaoua Occidental (Cameroun-Nigérie)'. Paper read at the Mega-Chad Network Seminar, *Datation et Chronologie dans le bassin du Tchad*. Bondy.

Hurault, J. (1993) Résumé – Abstract: Evolution récente des vallées de l'Adamaoua Occidental (Cameroun-Nigérie). In *Datation et chronologie dans le bassin du lac Tchad*, edited D. Barreteau and C. von Graffenried. Paris: Editions de l'ORSTOM, pp. 285–89.

Kopytoff, I. (1981) Aghem ethnogenesis and the Grassfields ecumene. In *Contribution de la recherche ethnologique à l'histoire des civilisations du Cameroun*, edited by C. Tardits. Paris: Editions du CNRS, pp. 371–82.

Laburthe-Tolra, P. (1981a) Essai de synthèse sur les populations dites 'béti' de la région de Minlaba (sud du Nyong). In *Contribution de la recherche ethnologique à l'histoire des civilisations du Cameroun*, edited by C. Tardits. Paris: Editions du CNRS, pp. 533–46.

Laburthe-Tolra, P. (1981b) *Minlaba I: Les seigneurs de la forêt*. Paris: Publications de la Sorbonne.

Lange, D. (1977) *Le Diwan des sultans du Kanem-Bornou: chronologie et histoire d'un royaume africain*. Wiesbaden: Franz Steiner.

Lange, D. (1987) *A Sudanic Chronicle: The Bornu Expeditions of Idris Alauma*. Stuttgart: Franz Steiner.

Lebeuf, A. M. D. (1969) *Les Principautés Kotoko: essai sur le caractère sacré de l'autorité*. Paris: Editions du CNRS.

Lebeuf, A. M. D. (1981) L'origine et la constitution des principautés Kotoko (Cameroun septentrional). In *Contribution de la recherche ethnologique à l'histoire des civilisations du Cameroun*, edited by C. Tardits. Paris: Editions du CNRS, pp. 209–18.

Lebeuf, A. M. D. (1992) Le site de Sou: étude d'une aire d'activité domestique. In *L'Archéologie au Cameroun*, edited by J. M. Essomba. Paris: Karthala, pp. 79–90.

Lebeuf, J.-P. (1962) *Archéologie tchadienne: les Sao du Cameroun et du Tchad*. Paris: Hermann.

Lebeuf, J.-P. (1969) *Carte archéologique des abords du lac Tchad*. Paris: Editions du CNRS.

Lebeuf, J.-P. (1981a) *Supplément à la carte archéologique des abords du lac Tchad*. Paris: Editions du CNRS.

Lebeuf, J.-P. (1981b) Le rôle de l'archéologie dans la connaissance de l'histoire (Cameroun septentrional). In *Contribution de la recherche ethnologique à l'histoire des civilisations du Cameroun*, edited by C. Tardits. Paris: Editions du CNRS, pp. 21–4.

Lebeuf, J.-P. (1992) Populations anciennes du sud du lac Tchad. In *L'Archéologie au Cameroun*, edited by J. M. Essomba. Paris: Karthala, pp. 91–100.

Lebeuf, J. P. and Lebeuf, A. M. D. (1977) *Les Arts Sao*. Paris: Hermann.

Lebeuf, J. P., Lebeuf, A. M. D., Treinen-Claustre, F. and Courtin, J. (1980) *Le Gisement Sao de Mdaga*. Paris: Société d'Ethnographie.

Lebeuf, J. P. and Masson-Detourbet, A. (1950) *La Civilisation du Tchad*. Paris: Payot.

Levtzion, N. and Hopkins, J. F. P. (eds). (1981) *Corpus of Early Arabic Sources for West African History*. Cambridge: Cambridge University Press.

Lewis, B. (1993) *Race et esclavage au Proche-Orient*. Paris: Gallimard.

Lovejoy, P. E. (1986) *Salt of the Desert Sun: A*

History of Salt Production and Trade in the Central Sudan. Cambridge: Cambridge University Press.

Maley, J. (1993) Chronologie calendaire des principales fluctuations du lac Tchad au cours du dernier millénaire: le rôle des données historiques et de la tradition orale. In *Datation et chronologie dans le bassin du lac Tchad*, edited by D. Barreteau and C. von Graffenried. Paris: Editions de l'ORSTOM, pp. 161–3.

Maret, P. de (1982) New survey of archaeological research and dates for west-central and north-central Africa. *Journal of African History*, 23:1–15.

Maret, P. de (1985) Recent archaeological research and dates from Central Africa. *Journal of African History*, 26:129–148.

Maret, P. de (1992) Sédentarisation, agriculture et métallurgie du sud Cameroun: synthèse des recherches depuis 1978. In *L'Archéologie au Cameroun*, edited by J. M. Essomba. Paris: Karthala, pp. 247–62.

Marliac, A. (1974) Prospection archéologique au Cameroun septentrionnal. *West African Journal of Archaeology*, 4:83–97.

Marliac, A. (1981) L'état des connaissances sur le paléolithique et le néolithique du Cameroun. In *Contribution de la recherche ethnologique à l'histoire des civilisations du Cameroun*, edited by C. Tardits. Paris: Editions du CNRS, pp. 27–78.

Marliac, A. (1991) *De la préhistoire à l'histoire au Cameroun septentrional.* Paris: Editions de l'ORSTOM.

Marliac, A. and Delneuf, M. (1984) *Reconnaissances archéologiques au Cameroun septentrional.* Paris-Yaoundé: ORSTOM-MESRES.

Marliac, A., Rapp, J. and Delneuf, M. (1983) *Reconnaissances archéologiques au Cameroun septentrional: les basses vallées des Mayo Louti, Tsanaga et Boula.* Paris-Yaoundé: ORSTOM-DGRST.

Mbida, C. (1992a) Fouilles archéologiques au sud Cameroun: résultats préliminaires de la mission de l'été 1990. *NSI*, 10/11:6–8.

Mbida, C. (1992b) Archaeological research in South Cameroon: preliminary results on the 1990 field season. *Nyame Akuma*, 37:2–4.

Mohammadou, E. (1981) L'implantation des Peul dans l'Adamawa (approche chronologique). In *Contribution de la recherche ethnologique à l'histoire des civilisations du Cameroun*, edited by C. Tardits. Paris: Editions du CNRS, pp. 229–48.

Nachtigal, G. (1980) *Sahara and Sudan.* Translated by A. G. B. Fisher and H. J. Fisher). London: C. Hurst and Co.

Ngijol Ngijol, P. (1980) *Les Fils de Hitong.* Yaoundé: Centre d'Edition et de Production pour l'Enseignement et la Recherche.

Ngoa, H. (1981) Tentative de reconstitution de l'histoire récente des Ewondo. In *Contribution de la recherche ethnologique à l'histoire des civilisations du Cameroun*, edited by C. Tardits. Paris: Editions du CNRS, pp. 547–62.

Ossah-Mvondo, J. P. (1990) Recherches archéologiques dans le nord-ouest: le site métallurgique de Ba. *Nyame Akuma*, 33:2.

Ossah-Mvondo, J. P. (1991) Problèmes et méthodes de la recherche archéologique en pays forestiers: la province du sud et ses environs. *Nyame Akuma*, 36:47–52.

Ossah-Mvondo, J. P. (1992a) Identification du site métallurgique de Mandoumba, centre Cameroun: les premières données archéologiques. *Nyame Akuma*, 38:17–19.

Ossah-Mvondo, J. P. (1992b) Prospection archéologique dans le département du Ntem, province du sud Cameroun. *NSI* 10/11:9–12.

Ossah-Mvondo, J. P. (1993) Prospection des sites d'habitat dans les arrondissements de Djoum et Mintom (sud Cameroun). *Nyame Akuma*, 39:15–19.

Packenham, T. (1991) *The Scramble for Africa: White Man's Conquest of the Dark Continent from 1876 to 1912.* New York: Avon Books.

Reyna, S. P. (1990) *Wars Without End: The Political Economy of a Precolonial African State.* Hanover, NH: University Press of New England.

Rowlands, M. (1986) Colonialism, archaeology and constituting the African peasantry. In *Comparative Studies in the Development of Complex Societies*; Vol. 3. Southampton: pre-circulated papers of the World Archaeological Congress.

Rowlands, M. and Warnier, J. P. (1993) The magical production of iron in the Cameroon Grassfields. In *The Archaeology of Africa: Food, Metals and Towns*, edited by T. Shaw, P. Sinclair, B. Andah and A. Okpoko. London and New York: Routledge, pp. 512–50.

Schmidt, P. and Asombang, R. (1990a) Rock-shelters and a greater history of the Bamenda Grassfields, Cameroon. *Nyame Akuma*, 34:5–10.

Schmidt, P. and Asombang, R. (1990b) Archaeological survey in northwestern Cameroon. *Nyame Akuma*, 34:10–16.

Seignobos, C. (1993) Des traditions Fellata et de l'assèchement du lac Tchad. In *Datation et chronologie dans le bassin du lac Tchad*, edited by D. Barreteau and C. von Graffenried. Paris: Editions de l'ORSTOM, pp. 165–82.

Tardits, C. (ed.) (1981a) *Contribution de la recher-*

che ethnologique à l'histoire des civilisations du Cameroun 2 vols. Paris: Editions du CNRS.

Tardits, C. (1981b) Le royaume Bamoun: chronologie – implantation des populations – commerce et économie – diffusion du maïs et du manioc. In *Contribution de la recherche ethnologique à l'histoire des civilisations du Cameroun*, edited by C. Tardits. Paris: Editions du CNRS, pp. 401–20.

Vansina, J. (1984) *Oral Tradition as History*. London: J. Currey.

Vansina, J. (1990) *Paths in the Rainforests: Toward a History of Political Tradition in Equatorial Africa*. Madison: University of Wisconsin Press.

Von Morgen, C. (1982) *A travers le Cameroun du sud au nord*. Paris: Publications de la Sorbonne.

Warnier, J. P. (1981) L'histoire pré-coloniale de la chefferie de Mankom (département de la Mezam). In *Contribution de la recherche ethnologique à l'histoire des civilisations du Cameroun*, edited by C. Tardits. Paris: Editions du CNRS, pp. 421–36.

Warnier, J. P. (1984) Histoire du peuplement et genèse des paysages dans l'ouest camerounais. *Journal of African History*, 25:395–410.

Warnier, J. P. (1985) *Echanges, développement et hiérarchies dans le Bamenda pré-colonial*. Wiesbaden: Franz Steiner.

Warnier, J. P. (1992) Rapport préliminaire sur la métallurgie du groupe Chap. In *L'Archéologie au Cameroun*, edited by J. M. Essomba. Paris: Karthala, pp. 197–210.

Warnier, J. P. and Fowler, I. (1979) A nineteenth century Ruhr in Central Africa. *Africa*, 49(4):329–51.

Wilhelm, H. (1981) Le commerce pré-colonial de l'ouest (plateau Bamiléké–Grassfields, régions Bamoun et Bafia). In *Contribution de la recherche ethnologique à l'histoire des civilisations du Cameroun*, edited by C. Tardits. Paris: Editions du CNRS, pp. 485–502.

Wulsin, F. (1932) An archaeological reconnaissance in the Chari basin. *Harvard African Studies*, 10:1–88.

Zeltner, J. C. (1980) *Pages d'histoire du Kanem: pays tchadien*. Paris: L'Harmattan.

9 An Americanist Perspective on African Archaeology: Toward an Archaeology of the Black Atlantic

THERESA A. SINGLETON

Introduction

It has been my goal for some time to engage Africanists and African-Americanists in a dialogue. As I learn more African archaeology, particularly the archaeology of the past 500 years, however, I have come to realize that this is no easy task. The previous papers highlight the difficulties of attaining this goal. A major problem is the uneven nature of archaeological data—many parts of West and West Central Africa are virtually unknown archaeologically, especially for the period of the trans-Atlantic slave trade. Even in areas where work has been undertaken, archaeological research is still quite preliminary. Another problem raised by MacEachern is the difficulty of distinguishing between activities associated with slaving and those associated with increasing political centralization. Finally, and perhaps most importantly, is the observation voiced by McIntosh as to whether or not the changes and transformations wrought by the Atlantic slave trade were any more significant than those of the Saharan trade, or other kinds of social transformations occurring in West Africa during the second millennium AD. While the trans-Atlantic trade is a critical frame of reference for the diasporist, this is not necessarily the case for the Africanist. These papers as well as others (e.g. DeCorse 1996) demonstrate that African indigenous developments played an equally significant role in the processes of change that occurred during the time of the Atlantic slave trade. Moreover, many of these developments were set in motion much further back in time.

Given these problems, is it possible for an African archaeology of the past 500 years and the archaeology of the African diaspora to inform each other? Agorsah has launched a spirited attack on the failure of both Americanists and Africanists to recognize the dual character of the archaeology of the diaspora, making it necessary for data collection to take place on both sides of the Atlantic. Additionally, he recommends the need for collaboration and exchange among both groups of scholars, and urges Africanists to go beyond ceramic sequences and to consider topics such as family, gender, race, or power relations in order to inform diaspora research (1996:222). While Agorsah's call for an archaeology of the Black Atlantic—research on people of African descent on both sides of the Atlantic Ocean—is overly ambitious at this juncture, this volume provides a major first step in bridging the interests of Africanists and African diasporists. This paper briefly examines ways in which the previous ones, as well as other archaeological studies undertaken by Africanists, contribute to the archaeological study of the African diaspora in the Americas.

Contributions of African archaeology to the archaeology of the Atlantic diaspora

When the archaeological study of the African diaspora was first initiated in the late 1960s and 1970s, few archaeologists were undertaking research in Africa on the period that coincides with the trans-Atlantic slave trade. Some Americanist archaeologists consulted with Africanists on an informal basis (Deetz 1996; Ferguson 1992: 9–10) to assist them in identifying alleged African influences from materials recovered from African-American sites, but there was no systematic effort to involve Africanist archaeologists in this work. Then, as is often the case now, efforts to link archaeological findings of the African diaspora with African origins utilized ethnographic studies of twentieth-century African peoples, not archaeological findings. This misuse of ethnographic models has come under attack by both those engaged in diaspora research (Thomas 1995) as well as by Africanists (e.g. Stahl 1993).

This collection of papers attests to the increased attention given to the archaeology of West Africa at the time of the trans-Atlantic slave trade. It also demonstrates that the failure of Americanists to consult African archaeology on archaeological questions is no longer warranted. Thus, this volume is valuable to the student of the Atlantic African disaspora for several reasons: it provides a long-overdue introduction to the culture history and material culture of diverse areas in West Africa before and after colonial rule; it places the complexities of the slave trade, its consequences, and its impact on the cultural landscape into sharp focus; and the recurrent discussion on the fluidity of African ethnicity studies casts serious doubt on assigning specific African ethnic provenances to archaeological finds recovered from African diasporic communities.

It is critical that students of the African diaspora understand the archaeology of West Africa during the time of the Atlantic slave trade. Even when the archaeological study focuses on those African societies who controlled and prospered from the slave trade (e.g. DeCorse 1992; Kelly and Gronenborn in this volume), rather than those who became captives of the trade, the archaeology of this

period holds great promise for elucidating material aspects of African life prior to European colonial rule. Pre-colonial burial customs provide an excellent example to illustrate this point. Excavations at the site of the early town of Elmina, the headquarters for the Portuguese and later the Dutch trade along the Gold Coast, yielded burials beneath African houses (De-Corse 1992). A similar practice of burials within houses has been reported from four slave quarters (c. 1670–1780) at the Seville Plantation along the north coast of Jamaica (Armstrong 1998: 389; 1999). That the practice of burial within houses was at least attempted by enslaved people is suggested in a written source from Barbados: 'negros are superstitiously attached to the burial places of their ancestors and friends . . . it is frequent to inter a near relation under the bed-place on which they sleep, an unwholesome and dangerous practice which they would think is the utmost tyranny to alter' (quoted in Handler and Lange 1978:174).[1] Other historical sources and archaeological research in Barbados suggest, however, that burial in cemeteries rather than sub-floor house graves was more commonly practiced on Barbadian plantations (Handler and Lange 1978; Handler et al. 1989).

The recovery of burials found underneath slave dwellings is one of the most convincing pieces of archaeological evidence for the transfer of an African practice in an African diaspora community uncovered to date. Mortuary practices suggestive of African customs have been identified elsewhere in the Americas. At Newton Cemetery on Barbados, the burial of a presumed religious specialist has been identified, and some of the artifacts found within the grave are suggestive of African religious practices (Handler 1997). Africanist archaeologists have noted similarities in burial practices between the interments of the African Burial Ground in New York and those found in West Africa (Warren Perry, pers. comm. 1999). In Cuba, religious paraphernalia comparable to that found at Newton, and other religious offerings similar to African religious practices, have been recovered from excavations of slave cemeteries (Domínguez 1999:33).[2]

The below-the-floor burials at Seville Plantation, however, also serve as a caution against assigning a specific African ethnic provenance to an archaeological find. It may be tempting to suggest that this custom is an Akan burial practice, given the archaeological evidence recovered from Elmina, a settlement historically associated with the Fante—a subgroup of the Akan ethnolinguistic family. The high concentration of enslaved persons referred to as 'Koromantin' or 'Coromantee' in Jamaica (see Higman 1984) and elsewhere in the British West Indies further suggests that these enslaved people departed from the Gold Coast, the cultural area of many Akan people.[3] Burial within houses, however, was not exclusively an Akan practice and was apparently widespread in West Africa at one time (Posnansky 1999:34).

It is equally important that Americanists understand changes in material culture resulting from European colonial rule in Africa. Stahl's case study discusses how British colonial policies may have led to the abandonment of some pre-existing African practices. Stahl discusses here and elsewhere (1994) that British administrators pursued a policy of village planning, wherein Africans were encouraged to abandon their old villages and resettle at new ones laid out in grids. These policies have direct archaeological implications because African villagers were persuaded to bury their dead in cemeteries rather than within their compounds, and they adopted new patterns of refuse disposal. Because many villagers did comply with colonial village planning, Stahl suggests many colonial and post-colonial studies of African village life are suspect for interpreting earlier archaeological findings.

The impact of the trans-Saharan, trans-Atlantic, and domestic slave trades on specific regions of West Africa is a major theme in many of these papers. These systems of slave trading were often intimately connected, and their effects varied from place to place. Where possible the authors have carefully distinguished the cultural groups who conducted slave raiding and slave trading from those groups who became the captives of these activities. This important distinction has often been overlooked by Americanists in drawing connections between African cultures and peoples of the African diaspora. This is just one of the many ways in which this collection serves as a powerful corrective in the search for African continuities in the Americas.

Several papers in this volume, most notably by de Barros, Holl, and MacEachern, examine the archaeological patterns associated with the social transformations that accompanied the three forms of slave trade. Research is still preliminary, but the impact of the slave trade as seen archaeologically includes: abandonment of settlements; relocation of people and production centers; the appearance of new forms of settlements—small dispersed settlements or densely populated settlements, fortified with walls, earth embankments or ditches; the cessation of some crafts—particularly production of certain types of pottery—and the appearance of new kinds of pottery; and modification of ritual practices. The result of these disruptive processes was the demise of some groups, the absorption of others into larger entities, and the creation of new cultural entities. This disruption may also be responsible for the present-day occurrence MacEachern observes of 'a bewildering constellation of ethnic, linguistic, religious, and economic groups' living in high densities for the last two centuries in the Mandara Mountains of the southern Chad Basin.

Africanist archaeologists have been able to detect only subtle differences or none at all in the material culture among groups who maintain separate ethnic identities, in situations of concentrated cultural diversity like that of the Mandara Mountains (e. g. DeCorse 1989; Stahl 1991). Ann Stahl's work in Banda (west central Ghana) is particularly instructive. She found that over the years non-Akan groups adopted Akan ethnic symbols—a process she calls Akanization—but maintained their separate identity in language and in certain ceremonies. She raises the question: 'How far back in time may we legitimately employ contemporary ethnic or cultural labels in our reconstructions of the past?' (1991:268). Her recommendation is that archaeologists must acknowledge the problems of contemporary labels and recognize that the boundaries implied by them may be highly permeable. Holl offers a similar comment from the vantage point of the Cameroons; 'social groups, be they characterized by shared worldviews, languages, or ethnic ascription, are products of historical processes not permanent essences.' Clearly, Africanists are ahead of some diasporists in moving away from essentialist notions of cultural identity, and in appreciating the problems of using present ethnic designations in the interpretation of the archaeological record.

Toward an archaeology of the Black Atlantic

In spite of the obstacles that may hinder collaborations between Africanists and diasporists, African archaeology is directly affecting the archaeology of the African Atlantic diaspora. Several Africanist archaeologists are undertaking archaeological research on sites of the African diaspora, and a few diasporists are beginning work in Africa. Africanists are involved in the analysis of the archaeological materials recovered from the African Burial Ground, the site of an eighteenth-century cemetery located in lower Manhattan in New York. Christopher DeCorse and I surveyed and tested several sites in coastal Ghana in 1993, dating between AD 1100 and 1900. DeCorse's students are presently developing dissertation projects on sites identified in the coastal survey, as well as working in northern Ghana where considerable slave raiding took place.

Two on-going projects initiated by Africanist archaeologists in the Americas incorporate Black Atlantic perspectives: Agorsah's study of Afro-Caribbean spatial organizations (Agorsah 1998, 1999) and Goucher's study on the transfer of African iron technology to the Americas (Goucher 1993, 1999).

Building on his research on African spatial patterns, Agorsah is comparing and contrasting the spatial organizations of pre-colonial African settlements in Ghana with those of maroon settlements in Jamaica and Suriname (Agorsah 1998). At the Jamaican maroon settlement known as Old Accompong Town, Agorsah observed connections between spatial configurations and social structure (kinship-based patterns), even though oral traditions claim there is no relationship between the two. He explains this discrepancy as resulting from 'true unconscious organization' that may be illusory or even contradictory in reality (1999:48). Agorsah interprets the formation and maintenance of 'yards' in Jamaican slave communities as another effort by Afro-Jamaicans to establish spatial patterns based on family relationships (1999:49).

Goucher's study on the transfer of African metallurgical technologies to the iron technology of the Caribbean combines archaeological, historical, and ethnographic research

(Goucher 1993, 1999). Goucher argues that ideological transfers associated with the transAtlantic journey of Ogun (the Yoruba deity associated with iron) to Haiti, Cuba, Brazil, and Trinidad have been investigated (see Barnes 1989), but the technological implications of these transfers have been ignored. The high value placed on enslaved people with ironworking and metalsmithing skills and the high status metalworkers occupied within slave communities are, for Goucher, strong suggestions that the prestige and empowerment bestowed on African ironworkers was transplanted to some degree to the Amercias. She has begun the archaeological study of metalworking at Reeder's Pen, the site of a foundry in Jamaica which produced iron and brass. The owner, John Reeder, was a coppersmith and according to written accounts he relied primarily upon the metallurgical expertise of African-Jamaican laborers—enslaved, free, and maroons. Excavations of portions of the foundry yielded a wide variety of iron and copper-alloy objects. Analytical studies of these metal objects, necessary to determine the kinds of technologies used to produce them, are now underway (Goucher 1993:212).

The ethnographic component of Goucher's research involved studying the work of present-day ironworkers and ritual performance involving ironworking symbolism. She interviewed one the of the last remaining blacksmiths in Jamaica who still refers to the anvil as the 'mother' of the forge. Identification of ironworking equipment with females is widespread in sub-Saharan Africa (1999:151). She has also studied African-derived religions in Jamaica and Trinidad, where ironworking is symbolically important in many of the ritual practices. In the Afro-Jamaican religion of kumina, she found numerous references to iron, including the use of archaic African terms for iron objects. In Trinidad, the oldest surviving Orisha shrine is dedicated to the Yoruba deity Ogun. Because Ogun is seen as both a violent warrior and a protector/nurturer, Goucher postulates that to enslaved Africans the relationship between Ogun and iron had a double meaning: one associated with the slaveholder's enslaving shackles; the other with iron tools that could be used to liberate enslaved persons from bondage. Both Agorsah's and Goucher's studies demonstrate the utility of an

Atlantic perspective in the study of African cultural survivals in the Americas.

Future work on the archaeology of the African diaspora will need to incorporate African archaeology for those practitioners who remain interested in establishing how an African heritage shaped the material lives of diaspora communities. As many of the preceding studies demonstrate, archaeologists of the African diaspora should not continue to follow the flawed methodological path of projecting the present onto the past. Additionally, these studies force us to come to the realization that even when more archaeological data are available for West Africa during the time of the trans-Atlantic slave trade, our interpretations of these data will be limited. All we might ever be able to say about a particular artifact or practice is that it represents what was, at one time, an African custom from an area either from which enslaved Africans were drawn or from where their captors once lived. This realization raises the question: will this result be worth all the effort? An equally pertinent question is: at what point in studies of the diaspora does Africa cease to be the reference point for our analysis? Indeed, these are difficult questions to answer. It is clear from the work of Agorsah, Goucher, and many other scholars that African customs and practices were incorporated into the worlds of people of African descent in the Americas. At the same time, if archaeology is to move beyond essentialist notions of cultural identity, diasporists need to evaluate and specify those situations wherein African data are useful for interpreting diasporic communities and those situations where they are not. We cannot generate dynamic models of cultural identity if we continue to see African peoples as static, or people of African descent in the Americas as conservative retainers of African worldviews.

References

Agorsah, E. Kofi (1996) The archaeology of the African diaspora. *African Archaeological Review*, 13(4):221–4.

Agorsah, E. Kofi (1998) 'Settlement pattern studies in the archaeology of the African diaspora'. Paper presented at the Society for Africanist Archaeology, Syracuse University, May 23.

Agorsah, E. Kofi (1999) Ethnoarchaeological consideration of social relationship and settlement patterning among Africans in the Caribbean diaspora. In *African Sites Archaeology in the Caribbean*, edited by J. B. Haviser. Princeton, NJ: Markus Wiener Publishers, pp. 38–64.

Armstrong, D. (1998) Cultural transformation within enslaved laborer communities in the Caribbean. In *Studies in Culture Contact: Interaction, Culture Change, and Archaeology*, edited by J. Cusick. Carbondale: Center for Archaeological Investigation, Southern Illinois University at Carbondale, Occasional Paper No. 25, pp. 378–401.

Armstrong, D. (1999) Archaeology and ethnohistory of the Caribbean Plantation. In *I, Too, Am America: Archaeological Studies of African-American Life*, edited by T. A. Singleton. Charlottesville: University Press of Virginia, pp. 173–93.

Barnes, S. (1989) *Africa's Ogun: Old World and New*. Bloomington: Indiana University Press.

Brandon, G. (1993) *Santeria for Africa to the New World: The Dead Sell Memories*. Bloomington: Indiana University Press.

DeCorse, C. (1989) Material aspects of the Limba, Yalunka, and Kuranko ethnicity: archaeological research in Northeastern Sierra Leone. In *Archaeological Approaches to Cultural Identity*, edited by S. Shennan. London: Unwin Hyman, pp. 125–40.

DeCorse, C. (1992) Culture contact, continuity, and change on the Gold Coast. *African Archaeological Review*, 10:163–74.

DeCorse, C. (1996) Documents, oral histories, and the material record: Historical Archaeology in West Africa. *World Archaeology Bulletin*, 7:40–50.

DeCorse, C. (1999) Oceans apart: Africanist perspectives on diaspora archaeology. In *I, Too, Am America: Archaeological Studies of African-American Life*, edited by T. A. Singleton. Charlottesville: University of Virginia Press, pp. 132–55.

Deetz, J. (1996) *In Small Things Forgotten: An Archaeology of Early American Life*. Expanded and revised edition. New York: Anchor Books.

Domínguez, L. (1999) *Los collares en el santería cubana*. Havana: José Martí.

Ferguson, L. (1992) *Uncommon Ground: Archaeology and Early African America, 1650–1800*. Washington, D.C.: Smithsonian Institution Press.

Gomez, M. (1998) *Exchanging Our Country Marks: The Transportation of African Identities in the Colonial and Antebellum South*. Chapel Hill: University of North Carolina Press.

Goucher, C. (1993) African metallurgy in the New World. *African Archaeological Review*, 11:197–215.

Goucher, C. (1999) African-Caribbean metal technology: forging cultural survivals in the Atlantic world. In *African Sites Archaeology in the Caribbean*, edited by J. B. Haviser, Princeton, NJ: Markus Wiener Publishers, pp. 143–56.

Handler, J. S. (1997) An African-type healer/diviner and his grave goods. A burial from a plantation slave cemetery in Barbados, West Indies. *International Journal of Historical Archaeology*, 1(2):91–130.

Handler, J. S., and Lange, F. W. (1978) *Plantation Slavery in Barbados: An Archaeological and Historical Investigation*. Cambridge, MA: Harvard University Press.

Handler, J. S., Conner, M. D. and Jacobi, K. P. (1989) *Searching for a Slave Cemetery in Barbados, West Indies. A Bioarchaeological and Ethnohistorical Investigation*. Carbondale: Center for Archaeological Investigation, Southern Illinois University at Carbondale, Research Paper No. 59.

Higman, B. (1984) *Slave Populations of the British Caribbean, 1807–1834*. Baltimore: Johns Hopkins University Press.

Palmie, S. (1993) Ethnogenetic processes and cultural transfer in Afro-American slave populations'. In *Slavery in the Americas*, edited by Wolfgang Binder, pp. 337–63. Würzburg, Germany: Königshausen und Neumann.

Posnansky, M. (1999) West Africanist reflections on African-American archaeology. In *I, Too, Am America: Archaeological Studies of African-American Life*, edited by T. A. Singleton. Charlottesville: University Press of Virginia, pp. 21–38.

Stahl, A. B. (1991) Ethnic style and ethnic boundaries: a diachronic case study from West-Central Ghana. *Ethnohistory*, 38(3):250–75.

Stahl, A. B. (1993) Concepts of time and approaches to analogical reasoning in historical perspective. *American Antiquity*, 58:235–60.

Stahl, A. B. (1994) Change and continuity in the Banda Area Ghana: the direct historical approach. *Journal of Field Archaeology*, 21(2):181–203.

Thomas, B. W. (1995) Source criticism and the interpretation of African-American sites. *Southeastern Archaeology*, 14(2):149–57.

Notes

1. There are also historical references for Jamaica that mention enslaved people burying their deceased family members under their houses. One such reference comes from a black loyalist (enslaved people who were granted their freedom by the British during the American Revolutionary War). He commented on the practice of Afro-Jamaicans burying their deceased loved ones under their houses (John Pulis, pers. comm., 1999).

2. In addition to Domínguez's work, there have been other slave cemeteries that have yielded suggestions of African religious practices.

3. Many of the ethnic labels given to enslaved Africans by slave traders refer to the places they were taken from, for example 'Cormantees' (Cormantin or Kromantin, a Dutch and English trading station on the Gold Coast), or 'Araras' (taken from the kingdom of Ardrah or Allada on the Slave Coast) rather than true ethnic designations (see discussion by DeCorse 1999:135–7 and Posnansky 1999:24–5). However, once in the Americas these designations often became the ways in which Africans and their descendants defined themselves. In many places, particularly in Latin America, Africans organized mutual aid and religious organizations based on these created ethnic labels. Although these ethnic designations have little or no historical or cultural meaning in Africa, they are often important to understanding identity formation among communities of the African diaspora (for examples see Brandon (1993) 55–9; Gomez (1998); Palmie (1993)).

Index

Abomey (Dahomey), settlement patterns as response to the slave trade 96

Adadiem (Banda), ceramics 50

Afade (*Afadena*) Kingdom (Chadian Plain, Cameroons) 168

Africanists, difficulties in the dialogue with African-Americanists 179–80, 182

Agarade rockshelter (Kotokoli region, Bassar) 63

Agokoli I (king of Notsé) 85

agriculture 3–4
  Bassar peoples 60, 63, 65
  commercial agriculture, Faleme River Valley (Senegambia) 30–1
  effects of resistance to the slave trade upon agricultural methods in Mandara Mountains 144–5
  Slave Coast 84–5, 96–7

Aho, Prince René (translator, French investigations into the ethnography of the Fon peoples) 84

Aja-Ewe peoples (Slave Coast) 84, 85, 86

Ajere (Yobe valley, Lake Chad), identification with Jaja/Kaka (Kanem-Borno) 107, 116

Akanization 44, 181

al-Idrisi (Arab explorer) 29
  accounts of slavery in Senegal 18–19
  description of Gesebi (Al-Qasaba) (waystation for trans-Saharan trade 108, 110

al-Kanemi, al-Hajj Muhammad al-Amin ibn Muhammad (*mallam*/scholar), on reorganization of political system of Kanem-Borno (nineteenth century) 118

al-Maqrizi (Egyptian historian)
  describes slave trade of Kanem-Borno 104, 108

description of ethnography of southern Lake Chad Basin 136

al-Muhallabi, slave trade in southern Lake Chad Basin 138

al-Qalqashandi (Egyptian geographer), description of Jaja (Kaka) 106

al-Qasaba (Gesebi, waystation for trans-Saharan trade from Chad regions) 108, 110

al-Yakubi
  slave trade in southern Lake Chad Basin 138
  Zaghawa state 135–6

Alat Makay (trading station) (Yaoundé-Lékié) 154

Allada (Slave Coast) 82, 86
  and the Atlantic trade 86–7
  metal artifacts 93

Almada, Alvarez d' (Portuguese explorer) 24

American Burial Ground (New York), burial practices, as illustrations of transfer of African practices to the African diaspora 180, 182

Amsaka (Chad Basin) 118

Anania, Giovanni Lorenzo (Italian geographer) 136, 142
  description of Chad Basin (1573) 116–17

Apetandjor (iron ore deposit, Bassar) 65, 73

Arab explorers
  accounts of slave trade in Western Sudan 16
  accounts of slavery in Senegal 18–19
  written accounts of West African cultural history 2, 3, 6

Arab trade networks 6

archaeology
  Cameroons 154
  contribution to dialogue between Africanists and

archaeology (*cont.*)
    African-Americanists and understanding of
      cultural practices 180–1, 182–3
  effects on understanding of Atlantic trade in
    Senegambia 15, 23–4, 32–3
  use in study of West African cultural history 1, 2,
    6–7, 9, 9–10
Archéologie de Sauvetage dans la Vallée du Mono
  (Togolais/Béninois salvage project) 85
aristocracy (Western Sudan), attitudes to the slave
  trade 16–17
Arondo (Faleme River Valley, Senegambia) 29, 30
Asante (Ghana)
  British colonial rule 44–6
  political history 40–1, 41–2
  slave trade 42, 44, 68–9
  see also Ghana
Atakpa (Bassar chief) 74, 76
Atlantic trade
  Asante involvement 68–9
  Cameroons 152, 153, 157, 173
  effects
    on Banda (west central Ghana) 38–9, 41–2,
      44, 53–4
    difficulties of determining effects on African
      indigenous developments 179
    on Senegambia 14–16, 18, 22, 31–2
    on West African cultural history 1, 2, 7–9, 10
  as market for slaves from southern Lake Chad
    Basin 146
  and the Slave Coast 81–4, 86, 86–7, 96–7
  see also slave trade; trade systems
Awdaghust (Tegdaoust) (Sahel), slavery 19, 32
Awing chiefdom (Ndop Plateau, Cameroons), iron
  industry 160

Baghirmi state (Chad Basin)
  independence of Kanem 136
  slave populations (early twentieth century) 146
Bambimbi (Ndom district, Cameroons), iron
  industry 155, 157
Bamenda Plateau (Western Grasslands,
  Cameroons), iron industry 159–62
Banda (Ghana)
  Akanization 181
  ceramics 47–9
  cultural life 39–40
  effects of the Atlantic trade 38–9, 41–2, 44, 53–4
  slave trade 42–3
Bandjeli (Bassar) 69
  ceramics 74
  iron industry 64, 65, *66*, 67, 73
Bangaler (Siin Salum region, Senegambia) (shell
  midden) 24

Bannock (Menoua, Cameroons) 158
Bantoma (trading fort) (Elmina, Ghana) 9
Banyo (Western Adamaoua, Cameroons),
  settlement patterns as defensive measures
  against Fulani conquests 163
Barbados, burial practices, as illustrations of transfer
  of African practices to the African diaspora 180
Barth, Heinrich (German traveler, in Kanem-Borno
  in 1850s) 118, 119, 124, 168
Bassa peoples (Yaoundé-Lékié, Cameroons) 155–6
Bassar peoples (Togo) 59–63
  colonial period 76
  cultural history 63
  effects of the slave trade 69–70, 70–5, 77
  iron industry 60, 64–8, 70, 71, *72*, 73–5, 76, 77
  trading links 68, 70
Bé (Upper Benue Basin, Cameroons) 166
Begho (entrepôt, Niger River) 40, 41, 47
Béhanzin (king of Dahomey) 84
Bénin, Bight of, *see* Slave Coast
Berlin Conference (1884–5), effects on Asante 45
Beti peoples (Cameroons), migration 155, 171, 173
Bibease (Ghana), European trading presence 9
Bidjilib-Liba-Wawa (iron ore deposit, Bassar) 65,
  73
big men (heads of families), existence among the
  Bassar questioned 67
Binaparba (Bassar), iron industry 73
Birim Valley (Ghana), cultural effects of the
  Atlantic trade 10
Birni Gazargamo (Kanem Borno capital) 103, *106*,
  110, 112–15, 118, 137, 146
Bissibe clan (Bassar peoples) 60
Bitampobe (Bandjeli area, Bassar) 73
Bitchabe (Togo) 64, 65, 67, 73
Bono Manso (entrepôt, Niger River) 41
Bono-Mansu (Ghana), trade developments 65
Bornu state (Chad Basin)
  independence of Kanem 136
  slave trade 146
Boubadkar, Almany Saada 30
Bowditch, T. E. (British explorer), Asante slave
  trade 69
brass-casting technology 3
Britain
  colonial policies, effects on African cultural
    practices 181
  colonial rule, Banda (Ghana) 40, 41, 44–6, 51,
    52–3
  trading practices, Faleme River Valley
    (Senegambia) 30
  see also Europe
Buduma/Yedina peoples (Lake Chad islands),
  resistance to slavery 143

Bui National Park (Banda) 42, 43
Bulala peoples (Chad Basin) 136, 141
Bunce Island (trading fort, Sierra Leone) 8
burial practices
   Chadian Plain (Lake Chad, Cameroons) 168–71
   Fali culture (Upper Benue Basin, Cameroons)
      166–7
   as illustrations of transfer of African practices to
      the African diaspora 180–1, 184 nn.1 & 2
   Saré Dioulдé (Senegambia) 25
   Senegambia 32
   Siin Salum region (Senegambia) 24–5
   Wopti-Tshalo culture (Upper Benue Basin,
      Cameroons) 167–8

Calfe (Gulfey) Kingdom (Chadian Plain,
      Cameroons) 168
Cameroons
   archaeological research 154
   settlement patterns 154–5
   and the slave trade (1500–1900) 152–4
   trade systems 173–4
   see also Lake Chad (Cameroons); Southern Lake
      Chad Basin (Cameroons)
Cape Coast, European trading forts 8
Cape Verde Islands, European settlement 7
Casamanca (Senegambia), shell middens 24
caste systems, West Africa 17
Central *bilad al-sudan* 101–3
ceramics
   Bassar
      effects on production of the iron industry 67–8
      effects of the slave trade 74–5, 77
   Kanem-Borno empire (Lake Chad) 106–7, 107,
      116, *117*, 118, 124, 125
   Kuula Kataa (Banda) 53
   Makala Kataa (Banda) 47–51
   Senegambia 25–9
   Slave Coast 86
      Savi and Ouidah 88–91, 94–5, 96
   Southern Lake Chad Basin 135
   see also iron industry; tobacco pipes
Chadian Basin, *see* Lake Chad (Cameroons)
Chadian Plain, *see* Lake Chad (Cameroons)
Chamba peoples (Cameroons), migration 171
chiefdoms, evolution among the Bassar 70–1, 77
Christiansborg (Danish trading fort, Asante) 8
cire perdue (lost wax) casting 4, 93
clans, Bassar peoples (Togo) 60, 63
Clapperton, Hugh (British expedition into Central
      Sudan) 108, 168
   description of Birni Gazargamo (1823) 113–14
climate change
   effects

Senegambia 29
   on settlement in Kanem-Borno 125
   links with slavery post-1600, in Sahel 19
cloth industry
   Asante (Ghana), British colonial period 45–6
   Slave Coast 86
clump furnace technology 159–60
colonialism, Southern Lake Chad 131
Copper Age, West Africa 4
copper artifacts, Savi (Slave Coast) 93–4, *94*
Côte d'Ivoire, *see* Ivory Coast
cultural practices, as guides to ethnic origins 181,
      183
currencies
   beads, Savi and Ouidah (Slave Coast) 91, *92*
   British currency replaces domestic, Northern
      Territories 45
   exchange rates, Fali culture (Upper Benue Basin,
      Cameroons) 167

Daccubie (Ghana), European trading presence 9
Dagomba (Ghana)
   slave trade 41
   and effects on Bassar 59, 65, 67, 69, 70, 71,
      73, 74, 75, 77
Dahomey, *see* Slave Coast
Daima (Lake Chad) 107–8, 118
Dalzel, A. (British merchant), observations about
      the Slave Coast 93, 94
Dekpassanware (smithing centre, Bassar) 63, 76
Denham, Dixon (British expedition into Central
      Sudan), description of Birni Gazargamo
      (*c*.1826) 115, 168
Denmark, trading presence 8, 9
dental pathology, as evidence of nutritional and/or
      health status 25
Dikre (sacred forest, Bassar) 65, 71, 75
Dikwa (Chad Basin) 123–4
   ceramics *117*, 124
Dimuri (Bassar) 67
Dioron Boumak (shell midden, Siin Salum region,
      Senegambia) 24
Djakpa (Gonja warrior) 69
Djowul (iron ore deposit, Bassar) 65, 73
Dogon peoples (middle Niger), opposition to slave
      trade 19
Dorbour (Banda), ceramics 50
Dumpo (Kuulo) peoples (Banda), assimiliation by
      the Nafana 40
Dupuis, J. (British merchant to Asante 1820s) 42

East Africa, European trading presence 7
Edea (Bambimbi, Cameroons), iron industry 157,
      173

El Hadj Omar, *jihad* movement (Senegambia 1850s) 26, 29

el-Bekri, slavery in the Sudan 16

Elmina (trading fort, Ghana) 8, 9, 9–10
burial practices, as illustrations of transfer of African practices to the African diaspora 180

English Royal African Company 87

Essomba Nagbana (grandfather of Otu Tambe) 155

ethnography
cultural practices not necessarily a useful guide 181, 183
ethnic labels as means of identifying slaves' departure point 181, 184 n.3
ethnic origins and spatial patterns 182
Slave Coast 83–4, 84, 85
Southern Lake Chad Basin 132–3, *134*, 135–6
study influenced by Atlantic trade 7

ethnology, West Africa 5

Europe
colonization of the Cameroons 153
documentary evidence of cultural effects of the slave trade in Senegambia 22–3
explorers, written accounts of West African cultural history 2, 3
trade links, Faleme River Valley (Senegambia) 30–1
see also Britain; France; Germany

explorers, written accounts of West African cultural history 2, 3

Faboura (shell midden, Siin Slaum region, Senegambia) 24–5

Fadl Allah (son of Rabeh) 123

Faleme River Valley (Senegambia), archaeological excavations 24, 29–31, 32, 33

Fali culture (Upper Benue Basin, Cameroons), burial practices 166–7

faunal remains, Savi and Ouidah (Slave Coast) 92

Ferguson, George W. (British colonial officer, Asante) 43

Fernandes, V. (Portuguese explorer) 24, 25

figurines, Savi (Slave Coast) 91

fisheries, Slave Coast 86

Fodio, Uthman dan, ban on alcohol in Hausaland (1804) 68

Fon peoples (Dahomey), ethnography 83–4, 85

Fort d'Estrees (trading fort, Goree Island, Senegal) 9

Fort Ruychaver (Dutch trading fort, Ankobra River, Ghana) 9

Fort St. Jago (trading fort, Ghana) 8

Fort Senudébu (French trading post, Faleme River Valley, Senegambia) 29, 30–1
archaeological excavations 24

France
colonization of Dahomey 83–4
colonization of Togo 76
trading practices, Faleme River Valley (Senegambia) 30, 31
see also Europe

Fula, *see* Banda

Fulani peoples (Cameroons)
influence over settlement patterns
Upper Benue Basin 165–8
Western Adamaoua 162–5
migration 172, 174
pastoralism 4

Fundong (Western Grasslands, Cameroons), iron industry 161

Fungom chiefdom (Western Grasslands, Cameroons), iron industry 162

Futa peoples (Senegambia) 29

Gambaru (royal palace, Yobe Valley, Lake Chad) *106*, 115–16, *117*, 118

Gambia, European trading presence 7

Garbai (son of Hashemi, and *shehu* of Dikwa and Kanem-Borno) 121, 123

Garoumélé (Niger), identification with Ni (Kanem-Borno royal city) 106–7, *106*, 115

Germany
colonization of the Cameroons 153
colonization of Togo 76
see also Europe

Gesebi (al-Qasaba, waystation for trans-Saharan trade from Chad region) 108, 110

Ghana
climate change and the economy (eleventh and twelfth centuries) 19
European trading presence 7, 8, 9, 10
population densities 6
social effects of the slave trade 17
spatial patterns 182
tobacco pipes 94–5
see also Asante (Ghana); Gonja (Ghana)

Glazed Sherd Industry (Western grasslands, Cameroons), iron industry *160*, 161–2

Glewhe, *see* Ouidah

Gold Coast, *see* Ghana

Gonja (Ghana) 44
involvement in the slave trade 41
relations with the Bassar peoples 59, 65, 67
slave trade, and effects on Bassar 69
see also Ghana

Gonja Chronicles (Kitâb Ghanjâ) 41

Gorée Island (Senegambia)
archaeological excavations 24
role in the Atlantic trade 14

Guinea, population densities 6
Gulfey (*Calfe*) Kingdom (Chadian Plain, Lake Chad, Cameroons) 168
Gyaman peoples (Ghana) 42, 43
Gyase family (Banda), slave origins 44

Hamdum ibn Dunama (*mai* of Kanem-Borno) (1717–31) 112
Hamei (Chadian Plain, Cameroons), burial sites 169
Hashemi (*shehu* of Kanem-Borno, nineteenth century) 119, 123
Hausa, trade links with Bassar 68, 70, 74, 76, 77
Houla (Pla) peoples (Slave Coast) 84
Houlouf (Chadian Plain, Cameroons), burial sites 169, 170, 171
Hueda peoples (Slave Coast) 85, 87
  slave trade 81–2, 96
Huede Archaeological Project 87
Huffon (king of Allada) 87
human sacrifice, archaeological evidence, as indicative of social status (Senegambia) 25

Ibn Battuta (Arab traveler)
  describes slave trade of Kanem-Borno 103–4
  description of the *mai* of Kanem-Borno 110–12
  slavery in the Sudan 16
ibn Dunama, Ali, *mai* (Kanem-Borno) (1750–91) 112
  reorganization of political and military structures of Kanem-Borno 110
Ibn Fartwa 136, 139, 141, 142
ibn Furtu, Ahmed (Arab traveler), description of *mai* Idris Alauma's reign (Kanem-Borno) 112, 117
Ibn Khaldun (Arab historian), description of Kanem-Borno trading practices 103, 107
ibn-Kutayba (Arab traveler), Zaghawa state 135–6
Ibn Said (Arab geographer)
  description of Chad Basin in relation to Kanem-Borno's capital cities 104, *105*, 106, 107
  description of ethnography of Southern Lake Chad Basin 136
Idris Alauma (*mai* of Kanem-Borno) (1564–1600) 112, 116, 117–18, 170
  conquest of Southern Lake Chad Basin 139, 141
Ignare (Bassar) 67
Iron Age 4
  Basso peoples (Togo) 63
  Southern Lake Chad Basin 133, 135
iron industry
  Asante (Ghana), British colonial period 45
  Bassar (Togo) 60, 64–8, 70, 71, *72*, 73–4, 76, 77
  and social rankings

Africa and the diaspora 182
  Western Grasslands (Cameroons) 174
Tado (Slave Coast) 93
Western Grasslands (Cameroons) 158–62, 174
Yaoundé-Lékié (Cameroons) 155–8
see also ceramics
Isge-Nguru (Marghi settlement, Southern Lake Chad Basin) 139
Islam
  cultural effects, Senegambia 26, 28–9
  effects, on the slave trade (Southern Lake Chad Basin) 146
  expansion 6
  influence over Kanem-Borno empire 110–11
  Southern Lake Chad Basin, adoption of Islam as means of avoiding slavery 138, 139, 144, 148
Isu (Western Grasslands, Cameroons), iron industry 161, 162
Ivory Coast
  European trading presence 8
  population densities 6
  trading presence 9

jaam (slave) 17
Jaja (Kaka) (Kanem-Borno capital city) 103, 104, 106, 107, 110
James Island (Senegambia), role in the Atlantic trade 14
Jimi (Kanem-Borno capital city) 104
Jola peoples (Senegambia), opposition to slave trade 19, 22
Jolof confederation (Senegambia) 29
Jukun peoples (Southern Lake Chad Basin) 137

Kabiye peoples (Togo) 60, 63, 64, 67, 75
Kabu peoples (Bassar)
  ceramics 75
  chiefdom 71, 73, 77
Kabu-Sara (Togo) 64, *66*, 67, 73, 76
Kaka (Jaja) (Kanem-Borno capital city) 103, 104, 106, 107, 110
Kanem-Borno, capital cities 104–10, 113, *117*, 125
Kanem-Borno empire (1400–1800) 110–18
  geographical extent 101–3
  influence over Southern Lake Chad Basin 136, 137, 138–9, 141–3
  in nineteenth and twentieth centuries 118–19, 122–3
  origins 103–10
  slave trade 103–4, 108, 110, 111, 123, 124, 125
Kano (Southern Lake Chad Basin), slave trade 146
Kasa (Banda) 42
Katcha Valley (Bassar) 73

Katsina (Southern Lake Chad Basin), slave trade 146

Kétou (Bénin), settlement patterns as response to the slave trade 96

Kintampo peoples (Ghana) 63

Kitâb Ghanjâ (Gonja Chronicles) 41

Klose, H. (German explorer), slave trade (Bassar) 69, 70

Kodjodumpa (Tyokossi clan) 70

kola nuts, trade 68, 70, 76, 77

Koli clan (Bassar peoples) 60

Koli Tengella (Peul chieftain) (Senegambia, fifteenth century) 29

Kom culture (Cameroons) 158

Konkomba peoples (Togo) 64, 67

Kotokoli (Tem) peoples (Togo) 60, 63, 64, 67, 68

Kribi (factory, Cameroons), foundation as part of the Atlantic trade, and population movements 173

Kuka peoples (Southern Lake Chad Basin), involvement in the slave trade 143

Kukawa (Southern Lake Chad Basin) 113, *117*, 118, 119–22, 123
   slave trade 146

Kumase (Asante capital, Ghana) 40–1, 41, 42

Kuranko (Sierra Leone), cultural effects of the Atlantic trade 10

Kusseri (*Uncusciuri*) Kingdom (Chadian Plain, Cameroons) 17, 168

Kuulo (Dumpo) peoples (Banda), assimilation by the Nafana 40

Kuulo Kataa (Banda) 47, 48, 53

Kwadwo, Asantehene Osei (Asante chief 1764–77) 69

Lagone (Logone) Kingdom (Chadian Plain, Cameroons) 170

Lagwen Kingdom (Chadian Plain, Cameroons) 169

Lake Chad (Cameroons) 102–3, 104
   Chadian Basin, population movements and settlement relocations 171–2
   Chadian Plain
      burial practices 168–71
      social ranking 174
   see also Cameroons; Southern Lake Chad Basin (Cameroons)

Lake Nokué (Slave Coast), lake villages 86

Lamba (Losso) peoples (Bassar) 67, 75

land-holding, Kanem-Borno empire 111

languages 3

Leo Africanus 136, 143

Lengam (Yobe Valley, Lake Chad) 116

Liberia
   European trading presence 8

Iron Age 4
   population densities 6

Liberty Village (Maiduguri, Chad Basin) 124

Limba (Sierra Leone), cultural effects of the Atlantic trade 10

Logone (*Lagone*) Kingdom (Chadian Plain, Cameroons) 170

Losso (Lamba) peoples (Gassar) 67, 75

lost wax (*cire perdue*) casting 4, 93

Lucas, S. (British traveler), description of Birni Gazargamo (early nineteenth century) 115

Maccari (Makari) Kingdom (Chadian Plain, Cameroons) 168, 170

Machina (Yobe Valley, Lake Chad) 116

Maga 136, 144

mai ('lord': Kanem-Borno) 103, 110–11

Maiduguri (Chad Basin) 124

Makal Kataa (Banda) 46–53

Makari (*Maccari*) Kingdom (Chadian Plain, Cameroons) 168, 170

Mali, influence on Senegambian cultural history 17, 32

Mamprusi (Ghana), relations with Bassar peoples 65, 67

Manan (Kanem-Borno capital city) 104

Manaouatchi-Gréa (north Cameroons), defensive walls *140*

Mandara Mountains (Southern Chad Basin)
   geographical effects of resistance to the slave trade 144–5
   settlement patterns 181

Mandarama, Sanda (*shehu* of Dikwa) 123

Manding peoples (Senegambia), burial practices 25

Mandinka peoples (Senegambia), burial practices 24

Mandja (Bagangté, Cameroons) 158

Mangwen I (Matomb, Cameroons), iron industry 155

Marghi peoples (Southern Lake Chad Basin) 141, 141–2

Massangui II (Bambimbi, Cameroons), iron industry 157

Matomb (Cameroons), iron industry 155, *156*, 157–8

Mauro, Fra 136, 141–2

Mayo Darlé (Western Adamaoua, Cameroons), settlement patterns as defensive measures 164–5

Mdaga (Chadian Plain, Cameroons) 170

Middle Senegal Valley project 26

Midigué (Chadian Plain, Cameroons) 170

Mmen (Western Grasslands, Cameroons), iron industry 162

Morocco, trading practices, Faleme River Valley
  (Senegambia) 30
mosques, Birni Gazargamo 115
Moteil, P.-L. (Lieutenant-Colonel), description of
  Kukuwa (Chad Basin) (1892) 120–1

Nababun (Togo), iron industry 64, 65, *66*, 67, 73
Nachtigal, Gustav (German traveler 1850s) 119,
  120, 168
  describes resistence to slaving raids of *mai* Idris
    Alauma 139
  description of Lake Chad area 108
Nafana peoples (Banda) 40
  slave origins 43–4
Nangbani (Bassar), smelting furnace *64*
Nassarao (Upper Benue Basin, Cameroons) 166
Nataka clan (Bassar) 71
Natchammba (Bassar) 67
Ndi (Western Adamaoua, Cameroons) 163
Ndom (Cameroons), iron industry 155, 157–8
Ndop Plateau Industry (Western Grassfields,
  Cameroons), iron industry 159–60
Newton Cemetery (Barbados), burial practices, as
  illustrations of transfer of African practices to
  the African diaspora 180
Ngala (Chad Basin) 108, *108*, 118
  ceramics 124
Ngalama Ibrahim Laminu, *mai*, instigates
  archaeological excavations at Daima (Lake
  Chad) 108
Ngambe (Bambimbi, Cameroons), iron industry
  157
Ngila (Cameroons), iron works 174
Ngock (Bambimbi, Cameroons), iron industry 157
Ngoutchoumi-Barki (Fali, Upper Benue Basin,
  Cameroons), burial practices *166*, 167
Nguilumlend (Bambimbi, Cameroons), iron
  industry 157
Nguru (Yobe Valley, Lake Chad) 116
Ni (Kanem-Borno royal city), identification with Tié
  (Chad Republic) 104, 106–7
Nigeria, Copper and Iron Ages 4
Nindje (Bambimbi, Cameroons), iron industry 157
Nkometou (Yaoundé-Lékié), iron industry 155
Nkongteck (Matomb, Cameroons), iron industry
  155, 157
Nkoranza peoples (Ghana) 42, 43
Northcott, Colonel H. P. (British colonial
  administrator, Northern Territories), imposition
  of British currency 45
Notsé (Slave Coast) 85–6
  potsherd pavements 93
Nyeng (Bambimbi, Cameroons), iron industry 157

Nyos chiefdom (Western Grasslands, Cameroons),
  iron industry 162

occupation mounds, Makala Kataa (Banda) 51–2
Ogun (Yoruba deity, associated with iron) 182
Old Accompong Town (Jamaica), spatial patterns
  182
oral traditions
  Bassar peoples (Togo) 59–60
  use in the study of West African cultural history
    2
organics, Savi and Ouidah (Slave Coast) 92
Otu Tamba (founding ancestor of the Beti peoples)
  155
Oudney, Walter (British expedition into Central
  Sudan), description of Birni Gazargamo (1823)
  113, 114–15, 116, 168
Ouidah (Glewhe) (Slave Coast) 8–9, 86, 87, 87–8
  ceramics 90–1, 95, 96
  organics 92
  settlement patterns 96
  tobacco pipes 95
Overweg, Richard (German traveler, Kanem-Borno
  1850) 119
Oyo peoples, domination of Dahomey 82

Peul peoples (Senegambia) 29, 32
Pla (Houle) peoples (Slave Coast) 84
plages (floodplain settlements) (Faleme River Valley,
  Senegambia) 31
plant food remains, Savi and Ouidah (Slave Coast)
  92
Pongsolo (Yaoundé-Lékié), iron industry 155
population levels 6
  Southern Lake Chad Basin, as affected by
    resistance to the slave trade 144–5
population movements, and settlement relocations,
  Chadian Basin (Cameroons) 171–2
Portugal
  trading practices, Faleme River Valley
    (Senegambia) 30
  trading presence in North Africa 8
potsherd pavements, Slave Coast 93
pottery, *see* ceramics
Pouss (Upper Benue Basin, Cameroons) 166

Rabeh (warlord, Sudan), investment of Kanem-
  Borno (late nineteenth century) 122–3, 124,
  170
Reeder's Pen foundry (Jamaica), as illustrative of
  social prestige attached to iron-working 182
Richardson, James (British traveler, Kanem-Borno
  1850s) 118–19

ritual practices, and the importance of iron working 182

Rohlfs, Gerhard (German traveler, Kanem-Borno 1850) 119, 124

Royal Niger Company 123

Saharan slave trade 19
  development in Western Sudan 16–17
  effects on Senegambia cultural history 16, 31
Sahel, slave trade 19
St. Louis (Senegambia), role in the Atlantic trade 14
Salih Isharku (Arab traveler), on population of Birni Gazargamo (c.1658) 115
Samori Turé, establishes empire from northern Sierra Leone to northern Ghana (1861–98) 43, 44–5
Sanda, Omar (son of Hashemi, *shehu* of Kanem-Borno) 123
Saninké clans, influence on Senegambian cultural history 17
Sao (*Sauo*) Kingdom (Chadian Plain, Cameroons), burial practices 168, 171
Sao (Saw) 136, 144
São Tomé
  European settlement 7
  Iron Age 4
Sara (Bassar), iron industry 73
Sarankye-More (son of Samori Turé) 43, 44
Saré Diouldé (Senegambia) (tumulus), evidence of human sacrifice 25
Sauo (Sao) Kingdom (Chadian Plain, Cameroons), burial practices 168, 171
Savi (Hueda capital, Slave Coast) 9, 82, 86–7, 97
  architectural remains 92–3
  ceramics 88–91, 94–5, 96
  currencies, beads 91, *92*
  figurines 91
  metal artifacts 93–4
  organics 92
  settlement patterns 96
  stone artifacts 93
  tobacco pipes 94–5
Saw (Sao) 136, 144
Sayfuwa dynasty (Kanem-Borno) 103, 118
Seetzen, Ulrich Jasper (German traveler), description of Birni Gazargamo 113
Senegal
  European trading presence 7, 9
  slave trade (twelfth century) 18–19
Senegal Tumulus Survey Project 26
Senegambia
  burial practices, archaeological evidence 24–5
  cultural history

    effects of slave trade 14–16, 18, 22–3, 31–2
    lack of archaeological evidence 23–4
  historical developments (tenth to nineteenth centuries) 20–1
  opposition to slave trade 19, 22
  see also specific peoples
Sereer peoples (Senegambia)
  burial practices 24
  caste systems 17
  opposition to slave trade 19
  and slavery as influenced by the Wolof 18
settlement patterns
  Cameroons 172
  as defensive measure against the slave trade, Western Adamaoua (Cameroons) 162–5
  as defensive measures against Fulani conquests, Upper Benue Basin (Cameroons) 165–8
  and population movements, Chadian Basin (Cameroons) 171–2
  as reaction to Fulani conquests, Western Adamaoua (Cameroons) 162–5
  Savi and Ouidah (Slave Coast) 96
  Slave Coast 96
  and the slave trade, Cameroons 172
  Yaoundé-Lékié (Cameroons) (trading station) 154–5
  see also slave trade
Seville Plantation (Jamaica), burial practices, as illustrations of transfer of African practices to the African diaspora 180–1
ShYTAQ (Sielɔngɔ) (Banda King) 41
Sierra Leone
  European trading presence 8, 10
  Iron Age 4
  population densities 6
Siin Salum region (Senegambia), shell middens 24–5
Sine Ngayéne (Senegambia) (megalithic circle) 25, 27
site densities, Senegambia 32–3
Slave Coast (Bight of Bénin)
  and the Atlantic trade 81–2, 86
    documentation 82–4, 86–7, 96–7
  cultural history (1500–1670) 84–6
  Dahomey Gap, physical geography 82
  European trading presence 8–9
  influence over Nigeria 6
  metal artifacts 93–4
  physical geography 82
  and the slave trade, effects on settlement patterns 96
Slave Coast, Dahomey 82, 83–4, 87
slave trade
  Banda (Ghana), nineteenth century 42–4

and the Cameroons (1500–1900) 152–4
cultural effects in Senegambia 22–3
distinctions between slavers and slaves important 181
effects
    on Bassar 59, 67, 69–70, 70–5, 77
    on cultural history of Senegambia 17–19, 22–3, 31–2
Faleme River Valley (Senegambia) 30, 31
incorporation of slaves into Kanem-Borno political system 118
Kanem-Borno 103–4, 108, 110, 111, 123, 124, 125
Kukaw (Chad Basin) 120, 122
opposition in Senegambia 19, 22
Sahara and Sahel 18–19
Southern Lake Chad Basin
    effects 131–2, 147–8
    origins 137, 138–9, *140*, 141
    resistance to slave trade 143–4
    routes and markets, nineteenth century 145–7
    sub-contracting 141–3
see also Atlantic trade; settlement patterns; trade systems
Snelgrave, Captain William, observations on the Slave Coast 83
So (indigenous groups: Kanem-Borno) 111
social rankings
    and iron works, Western Grasslands (Cameroons) 174
    and trade systems, Cameroons 174
Songhay empire
    relations with Kanem-Borno 112
    social effects of the slave trade 17
sorcerers, social standing (Banda) 43
South Africa, European trading presence 7
Southern Lake Chad Basin (Cameroons)
    geography and ethnography 132–3, *134*, 135–7
    slave trade
        effects 131–2, 144–5, 147–8
        origins 137, 138–9, *140*, 141
        resistance to 143–4
        routes and markets, nineteenth century 145–7
        sub-contracting 141–3
    see also Cameroons; Lake Chad (Cameroons)
spatial patterns, and ethnic origins 182
Stone Age
    Bassar peoples (Togo) 63
    West Africa 4
stone artifacts, Savi (Slave Coast) 93
Sukur peoples (northern Nigeria), chiefdom 71
Sumpra Cave (Upper Benue Basin, Cameroons) 166
Surinam, spatial patterns 182

Tado (Slave Coast) 85
    iron industry 93
    potsherd pavements 93
Tarrikh el-Fettach, slavery in the Sudan 16
Tarrikh es-Sudan, slavery in the Sudan 16
Tata Almamy (Faleme River Valley, Senegambia) 29–30, 30–1
tata (fortified strongholds) (Faleme River Valley, Senegambia) 31
technology, West African 4
Tegdaoust (Awdaghust) (Sahel), slavery 19, 32
Tem (Kotokoli) peoples (Togo) 60, 64, 67, 68
Tié (Chad Republic), identification with No (Kanem-Borno royal city) 104, 106–7
Tinipé (Danyi Plateau, Togo), settlement patterns as response to the slave tade 96
Tipabun (iron ore deposit, Bassar) 65, 73
Titur (Bandjeli area, Bassar) 73
tobacco pipes
    Kuulo Kataa (Banda) 53
    Makala Kataa (Banda) 51, *52*
    and pottery development, Senegambia 25, 26
    Savi (Slave Coast) 94–5
    see also ceramics
Togoland, *see* specific peoples
Togudo-Awute (Allada, Slave Coast) 86
trade systems 4, 6
    Banda (Ghana) 39–40, 40–1
    Bassar 68, 70, 74, 76, 77
    Cameroons 172–4
    Chadian Basin (Cameroons) 171
    Faleme River Valley (Senegambia) 30
    markets, Kanem-Borno, in nineteenth century 120
    salt trade, Slave Coast 86
    Slave Coast 86
    and social rankings, Cameroons 174
    trans-Saharan trade from Chad region 108, 110
    see also Atlantic trade; slave trade
trans-Saharan trade, links with the Cameroons 152, 153
Tuareg peoples, relations with Kanem-Borno (seventeenth century) 112
Turkish Ottoman empire, relations with Kanem-Borno (sixteenth century) 112
Tyokossi peoples (Togo) 60, 67, 68
    slave trade and effects on Bassar 69–70, 71, 73, 74, 75, 77

Ukpwa (Western Grasslands, Cameroons), iron industry 161
Ulichi (Wulki) Kingdom (Chadian Plain, Lake Chad, Cameroons) 168

Umar (*shehu*, Kanem-Borno, nineteenth century) 118–19

Uncusciuri (Kusseri) Kingdom (Chadian Plain, Cameroons) 17, 168

Upper Benue Basin (Cameroons), settlement patterns as defensive measures against Fulani conquests 165–8

Usuman dan Fodio (Fulani Islamic scholar), *jihad* against non-Islamic practices in west central Sudan (1804) 118

vegetation, West Africa 3, *4*

Vouté peoples (Cameroons), migration 171, 174

Wandala peoples (Southern Lake Chad Basin), involvement in slave trade 141–3, 145–6, 147, 148

Wawandera (Western Adamaoua, Cameroons) 163

We (Western Grasslands, Cameroons), iron industry 162

West Africa
  cultural history
    effects of the Atlantic trade 1, 2, 7–9
    effects of the slave trade 17–19, 22–3, 31–2
    study 1–3, 6, 9–10
    geography 3–4

Western Adamaoua (Cameroons)
  settlement patterns as reaction to Fulani conquests 162–5
  social rankings 174

Western Grasslands (Cameroons)
  iron industry 158–62
  social rankings 174

Western Sudan, cultural history, effects of Saharan slave trade 16–17, 18

Wolof peoples (Senegambia)
  burial practices 24
  caste systems 17
  and slavery 18, 22

Wopti-Tshalo culture (Upper Benue Basin, Cameroons), burial practices 167–8

written records, use in the study of West African cultural history 2, 3, 6

Wulki (*Ulichi*) Kingdom (Chadian Plain, Lake Chad, Cameroons) 168

Wum (Western Grasslands, Cameroons), iron industry 161

Ya Na 'Abdullah (Dagomba chief, *c.*1864–76) 69

Ya Na Ya'qub (Dagomba chief, *c.* 1833–*c.*1864) 69

Yalunka (Sierra Leone), cultural effects of the Atlantic trade 10

Yaoundé-Lékié (Cameroons), settlement patterns 154–5

Yaqut (Arab historian), description of Kanem Borno 103

Yau (Yobe valley, Lake Chad), identification with Jaja (Kaka) (Kanem-Borno) 107, 116

Yedina/Buduma peoples (Lake Chad islands), resistance to slavery 143

Zaghawa state (Southern Lake Chad Basin), extent of rule 135–6

Zoa chiefdom (Western Grasslands, Cameroons), iron industry 162